The Rise of Modern Jewish Politics

The path toward modern Jewish politics, a process that required a dramatic reconstruction of Jewish life, may have emerged during a far earlier time frame and in a different geographic and cultural context than has previously been thought. Drawing upon current sociological understanding of social movements, this book places the 1827 organized protest in London at an important point along a transnational social movement continuum—similar to the abolitionist and women's rights movements—that waxed and waned throughout the nineteenth century. From its early origins in London in 1827, to Moses Montefiore's gallant style of leadership in the Middle East, to the rise of the "Mourning March" and street processions of the early twentieth century, and then on to the civil disobedience of the 1980s, the movement evolved, shifted its contentious center from England to the United States, and adapted to a dramatically altered post-Holocaust environment. This multifaceted and often fractious campaign was never monolithic by nature and was often rife with internal disputes. It ran the gamut between stirring accomplishments and mobilizations that fell far short of expectations. Any attempt to view the lengthy series of international protests as a steady progression of liberality and advancement would be at odds with a far more ambiguous reality.

The Rise of Modern Jewish Politics argues that the numerous protest insurgences strengthened Jewish participation in the public sphere and further defined a public political culture. While the movement certainly evolved through the decades, the core values that first arose in London were retained during the course of several contentious cycles that later surfaced in both Britain and the United States. This book utilizes an innovative interpretive framework to formulate a new paradigm of how Jews entered the modern world. The struggle for Jewish rights remains one of the most enduring social movements in modern history.

C.S. Monaco is a research associate in the Department of History at Oxford Brookes University, UK and courtesy professor, Department of History, University of Florida, USA. He has published articles in *Jewish Social Studies*, the *Journal of Modern Jewish Studies*, and *American Jewish History*. His research interests include modern Jewish history, Jewish Atlantic studies, social movements, and Diaspora studies.

Routledge Studies in Religion

1 **Judaism and Collective Life**
Self and Community in
the Religious Kibbutz
Aryei Fishman

2 **Foucault, Christianity and Interfaith Dialogue**
Henrique Pinto

3 **Religious Conversion and Identity**
The Semiotic Analysis of Texts
Massimo Leone

4 **Language, Desire, and Theology**
A Genealogy of the Will to Speak
Noëlle Vahanian

5 **Metaphysics and Transcendence**
Arthur Gibson

6 **Sufism and Deconstruction**
A Comparative Study of Derrida and Ibn 'Arabi
Ian Almond

7 **Christianity, Tolerance and Pluralism**
A Theological Engagement with Isaiah Berlin's Social Theory
Michael Jinkins

8 **Negative Theology and Modern French Philosophy**
Arthur Bradley

9 **Law and Religion**
Edited by Peter Radan, Denise Meyerson, and Rosalind F. Atherton

10 **Religion, Language, and Power**
Edited by Nile Green and Mary Searle-Chatterjee

11 **Shared Idioms, Sacred Symbols, and the Articulation of Identities in South Asia**
Edited by Kelly Pemberton and Michael Nijhawan

12 **Theology, Creation, and Environmental Ethics**
From Creatio Ex Nihilo to Terra Nullius
Whitney Bauman

13 **Material Religion and Popular Culture**
E Frances King

14 **Adam Smith as Theologian**
Edited by Paul Oslington

15 **The Entangled God**
Divine Relationality and Quantum Physics
Kirk Wegter-McNelly

16 **Aquinas and Radical Orthodoxy**
A Critical Inquiry
Paul J. DeHart

17 **Animal Ethics and Theology**
The Lens of the Good Samaritan
Daniel K. Miller

18 **The Origin of Heresy**
A History of Discourse in Second Temple Judaism and Early Christianity
Robert M. Royalty, Jr.

19 **Buddhism and Violence**
Militarism and Buddhism in Modern Asia
Edited by Vladimir Tikhonov and Torkel Brekke

20 **Popular Music in Evangelical Youth Culture**
Stella Sai-Chun Lau

21 **Theology and the Science of Moral Action**
Virtue Ethics, Exemplarity, and Cognitive Neuroscience
Edited by James A. Van Slyke, Gregory R. Peterson, Kevin S. Reimer, Michael L. Spezio, and Warren S. Brown

22 **Abrogation in the Qur'an and Islamic Law**
Louay Fatoohi

23 **A New Science of Religion**
Edited by Gregory W. Dawes and James Maclaurin

24 **Making Sense of the Secular**
Critical Perspectives from Europe to Asia
Edited by Ranjan Ghosh

25 **The Rise of Modern Jewish Politics**
Extraordinary Movement
C. S. Monaco

The Rise of Modern Jewish Politics
Extraordinary Movement

C. S. Monaco

NEW YORK AND LONDON

First published 2013
by Routledge

605 Third Avenue, New York, NY 10017
4 Park Square, Milton Park, Abingdon, Oxon OX14 4RN

First issued in paperback 2017

*Routledge is an imprint of the Taylor & Francis Group,
an informa business*

© 2013 Taylor & Francis

The right of C. S. Monaco to be identified as author of this work has been asserted by him/her in accordance with sections 77 and 78 of the Copyright, Designs and Patents Act 1988.

All rights reserved. No part of this book may be reprinted or reproduced or utilised in any form or by any electronic, mechanical, or other means, now known or hereafter invented, including photocopying and recording, or in any information storage or retrieval system, without permission in writing from the publishers.

Trademark Notice: Product or corporate names may be trademarks or registered trademarks, and are used only for identification and explanation without intent to infringe.

Library of Congress Cataloging-in-Publication Data

The rise of modern Jewish politics: extraordinary movement /
   by C.S. Monaco.
       p. cm. — (Routledge studies in religion ; 25)
   Includes bibliographical references and index.
1. Jews—Europe—History—19th century. 2. Jews—Europe—History—20th century. 3. Jews—Europe—Politics and government—19th century. 4. Jews—Europe—Politics and government—20th century. 5. Jewish leadership—Europe—History—19th century. 6. Antisemitism—Europe—History. I. Title.
   DS135.E83M66 2012
   320.94089'924—dc23
   2012027232

ISBN 13: 978-1-138-11863-8 (pbk)
ISBN 13: 978-0-415-65983-3 (hbk)

Typeset in Sabon
by Apex CoVantage, LLC

In memory of my father-in-law Adolf Widman (1906–1980)

Contents

List of Figures xi
Acknowledgments xiii

Introduction 1

PART I
The Extraordinary Movement

1 Movement Origins 19
2 "To Rise and Shew Themselves Men" 36

PART II
The Damascus Affair

3 Blood Libel 57
4 Mansion House and Beyond 72

PART III
The Mortara Affair

5 "A Mighty Outcry Resounds" 91
6 Toward Unity 106

PART IV
Romanian Pogroms

7 "A Scandal to Civilization" — 123

PART V
Russian Crises

8 "A Crisis in Jewish History" — 141

9 The Kishinev Massacre — 160

Epilogue — 171

Conclusions — 177

Notes — 185
Appendix — 221
Selected Bibliography — 231
Index — 249

Figures

1.1	A public meeting at Freemasons' Hall, circa 1820s. [Source: *A History of the British and Foreign Bible Society*, vol. 2 (London, 1910).]	31
2.1	Jewish peddler at House of Commons, William Heath caricature (1829). [Private collection of the author.]	50
3.1	Portrait of Sir Moses Montefiore. [Source: *Illustrated London News*, 3 November 1882.]	70
4.1	Montefiore "Testimonial Monument in Silver." [Source: *Illustrated London News*, 27 February 1843.]	87
5.1	Map of Italian peninsula and the Papal States. [Source: *Efter Stielers Hand-Atlas* (Stockholm, 1852).]	92
6.1	Pope Pius IX, caricature. [Source: *Punch* (London), 13 April 1861.]	117
7.1	Moses Montefiore addresses an angry crowd outside his Bucharest hotel room. [Source: *Diaries of Sir Moses and Lady Montefiore*, ed. L. Loewe., vol. 2 (Chicago, 1890).]	128
8.1	"Ill Treatment of the Jews in Russia." [Source: *Illustrated London News*, 4 June 1881.]	147
8.2	"Great Public Meeting at Guildhall." [Source: *Illustrated London News*, 20 December 1890.]	157
9.1	Assembled corpses of Kishinev victims. [Source: *Kishinevskii Pogrom* (Stuttgart, 1903).]	162

Acknowledgments

Historical research is seldom a solitary venture, and so I naturally owe debts of gratitude to a number of people who have aided my arrival at this stage in my career—far too many to adequately thank here. There are, nevertheless, several individuals who I would like to single out for special consideration. Two emeritus history professors at the University of Florida, Samuel Proctor and Neill Macaulay (both now deceased), shared my initial fascination with Moses Levy at a time when few scholars would have deemed this figure worthy of serious consideration and thus helped set the stage for this present work. Similarly, the advice and encouragement of the late John Klier (University College London) proved vital to the development of this book.

I am indebted to Laura Stearns at Routledge for her steadfast support for this project, and I am obliged to the anonymous reviewers for their constructive comments. In addition, Fred Krome (University of Cincinnati) provided feedback on the initial manuscript at a critical juncture; sociologist Peter Stamatov (Yale University) graciously reviewed an early article of mine regarding the formation of the Jewish rights movement; and Michael Stanislawski (Columbia University) helped place the 1827 Russian *ukase* that sparked London's "extraordinary movement" into proper perspective. Kind assistance was further rendered by the following organizations: the Board of Deputies of British Jews, the British Library, London Metropolitan Archives, Bodleian Library (Oxford), American Jewish Historical Society, American Jewish Archives, YIVO Institute for Jewish Research, Library of Congress, and the Bibliothèque Nationale de France. While I acknowledge the suggestions and input of colleagues, I, of course, take entire responsibility for any inaccuracies that may be included herein.

Finally, I am indebted to my wife Rose. She proofread my manuscript, provided numerous pertinent comments, and followed each stage of this book with heightened interest. She ran all aspects of our household for two years and provided an atmosphere of solitude and encouragement. Without her assistance this book would not have been possible.

Introduction

> *At the present moment, the eyes of England, of Europe, and of a great part of the civilized world seem to be directed toward us, and . . . men are looking with something approaching anxiety for the result of the Public Meetings of the Jewish Nation that have been called (the first time for many centuries).*
> —Moses E. Levy, 1827[1]

In London during the winter of 1827, a unique series of public meetings between Jews and Christians had escalated into what some in the newspaper press deemed an "extraordinary movement." A cohort of predominately middle-class Jews led by Moses E. Levy (1782–1854)—a cosmopolitan reformer from the United States—joined affluent members of the evangelical Philo-Judaean Society (1826–1831) in an unprecedented political coalition.[2] Both parties met on equal footing to debate the essentials of their respective faiths; influential evangelicals lobbied for the end of Jewish civil disabilities in England; schools and other philanthropic endeavors were established for the benefit of the Jewish poor; and in what became an international cause célèbre, hundreds of Anglo-Jews expressed solidarity with their coreligionists in Russia by denouncing the antisemitic policies of Tsar Nicholas I. This dramatic foray into the public sphere by one of England's most stigmatized minorities garnered the interest of the world press and stirred significant controversy. The magnitude of press exposure would indeed dwarf all other contentious meetings in Britain during the same period.[3]

As conspicuous as the "extraordinary movement" was, it has nevertheless been bypassed by historians—an astonishing omission by any standard. The reasons behind this lacuna may have been complex, but, as we shall see, the movement certainly did not lack deep notoriety or far-ranging influence. Indeed, this unparalleled endeavor had a profound impact on national political agendas and major legislative reforms in England and resulted in striking changes within the Anglo-Jewish community. Jews cast off their traditional "mask of quietism";[4] presented moral claims that challenged the marginalized position of Jews in society; fashioned an autonomous expression of Jewish nationalism; and utilized an array of injustice frames to forge a modern political consciousness—all during a far earlier date than scholars have considered.

The "extraordinary movement"—or what I will more broadly refer to as the Jewish rights movement—adhered to a sequential pattern that followed in much the same manner as the antislavery crusade, Catholic emancipation, and women's rights. Accordingly, the London movement did not merely come to an end after a limited protest phase. Following a period of relative inactivity or *abeyance*,[5] and drawing upon now-established coalitions and political networks, the movement remobilized in response to the horrific persecutions against the Jews of Damascus in 1840 (Part II). Compared to the 1827 Russian *ukase* that sparked the initial London protests—an imperial decree that ostensibly forced unknown numbers of Jews in the Russian interior to abandon their homes and property and banished rabbis—the Damascus affair was rife with accounts of barbaric torture and murder. This 'blood libel' cast innocent Jews as ritual killers, a spurious accusation rooted in the Middle Ages that became a bitter affront to all Jews. Protest meetings emerged again, this time at London's Great Synagogue, to be followed by a mass protest at Egyptian Hall, Mansion House—the lord mayor's town palace located in the center of the City of London. Newspaper coverage inspired an upsurge of similar protests elsewhere in the United Kingdom as well as Hamburg and Altona, the Caribbean, and in cities throughout the eastern United States.[6] In contrast, the notorious Mortara affair of 1858—which involved the abduction of an Italian Jewish boy by papal authorities—may have provoked worldwide indignation and resulted in major political reverses for the papacy, but on this occasion widespread demonstrations emerged primarily in the United States (Part III). Even so, Abraham Benisch, editor of London's *Jewish Chronicle*, surfaced as an influential Jewish rights advocate and accurately predicted that "the *movement* in America is likely to assume gigantic proportions."[7] Next, the brutal and systematic persecution of Romanian Jews sparked a resurgence during the 1860s and 1870s (Part IV). For the first time, the subject of mass emigration came to the fore, a topic that was considered unacceptable by a Jewish elite who still adhered to the principle of assimilation. In 1881 a massive outbreak of rioting and pillage, directed at Russian Jews in the Pale of Settlement, shocked the Western world and convinced many Jews of the necessity of emigration (Part V). Britain's chief rabbi, Hermann Adler, remarking on the public protests in London, placed his faith, as did most others in the movement, in the "influence of public opinion" to offer deliverance from "the darkness which overshadows my brethren."[8] During the next forty years, hundreds of thousands of Jews departed the Pale in the hope of finding both a safe haven and better economic opportunities in the New World. During this time, the contentious center of the Jewish rights campaign shifted from England to the United States—a turnaround that became strikingly obvious during the enormous American response to the

Kishinev Massacre in 1903 (chapter 9). The emphasis of this study therefore centers on the movement's first seventy-six years and will pay particular attention to the social, religious, and political climate in England that gave rise to this unprecedented and influential human rights campaign.

Most of these protest episodes, with the exception of the initial 1827 movement and the relatively obscure Romanian pogroms, have been recognized as significant chapters in Jewish history.[9] Each insurgence, however, has previously stood alone and disconnected in the historiography, a scholarly propensity that theorist Verta Taylor has disparagingly referred to as the "immaculate conception" model of social movements.[10] The idea that each of these transatlantic protests could be interpreted as an expression of an enduring Jewish rights struggle has never been broached by modern historians. But just as the British antislavery crusade did not terminate after Parliament passed the Foreign Slave Trade Act (1806), but reemerged, after a period of abeyance, during the mid-1820s with a different agenda (immediate emancipation) as well as a leadership that combined both newcomers and old stalwarts, one can also appreciate that the struggle for Jewish rights manifested a similar cyclical framework.[11] Most importantly, however, even if one's historical sensibilities preclude such notions as movement continuity (for whatever reason), it is indisputable that each of the episodes that will be examined in this book constituted a social movement by itself. Moreover, each of these mobilizations followed a similar contentious framework that centered on the human rights sufferings of *foreign* Jews rather than on injustices at home. And all witnessed the startling entry of Jews into the political public sphere. Thus, I believe that full contextual understanding is only possible by examining the succession of Jewish rights protests in their entirety rather than partitioning them as lone and disparate entries in the historiography.

The idea that each insurgence was an integral part of a transnational social movement continuum that waxed and waned through the years is well supported by the historical record.[12] Indeed, this very continuum, especially Anglo-Jewry's leading role within it, was once a matter of deep communal pride. For example, Herbert Bentwich (1856–1932), a prominent attorney and a member of the Board of Deputies of British Jews, responded to the board's policy of nonengagement during the Kishinev Massacre by reminding his colleagues that their objections were essentially "the same raised in 1827, 1872, 1881, and 1890," and that despite the dire warnings of the past, successful protests were held nonetheless (chapter 9).[13] As an attorney, Bentwich felt particularly justified in referring to historical precedent to make his case for communal protest. But he was certainly not alone in this regard. Sir Moses Montefiore's former rabbi from Ramsgate, Herman Shandel, also publicly lamented the Board of Deputies' inaction and elaborated on the movement's past achievements and victories, extolling not only Montefiore's former efforts on behalf of the cause but the leadership of Adolphe Crémieux, Francis H. Goldsmid, David Salomons, and other revered figures whose actions spanned much of the nineteenth century.[14] Moreover, as early as 1841, directly following the successful conclusion of the Damascus affair, London's *Voice of Jacob* portrayed the position of Anglo-Jewry as possessing a new sacred obligation: that of being "champions for the rights of their brethren everywhere."

> The exertions for the interests of Judaism will here find its centre, and hence will they diverge to a circle that will embrace the whole earth. It is for this purpose that Providence seems to have held back the English Jews for so long, in order that they might profit from the experience of others. Happy the Jews of the Universe, if their British brethren understand their position—if they render themselves equal to its duties. Happier still the British Jews to whom such a future is vouchsafed.[15]

Pride in assuming the mantle of Jewish rights permeated communal discussions for decades. Jews had taken on a righteous and judgmental role in society and dared to hold foreign leaders accountable for their moral and ethical transgressions—a deeply empowering obligation, to be sure.[16] After the first suggestion of abandoning this weighty responsibility arose in 1881, this position was not only denounced in the editorial pages of the *Jewish Chronicle* as a heartless betrayal but as representing a "crisis in Jewish history" and a regression toward a ghetto mentality.[17] Unfortunately, any comparable sense of mission and historical continuity has been lost through the years, a tendency that has undoubtedly been influenced by present historical trends. "The historian," notes one scholar, "does not see the past as recurring but rather as made up of unique events, each to be understood in its own context."[18] Some scholars have learned to distrust linkages between past and present (such are the pitfalls of Whiggish history, so it is warned). Furthermore, a postmodern view of Jewish history has also entered the equation. According to certain proponents of this theory, any "essential" connection between Jews in various times and places is contested. Rather, Jewish history is simply seen as "an imagined construction" based on an accumulation of exceedingly different and unique histories.[19] Such a perspective certainly does not bode well for understanding social movement dynamics. Among other problems, to ignore the claims of Bentwich, Shandel, and Benisch—as well as similar assertions of movement continuity from a host of activists—is to risk losing sight of the very campaign for Jewish rights that once held such high communal authority.

Adding yet another level of difficulty in understanding contentious phases is the fact that the physical and emotional environment of Jewish protest—unlike similar efforts on behalf of antislavery—has not been awarded much scholarly attention. Despite the fact that these affairs often included eminent individuals; took place at symbolic, elite venues such as London's Mansion House and New York City's Carnegie Hall; and largely adhered to parliamentary rules of order, these nineteenth-century protests were

detached from the political mainstream and were often highly emotive—
reasons enough, it seems, to have been sidelined by historians. Emotions
have indeed "seemed tangential (if not fundamentally opposed) to the historical enterprise," as one author has acknowledged, and the very swirl of
politics is either depreciated or avoided entirely.[20] Yet language that is stigmatized as "purple prose" or dismissed as "hot air" today was the actual
lingua franca of all successful movements. In a sense, the "extraordinary
movement" drew upon the precise element that has been rigorously downplayed since Jewish historians Salo Baron and Cecil Roth first took a stand
against the impassioned "history of suffering" (or "lachrymose history,"
to use Baron's term) that infused the work of their nineteenth-century predecessors.[21] Particular attention will nevertheless be given to the language
and imagery employed by Jewish political entrepreneurs, underscoring the
critical role of movement narratives in rousing and sustaining activism.[22]
Deliberate effort will be made to engage activists on their own turf, so to
speak, and to assess the transnational movement they participated in as
realistically as possible.

Because these mobilizations were separated by fairly lengthy periods of
seeming inaction and focused on incidents in diverse regions of the world, it
is hardly surprising that a unifying framework has been lacking. Christian
participation at many of these mass meetings has also blurred usual Jewish historical boundaries, adding to the overall difficulty. Yet a few recent
scholars, including Carol Fink, Abigail Green, and William D. and Hilary
L. Rubinstein, have noted a substantial, albeit ill-defined, transformation
among the international Jewish leadership during the nineteenth century,
a behavioral change whereby leaders openly promoted the welfare of Jews
worldwide.[23] Explanations for this dramatic shift range from: the ascendance
of "liberal values" during the era; the rise of Christian Philo-Semitism; and
the assumption that certain technical innovations such as railways, steamships, and the telegraph contributed to the growth of a global public sphere,
a milieu in which Jews naturally took part.[24] Abigail Green has relegated
the interfaith protest meetings in London as well as the support they garnered overseas (beginning in 1840) under the rubric of empire; a so-called
"imperialism of human-rights."[25] This motif not only ignores the fundamental processes of social movements, but it consigns all behavior under
the interests of the nation-state, precisely at a moment when the Jewish
rights movement was becoming increasingly transnational in character. As
will be amply demonstrated, however, any attempt to come to terms with
the transformation of the communal leadership without first recognizing
the movement in which they were participating clearly misses the proverbial
forest for the trees.

Intense public indignation can sustain itself for only a limited time, and
active movement phases are especially vulnerable to changes in the political
environment.[26] Most social movements do not reach a national level (let alone
an international one) and often terminate in obscurity. A fortunate few,

however, not only manage to persist but do so on an impressive scale. Quite often, activists sustain their goals during periods of relative calm by their involvement in less contentious organizational forms. In the case of Jewish rights, movement continuity was upheld for a significant duration by such organizations as the Alliance Israélite Universelle (1860), the Anglo-Jewish Association (1871), and the Israelitische Allianz zu Wien (1872) as well as the sudden proliferation of Jewish newspapers that first arose in response to the Damascus affair. Each of the above-mentioned organizations exhibited key elements of what social theorists identify as "abeyance structures." *Temporality, commitment, exclusiveness, centralization,* and a distinct movement *culture* are all traits that are manifested by such groups.[27] Of these characteristics, *exclusivity* deserves brief note, because it counters feelings of inclusiveness that are generated during social movement mobilizations. Exclusiveness fosters a sense of a "chosen few," a core group who maintain the flame during periods of political opposition or uncertainty. A Jewish elite faction, as will be demonstrated in the following chapters, did indeed dominate Jewish rights organizations for decades. Overt protests may be placed on lengthy hold, but the most successful movements reemerge during times of crisis and when the political environment allows. According to some theorists, a small number of enduring social movements, such as women's rights, may actually never come to a complete end.[28] The struggle for Jewish rights, I believe, fits this durable framework.

Despite the 180-year absence of the original London meetings from standard histories of the era, a wide range of newspapers and periodicals of the period reveal a heightened level of public awareness. With few exceptions, the major metropolitan press was supportive or at least dispassionate in their coverage, a marked departure from the mocking and derisive tone typically reserved for the Jews. Renowned Protestant periodicals included significant mention, and much of the provincial press in England reprinted the London reports in their entirety.[29] On the Continent, the influential *Allgemeine Zeitung* (Augsburg) placed the London protests on its front page, and in the United States, leading papers along the eastern seaboard remarked upon "the extraordinary movement of the Jews of Great Britain."[30] This far-flung media prominence was a direct indication of the degree to which this distinctive social movement resonated throughout much of the Western world.

Given the obvious import of this undertaking, what could reasonably account for such long-standing disregard? The answer resides in an array of circumstances. For one, the periodical press, which serves as the best starting place for reconstructing social movements, has often been an underutilized historical resource. Additionally, the leading Jewish figure during the movement's initial phase, Moses Levy, was a foreigner, and his limited residence in the metropolis as well as his subsequent historical neglect in the United States only increased his liminality and further obscured Levy's unique activist role in London.[31] Perhaps the foremost reason behind this lacuna, however, can be traced to the late nineteenth century, when communal historians omitted any mention of this episode in published accounts. At this juncture, the Jewish elite strived to maintain a unified public image that reaffirmed their place in the national polity. Amateur communal historians willingly advanced this ideal; controversial events were censored, and a filiopietistic style predominated. Because the middle-class activists of 1827 blatantly rebelled against synagogue strictures, were led by Moses Levy (an obstreperous outsider from frontier Florida), associated with "fanatic" Christians, and even mocked the oligarchs for their initial avoidance of the movement, it was perhaps inevitable that this undertaking was thoroughly excised from collective memory. This type of response is actually one of the more predictable outcomes of social movements; power-holders often go to great lengths to ignore the insurgent reality that inevitably surfaces during contentious periods.[32] It should also be emphasized, however, that this same select group later co-opted the movement as their own during the resurgence of 1840, while many of their descendants followed suit during later manifestations. By asserting control, the communal elite altered the symbolic environment in their favor, as they now embodied lofty British virtues of philanthropy and benevolence (a scenario that actually reinforced their own legitimacy) and in the process became caretakers of a new collective identity. The fact that Jewish historical identity in England precluded the mere mention of internal strife during the movement's earliest phase is indicative of a heightened degree of communal insecurity, a propensity that recent historians have been keen to recognize.[33] As will be demonstrated, however, the latter part of the nineteenth century was also the precise period when the Anglo-Jewish elite not only began to disassociate themselves from active protest but castigated all those who dared to engage in the public sphere. The leadership had thus gone full circle. Hence, a convergence of circumstances has arisen that has transformed the groundbreaking events of 1827 into an anomalous blank slate.

Prior to the Jewish rights movement, British Jews, just as their continental brethren, studiously averted the public sphere. Compliance, not activism, was still the norm, and the rabbinic axiom *dina de malkhuta dina* ("the law of the kingdom is the law [for the Jews]") was much intact. During the latter half of the eighteenth century, a handful of Anglo-Jewish authors may have articulated their identities through the literary medium, but this apolitical "literary public sphere"—what theorist Jürgen Habermas defines as "a process of self-clarification" that emphasized the private intellectual world—was quite distinct from the appearance of a fully political public sphere.[34] On the other hand, political matters that concerned the Anglo-Jewish community remained within the purview of the Jewish gentry, who were expected to act as discreet, behind-the-scenes intercessors (or *stadlanut*) with government officials. Jewish traditionalists still looked upon the political public sphere with profound distrust, and the solemn work of ensuring the communal welfare was generally understood only within a circumspect chain of command.[35]

Viewed from this perspective, the first expression of the Jewish rights movement clearly manifested a quantum shift in consciousness and thus deserves special consideration. Once the medieval "law of the kingdom" *mentalité* had been breached, many believed the old ways were rendered obsolete. Identity formation indeed surfaces as a central factor during collective action, a transformational process that helps shape future behavior.[36] This is not only a psychological phenomenon but an inherently social one as well. Consequently, recognition of this episode not only adds appreciably to our knowledge of social movements and interfaith activism in late Georgian England, but it challenges a variety of preconceptions, including the emergence of modern Jewish political identity.

Scholars have typically looked to events in late-nineteenth-century Russia as a historical "big bang," a cognitive liberation that rejected centuries of political passivity in favor of self-determination.[37] Jonathan Frankel, for example, has portrayed this period as a "revolution in modern Jewish politics."[38] What is more, some have also envisioned Jewish political endeavors prior to this time as virtually nonexistent; Jews were apparently "washed clean," as David Vital put it, "of political habits and political ideas, let alone political capabilities."[39] With respect to the celebrated actions surrounding the Damascus affair, David Biale posited that, "perhaps for the first time since antiquity, Jews acted to defend the rights of Jews in other countries."[40] Earlier in London, however, Jews publicly castigated the Russian tsar and proudly proclaimed that all their brethren were "flesh of their flesh and bone of their bone."[41] The fact that this event occurred in London, the leading cultural and intellectual metropolis, enhanced the movement's standing and facilitated the diffusion of ideas. The significance of the Jewish rights movement thereby transcends national borders and offers historians a radically different perspective on the development of modern Jewish politics.

The success of the movement owed much to the innovative contributions of Moses E. Levy—a peripatetic figure who has formerly been relegated to the margins of Jewish history.[42] In fact, his promotion of Jewish nationalism, as well as his resolute stand against assimilation, evokes the position of a much later group of Zionists. During Levy's relatively brief tenure in England (1825–1828), this former Caribbean merchant-shipper turned philanthropist and activist not only established the case for a Jewish homeland as the necessary fulfillment of biblical prophecy, but—in a manner akin to Leo Pinsker's treatise *Auto-Emancipation* (1882)—he advanced a deep skepticism regarding the future of Jews in gentile society. "Barbary, Turkey, Poland, the wilds of Prussia, [Jews] tried them all," Levy declared at London's elite Freemasons' Hall, "and every where found an enemy in man."[43] Some fifty years later, Pinsker employed a similar fatalistic approach: "[all] nations, by reason of their eternal, *natural* antagonism, will forever reject us."[44] Levy often resorted to an emotion-laden rhetoric and used injustice frames that were in keeping with the rhetoric of sensibility that pervaded the abolitionist crusade but had yet to be applied to the Jews in a social movement context. He claimed, for instance, that without a country of their own, Jews would inevitably face the "persecution of contempt" and thus be forced to "drag the chain of servitude." Levy even equated this dysfunctional state, as Pinsker did later, to a kind of death.[45] The appearance of these claims in 1820s England counters numerous historical assumptions vis-à-vis the rise of Jewish self-emancipation and even the origins of political Zionism.[46]

By virtue of Levy's leadership and celebrity standing in London, this "gentleman of the first respectability"[47] and intimate of colonial governors, generals, and bishops also established an entirely novel benchmark for the communal magnates. The acquisition of wealth and devotion to pious learning could no longer be seen as exclusive guarantors of privileged standing; instead, principled and courageous action—following the evangelical norm—was required to make these traits worthy of respect. Contiguous with Levy's final months in the metropolis and immediately following his departure for the United States, illustrious figures such as Moses Montefiore and Isaac L. Goldsmid also became exemplars of this new standard; rather than shun the limelight, they now openly advanced altruistic agendas. During the Jewish rights resurgence of 1840, Montefiore journeyed on a high-profile mission to the Middle East and, in conjunction with his French counterpart Adolphe Crémieux, negotiated with the viceroy of Egypt in an attempt to free imprisoned Damascus Jews and to assure that their innocence in the matter was properly adjudicated. Both Montefiore and Crémieux, in other words, had stepped beyond their own domestic boundaries and adopted the persona of transnational activists.[48] In Montefiore's case, the role of a diaspora nationalist was also reprised. And, as has been noted, among the other Anglo-Jewish notables who had previously shunned the initial solidarity movement, many now assumed a quite visible and respectable presence in 1840. The struggle for Jewish rights had evolved to reflect the interests of a growing number of the communal elite who were no longer averse to joining with Christians to zealously promote Jewish rights abroad.

A basic tenet of all social movements, according to historical sociologist Charles Tilly, posits that "the prior path of collective claim-making constrains its subsequent forms, influencing the very issues, actors, settings, and outcomes of popular struggle."[49] While the "extraordinary movement" surely reflected previous modes of collective action in Britain, it also reshaped and informed contemporary endeavors as well. If one considers that the repeal of the Test and Corporation Acts (1828), the newly invigorated drive for Catholic emancipation (1829), and the Anglo-Jewish elite's sudden efforts (after a legacy of indifference) to press for the removal of Jewish disabilities were all concurrent with the initial London movement, then this episode assumes even greater relevancy. None of these collective efforts stood in isolation from each other; as evidenced by the fact that Jewish leaders began to form a discreet alliance with Catholic activist Daniel O'Connell in July 1828 in order to advance Jewish emancipation.[50] The original London movement, as will be demonstrated, can now be seen as an *initiator movement*.[51] Neophyte Jewish activists defied the privileged reality of the British establishment and simulated a degree of civil equality not yet awarded to disenfranchised Jews. This climate of insurgency actually gave rise to a significant *spin-off movement*: the thirty-year campaign for Jewish political emancipation in England.

The Jewish rights struggle certainly evolved and adapted over time, but its core goals remained solidly in place. The movement fostered Jewish unity and nationhood and made explicit demands on all Jews to rise up in defense of the human rights and dignity of all their brethren. Initial protests were a passionate reaction to a highly stigmatized identity, and, as we shall see, bonds of trust and fidelity emerged along with a newfound sense of strength and solidarity. For these activists, their oft-repeated declaration, "to shew that they were men,"[52] resonated far beyond class boundaries and struck at the core of their identities. This defiant rhetoric adhered to modern concepts of universal rights and contested the rabbinical construction of masculinity that held self-restraint and Torah scholarship as paramount. A muscular style of Judaism surfaced in London; a passionate politics laden with symbolic meaning. This reordering of the hierarchies of identity would resonate far beyond the metropolis.

Another measure of the Jewish rights movement's success was the establishment of organizations that provided a more formalized, institutional structure. The emergence of the Alliance Israélite Universelle in Paris, an event that was precipitated by righteous anger over the previous Mortara incident, reflected a significant alteration in mainstream attitudes toward Jewish rights. After the first few protest cycles, advocacy of Jewish rights had progressed to such a point that professional organizational networks could evolve to provide needed services and to lobby against persecution throughout the world. While organizations in Britain, France, Austria, and America each developed their own agenda, all would be in general accord with the original motives of the Alliance, which was envisioned in 1860 as "a home of moral progress, religious solidarity, and protection for those who suffer on account of being Israelite."[53] These systematic and bureaucratized approaches, however, operated on a very different level from the protest mobilizations that surfaced in response to persecution. In time, the preservation of the organization itself rather than the original ideals of the movement often becomes a primary concern. Indeed, such a broad dependence on hierarchical organizational networks could have signaled the end of the contentious phase of the movement.[54] As it happened, a much more conservative orientation surfaced among the Jewish leadership during the last decades of the nineteenth century, and any form of passionate expression was actually denounced. But, as the Russian crises and indeed the twentieth-century anti-Nazi protests (1933) in New York City attest, spontaneous and highly emotive public demonstrations erupted in full force whenever gross violations of the rights of Jews became known and when the political environment permitted. A new nonelite leadership—composed primarily of socialists, Zionists, and other Eastern European émigrés—began to fill the void that had been caused by the abdication of the communal magnates in the political public sphere.

What forces were present in early-nineteenth-century Britain that allowed the Jewish rights movement to take hold? Historians, after all, have long regarded the Anglo-Jewish community as being particularly nonreceptive to change or social innovation of any kind. Historian Todd Endelman has maintained that "no new ideological or cultural current in modern Jewish history was launched or found fertile ground in Britain." According to Endelman, the real forces that "reoriented modern Jewish consciousness" originated solely in Eastern and Central Europe, where persecution "bred discontent with traditional norms and values."[55] The supposed permissiveness and liberality of England did not furnish the necessary edge, or so it is assumed, that results in rebelliousness, creative vigor, and intellectual achievement. "Anglo-Jewish history," Endelman thus contends, "is undramatic," at least compared with Jewish life on the Continent.[56] This thesis resounds throughout the historiography. England is seen as predominately liberal and munificent; Jews were thus lulled into "a sense of unpressured timelessness."[57] Another historian has recently envisioned the formation of modern Anglo-Jewish identity as a "gradual and unconscious absorption of thoughts and actions," an exceedingly passive and disinterested stance that the author likens to "osmosis."[58] The dominant view of English liberalism is given a more nuanced interpretation in David Feldman's influential study, *Englishmen and Jews: Social Relations and Political Culture, 1840–1914*, although Feldman's essential claims differ only marginally from Endelman's thesis. Feldman thus focuses upon "the extent to which different institutions and collectivities were able to accommodate the Jewish minority."[59]

Accommodation—certainly not activism on the part of Anglo-Jewry—becomes the overriding focus. The author views the steady progression of political and legal advances that benefited Jews between 1830 and 1914 as an achievement devoid of any trace of social movement activity. And he interprets the relatively "passive response" that marked the communal leadership during the Russian pogroms of 1881–1882 as normative and not as the controversial abnegation that it actually was.[60] As we shall see, however, London Jews actually did forge a fundamental break with the past and constructed an original political consciousness in the process. They bypassed traditional authority in a direct appeal to public opinion, exhibited forceful reactions against antisemitism, and contributed to striking, long-term changes in the Anglo-Jewish community. Throughout most of the nineteenth century, in fact, metropolitan Jews, in conjunction with high-ranking Christians, set the pace for a substantial movement that took hold on both sides of the Atlantic and made abundant use of the public sphere.

To fully assess the Jewish rights campaign and the circumstances that gave rise to it, one has to come to terms with the social and political standing of Jews during the premovement era. Although an ennobling picture of the Anglo-Jewish "cousinhood"—the interrelated Montefiores, Rothchilds, Goldsmids, Mocattas, and other wealthy families—abounds in the historiography, within the social imaginary of early-nineteenth-century England, all Jews, regardless of means, were conspicuous as the consummate "other." The closest parallel to Jews, as clearly evidenced within the literature of the period, was in fact the despised Gypsy. While Jews filled a cultural niche as urban domestic aliens, Gypsies were consigned as their rural counterparts.[61] Condescension cut across all income levels, from ubiquitous "old-clothes men" (street peddlers) to the comparatively small number of "stockjobbers" on the London Exchange, who, under the dictates of caste, were stigmatized by upper-class Anglicans as parvenus and "plebeians."[62] Naturalization was denied all foreign-born Jews (the majority status of Jews in England); education and employment was severely restricted; and even the most talented were barred from the professions—with the exception of foreign-trained physicians who served the insular Jewish community. Anglo-Jews could not vote, hold public office, or attend university (as was the case with all non-Anglicans during the initial phase of the movement). Simple prejudice, however, further excluded Jews from "common seminaries" or trade institutions. The City of London had barred Jews from the "freedom of the City," thereby excluding them from owning or operating retail shops and preventing Jews from holding city office. While Anglo-Jews worshipped freely and did not suffer the same type of overt oppression that was widespread on the Continent, there was, nevertheless, a palpable "persecution of contempt," as Moses Levy phrased it.[63] Indeed, he surmised that this "refined malice" was an even greater malevolent force than "torture, the sword, or the fagot." These latter afflictions "only destroyed the body," he asserted, but unremitting contempt "ruined the soul."[64] Philo-Judaeans were similarly cognizant of an "open spirit of hatred" against Jews and deliberately set out to undermine this centuries-old prejudice.[65]

Counterpoised against such narrow-mindedness was the image of England as an international center of humanitarian-based social movement activity. An almost obsessive desire for human improvement marked most of these efforts, and a concomitant belief in the creation of a new moral order was routinely cast under the mantle of liberalism. Indeed, London's vaunted reform culture—an outgrowth of evangelical Protestantism—fostered expectations for social transformation that far exceeded any other city in Europe or the United States. Much of the nation's moral authority was vested in the emancipation of enslaved blacks in the British Caribbean, a social movement of impressive proportions (and an endeavor that threatened vested economic interests).[66] As historians Robin Blackburn and Eric Foner both suggest, the abolitionist movement served a pivotal role in formulating the notion of universal human rights, a radical concept unrestrained by race or national origin.[67] According to this historical perspective, nothing less than a new understanding of human freedom and unity emerged as a result of the antislavery crusade. Redefining moral concepts was one thing, but taking remedial action in the public sphere was an innovation of a far different order—a path that endowed enlightened political actors with "moral capital."[68] It is thus most significant that Moses Levy strongly identified as an abolitionist; attended and spoke before antislavery meetings; and published his own plan for gradual emancipation while in London (1828)—a Jewish contribution to antislavery that has long gone unacknowledged.[69] In addition to abolitionism, a diverse range of benevolent societies in England also sought to mitigate the suffering of local working-class children, elderly pensioners, industrial laborers, and other marginalized groups. An organizational, tactical, and philosophical foundation for radical reform therefore existed for others to emulate. Reformers were grounded in well-honed public relations techniques that were used to manipulate public opinion, and ascendant bourgeois virtues of altruism and philanthropy were held aloft for all to follow. These were "social virtues" and "moral sentiments" that had particular resonance within Britain. Unlike the French *philosophes*, whose ultimate appeal was to reason, exponents of the British Enlightenment centered on a moral philosophy of compassion. By the time of the Jewish rights movement, the virtues of benevolence and philanthropy were deeply engrained, particularly among the middle classes.[70] While religiously based "benevolence" remained the cultural ideal, it should also be understood that Anglo-Protestantism was undergoing severe fractionalization and in-fighting during the late 1820s—a fact that has eluded most historians of Anglo-Jewry. Romanticism was beginning to make deep inroads, especially within the emergent apocalyptic branch of the evangelical movement.[71] For this ultraconservative group particularly, all Jews had an exceptional role to play during the end-times. Whatever the motivation, the scathing image of the Jew in British society and the marginalized existence of most Jews as social and political pariahs remained wholly at odds from those hallowed ideals that ostensibly set England apart and increasingly validated the nation's sense of self-worth, a society committed to the ideal of natural liberty.

The appearance of mechanized, steam-powered presses led to the proliferation of print culture in Britain (there were more than three hundred newspapers in the country by 1828), a factor that proved indispensable in disseminating social movement goals.[72] The country became enamored by the idea of self-improvement, particularly for the working classes, and a heightened desire for knowledge resulted in a nation "obsessively communicating with itself."[73] Often overlooked, but of at least equal significance, was the centrality of public speaking. Successful orators of the era, such as William Wilberforce, Daniel O'Connell, and Rev. Edward Irving, became powerful agents of cultural change and aroused almost cultlike celebrity. As both a foreigner and a Jew, Moses Levy may at first seem a most unlikely candidate for such renown. While very much an outsider, by all accounts Levy met the lofty British standard of gentility, drew upon the rhetoric of sensibility, manifested striking oratorical skills, and was praised, even by those who disagreed with his views, for "his great benevolence of soul, and deep and enlightened piety."[74] Levy idealized London as "an emporium of civilization and religion, where man appears in the advanced post of improved character."[75] The metropolis strongly beckoned to him, as well as other believers in human progress, and afforded unique prospects for someone of Levy's talents. This city of one and a half million (which included 15,000 Jews) became a natural base from which the movement could make its debut and evolve over the ensuing decades.

A NOTE ON SOCIAL MOVEMENTS

While modern historians may routinely label such seminal undertakings as women's rights, for example, as a social movement, with few exceptions—such as the eminent Zionist historian Jacob Katz—most are unwilling to immerse themselves in the current sociological literature and apply these concepts to historical phenomena.[76] The reason for this reluctance appears to stem from an inherent tension between disciplines.[77] Suffice it to say that sociology, with its emphasis on broad generalizations, theory, and an often dense terminology, may seem antithetical to the historian's traditional focus on empirical research, historical narrative, and the attention usually given to societal differences, changes that occur through time, and the importance of the individual. "Sociologists . . . are trained to notice or formulate general rules and often screen out the exceptions," observes Peter Burke, "while historians learn to attend to concrete detail at the expense of general patterns."[78] This book attempts to bridge the gap between these disciplines (along with their intrinsic universal/particular divide) and stems from very pragmatic concerns. The social movement model, as I discovered, offers the only viable means with which to identify and analyze the previously "hidden" events of 1827 as well as those that followed. Once equipped, one can excavate the archival sources and actually discern a foundation, so to speak. Initial clarification is needed, however, as common understanding of social movements may differ dramatically from the particular sociological model used here.

On the most basic level, social movements consist of organized public challenges that are directed at society's power-holders. These movements are innately political, aim at redressing specific wrongs, and are conducted on behalf of a needy or disenfranchised group of persons who reside under elite authority.[79] The goal of social and political change is enacted through a set of strategies—a contentious repertoire consisting of parliamentary petitioning, pamphleteering, street demonstrations, committees, public meetings, and so forth. In the process, activists openly proclaim their grievances. These actions may be intrinsically political, but they also take place outside the mainstream and are skewed to attract maximum media attention. Indeed, a sense of moral outrage is often a key element. Protesters nevertheless gain strength and influence only when they are perceived as a creditable, united body and after they risk antagonizing the establishment in pursuit of a worthy agenda. Finally, it should be noted that this kind of venture is a relatively modern construction; in fact, national social movements, according to Charles Tilly, only emerged as a significant form of contention in Great Britain after 1815.[80] The "extraordinary movement" was certainly a singular event in modern Jewish history, but it still adhered to a well-recognized form of contentious politics that has evolved and flourishes to the present day. The initial expression of the movement actually formed a collective action *master frame* for future events: it established the key issues of protest; set a common perspective for analyzing and resolving crises; utilized symbols, metaphors, and catchphrases that aided in conveying movement goals; defined the makeup and responsibilities of coalition members; and even established criteria for protest venues.[81]

Certain social movements, known as solidarity movements, direct their claims toward human rights issues abroad.[82] This was certainly the case with the struggle for Jewish rights. In each instance, the existential threat was perceived as external. An overriding sense of altruism is thus one of the most distinguishing aspects of solidarity movements; activists are perceived as taking part from an explicit sense of moral obligation and not from motives of self-interest. Adding another layer of complexity to the solidarity movement paradigm is the fact that the "extraordinary movement" drew upon an unparalleled interfaith coalition of Jews and Christians. For Jews, *tzedakah* (charity and social justice) is both a religious obligation and a collective responsibility, as is the concept of *Kelal Yisrael* (fidelity to a world Jewry). "They [the Jewish nation] are like one body," wrote the renowned second-century sage Rabbi Shimon bar Yohai. "When one is injured, all feel the pain."[83] This particular tenet emerged as a kind of rallying cry at one point during the early meetings in London and in fact became a recurrent theme during subsequent phases of the movement as well. While such sentiments were ancient and deeply felt, organized and heated public expressions of *Kelal Yisrael* were entirely novel phenomena at the time. Hence the Jewish rights campaign may have been an indication of altruistic intent among Christian coalition members; indeed, their support was a milestone of sorts. Jews no longer presented "an obstacle to the brotherhood of the Christian world," or so it was thought.[84] But from a Jewish standpoint, persecution was felt on a far more intimate and direct level—they were the ones, after all, who were the stigmatized "other"—and their reaction to oppression actually reinforced a diaspora identity. "Our tie is a sincere brotherly love," as Isaac Leeser, a leading figure in American Jewry, declared during the height of the Damascus affair. "Our patriotism is the affection which unites the Israelites of one land to that of another."[85] Jews were now willing to publicly admit that diaspora loyalties could coexist with (indeed even transcend) their sense of obligation to their own countries during times of exceptional crisis. A curious tension arose as the movement seemed to encourage two apparently divergent paths: an increased sense of transnational identity and a striving for enhanced rights of citizenship.

Although a significant portion of the British press may have been supportive of the campaign for Jewish rights, there was nonetheless a conservative faction that looked upon these newly engaged activists with intense displeasure and genuine alarm.[86] The majority of high church Tories, for instance, still conceived of Jews as "aliens," and so they were deemed undeserving of all political rights. Yet negative reactions never reached a boiling point; a situation that was undoubtedly mitigated by the fact that the movement focused attention on the human rights shortcomings of a distant ruler rather than finding fault at home and also held the support of politically influential evangelicals as well. This unique display of Jewish autonomy did not provoke violence or serious retaliation toward the Anglo-Jewish community, a situation that was certainly welcomed by those early activists who dared to take up the banner of Jewish rights. Indeed, the relative ease with which this novel undertaking took place proved to be a most reliable blueprint for the future. This framework portrayed Jews not only as possessing fundamental human rights but as persons capable of legitimately defending these rights. What was formerly understood as unjust (but nevertheless bearable) was now redefined, using modern norms, as grossly intolerable and meriting urgent remedial action. Traditional acquiescence was replaced by active resistance. In most instances, the movement projected an aura of inevitability, modernity, and of moral and intellectual advancement. "Progress of liberal ideas," proclaimed a New York City protestor in 1858, "can no more be stopped than the lightning's message along the telegraph wires."[87] This was a righteous endeavor that appeared to effortlessly transcend national boundaries, and, once having gained the moral high ground, participants claimed to be undeterred by the decisions of governments. All "friends of humanity" were united, no matter their faith, and if national officials proved unsympathetic to their cause, the censure of the world press would ultimately prove "more potent to correct the evil."[88] As we shall see, the Jewish rights campaign eventually established itself as one of most prevalent and enduring social movements of the nineteenth century; its early success formed a foundation for future endeavors in the twentieth century and beyond.

While the main focus of this book will cover a substantial time frame—1827 to 1903, with a brief overview of the twentieth century—it is not by any means intended as a comprehensive historical survey. The historiography already abounds with excellent studies of this lengthy period. Instead, discussion will necessarily be restricted to the major phases of the movement itself, which will be presented here in five sections. Historical context is obviously vital to this undertaking, but the most cogent historical markers will be evidence of communal insurgency, protest, and collective action. In this sense, the present study will depart rather dramatically from the principal concerns of most historical narratives. On the other hand, it will more closely adhere to how actual participants in the movement saw themselves and their place in society.

Part I
The Extraordinary Movement

1   Movement Origins

Inextricably linked to society as a whole, successful social movements draw the interest of the mass media and the scrutiny of governments; enlist a range of political allies and generate fierce adversaries; and are specially attuned to other collective endeavors and countermovements.[1] Thus, it is especially notable that the emergence of the Jewish rights movement (itself a passionate form of politics) corresponded with a period of ideological conflict and political uncertainty in England; a veritable "crisis of the old order," as one historian has phrased it.[2] Conservatives experienced major legislative reversals, and signs of increasing democratization caused many to bemoan both their "perishing Epoch"[3] and their previously favored status within it. A financial crisis that began in 1825 shook many people's faith in the monetary system. Furthermore, a period of political unrest surfaced in February 1827 after the lengthy ministry of Lord Liverpool (along with the entire Tory party) was thrust into disarray following the prime minister's debilitating stroke. The appointment of George Canning in April resulted in virtual rebellion by the "old Tories," but the Canning ministry proved short-lived, as he also died unexpectedly.[4] Canning was succeeded by the highly ineffectual Lord Goderich, whose weak cabinet collapsed after three months—a period marked by a problematic military alliance with Russia and the latter's unsettling gains after the Battle of Navarino (Greece) in October. George IV, after some initial hesitancy, then appointed the more forceful Duke of Wellington as prime minister in January 1828, a ministry that managed to endure for a tumultuous two years. Heightened periods of governmental flux and instability, social theorists observe, offer increased opportunities for political protest, as new players will often seek to fill any perceived power vacuum.[5] The emergent Jewish rights movement, falling as it did within the one-year time line between Liverpool's departure and Wellington's appointment, appears to reaffirm this thesis—both on the national level and, as we shall see, the communal as well.

A corresponding period of crisis and fragmentation also marked much of Anglo-Protestantism. "Parties in the religious world, as in the political," as a journalist lamented in 1827, "are exceedingly confused."[6] Anglicans, for example, were not only separated into three "parties" (high, low, and evangelical), but the evangelical branch was exceedingly prone to internal splintering and infighting. The most important of these divisions was the deep antipathy that developed between post- and pre-millennialists. This evangelical schism was so profoundly felt and theologically divergent that, according to historian Boyd Hilton, they virtually composed two separate religious sects.[7] Prominent post-millennialists included such figures as William Wilberforce and the Clapham "saints." On a basic level, these evangelicals believed that the second coming was reserved for an indeterminate future; in the meantime, an ongoing measure of "good works" was vital in order to prepare the way for this event. Ironically, it was from this branch that the notorious culture of conversion in Britain emanated. In contrast, pre-millennialists, exemplified by the noted Scottish preacher Rev. Edward Irving and the wealthy, influential layman Henry Drummond, vehemently rejected their colleagues' optimistic eschatology (Drummond actually considered liberality as intrinsically evil). Pre-millennialists were convinced, based on their understanding of prophetic scripture, of a forthcoming and dreadful apocalypse, and that human intervention should therefore be restricted to a very select agenda in order not to interfere with God's plan. A resurgence of apocalyptic fervor arose during the mid-1820s—the beginning of the so-called London prophetic revival.[8] Romanticism made a significant impact: healings, miracles, prophecy, and various other phenomena were taken as direct proof of the approaching end-times. A predominant sense of the transcendent, as well as an overriding pessimism and rigidity, was manifested in the pre-millennial eschatology. In a curious twist, the prophetic revival first made major advances not among the poor and uneducated, but among the upper classes. The American Revolution, the excesses of the French Revolution, the rise and fall of Napoleon, the emergence of working-class radicalism, and a growing democratization were all transformative events that generated a disturbing sense of instability for many staunch conservatives. The entire social order, it appeared, was steadily being dismantled, and increasing numbers believed that God's hand was the only cogent explanation for these unsettling circumstances. Numerous "signs of the times" confirmed that a cataclysmic future was literally unfolding in the present; such distinctions are fundamental to a full contextual understanding of subsequent events.

THE JEWS OF LONDON

Compared to the cosmopolitan reputation of the Jews of Berlin or Amsterdam, London Jews were often cast as culturally and intellectually inferior to their continental brethren. Contributing to this negative perception was the sizable influx of poor and illiterate newcomers, primarily from Central and Eastern Europe, who settled in the city's East End slums. Their ragged countenances could hardly have been more antithetical to the bourgeois ideal sought by communal leaders. Faced with few options, many immigrants became street peddlers; they went about in traditional Ashkenazi garb—black cloaks and broad-brimmed hats—and aggressively hawked their wares with loud, coarse-sounding Yiddish accents. In addition, "a small army of Jew boys," according to one contemporary account, would converge en masse toward any well-to-do traveler in the city for the chance of a quick sale of a comb, sealing wax, or perhaps a lemon.[9] Whether adult or child, "street Jews" seemed to epitomize all that was uncanny and un-English; their visible presence, numbering in the thousands, overshadowed the more respectable demeanor of the Jewish "middling classes"—the petty merchants and artisans. Eventually the new arrivals would eschew their traditional attire and adapt more fully to the rough-edged culture of the East End, often evincing a swaggering aggression that could easily degrade into anger and conflict.[10] Such streetwise assertiveness and spiritual torpor differed sharply from the more subdued conformity of their continental brethren. The truculent image of the uneducated, Anglo-Jewish masses—what the writer Thomas Carlyle rendered as "all the hungry ugliness of creation"[11]—was the result of waves of impoverished immigrants and mirrored the radical diminution of conventional synagogue authority in England.

In dramatic contrast to the pauper underclass were the acculturated intellectual elite such as Hyman Hurwitz, a respected scholar in rabbinic literature, head of a private Hebrew academy in Highgate (north of London) and later appointed professor of Hebrew at the newly established University of London (1828). Hurwitz, born and raised in Poland, may have been praised by no less a personage as Samuel Taylor Coleridge as "most deserving the name of a *philosopher*,"[12] but such tributes were exceedingly rare. The renowned political economist David Ricardo (a Christian convert); the writer and essayist, Isaac Disraeli; and the brilliant mathematician and autodidact, Benjamin Gompertz were also singled out on occasion. And in the arts, the operatic tenor John Braham attained international distinction. Despite the demonstrable talent of these individuals, detractors of Anglo-Jewry followed a peculiar conceit of the period and chided London Jews as being incapable of producing their own preeminent thinkers, scholars who could equal the stature of Moses Mendelssohn or Baruch Spinoza. The supposed dearth of "great men" contributed to the perception of English Jewry as cultural and intellectual subalterns.[13] To be sure, London lacked a robust community of *maskilim*, and refined, anglicized Jews did not generate the sort of elevated literary and artistic salons that thrived in Berlin and Vienna. Whatever the diverse merits of London's fifteen thousand Jews, it should be recalled that all were barred from attending the universities of Oxford and Cambridge and that basic secular education was restricted to a fortunate few. Moreover, following universal expulsion in 1290, Jewish resettlement was a tentative process that began some 350 years later, with small numbers arriving in England beginning in the mid-seventeenth century. Hence, not only did the Jews of London (circa 1820s) lack the same sense of continuity and authoritative control that pervaded much of the Continent, but the "community" consisted of a broad mosaic of unlettered and impoverished foreigners who knew little of their religious traditions, inhabited squalid tenements, and overwhelmed meager communal resources. All things considered, any limitation in cultural and intellectual attainment would hardly be unexpected.

Positioned at the apex of Jewish society in the metropolis was a wealthy stratum of merchant bankers, bullion brokers, stockbrokers, and international investors—a close-knit "cousinhood" who kept to their peers and distanced themselves from the pressing concerns of the lower classes.[14] With few exceptions, these communal aristocrats did not follow strict orthodox lifestyles; even so, many upheld at least the pretense of traditional Judaism in their personal lives and maintained strong institutional links with their respective synagogues. Unlike their counterparts in Europe and the United States, reform currents within Judaism generated comparatively little interest among the Cousinhood at this time. Conservative upper-class conformity (patterned after the Anglican gentry) held sway, and, in keeping with this tendency, communal magnates typically turned a blind eye toward religious and social innovation of any sort.

By the early nineteenth century, a segment of prosperous Jews had already moved into imposing town houses in the capital's fashionable West End, where they could maintain a sense of aristocratic decorum and social exclusivity, despite the fact that they were often subjected to ostracism themselves. The entry of wealthy Jewish stockbrokers into genteel neighborhoods was regarded as a sure sign that persons of "high caste" would soon leave, property values plummet, and "plebeianism" would, in all certainty, run rampant. Some residential leases expressly prohibited "that any Jew should occupy their houses."[15] Even Coleridge, who truly admired his accomplished neighbor, Hyman Hurwitz, was nevertheless convinced that "the Jews on the Stock-exchange & their compeers" constituted "the lower classes."[16] Such a distinction would, of course, include some of the most affluent persons in England. Similarly, the historian and Whig politician, Thomas Babington Macaulay (1800–1859), known for his vigorous defense of Jewish emancipation during his first speech in Parliament, still harbored deeply engrained feelings of Jewish otherness. In 1831, after being personally invited to a fancy-dress ball by one of the Cousinhood's grandees, Isaac L. Goldsmid, Macaulay later mocked the exchange in private, equating it with a scene from Boswell's *Tour to the Hebrides*. Macaulay envisioned himself as Boswell's honored friend, Dr. Johnson, and placed Goldsmid, quite tellingly, as a Hebridean goatherd.[17]

The Cousinhood therefore possessed a highly ambiguous standing. Their influence on the Royal Exchange, for example, may have been substantial, but the City of London restricted Jewish brokers to a dozen individuals. A consequence of this arbitrary regulation, noted one observer, was "that enormous sums have, since time immemorial, been extorted from the

Jew brokers, as the price of this privilege," amounts that could run as high as two thousand pounds.[18] Furthermore, even if an individual secured a coveted broker's medal or achieved success as a "stockjobber" (a pejorative that was virtually synonymous with financial trickery, amorality, and avarice[19]) on the far less restrictive London Stock Exchange, this hardly allowed Jews to recast themselves as bona fide members of the English upper class. Stockjobbing was routinely compared to "gambling with loaded dice" and was supposedly the means by which "some of the greatest Jewish fortunes" were made.[20] Philosopher David Hume wrote that the stock market was in "the hands of idle people, who live on their revenue, our funds, in that view, give great encouragement to an useless and inactive life."[21] Ultimately, societal prejudices applied to all Jewish classes; as the *Eclectic Review* (1829) noted when the subject of Jewish civil liberties came to the fore in London: "The truth is that all over the world, the word Jew is an indefinite synonym for anything bad." In Great Britain, the magazine concluded, where commerce was paramount, "a national feeling of contempt for the Jews" arose as "Jew" became tantamount to "cheat."[22] Immense wealth could not offset Anglo-Jewry's highly diminished "cultural capital"; indeed, according to theorist Pierre Bourdieu, success in the marketplace often serves as an obstacle to cultural or "symbolic" power.[23]

Given their inclusion as figures of contempt within gentile society, it is not unexpected that the Jewish elite would also assume a distinct ambiguity within the communal realm as well. The oligarchs actually exerted scant control over the broader Jewish community (as most immigrants were not members of any synagogue), and, unlike their continental brethren, Anglo-Jewish leaders lacked the coercive force of law. Within their own congregations, however, these figures dominated internal affairs with a fairly arbitrary hand. The Cousinhood had long barred the predominately middle-class "seatholders" from any share in congregational decisions, imposed a wealth-based standard of virtue, envisioned poverty as a character flaw, and absolved themselves from coming to the aid of their distant brethren.[24] Furthermore, the chief Ashkenazi rabbi, Solomon Hirschell, was firmly under elite control and rarely exerted any independence. A Board of Deputies, consisting of leading members of London's five synagogues, was established in 1760; this body nevertheless remained a mere ceremonial vestige by the time of the Jewish rights movement, lacked statutory power, and had never advanced Jewish interests to any significant level. By failing to keep up with an evolving social reality and by insulating themselves from the community at large, Jewish notables had unwittingly eroded their own legitimacy. This social and cultural dislocation was at variance with the rising norms of equality, participation, and self-realization; modern attributes that were much in alignment with London's culture of reform, with its appeal to activism, public dialogue, and moral regeneration.

Jews were also divided among Ashkenazi and Sephardi factions; each maintained its own synagogues and did not permit communal largesse, such as it was, to extend beyond rigid demarcations. Both groups, however, were entirely ill-equipped for the rapid influx of immigrants and the subsequent formation of an expanding underclass. A single Jews' Free School, which offered basic instruction in secular and religious subjects, was established by members of the Great Synagogue (Ashkenazi) and operated in the East End beginning in 1822.[25] The number of students who could be accommodated at this school, however, fell dramatically short of the community's actual requirements. The prevailing observation, apart from the Cousinhood, was that basic necessities were being woefully ignored. Rabbi Joseph Crooll (1760–1829), a Hebrew instructor at Cambridge University who became a supporter of the Jewish rights movement, reflected this attitude when he criticized the general state of inaction in a letter published in the London press in 1828. "Our faces ought to be covered in shame," he declared emphatically, "when we see daily the Christians join, the rich and the poor together, to instruct their poor, and sparing no expense. But we, who are the children of Abraham, the friend of God, and the people with whom God made a covenant, are lying in a deep sleep."[26] Jews were unquestionably experiencing a profound sense of cultural and social dislocation; the elite simply failed to come to terms with this crisis. Evangelicals, on the other hand, realized an opportunity and began to reach out to destitute and uprooted Jews, offering food, employment, and educational resources in an aggressive bid for converts. While this proselytizing met with very limited success, the breakdown of communal identity and cohesion continued unabated. The haphazard resettlement and pauperization of thousands of Jewish arrivals in the city, a scene that has been aptly equated to a "frontier boom town,"[27] as well as a dearth of effective leadership created a political, religious, and moral vacuum of serious dimensions. Compared to any traditional Jewish community on the Continent, where the primacy of Jewish law was enforced and communal authority was staunchly maintained, the Jews of London stood as a strange and discomforting anomaly. Indeed, the metropolis surely exemplified all that could go awry if the social, spiritual, and economic hazards of the modern industrial age were not substantially addressed.

A CAST OF CHARACTERS

It was amid this fractious setting that Moses E. Levy first made a name for himself in the metropolis. In contrast to his better-known Jewish and Protestant contemporaries, Levy has eluded historical interest in England and, until recently, has also remained a marginalized figure in the United States. The son of a high-ranking Sephardic Jewish courtier to the sultan of Morocco, Levy was a sophisticated, transnational figure whose far-ranging travels and avoidance of any kind of self-promotion in his later years made him especially vulnerable to historical omission.[28] Before relinquishing a flourishing business career, Levy—the father of future United States senator, David L. Yulee (Florida)—was a leading Caribbean merchant-shipper based in St. Thomas, Virgin Islands, and supplied General Pablo Morillo's massive expeditionary forces in Venezuela with food and munitions. Focused on his new philanthropic agenda and distraught by the waves of anti-Jewish violence in post-Napoleonic Western Europe—known as the *Hep! Hep!* riots of 1819— Levy arrived in the newly acquired U.S. territory of East Florida in 1821 with the intention of settling a vast 100,000-acre agrarian refuge for oppressed Jews, an idealistic "asylum" based on communitarian principles.[29] To avoid any prospect of controversy, Levy cautiously kept his plans out of the public eye. But the myriad difficulties of forging a colony in a subtropical wilderness, funded at his own expense, seriously impeded his ambitions. Even so, Levy, who became a U.S. citizen during this time, founded Pilgrimage Plantation (1822–1835), a large agricultural venture replete with citrus groves, livestock, a sugar mill, plantation house, and various dwellings where a half-dozen immigrant Jewish families resided in the isolated Florida interior, including a young scion of the Warburg banking dynasty.[30]

In 1825 Levy arrived in London, where he immediately tried to persuade members of the Anglo-Jewish elite, such as Isaac L. Goldsmid, of the efficacy of his colonization project.[31] Unfortunately, Levy's arrival coincided with negative publicity surrounding Mordecai M. Noah's proposal for a Jewish colony in upper New York State a few months earlier.[32] Despite Levy's efforts to disassociate his venture from Noah's grandiose and widely spurned "Proclamation to the Jews," the topic of Jewish colonization in America had already been seriously tarnished. After Levy's solicitations went unheeded, he traveled to Paris, where a long-standing business friendship facilitated the mortgaging of a portion of his Florida landholdings. Returning once more to London, Levy took up residence at 1 Park Row in Knightsbridge, a spacious yet unpretentious address near Hyde Park. His original territorialist goal was soon eclipsed by what he considered to be a more urgent and practical necessity: to inculcate a Jewish national consciousness. Levy's commitment to the London reform movement, including his participation in the antislavery campaign, coupled with a personable manner and an impressive command of Hebrew and the Bible—qualities that certainly aided in advancing his ambitious cause. Among a variety of influential friendships and alliances that were formed at this time were members of the newly formed Philo-Judaean Society, an organization that was much under the influence of pre-millennial fervor.

On 9 March 1827, the Philo-Judaean Society sponsored a unique interreligious debate held at the headquarters of the Anti-Slavery Society (in close proximity to Guildhall). This meeting was in answer to a rather audacious public challenge made by the noted Hebraist Selig Newman (1788–1871). Educated in Posen, Poland, Newman was awarded a position at the leading synagogue in Berlin at a young age and eventually moved to England, where he was appointed minister of a congregation in Plymouth. Like his colleague Rabbi Crooll at Cambridge, Newman's scholarly achievements—he authored an esteemed Hebrew-English lexicon, among other works—were recognized by his appointment as a quasi-official instructor of Hebrew at Oxford University.[33] Jews, of course, could not hold genuine faculty positions at either Oxford or Cambridge. Even so, Newman yielded some influence, as his pupils included the future Archbishop of Canterbury and, outside of Oxford, the respected rabbi, Dr. Morris Raphall (1798–1868).[34] Like Crooll, and doubtless influenced by their mutual positions of authority over earnest Oxbridge students, Newman was entirely heedless of long-standing communal prohibitions regarding public religious disputes. Newman later admitted that he could never "deign to play the hypocrite" or to act contrary to his convictions and was "determined not to swerve from the path of truth."[35] Thus, in what he considered a principled and forthright appeal to pure reason (rather than blind faith) as well as manly engagement, he confidently challenged "any Jewish convert or learned Christian" who would defend "scriptural proofs of Jesus being the Messiah"—a radical proposition by any measure. By making this claim in public, Newman had in effect brazenly announced his entry into the modern political arena and had thereby broken with an earlier precedent set in the late eighteenth century by such Jewish writers as David Levi, all of whom confined their polemics to the printed realm. Indeed, to take aim at the core of Christian precepts via public debate was perhaps the intellectual counterpart to the city's popular Jewish-versus-Christian prizefights.[36] A Jewish observer actually noted that a faction of lower-class, "unenlightened" Jews looked upon this event as a form of religious warfare.[37] Be that as it may, the challenge was surely intended to counter a particularly offensive tactic used by evangelicals: Jewish apostates were often sent as newly converted Protestant missionaries into poor Jewish neighborhoods, where they provoked much unease. The formal debate format would nonetheless render any form of unruliness off-limits; proper order (at least in theory) was expected to dominate.

Accepting Newman's offer was Rev. Joseph Wolff (1795–1862), a former German Jew turned Christian provocateur and millennialist who consistently demonstrated an odd zeal and eccentricity throughout his lifetime.[38] He was considerably ill-equipped for any role that required a modicum of diplomatic tact, and his reputation (he was also engaged in proselytizing East End Jews at this time) surely preceded him. After Newman's opening address passed by without excitement, Wolff approached the lectern and embarked on a fiery sermon rather than adhering to the rules of cool argument. His remarks soon sparked outrage from a hostile portion of the approximately five hundred "Israelites" in attendance: a loud and continuous uproar—a shaming ritual known in England as "rough music"—overwhelmed Wolff's every word. His voice at a fevered pitch, holding a Bible in one hand and waving the other in "violent gesticulations," Wolff, according to the correspondent for the *Times*, seemed the very epitome of a madman.[39] A Jewish observer asserted that only a small faction of "malcontents" was responsible for the disruption; most middle-class Jews, according to this account, sat by quietly and "blushed for the indecorous conduct of those persons."[40] Any raucous behavior defied traditional Jewish conceptions of proper male conduct; self-restraint was to be maintained at all times. Communal leaders, one can safely assume, were entirely absent. Their nonattendance was perhaps wise given that the unseemly chaos relegated all Jewish participants into a kind of mob. After failed attempts to restore calm, this discomforting experiment in Jewish-Christian dialogue never regained order and eventually adjourned early.

As unlikely as it may seem, the Newman-Wolff debacle did not signal the end of Jewish engagement in the public sphere; to the contrary, this faltering effort would lead to far more productive endeavors. Even so, one may naturally question the motives of the Philo-Judaean Society. Their involvement, however, actually ran counter to the usual evangelical or conversionist orientation—an aggressive mind-set that was so intently rendered by Joseph Wolff. At first glance, Philo-Judaean efforts may in fact evoke a liberal-humanist orientation; indeed, this has long been the view of historian Todd Endelman.[41] Yet upon close examination, it becomes quite clear that the Philo-Judaean leadership adhered to the precepts of the ultraconservative, pre-millennial wing of evangelicalism and actually considered liberalism anathema.[42] Because historians have never delved very deeply into the character of this little-known organization, it becomes necessary to cast a fresh perspective on this seemingly paradoxical and enigmatic group.

The Philo-Judaean Society was an association of predominately Anglican evangelicals whose wealth, high social ranking, and political connections starkly contrasted with the more modest standing of the Jews who attended the Newman-Wolff debate. The society's inner circle consisted of such eminent personalities as Henry Drummond MP, Viscount Mandeville MP (sixth Duke of Manchester), Rev. Hugh McNeile, Hon. J. J. Strutt (Baron Rayleigh), and General Charles Neville.[43] Their allies in Parliament included Robert Grant and Spencer Perceval (son of the late prime minister) in the House of Commons; the cabinet minister Lord Bexley; and the Earl of Shaftesbury and Baron Vernon in the House of Lords.[44] Most of these influential individuals were proponents of the imminent second coming of Christ and believed that Jews had been ordained by God to play a fundamental role during the end-times, prior to the founding of the millennial kingdom.[45] By virtue of this privileged position, anti-Jewish bias and maltreatment needed to be quashed and immediate measures taken to educate and employ the masses of illiterate Jewish poor in London and eventually the world at large. The society was founded in 1826, following the first of an annual series of prophetic conferences held at Drummond's Albury estate in Surry, in order to specifically advance these goals.[46]

Strikingly at odds with the hard-line proselytizing that had grown to dominate evangelical dealings with English Jews, the Philo-Judaean Society focused on temporal needs and eschewed conversionist tactics.[47] Proselytizing, on the other hand, was the exclusive concern of the separate and far better known London Society for the Promotion of Christianity among the Jews, an older organization commonly referred to as either the London Society or, more frequently, the Jews' Society. [Wolff was actually employed by the Jews' Society and, as it happened, never again appeared in connection with the Philo-Judaeans.] Unlike the Church of England–sponsored Jews' Society, the Philo-Judaean schema relegated the possibility of conversion to the final moment when "the Lord [comes forth] from the holy of holies ... surrounded by angels, and arrayed in the robes of glory."[48] Only then, according to this view, would Jews have the choice to accept the Messiah. Perhaps the best way to distinguish between the Philo-Judaeans and the Jews' Society is to consider what is usually referred to as Christian philo-Semitism. As one scholar has summarized it, "philo-Semitism promoted love of Jews not *as Jews* but as potential converts who might be redeemed from scorn by becoming Christians."[49] This is all very well, but in the case of the new pre-millennial (Philo-Judaean) standard, it is obvious that Jews were indeed esteemed *as Jews* (although not without ambivalence) and conversion was to be left in God's hands. It is apparent, therefore, that a critical conceptual modification was made at this time—ironically the result of apocalyptic fundamentalism—that allowed Christians to view Jews as intrinsically worthy in and of themselves.[50]

The Philo-Judaean rank and file may have varied in their reasons for supporting the society; some indeed were members of both the Jews' Society and the Philo-Judaean Society. But organizational direction was clearly set by the Philo-Judaeans' founding officers, who included the influential Drummond and the prophetic author John Aquila Brown.[51] These men and women—there was a separate and quite active Ladies Association as well—considered themselves as bulwarks against liberalism. The leadership held a unique doomsday interpretation of the Bible that restricted their philanthropic efforts to the amelioration of the Jews and, as can be seen by their parallel labors on behalf of the abolitionist movement, the emancipation of slaves;[52] the rest of humanity would simply have to bear their sufferings until the impending divine judgment. The rising tide of English liberalism was actually adjudged by Drummond as the "very principle of Satan."[53] To be sure, this manifest illiberality and exaggerated fatalism resided outside mainstream Protestantism. But this privileged faction was hardly marginalized in any real sense and possessed significant social and political resources.

A MOVEMENT EVOLVES

The repercussions of the Newman-Wolff affair continued for several more months, as Wolff sought retribution for his public humiliation through the London press. The demonstration of rough music left him in a prolonged state of pique. In June, before leaving for the Holy Land, he delivered a parting shot at the very people who were the supposed focus of his Christian mission. "The Jews of London," he fumed in a letter published in the *Morning Chronicle*, were "not much better than Gypsies . . . the most hopeless set of all the Jews that I ever saw." These were "barbarians" who only cared for money and bereft of any measure of intellectual achievement (failing to equal their more cultured brethren in Europe), Wolff berated and openly "abhorred the character of the Israelite, at London."[54] This invective spawned a stream of mostly pseudonymous Jewish rejoinders, also published in the *Chronicle* (Selig Newman apparently refrained from commenting). And so the winner-loser dynamic that had framed the initial, ill-fated meeting continued to play itself out in the press. Wolff's base portrayal of London Jews as ignorant street peddlers and old-clothes men reeking of garlic (and avarice), coming as it did from a supposed "Reverend Gentleman" and former Jew, attracted a range of newspaper coverage on both sides of the Atlantic.[55] Still not content, however, the vengeful missionary delivered another missive, republished in the influential *London Magazine*, wherein he pledged to continue "TO HATE FATHER, MOTHER, BROTHER, AND SYSTER [*sic*], FOR THE SAKE OF JESUS MY LORD." The growing oddity and unhinged quality of Wolff's correspondence was becoming self-evident, even to the editors of the *London Magazine*: "Considering Mr. Wolff's manner of making converts by the method of hating father, mother, brother, and sister, one cannot be surprised at the circumstances of his having found the Jews of London such obstinate Jews as he represents them."[56]

Let us take a moment and review this unusual incident. First, the peculiar status of religious apostates arises as a special topic. In an effort to prove their loyalty to their newly adopted religion, such persons often feel compelled to perform various symbolic acts of revenge against their earlier spiritual tradition, and so evoke highly distorted and negative imagery in the process.[57] Wolff's personal idiosyncrasy was certainly his own, but on a broader level he did manage to follow well-recognized patterns—the pathology of Jewish self-hatred, as can be readily perceived, also came to the fore. Second, this episode was marked by a passionate desire to uphold individual and collective honor. While hardly an impulse rooted in modernity, it should be recalled that the debate was originally intended as a rational and "modern" means by which to fend off an increasingly aggressive conversionist culture (redeeming Jewish honor in the process). But the shaming ritual that was enforced upon Wolff was precisely what Newman wished to avoid, for all such displays merely reinforced a negative perception of Jews. Moreover, the letters that were published in reaction to this incident were written by fairly well-to-do, literate Jews who professed that they could not stand by idly and allow Wolff, who they disdained as a rank opportunist and "turncoat," to cast aspersions and defame the community at large.[58] In fact, the traditional honor code that still pervaded British culture dictated an immediate and forthright response.[59] All such actions could thus be readily understood and even sympathized with among gentile observers. Seen as a

30 *The Rise of Modern Jewish Politics*

whole, therefore, one can detect a tangible behavioral shift. Jews were now willing to disobey time-honored communal dictates and project themselves onto the political public sphere. Once-formidable obstacles based on ancient patterns of thought and religiously based traditions of passivity were beginning to erode. Finally, this contentious chapter exhibited a masculinist discourse and embodied a core struggle against shame and powerlessness and between Jewish quietism on the one hand and the new British model of manly self-determination on the other—a recurrent theme that will become more apparent later on.[60]

What may have induced Wolff to launch his harangue in June (three months post-debate) may never be known precisely, but a contributing factor was undoubtedly Moses Levy's oratorical debut during the previous month. Indeed, Levy's speech before the Philo-Judaean Society's annual meeting at Freemasons' Hall on 18 May 1827 drew widespread favorable notice in the metropolis and cast Jews in an entirely different light. Among other advances, Levy's address stood as an unprecedented Jewish foray into the elite public sphere. The Great Hall, with its central chamber looming sixty feet in height, surrounded "by an entablature and cornice, supported by pilasters and square fluted columns,"[61] was adorned with Masonic symbols, portraits of the nobility, and a ceiling burnished in gold and encircled by signs of the zodiac—an imposing structure that could easily accommodate a thousand persons in luxurious style. Architecturally, this building mirrored the pretentions of Britain's ruling class and thus served as a setting where notables could advance their ideas in a milieu of power and influence. Freemasons' Hall was thus a public space laden with symbolic import. It was from here, for example, that the vaunted figures of the Anti-Slavery Society—William Wilberforce, Thomas Buxton, Zachary Macaulay, Thomas Denman, and others—held their anniversary meetings, along with hundreds of the rank and file.[62] On this occasion, however, the hall was not only filled to capacity with a "highly respectable company of ladies and gentlemen," but among these were a notable contingent of Jews.[63] Despite the genteel trappings, public meetings in Great Britain generally included a large cross-section of the populace, and most were in fact conducted at far more humble venues. As a whole, the institution of the public meeting reflected the powers inherent within the British citizenry, and their rising popularity was an indication of a growing shift toward democratization.

Following official business, including a prayer that equated the new Philo-Judaean cause to "laying a foundation-stone for the second temple," Levy was introduced to the assembly by the chairman, Viscount Mandeville. Despite Levy's lack of experience speaking before any large gathering, he confidently proceeded to detail past and present abuse toward the Jews throughout the world; demanded atonement for this maltreatment; rebuffed conversion efforts; and asserted that "the continuation and existence of the people of Israel manifest to the world a miraculous living monument of the truth of Revelation" [for the complete address, see the Appendix]. Hence it

Figure 1.1 A public meeting at Freemasons' Hall, circa 1820s.
Source: *A History of the British and Foreign Bible Society*, vol. 2 (London, 1910).

was the duty of Christians, Levy declared (echoing the goals of the Philo-Judaeans), to help raise the Jews from their subjugated state. Centuries of hatred and derision had taken a toll and "brutalized the mind." While his speech was vigorously pursued, Levy couched his ideas in terms of a mutual undertaking and flattered his audience's nobility of purpose. "For thus is the human heart acted upon," he surmised, "it knows no medium; when hatred cannot be indulged, love must; and when love is once roused, it necessarily will attract a corresponding sentiment." He insisted that by atoning for past wrongs, Christians would "accelerate that period foretold in the Bible when Jew and Gentile shall unite in one faith." By asserting that mankind could claim some agency in the impending end-times, Levy ran counter to centuries of Jewish tradition—any desire to "force the End" had been renounced throughout the ages by nearly all Jewish authorities.[64] Much like secular and religious Zionists of a much later generation, Levy promoted human action over passive expectations of divine intercession; an anthropocentric rather than theocentric orientation. In another radical departure, this "gentleman of the Hebrew nation" avoided the more conventional, scripturally based defense of Judaism undertaken by Selig Newman and ventured into wide-ranging topics that had never been openly broached before. Levy was convinced that even the most liberal gentiles would never be truly free from prejudice and would always hold Jews in disdain; a situation that he repeatedly labeled as the "persecution of contempt." Furthermore, he invoked emotional appeals to nationalism to communicate a universal plan of redemption and claimed that only by forming their own nation would Jews be able to fulfill their sacred destiny:

> Without a country,—without a field of action for intellect to expand, or for virtue to be exercised—without any food for reflection—the Israelite is compelled to centre all his comforts and the powers of his noble faculties, in his miserable self. And while inhaling the moral pestilential atmosphere that surrounds his contracted sphere, he is made to drag the chain of servitude, and is prevented from soaring beyond himself. . . . [But] at the magic sound of nationality, the hearts of all Israel, both far and near, will be moved, and the mind will necessarily soar above itself in the spirit of revelation; for to an Israelite, nationality and the Bible are synonymous: he will seek it with a proportionate degree of avidity, as the patriotic flame rages within in his breast; he will attend to its whole structure, instead of its mere disjointed parts; he will be led to the knowledge of the importance of the office consigned to the house of Israel.[65]

Despite Levy's dramatic nationalist invocation, he realized that the times were ill-suited for any large-scale colonization scheme. [Noah's debacle was still fresh in many people's minds.] Furthermore, Levy's financial difficulties, largely stemming from the legal uncertainty attached to his large purchase of former Spanish land grants in Florida, prevented him from vigorously pursuing his own territorialist agenda beyond what he had already started. His Freemasons' Hall speech was therefore an attempt to lay groundwork for the future by instilling a Jewish national consciousness. Levy intended to "excite compassion" among Jews toward the sufferings of their brethren and to oppose antisemitism through the founding of a new social movement. Pointing to the antislavery crusade that had originated in Britain as an exemplar of how "great works" can be enacted through comparatively small means, he appealed to the Philo-Judaeans to become vital partners in what Levy rather presciently envisioned as a robust worldwide movement.

> Thus we see, from a handful of men, occupying an insignificant spot on the earth, the British nation is made an instrument in the hands of God to propagate the light which revelation furnishes for the progressive civilisation to a great portion of the habitable world. . . . Let the standard be raised by pious persons, it would soon take root among the generous sons of Great Britain, and the voice of sympathy towards the fallen children of Israel will be echoed by their offspring, the people of the United States. Their condemnation of past persecutions will be sufficient to deter all tyrants from exercising the inhuman cruelties that so much degrade human nature: whether they be in Asia, Africa, or Europe.

The Freemasons' Hall address incorporated the same type of religiously based, good-versus-evil master frame that had proven so effective in rallying support for the antislavery movement in Britain. On the one hand, there was a distinct pessimism whereby Jews were rendered as perpetual slaves. They would continue to be locked into this degraded state, according to Levy, unless the Christian world began to look upon Jews—"whom they have so long persecuted and vilified"—with genuine affection and pledged themselves to atone for centuries of ill treatment. Only collective action, where the will of many "would be made an instrument in the hands of God," was thought capable of ending this cycle of abuse, just as abolitionism promised to rescue the "benighted sons of Africa" from their ancient bonds. Levy not only identified the essential problem in collective terms but claimed that the extreme gravity of this situation, which flew in the face of divine will, necessitated a united mobilization of pious and like-minded people. By appropriating many familiar ideas and symbols from the abolitionist crusade, Levy was able to establish a human rights–based social movement framework that had particular cultural resonance in England.[66] Moreover, he went far beyond any of his Jewish contemporaries by his willingness to confront Christian antisemitism on its own turf and to directly engage in the political and cultural sphere. The address may have been infused with moral rhetoric and divine invocations, but it can also be viewed as a rather masterful act of negotiation. Levy emphasized commonalities rather than differences and avoided contention; his leadership style thus made ample use of his abilities as a social broker.[67] Given the profound level of distrust that most London Jews felt toward evangelicals, the role of an effective intermediary was of inestimable value. Levy certainly infused his arguments with a millenarian idiom that deeply resonated with Philo-Judaeans. For over an hour, Levy, flanked on the speakers' platform by some of England's leading pre-millennialists, was interrupted by approving cheers and loud applause. Rev. Hugh McNeile, reckoned by some to be the "greatest Evangelical preacher and speaker in the Church of England" during the nineteenth century,[68] was visibly moved by Levy's address and flattered him by stating that "though he had often been instructed by the writings of a Jew, it was never till that day that he had derived knowledge from the speech of a Jew."[69] Despite the exceeding novelty of the proceedings, and unlike the previous episode with Joseph Wolff, nothing arose to mar the occasion. In a manner analogous to religious revival, unanimity and ardor prevailed in common pursuit of a lofty cause.

Moses Levy's intentions of launching a movement was given a significant boost by glowing reports of his performance as well as entire transcripts of his address that were published in the *World*, London's sole evangelical newspaper at the time (owned and operated by the Congregationalist church).[70] This speech, therefore, became a defining moment and transformed Levy into a Jewish activist and non-Christian religious celebrity, a type of figure previously unknown in the metropolis. It should also be noted that the editor of the *World*, Stephen Bourne (ca. 1792–1868), was genuinely committed to the ideal of universal religious liberty and was on close terms with Lord Holland, the eminent liberal Whig politician.[71] Bourne was certainly no end-times zealot, and his religious views were aligned within the tolerant, nonapocalyptic, evangelical camp. He would become Levy's constant enthusiast, publishing his letters and articles weekly and favorably commenting on virtually his every move and chastising those who treated him unjustly. This was during a period when anything less than a sterling reputation could sink any fledgling organization and when the exclusion of the Jews from the press—other than occasional, sneering missives—was the rule. In essence, the *World* became the unofficial organ of the movement and a fiery advocate for Jewish liberties. "Every Jew that lives," Bourne would later write, "is a reproach to those who deny to their fellow subjects equal rights."[72]

Although Levy's speech proved successful, the nascent Jewish rights movement had yet to coalesce into a fully functioning coalition; social movements, of course, do not suddenly emerge fully formed upon the scene. But if any single moment could be considered as the birth of the movement, it would surely be the event at Freemasons' Hall. For only after activists form a mutually beneficial alliance with sympathetic elites whose social ranking and political networks offset the inherent weaknesses of marginalized groups does any movement have a practical chance at success.[73] Levy's exceptional debut as a charismatic Jewish orator, combined with the organizational and political resources of the Philo-Judaeans and the support of the *World* newspaper, created an impressive foundation for the future. Levy recognized that any move toward true emancipation, as opposed to the mere acquisition of formal political rights, also necessitated a fundamental alteration in societal attitudes. A sense of political awakening emerged, and, among other contributions, the movement would provide a practical means by which Jews and Christians could mutually redefine their relationship to each other in an atmosphere of respect. Strikingly similar to later efforts by American feminists in the 1830s, whereby women's liberation appropriated the universal human rights posture of abolitionism, it is most noteworthy that Levy equated the metaphorical status of Jews to slaves.[74] Antislavery was, after all, the ultimate expression of the politics of atonement and, according to Boyd Hilton, "provided public evangelicalism with its most potent *raison d'être*."[75] The assumption of a core set of humanitarian principles as well as a broad "culture of sympathy" also entailed a new state of consciousness, an altered awareness, and a specific rhetoric that Levy utilized very effectively. From this time onward, Jewish and gentile activists would consistently cast themselves, as well as the dark forces they saw aligned against them, in Manichean terms. Movement participants would eventually become far less influenced by evangelicalism but would retain their sense of enacting a powerful moral crusade. "It is the principle of humanity that has been awakened . . . the prerogative of man that has been usurped," declared a rabbi during a Jewish protest meeting in New York City in 1858.[76] Much later in Paris, Victor Hugo characterized the *phénomène horrible* of the 1881–1882 Russian pogroms as a choice between the continued progression of civilization or a disastrous regression toward barbarism: "The past . . . is holding mankind in its deadly grasp. The thread of life is still between its spectral fingers; on the one side the people; on the other the rabble; on one side light, the other, darkness. Choose!"[77]

2 "To Rise and Shew Themselves Men"

Three groups had been drawn together in a loose alliance following Moses Levy's oratorical debut in London: Levy and a growing cohort of Jewish supporters (including Selig Newman); Stephen Bourne and the editorial resources of the *World*; and the Philo-Judaean Society with its secretary John Aq. Brown assuming the primary public role. In June 1827, in what would be their first legislative move, the Philo-Judaeans presented a unique petition to the House of Lords through the efforts of the sixth Earl of Shaftesbury.[1] The Lords were asked to repeal a set of ancient oppressive laws directed at the Jews of England—a body of feudal, "dead letter" statutes that relegated Jews to mere chattel (some dating to Henry III). Legally valid but nevertheless ignored for centuries, draconian statutes still existed that prohibited Jews from entering any town or city without a special license from the king, for example, and, among a host of similar strictures, also required the wearing of distinctive badges on clothing. While unenforced, the continuation of these medieval laws, according to the petition, constituted a grave affront to the dignity of Anglo-Jewry and could provide the legal means for renewed repression in the future (a modus operandi that Pope Leo XII had recently followed vis-à-vis the Jews of Rome). Philo-Judaeans utilized great diligence, however, in distinguishing between *civil* injustices and the goal of Jewish *political* rights (the right to vote and hold elective office)—the latter still remained uncontested at this time. Despite the petition's modest demands, the appeal floundered in the upper house. The same agenda was also tried unsuccessfully in the lower house.[2]

Following this petition, events soon took place outside the environs of Parliament that allowed the embryonic movement, mostly through trial and error, to develop its own tactical repertoire and to select a contentious rights issue that all coalition members could unite behind. This evolutionary course made substantial headway in September, when, ostensibly from pure curiosity, Levy attended two open meetings sponsored by the Society for Investigating the Prophecies of Scripture that were held at Salvador House, a venue located in the city's Bishopsgate district.[3] Unlike the Philo-Judaeans, this particular gathering vehemently rejected the theology of Jewish restoration and looked to Great Britain as the fulfillment of biblical prophecy instead.

The organization's leadership included Captain J.E. Gordon, head of the rising ultraconservative wing of Anglican evangelicalism, an anti-Catholic agitator, and founder of the Protestant Reformation Society. After listening attentively for some time, Levy felt obliged to rebut the various "fallacious" interpretations of scripture that were being espoused, and, by drawing upon both the Hebrew Bible and the New Testament, he attempted to show that "[Israel] will return as a distinct nation to fulfill the as yet unfulfilled redemption of man."[4] Similar to what occurred during the Newman-Wolff episode, Levy was vigorously shouted down by many in attendance and was confronted head on, in his words, with the "spirit of persecution." As a Jew who dared to contradict this group's deeply engrained anti-Judaism (and by attempting to quote from the New Testament in the process), it seems improbable that Levy would have been oblivious to the kind of reaction that was likely to ensue. Nonetheless, once having denied Levy a fair hearing, this faction was roundly criticized by the *World*, and so an obscure episode was thrust into the limelight, with Levy depicted as a pious and accomplished gentleman who had suffered rude indignities.[5] Levy was therefore encouraged when he, in conjunction with fifty of his coreligionists and an indeterminate number of Philo-Judaeans, returned to Salvador House to complete his initial argument. This sudden influx of people prompted Gordon and others to issue a formal challenge to "the most learned of Modern Judaism" to defend oral law, which was heatedly condemned as "the worst species of Idolatry."[6]

A round of contentious meetings between Gordon's faction—now calling itself the Society for the Investigation of Modern Judaism—and Levy's supporters took place, with fiery arguments centered on Judaism's oral tradition. "A tremendous uproar" greeted any Jewish speaker, according to one witness, who dared "mention anything that seemed to reflect upon the Hebrews for their rejection of Christianity."[7] After several such incidents, Levy, along with Newman and a diverse group of Jews, now numbering 150, managed to assert their own voices over the fray. Levy and Newman each offered a working definition of oral law, discussed its origins and purpose, and compared this tradition with the written law or Torah. Both agreed upon the necessity of oral law. Gordon's supporters, as well as other evangelicals who were less antagonistic, delivered their own counterarguments; from their Bible-centered perspective, the "undefiled" word of God was paramount. The "spirit of rancour and hatred" eased remarkably after the Philo-Judaeans eventually gained control (Gordon stopped attending altogether). At the end of a year, this unlikely interfaith forum, now covering a variety of religious topics, and "having aroused the Jewish people to the essentials of their faith,"[8] managed to assume a congenial—indeed, some would actually say "brotherly"—demeanor.[9] These proceedings were considered of such import that entire debates were included verbatim in such papers as the *Times* and *Morning Chronicle* as well as the *World*.[10] What initially began as a volatile and contentious experiment in interfaith relations eventually took on an air of comity and forbearance and, despite the clear disapproval of Britain's chief rabbi, became a regular feature of life in the metropolis, continuing for several years.

Joining Levy and Newman in the Jewish-Christian debates were a core group that included Isaac Vallentine (who later published the *Jewish Chronicle* newspaper), Moses Lyon, Charles Samuel, and Messrs. Polack, Israel, Silver, Solomon, Johnson, and Tobias, and many others who remain unidentified.[11] Some were Freemasons, and all who were noted by name in the press appeared to be literate and well-informed individuals who regularly contributed toward discussions. Many more were drawn to the debates, however, who may have been wanting in education and ill-informed about Judaism yet were highly motivated and identified strongly as Jews. This bloc included petty merchants and tradesmen and, it appears, some street peddlers. A social hierarchy may have been present, with the most learned and polished element at the vanguard, but there was still a remarkable degree of inclusiveness. As the majority was religiously conservative, Levy kept his more radical reform agenda to himself (not wishing to alienate potential followers) and adopted a more traditional religious stance.[12] Levy may have tempered his millennial allusions, but he still infused his arguments with a vigorous Jewish fundamentalism that most others seemed more than willing to accept. In actuality, however, his religious views were a unique amalgam of messianic fundamentalism and a *Haskalah*-inspired reform agenda that was all his own.[13]

The interfaith forum at Salvador House represented a milestone in the development of Christian-Jewish dialogue in England. Until then, nothing remotely similar had presented itself. The unencumbered rhetorical defense of Judaism unleashed a new level of confidence among Jewish participants. Because the proceedings now maintained civility and order, they could also claim a degree of respectability; and by defending their religious tradition in such an erudite manner, Jews could now bask in the elevated stature of public debate in England. Successful rhetors were not only highly educated citizens and hence entitled to esteem, but the rhetorical art was imbued with authority and deemed vital to the maintenance of public welfare, justice, and social ethics—indeed, the entire political process.[14] Its raison d'être stemmed from the classical Roman model; that is, rhetorical discourse was intended to shape and maintain public consensus as the foundation of civic accomplishment.[15] While Mordecai M. Noah had already emerged in the United States as a Jewish orator of renown, England still lacked an equivalent public figure. One can thus better appreciate the sense of incredulity that followed in the wake of Levy's Freemasons' Hall address. The Salvador House debates should also be seen within a similar perspective. Formal public debate in England was embedded within an elite collegiate culture, and so was restricted to gifted Anglo-Protestant men who adhered to the old-style Oxbridge debating society culture. On the opposite end of the spectrum was the more informal tradition of alehouse debating clubs that were often hosted in small pubs throughout England. Their frequent antiestablishment, working-class tenor often placed these "debates" in conflict with the government, and because such groups were at times suspected of outright insurrection, they were regularly infiltrated with Home Office spies and informers.[16] The radical culture of the alehouse clubs was actually in decline by the 1820s, and a new standard of "respectability" and embourgeoisement was in ascendance. The Salvador House events were therefore of an intrinsically different order and, given their intense scrutiny by the press, went to great lengths to assure a suitable, parliamentary-style format that was enforced by an authoritative chairman. Neither Jews nor Christians wished to be placed in a "radical" framework. In addition to contributing toward a more democratized conception of formal debate, Jews had—by their admission into the political public sphere and the resultant recognition by the press—entered the body politic. Hence as a de facto citizenry, loosely defined, they began to reconstruct their own identity. Scholars have long noted that these types of innovative collective endeavors transform "cultural representations" and substantially alter how "groups see themselves and how they are seen by others."[17] Protestant reformers could no longer complain that Anglo-Jews kept entirely to themselves or that they neglected "to lead forth their troops into the open field of fair argument."[18] Once established, however, these discussions would shift into a public platform of a far different order.

In late October 1827, details of a Russian ukase, or imperial edict, issued by Nicholas I some months earlier first began to be noted in the London papers. This decree banished Jews from "any of the Cities of Russia" [aimed at those who resided outside the Pale of Settlement and within ethnic Russia] who did not at least hold artisanal status. All rabbis and "religious functionaries" were also slated for immediate expulsion. Prior to the meetings of Christians and Jews, one would hardly expect that news of any foreign ordinance that forced Jewish families from their homes and also expelled rabbis would have stirred a ripple of interest in England. On 30 October, however, John Aq. Brown provided an English translation of the ukase's thirteen articles, which appeared in the *World*, wherein he vehemently cautioned readers that God would soon "avenge his own elect (his chosen people)" for such gross injustices.[19] Due largely to Jewish participation at the Salvador House debates, the novel theme of Jewish rights now held a degree of cultural resonance in the metropolis.

One of several harsh directives aimed at Russian Jewry in 1827 (which included an infamous military conscription decree), Moses Levy joined Brown in casting this particular ukase as the coalition's most central concern. As with the antislavery crusade, the humanity of the oppressed along with their presumed right to worship freely and to engage their own religious functionaries would be accentuated to gain general sympathy. Certainly, neither Brown nor Levy was cognizant of the precise number of Jews who were affected by this imperial edict. It is difficult, even now, to determine how many Jews resided, legally or otherwise, outside the Pale and within the Russian interior at this particular time. According to one account, there were 159 Jewish families living in St. Petersburg in 1826; most of these are listed as merchants and artisans.[20] Even if one assumes an equivalent number in Moscow, and perhaps a smaller cohort in other cities, it is difficult to imagine that the ukase would have resulted in mass expulsion—even if it had been rigorously enforced by local police.[21] The number of rabbis is even more uncertain. Yet, as it often happens with social movements, the very timing of the edict proved most vital; as was the heightened interest of the press. The mounting rumors painted an urgent and extremely dire situation in Russia, and the degree to which Anglo-Jews now felt empowered to publicly announce their concerns and to risk actual protest enabled the transformation of a comparatively obscure Russian edict into a substantial human rights issue.

A few weeks following the publication of the ukase, the subject of Russian abuses entirely dominated the Bishopsgate meetings. Religious debates were suspended in order to address the urgent plight of Russian Jewry, with Moses Levy taking the lead. The tenor of these assemblies increasingly resembled attempts at crisis management.[22] By the second meeting, many in the national and international press had been alerted to the radically distinctive voices of the "Jews of England" railing not only against the tsar but the harsh policies recently enacted in Frankfurt and Darmstadt and by the pope in Rome as well. Additional details concerning the ukase also came to light, ostensibly from reliable sources in Russia, and gave rise to serious alarm.[23] Seeming to adhere to the centuries-old *silihot* tradition, wherein all disasters and persecutions were deemed as divine punishment for communal sins, congregations were reported to be fasting and praying at the graves of their forefathers in an effort to avert further catastrophe.[24] Rumors also circulated that large numbers of men, women, and children had been driven from their residences in the cities and thus faced the Russian winter without shelter, all the while suffering from "the pangs of hunger." For the skilled tradesmen and their families who were allowed to remain in such cities as Moscow and St. Petersburg, children would now be deprived of religious instruction as rabbis were now officially banished. A few vociferous Jewish dissenters at Salvador House, however, sought to minimize the impact of the tsar's edict and claimed that not enough was known about the subject to warrant any action. Levy had little patience with these individuals and heaped substantial ridicule upon them. If the ukase had been a "money-making" scheme, he declared, "the Stock-jobbers would have adopted every means to obtain the earliest intelligence and they would have speculated upon it even before its promulgation." But now this same "class" felt obligated to wait indefinitely for the highest standard of proof, despite the fact that the lives of "helpless widows and orphans" were in jeopardy—a riposte that drew a wave of tumultuous cheers. Still troubled by those who maintained a "heartless insensibility" toward the plight of the destitute, Levy asked rhetorically: "If a person received a wound in one of his members, was it not natural that the whole body should be affected? But what would they conclude, if this body betrayed no sensibility to the wound?" After a pause, several persons replied in unison: "In a state of mortification."[25] Such fine details were reported on with intense interest by the press. By meeting's end, following Levy's appeal that "the more frequently they met together the better they would cultivate that feeling of kindness and goodwill which should distinguish the House of Israel," it was agreed that the Jews would hold their own separate assembly, led by representatives of their own choosing, at the venerable London Tavern on Bishopsgate Street. This was a much larger and far more imposing establishment than Salvador House and was on equal stature with Freemasons' Hall.[26]

Those Jews who gathered in the grand, chandeliered meeting room of the London Tavern on the evening of 5 December were surely mindful of the torrent of publicity that was directed at them. News of the "extraordinary movement" had already begun to circulate overseas. Levy's observation that "the eyes of England, of Europe, and of a great part of the civilized world seem to be directed toward us,"[27] as well as the anxiety that this situation caused Jews whose very laws precisely forbade this sort of contentious politics, certainly placed their actions into appropriate context. Indeed, the large crowd and the presence of the national and foreign press was an indication that these individuals had tapped deeply into the inherent power of social movements. What is more, now that the Jews remonstrated against the "Autocrat of the North," as the press dubbed the tsar, their actions played directly into a rampant British Russophobia.[28] Conditions were thus ripe for a heretofore reclusive category of Britons, long subjugated by the stigma of deicide and perceived for centuries "as not like other men,"[29] to utilize the techniques of collective action to enter the national and international political sphere.

"M. E. Levy, Esq. of Florida, having been instrumental in convening the Meeting and being familiar with its objects," was unanimously elected chairman.[30] After the ukase was read in full, the meeting secretary, Mr. Israel, reminded all those in attendance of the historic nature of their enterprise: "By coming forward in a proper manner, the English Jews would not only shew to the people of England, but to the inhabitants of Europe, that when they touched one of their nation, his brethren felt that he was flesh of their flesh and bone of their bone." No longer, it appeared, would the Jews of London suffer scorn for their supposed selfishness and indifference. To the contrary, as they now drew world attention to the plight of their downtrodden brethren, they had become exemplars of a new and enlightened philanthropy, a position in keeping with elevated British sensibilities. Despite persistent challenges from two individuals, Messrs. Cohen and Herrman, both of whom continued to reject the gravity of events in Russia, the "Meeting of the Jews" exhibited a passionate solidarity and succeeded in doing so entirely apart from the communal magnates. Levy then used the occasion to censure what he perceived as the indifference of the Cousinhood, all of whom were conspicuously absent. "Those who had money, for the greater part appeared to be destitute of proper feeling," he asserted, "and were so engaged in the improvement of their fortunes or in fashionable amusements, or else were so much in dread of exciting any hostile feelings in persons possessed of power," that Levy deemed any appeal to them as futile. In essence, he dared to render the authority of the oligarchs superfluous and cast those who gathered at the London Tavern as the legitimate standard bearers. A resolution was passed that requested that "Mr. Levy frame an address to the various congregations of the Jews of Great Britain" in a move to gain wider support for the Russian protests.[31] Remarkably, the communal elite failed to publicly question the meeting's presumed right to make claims on behalf of Anglo-Jewry. An astonishing scenario, especially as these unprecedented proceedings had actually evolved into, among other things, a blatant and rapidly escalating communal rebellion.

During the next "Public Meeting of the Jews" held on 19 December (also at the London Tavern), Levy's "Address to the Captive Children of Israel, inhabiting the Dominions of his Britannic Majesty" was read and then unanimously adopted. The entire address, ostensibly for Jews only, later appeared in mainstream religious periodicals in England and the United States.[32] Levy's condemnation of Russian abuses was compelling, but his scripturally based phraseology held special allure for Christian readers. "These chastisements which have been heaped upon our devoted heads," Levy wrote, "are, as it respects the Almighty, merited by our sins and that of our forefathers, as denounced by our lawgiver and the prophets." Levy's invocation of the timeless rebuke of the Prophets therefore gained the special approbation of Christians, many of whom openly welcomed such self-effacing language from the Jews.[33]

"Mr. Israel, Mr. Tobias, Mr. Lyons, Mr. Samuel, and several other gentlemen" then addressed the assembly and "urged Jews to arouse their dormant energies, and to present themselves to the different governments of the world as men meriting and claiming equal rights with their fellow citizens."[34] Political claims suddenly escalated to a higher level. In so doing, the protestors not only defied the privileged reality of the British and communal establishment but quite wittingly advanced an alternate, insurgent reality as well. Various speakers promoted the traditional Jewish paradigm of a distinct nation; nevertheless, it was also claimed that certain basic rights could never be denied, regardless of religion or nationality. While this position reflects the present-day legal consensus, these assertions were exceedingly bold at the time. Following the Napoleonic formula established in the late eighteenth century, most European nations conceived of Jewish civil rights in a contractual framework. Equal rights were reserved as a reward for Jews who were willing to forsake traditional notions of nationhood and exclusivity and accepted their inherent obligation to assimilate into the national fabric. This quid pro quo rationale was widespread and in fact was adopted by the Congress of Vienna (1815). The European *maskilim*, of course, fully ascribed to the assimilationist path and placed it as an ultimate objective.

The notion of Jews becoming "children of the country" with full rights and responsibilities may have remained a highly debated issue in Europe (with the exception of the Netherlands and France, where political emancipation had been in force for decades),[35] but in England the "Jewish question" had yet to arise as a significant issue.

The Meetings of the Jews should therefore be seen against the backdrop of assimilationist politics that pervaded Europe; a specific context that Levy was keenly aware of. Because he considered *natural rights* (life, liberty, and the pursuit of happiness) and *civil rights* (protection by law, owning property, recognition of marriage, trial by jury, etc.) as universal but excluded *political rights* from consideration, any reciprocal obligation to assimilate was diminished. At first glance, Levy's limited claims may be reminiscent of the later "separate but equal" paradigm of American jurisprudence—with the exception, of course, that Levy quite vigorously demanded (and expected) legitimate parity in everything other than voting and elective office. Still, he freely admitted that any type of exclusion from the ordinary rights of citizenship was an inherently inferior and "inconvenient" position. Yet, in this one aspect, Jews simply had no choice. "The Jew must love the country where he lives, but the world more, for whose welfare our separation from the mass of mankind is by the Most High ordained."[36] In as much as the British government was inseparable from the established Church of England, the significant obstacles of oath taking and nonrecognition of the Jewish Sabbath merely reinforced, at least in the minds of Levy and his colleagues, the inherent impracticality of political rights. Levy insisted that Jews could never have dual allegiances; no matter where they turned, "the nationality of Israel stares him in the face."[37] Seen as a whole, this point of view blended the nationalist and communitarian ideals that resided within traditional Judaism with the activism and universalism of the reform movement while vehemently rejecting the path of assimilation; an amalgam that, once again, bears a marked resemblance to a much later generation of Zionists.[38]

The speakers at the London Tavern also carefully framed their remarks within the new civic standard of "manly" forthrightness, a significant, albeit unusual, feature—at least within the context of Anglo-Jewish historiography—that requires some clarification. The era of the Regency dandy was in an obvious state of decline, while the standard of plainspoken manliness, originally ushered in by evangelical culture, was on the rise in Britain. Unlike the former model of gentlemanly politeness, where breeding, gentility, and elite education predominated, manliness was a distinction that had to be earned—an egalitarian construction that was within reach of any person who "practiced self-help with a single-minded determination."[39] This emphasis on interiority, earnestness, and strength of character mirrored the growth of the middle class and thus held particular meaning for the Jewish business class, who held sway over the public meetings. Religious and moral principles were judged vital to a masculine character and were expected to be implemented through action as well as fellowship with like-minded individuals;[40] qualities that were especially apparent during a speech by Mr. Israel.

> When I address my brethren, they should consider that although they may be safe in England, they are only a part of a larger family of a great nation; they should feel it to be their duty to come forward manfully and bear their protest against such injustice. I ask this meeting to call upon all Governments to act justly toward our nation, and I think the time is not far distant when they will be willing to do so. At present it is our duty to stand forward and say to the world, we are men, we call for the rights of men, we ask for nothing inconsistent with the safety or good government of any state. We wish not to injure others, but to be put on a level with them. Our religion is not inimical to good government; it has been tried and never found intolerant or injurious to the interests of freedom. . . . I would not have my brethren keep back their sentiments through fear. The world will respect them better if they stand forward manfully and unite in protesting cruelty and oppression, displayed by whomsoever it may. For a long time have they been afflicted, persecuted, and degraded; it ought not have been so—let them say so to the world, and I have no doubt these oppressions will cease.[41]

Though at times quite eloquent, these early activists still recognized that there was a reluctant faction of their members in the city who avoided the movement entirely. The righteousness of their cause may have been self-evident to many, but the unprecedented nature of this engagement still produced apprehension. The stakes had in fact been raised exponentially by the fact that this modest group had been thrust onto the world stage via the press. Whether from fear or plain indifference, however, outright dismissals of suffering seem to have been routine and so presented a curious challenge. In recognizing this formidable obstacle, Levy compared the mentality of Jews who refused to come to the aid of other Jews to a "slavish state of mind." Like blacks in the West Indies, Levy declared, a steady regime of psychological abuse had stifled every feeling other than blind submission to authority. As a result, Jews needed to liberate themselves; indeed, the time was right, he stressed, to strive toward the "amelioration of our condition." Not only did God demand this, but "all civilized nations" were also in accord with their cause.[42] By engaging in this type of rhetoric, Levy sought to disassemble the Jewish mask of quietism; only by doing so, he believed, could they fulfill their destiny in the modern world.

A MOVEMENT REDEFINED

The media inevitably perform a central role in the success (or failure) of social movements, and the beginning of the Jewish rights movement was surely

"To Rise and Shew Themselves Men" 45

no exception. As noted, press coverage was extensive, yet a few London papers chose to ignore the movement entirely, while a virulent antisemitic invective surfaced elsewhere. In a column in the elite *London Magazine*, for example, an anonymous editorialist feigned enthusiasm for the past horrors of the auto-da-fé and hoped to deflate all Jewish pretensions of equality or moral suasion: "When they [Jews] were roasted, they were content; now they are uneasy and complaining of all manner of little nuisances."[43] A similar intolerance surfaced in the working-class *Cobbetts Weekly Political Register*: "the banishment of the *Christ-killers* from Russia is really a good proof . . . that the Emperor of Russia is *not* a tyrant."[44] Both mockery and omission are standard media responses to social movements, as these contentious endeavors defy the existing power structure in ways that many find intolerable. As we have seen, however, influential papers such as the *Times* and *Morning Chronicle* were prominent in setting a new editorial criterion in regard to the Jews and, in addition to the more zealous reportage of the evangelical *World*, covered the movement in detail—by itself, a notable advancement. There was a strong sense, as Stephen Bourne stated, that whenever any "body of men who were suffering unjustly . . . had the spirit and courage to meet together" and presented their case to the public, then the press of England had a special obligation to support such noble efforts.[45] The meetings were also viewed favorably because they adhered to a parliamentary ethic, were solidly middle class, and followed a standard long established by countless antislavery meetings throughout Britain by presenting grievances in a moral, righteous, and passionate framework. Major Protestant periodicals in Britain and Ireland included significant mention and usually voiced strong sympathy, and the provincial press throughout England and Wales followed suit. News of the protests even traveled to the margins of empire, including Sydney, New South Wales.[46] The *Allgemeine Zeitung* (Augsburg), a leading German-language daily, assigned the protest meetings to the front page and presented the affair as a genuine British phenomenon, as did the *Dagblad van's Gravenhage* (The Hague) in the Netherlands. In the United States, the *New York Observer*, the *Philadelphia Gazette and Daily Advertiser*, and the *American Baptist Magazine*, among others, all observed "the extraordinary movement of the Jews."[47] Hence, the emergent Jewish rights movement easily broke through the general press tendency to either withhold notice of social movement activities or to indulge in haughty rebuke.[48] Thereupon the episode promptly spread throughout much of the Western media, yet other factors were present that impeded future efforts in London.

Amid a flurry of public interest that followed the London Tavern meetings, many of the same Jews joined the Philo-Judaean Society in a demonstration of solidarity on New Year's Day among a capacity crowd at the King's Head Tavern—thereby gaining still more notice.[49] The cumulative impact of these gatherings, with their mounting sense of urgency, was widespread, but a perplexing scenario manifested itself by mid-month. With no forewarning, the winter's most distinctive news event simply dropped from public notice; no further commentary concerning the ukase, Russian Jewry, or the public protests ensued in London. If much of the press had proven itself more than willing to support a just cause, one may reasonably suspect that a still-undefined force had stifled these lofty impulses. Social movements, especially after experiencing such a rapid and extensive escalation in publicity, do not stop abruptly or change direction without substantial cause. As the Jewish rights movement challenged authority and also claimed a degree of popular sovereignty, its continuance was dependent on the receptiveness of the political and cultural climate in London.[50] The tenor of the political environment had, in fact, been altered by a sudden change of government early in 1828.

The resignation of the ineffectual Lord Goderich as prime minister on 8 January and the subsequent appointment of the Duke of Wellington obviously presented a more forceful political milieu. No friend of Jewish liberties (or public meetings for that matter), and oblivious to public opinion, Wellington's conception of Anglo-Jewry reflected a quasi-medieval worldview. Jews, according to the prime minister, were perpetual "aliens" who were no different from adherents of any other "infidel or pagan superstition on the face of the earth" and were thus inherently unworthy of a legitimate place in "Christian Britain."[51] Adding to this scenario, Great Britain was also engaged in joint military operations with Russia against Turkey, a precarious and controversial alliance that the "hero of Waterloo" had been personally involved in. What is more, the tsar had grown increasingly irritated at the antagonistic tone of the English press during this period and obliged his ambassador in London to lodge a complaint with the British government.[52] Given the new prime minister's predisposition, the rapidly mounting publicity concerning London Jews, their defiant anti-tsarist rhetoric, the increasing delicacy of the Russian alliance, and the explicit threat that these demonstrations presented to the Establishment, then it is not unexpected that the movement would undergo a significant alteration. Although the social movement model would suggest some type of intervention by ruling elites, documentary evidence is still lacking, and so any causal scenario will have to remain conjectural.[53]

While the Meetings of the Jews as well as the interfaith protests ceased entirely, the original Salvador House debates continued without interruption and with strikingly increased numbers of Jewish participants. In January these deliberations relocated to the King's Head Tavern, with Moses Levy and his supporters again in attendance, and with Philo-Judaeans in the chair. Levy kept a conspicuous presence within the metropolis for an additional eight months, but he now uncharacteristically refrained from all commentary regarding foreign oppression of the Jews (Russian or otherwise). Even though Levy would never again mobilize his coreligionists using the venue of a public meeting house, he soon entered the realm of a respected religious celebrity. The *World* continued publishing Levy's many letters and articles; his stances on educational reform, Jewish nationalism, assimilation, antislavery, irreligion, and other issues were eagerly received and often debated.[54]

Despite significant changes, much of the movement's original momentum managed to survive intact by shifting focus from the plight of foreign Jewry to consolidating all efforts on behalf of Anglo-Jews. What had surfaced in the international sphere as a Jewish solidarity movement transitioned into a period of abeyance, while a new direction allowed Jewish activists to further many of their general goals and to maintain a sense of cohesion by applying their energies toward local concerns. Levy and his protégés centered their labors on providing basic religious and secular education to the poor and lower middle classes in London. The discussions held at Salvador House and King's Head Tavern demonstrated, according to Levy, "the deficiency of many of my brethren in the learning with which they should be well acquainted."[55] Following Levy's persuasive arguments, Selig Newman and others founded the Light of Torah Society, which initiated free adult schools as well as a weekly series of open religious lectures in the city, and a newly organized religious tract society distributed an accessible adult Jewish catechism in pamphlet form (also gratis).[56] These actions were especially valued since previous schools set up by the Philo-Judaean Ladies Association to instruct Jewish women in basic literacy skills were condemned by the chief rabbi, Solomon Hirschell, who considered them conversionist fronts; Hirschell then threatened to withhold Jewish burial to all who attended.[57] It was thereby incumbent upon Jews to carry out their own agenda. Moreover, as most Jewish children in the city lacked even the most rudimentary knowledge of the Hebrew alphabet, Levy appealed for increased instruction in their "sacred tongue," urging the implementation of "scientific" (non-rote) teaching methods. He went even further by strongly advocating the novel scheme of forming a Jewish college in London, an innovation that would not see fruition until 1855.

Although the Philo-Judaean Society also supported this renewed local commitment, they now placed Anglo-Jewish political emancipation as a major goal—a change in strategy that marked a substantial rift within the movement.[58] Both Levy and the Philo-Judeans initially considered the continuance of the Jews as a "distinct and separate people among the nations" a sine qua non.[59] But now, for reasons that still remain unclear, the Philo-Judaeans reversed themselves on this key issue.

In April 1828, while the Jewish-Christian debates continued in full force at the King's Head Tavern, Philo-Judaeans pursued their separate course and submitted a new round of petitions to Parliament, this time in regard to the repeal of the Test and Corporation Acts. These petitions supported an amendment that would have permitted Jews to omit the words "upon the true faith of a Christian" while taking an oath of office. When Lord Bexley, a senior member of the London Society and a crucial ally of the Philo-Judaeans, moved for the inclusion of the amendment in the House of Lords, he remarked that "he could not see how their lordships could have any objection, when they recollected that the Act of Toleration had hitherto authorized the Jews to occupy civil offices, and the words alluded to in this bill would infuse a drop of bitterness into their cup where it might easily have been spared."[60] Significant objections nevertheless surfaced. Lord Eldon, the former chancellor, presumed to reflect majority opinion by a particularly mocking assessment: "Let it be remembered that the Jews were here and there and every where, and yet they were no where (*a laugh*); and that they were a people whom their Lordships did not acknowledge."[61] Wellington concurred: "There was no instance in which the legislature had sanctioned the admission of such persons into office." Moreover, according to the prime minister, the very idea of Jews holding elective office was wholly "disliked by this country."[62] The subsequent rejection of the amendment did indeed serve to isolate Jews even more; though the eventual repeal of the Test and Corporation Acts certainly benefited Dissenters, it also verified, according to the Philo-Judaeans, "that much national antipathy still exists against them [the Jews]."[63] Although Moses Levy's cohort remained detached from these parliamentary efforts, one of the Cousinhood's leaders, Isaac L. Goldsmid, focused intently on this issue and on 5 May sent a letter to Wellington urging his support—with no discernible effect.[64]

Goldsmid's tentative involvement at this juncture, as well as the interest of other members of the communal inner sanctum, including Moses Montefiore, Nathan Rothschild, and Moses Moccatta, is of course most noteworthy and has been well acknowledged in the Anglo-Jewish historiography. Unaware of the "extraordinary movement," however, modern historians have been at a real disadvantage regarding any appraisal of this unexpected political turn. A common view regarding the communal leaders' new course is that the passage of the Catholic Emancipation Bill (1829) functioned as a prime motivator as it created political liberties for the Catholic minority while continuing to omit Anglo-Jewry from equal consideration, and thus fomented a heightened sense of injustice. As scholars have also noted, however, elite involvement actually preceded the passage of the bill.[65] We can now see that the uncharacteristic engagement by communal leaders succeeded the first stirrings of the "extraordinary movement" by about a year. The beginning of the campaign for Anglo-Jewish emancipation can thus be properly understood as a spin-off political movement. The previous movement's sense of agency (substantive societal change no longer appeared implausible for the Jews), its collective action frame as well as its dependence on interfaith coalitions was adopted and reinterpreted by the Jewish notables in the form of a political rights struggle, a testament to the success and influence of the first wave of protests. Both the repeal of the Test and Corporation Acts and the passage of Catholic emancipation were undoubtedly precipitating events and clearly demonstrated what could be achieved through "organized agitation" by the disenfranchised.[66] The foundation for Jewish participation in the political public sphere, however, had already taken place in 1827.

The Jewish rights movement had established the effectiveness of protest that was devoid of any explicit or implicit threat of force or fear of the crowd, the latter being virtually synonymous with Catholic emancipation. Anglo-Jewry, as Isaac Goldsmid's son Francis observed much later, had to comport themselves using a higher standard, by applying "the force of public opinion, influenced by a sense of moral right."[67] Without acknowledging any debt to the previous master frame enacted by the Meetings of the Jews, Goldsmid's comment unwittingly underscored just how instrumental this earlier chapter was to subsequent events. Here we can discern what has now become axiomatic among social movement analysts—that the previous path of claim making did indeed "constrain its subsequent forms," as Charles Tilly has stated, "influencing the very issues, actors, settings, and outcomes of popular struggle."[68]

The emergence of the Jewish rights movement inspired more than just the communal elite to regard political emancipation as a pressing issue. On 19 June 1828, a certain Moses Levy of Great Alie Street (London) became the first Jew to petition Parliament for the political relief of Anglo-Jewry; this was followed on 10 July by a similar petition "from certain persons belonging to the very ancient faith of the Jews."[69] Just as the Philo-Judaean petition, however, these efforts came to naught. Furthermore, some meetings were held in the city that summer and a circular was distributed by Samuel Levy Keyzer, a Brussels merchant and a former associate of Moses E. Levy, appealing to "all distinguished friends of civil and religious liberty" to meet together for "the relief of the Jews of England."[70] But these gatherings, held in conjunction with a number of Catholic activists, lacked effective leadership and elicited little more than mild curiosity from the Jews.[71] Nevertheless, the prospect that some future charismatic figure, following in the mode of Moses E. Levy, could have surfaced during another unsanctioned wave of protests was certainly not far from the minds of communal leaders. Be that as it may, Isaac L. Goldsmid was particularly receptive to the notion that the Cousinhood had to enter the political public sphere straight away and begin to utilize the techniques of public persuasion in the process.[72] Also influenced by a number of progressive figures of the era, such as Jeremy Bentham and Lord Holland, Goldsmid committed himself to the cause of Jewish political liberty and, together with his son, evolved into an indefatigable campaigner. On 26 June, in the company of the more traditional communal luminary, Moses Montefiore (the dominant figure among the Board of Deputies), Goldsmid met with a group of Protestant Dissenters and Catholics "for the purpose of consulting as to the best mode of obtaining privileges for Jews."[73] Thereafter, Nathan Rothschild joined with Montefiore and Goldsmid in working toward a unified strategy. Apparently in keeping with these private talks, the following month, I. L. Goldsmid dispatched an emissary to Ireland with the intention of creating a political alliance with the recently elected Irish MP, Daniel O'Connell.[74] Thus, a select few within the ranks of the Cousinhood took it upon themselves to enter the political fray during the summer of 1828, a seemingly inconspicuous start to what would evolve into a thirty-year drive for full Anglo-Jewish political rights.

By the end of the summer, Moses Levy departed London and returned to the United States, where the affairs of his communal venture in Florida required urgent attention. Levy faced a surfeit of difficulties upon his return: legal problems regarding his land grant purchases continued unabated, and

Figure 2.1 Caricature by William Heath (1829) showing a Jewish peddler knocking at the door of the House of Commons while Protestant Dissenters and a Catholic—recently awarded the right to serve in Parliament—thumb their noses from above. The addition of a ladies' bonnet was a further effort to mock Jewish pretentions of equality.

Source: Private collection of the author.

occasional raids by Seminole Indians increased tensions on the frontier. Even so, Levy's advancement of free public school education in one of the least populated areas of the United States resulted in a groundswell of popular support for this much-needed reform. The outbreak of the Second Seminole War in 1835, however, put an end to Levy's idealistic endeavors, including his Jewish agricultural colony. Pilgrimage Plantation was destroyed along with virtually every other homestead and plantation in the East Florida interior. While none of the Pilgrimage inhabitants were harmed, the region was thrust into a ruinous seven-year war and, together with the financial panic of 1837, created a rather grim situation for Levy.[75] His estranged youngest son David, however, would benefit politically from the crisis milieu as well as his family's continued status as one of the region's largest landholders. Defying the elder Levy's staunch prohibition against seeking elective office, David's entry into local Democratic Party politics, his considerable talent as a stump speaker, and his advocacy of Jacksonian democratic ideals aided his election as the first Jewish U.S. congressman and ultimately the first senator as well.

Even though Moses Levy never returned to England, his earlier contributions in the metropolis, as we have seen, made a durable impact in a number of areas. Not long after Levy left the London scene, for example, Montefiore first began to establish himself as a distinct public personality and initiated a sustained effort to reconstruct the traditional role of the *shtadlan* or high-level Jewish intermediary. In doing so, he astutely reaffirmed the legitimacy of the communal elite, not through the standard displays of power and privilege but by cultivating a unique position in society that stressed interfaith cooperation, philanthropy, and, most especially, asserting the basic rights of foreign Jews. Montefiore was more cautious vis-à-vis Anglo-Jewish emancipation than Goldsmid, and the former would consistently resist his colleague's more aggressive inclinations.[76] Yet the manner in which both these men reinterpreted their leadership roles and their sudden eagerness to take part in the political public sphere and to form alliances with an array of evangelicals, Protestant Dissenters, and Catholics can no longer be viewed in isolation from the Jewish rights movement, the interfaith debates, and the previous public persona of Moses Levy.[77]

In November 1828 Montefiore demonstrated his willingness to cooperate with evangelicals by his mutual support of aid to Palestinian Jews, a position that the Philo-Judaean Society was quick to laud as a significant milestone. The society also noted that their contributions toward the relief of London's Jewish poor induced a number of wealthy Jews in the West End to establish their own "Benevolent Society" (i.e., the Society for Relieving the Aged Needy of the Jewish Faith).[78] Ostensibly, Philo-Judaeans were pleased that their charitable efforts "provoked the Jews to jealousy," since this ultimately resulted in "a more powerful excitement of that national spirit, which, once aroused, will not fail to produce rich fruits."[79]

Also during this period, John Aq. Brown and fellow Philo-Judaean Apsley Pellatt—a London glass manufacturer and member of the Court of Common

Council—were both intent on overturning the prohibition of Jews from the freedom of the City. Isaac and Francis Goldsmid joined Philo-Judaeans in petitioning for the reversal of this long-standing ban, and in 1830, City officials finally relented; a substantial social and economic boost to the Jewish middle classes. As I. L. Goldsmid observed some years afterward, not only did the admission of the Jews to the freedom of the City enable them "to earn their living as shopkeepers," but the collapse of this prohibition opened the way for the election of Jews to civil office in London.[80]

Additionally, the first of a series of Jewish Disability Bills were introduced by Robert Grant and Lord Bexley in both houses that same year—a move that Rothschild, Montefiore, and Goldsmid openly endorsed. Goldsmid chaired his own organization, the Association for Obtaining for British Jews Civil Rights and Privileges, and worked diligently behind the scenes.[81] But none of these early, pathbreaking attempts at Jewish political emancipation succeeded, despite a mass petition signed by fourteen thousand supportive Londoners that included a large percentage of eminent merchants, bankers, medical practitioners, and attorneys.[82] Indeed, by 1848, Goldsmid grew weary of limiting tactics to lobbying, petitioning, and pamphleteering and urged that the Jewish Board of Deputies allow the formation of public meetings to advance their cause more effectively; the board nonetheless failed to pursue this idea.[83]

Following the dissolution of the Philo-Judaean Society in 1831, due to internal splintering caused by Drummond's departure from the Church of England and his espousal of the newly formed Catholic Apostolic Church, there was little outward evidence of the original movement that had spawned so much excitement a few years earlier.[84] The Jewish-Christian debates, after several impressive years of interreligious dialogue, also concluded about this same time. Even though the initial "extraordinary movement" had gone into abeyance, the overall standing of Jews in England had altered quite perceptively. Jews had begun to be recognized as political participants rather than an exclusively alien population who, like Gypsies, were merely tolerated. London Jews were now left unfettered in the practice of their trades and were gradually allowed into the professions as well. Earlier in 1828, University College London opened as a nondenominational institution that admitted students regardless of religious beliefs, an endeavor that owed much to the philanthropic contributions of I. L. Goldsmid. As a whole, the Cousinhood began to commit more financial resources on behalf of the metropolitan Jewish poor. The campaign for Jewish political liberties also started to show tangible results. In 1835 Parliament formally enfranchised Jews, provided they met the standard qualification as propertied males; a decade later, Jews could hold municipal offices without taking a Christian oath. By 1858, as is well known, Baron Lionel de Rothschild was finally allowed his seat in Parliament, ending a prolonged struggle to sit for the City of London. Thus, a political movement that spanned several decades, headed mostly by an acculturated and superiorly advantaged faction of Anglo-Jewry, came to a close.

Unlike similar emancipatory efforts on the Continent and despite the heated opposition of high church Tories and a right-wing evangelical faction who loathed Jewish otherness and believed that modern Judaism had been utterly corrupted by rabbinism, during the first phase of the political campaign at least, neither the Jewish elite nor their gentile allies were compelled to draw upon the European contractual standard. Similar to what Levy and his followers had espoused in 1827, Anglo-Jewish rights were conceived as universal and not as a form of recompense for assimilation or for implementing radical religious reform. In reaction to the continued refusal of the legislature to allow Jews to sit for Parliament, however, Goldsmid altered his strategy. In a move that further severed his relationship with the London Committee of Deputies of British Jews, in 1845 Goldsmid (now a baronet) approached Prime Minister Robert Peel and made his case for full Jewish political liberties by pointing to the formation of the first reform congregation in London, an organization that Goldsmid led, and the presumed desire of British Jewry to conform to a more conventional (assimilationist) standard.[85] In another notable change from the earlier movement, the subject of Jewish emancipation (broadly construed) became, in a crucial respect, another manifestation of elite authority; paradoxically, this democratic ideal had separated from the egalitarian social movement process that had originally given rise to it. Although the Cousinhood managed to reestablish their sovereignty, they had also redefined the role of the Jewish upper class to include a far more visible and magnanimous public function; and so these men of property and distinction found themselves in a greatly enhanced position both as Englishmen and as communal leaders.[86]

Part II
The Damascus Affair

3   Blood Libel

Between 1827 and 1840, England experienced quite visible growth in virtually all aspects of its economy, but it also suffered a corresponding increase in environmental squalor set in motion by unrestrained industrialization. Some of the most noteworthy events in modern British history occurred at this time; paramount among these was the rapid demise of the ancien régime. In brisk succession, the repeal of the Test and Corporation Acts ended Anglican political privileges, and the passage of Catholic Emancipation dispatched the notion of Britain as an intrinsically Protestant nation. Then, in another sweeping legislative move, the Great Reform Act (1832) significantly reduced monarchical authority and curtailed the House of Lords. While the cultural and intellectual hegemony of both the aristocracy and the established church was dealt a significant blow, these vested interests still remained formidable forces. Moreover, the antislavery movement that had originated in the late eighteenth century as a modest coalition of Quaker and evangelical activists and endured through several cycles of heightened mobilization as well as abeyance, rallied once again to claim final victory. In 1833 both houses of Parliament voted to emancipate slaves in Britain's Caribbean sugar colonies, allowing for a short transitional period, an unprecedented event in world history that became an exemplar for all other Western nations. "For the first time in history," historian David Brion Davis has observed, "the more enlightened nations were beginning to understand that morality, self-interest, and human progress were mutually interdependent and were to be achieved by the same means."[1] Enlightenment ideals and notions of benevolent progress were becoming more prevalent, yet there were significant signs of traditional revival in England as well, especially in religion and the arts.

Strongly impacting the social consciousness of the early Victorians was the ascendance of humanitarianism; a sentiment that became a virtual trademark of the popular press.[2] While not an ideology in the strictest sense, this sensibility nonetheless served as a compelling political force for social change and was responsible for ever-increasing calls for voluntarism and governmental reform. This perspective, it should be said, differed appreciably from the "earnest philanthropy" of the evangelicals; at its core, the humanitarian ethic did not focus on saving souls. "In the fight for humanitarian causes," as one scholar of the early Victorians observes, "reason was invoked more often than religion."[3] Largely unencumbered by organized religion and sometimes prone to sentimentality, humanitarianism expressed an unabashed compassion for the unwarranted pain and suffering of individuals—be they oppressed factory workers, miners, child laborers, the famine-ravaged Irish, or any number of subaltern groups—and found a receptive audience in an expanding, literate middle class. "Charity, mercy, forbearance, and benevolence," as Charles Dickens's character Jacob Marley phrased it, "were, all, my business. The dealings of my trade were but a drop of water in the comprehensive ocean of my business!"[4] While predominantly secular, aspects of this inclusive standard were nevertheless adapted into a religious framework by a group of broad-minded evangelicals. Rev. Baptist Noel, the queen's chaplain who helped found the London City Mission, was clearly influenced by humanitarianism and was in fact criticized for being "a great deal too liberal for the church."[5] Other socially concerned evangelicals such as Lord Ashely, the future Earl of Shaftesbury, can also be counted within this cohort. By the 1840s, both liberals as well as some Tories united in proclaiming a "great movement of humanity"[6] that seemed to spring forth as a natural countervailing force against the excesses of laissez-faire capitalism. At its best, humanitarian discourse not only stressed the unity of mankind but the intrinsic worthiness of individual lives as well; it shaped British perceptions (as well as increasing numbers in Europe and the United States) toward the "other" at home and abroad.[7] Self-reliance was certainly held as a virtue, but humanitarianism specifically looked to wealthy and kindhearted individuals who had the means to combat social evils. In London, Dickens became one of the most recognizable advocates of this social consciousness, but there were myriad other novelists, journalists, poets, and visual artists of varying degrees of distinction who also espoused this vital sensibility. Ironically, however, many of these same writers and artists also perpetuated a grossly caricatured representation of Jews.[8]

International intervention that claimed to act on behalf of humanitarian principles (what would later be referred to as human rights) was not wholly unknown in the nineteenth century. The presumed right of Christian European powers to come to the aid of various religious minorities abroad was enacted in greater or lesser degree by military interventions in Greece (1827–1830) and Syria (1860–1861), and through diplomatic negotiations in Crete (1866–1868). Although historians are understandably reluctant to attribute such complex actions under a humanitarian aegis, especially during an age of empire, there was at least the public perception that humanitarian-based intervention, either through diplomatic means or, as a last resort, military might, was not only viable but morally necessary. In the case of Greece, the cruelties that were inflicted against the Christian Greek population in their struggle for independence against the Ottoman Turks stirred widespread popular sympathy for the Greek cause. The motivations behind the military alliance that was brought to bear against Turkey by Great Britain, France, and Russia are open to question, however.⁹ But a more straightforward scenario presented itself in Syria. Following the wholesale massacre of an estimated eleven thousand Maronite Christians by the Druze population and the resultant flux of homeless refugees, an international agreement by five European powers (including Britain) mandated the occupation of the region by French troops. In this instance, the case for humanitarian intervention seems more convincing as the French held to their stated mandate and withdrew all their forces within the allotted time.¹⁰

The major point here is not whether nineteenth-century nation-states could ever act in a truly virtuous or altruistic manner (at least when it concerned an imperiled group of fellow Christians) or indeed whether the multitude of editors, authors, and publishers in the periodical press were bona fide humanitarians or merely cynical manipulators of public opinion. What is of central importance, however, is recognition of the predominant cultural and intellectual trends from which social movement participants could draw upon in their tactical repertoire. Hence, when news of the torture, imprisonment, and deaths of some of the prominent Jews of Damascus began to surface in London—as well as the deployment of the ancient ritual murder tale—the solidarity movement that arose in response to this oppressive upturn did not represent the same radical break with the past that occurred in 1827. The former quietist standard had already been effectively cast aside in England, thanks in large part to the previous Meetings of the Jews. The resurgence of 1840 nevertheless utilized the basic injustice frame of the prior "initiator movement." As we shall see, this mobilization again focused on a human rights incident abroad—one that involved grievous acts of wrongdoing toward Jews. The resurgence was also in reaction to a rampant stigmatization that ensued from this incident. The movement employed a familiar rhetoric in calling for international Jewish solidarity; relied on an interfaith alliance to bolster political leverage; fashioned direct appeals to the press; directed claims at a foreign head of state; and held public events at elite city venues to augment their standing. Although impassioned, activists exhibited considerable restraint and conformed to conventional (nondisruptive) protests. And the principal Anglo-Jewish leader, Moses Montefiore, was vigilant to separate this solidarity campaign from the drive for Jewish political rights. The master frame of the previous "extraordinary movement" was therefore much in evidence, but a new leadership and an altered political environment naturally required certain modifications that would place this mobilization more in line with existing standards. In this case, a broad humanitarian ethic had indeed become fixed in the mainstream consciousness and was actively promoted in the Western press. Humanitarian ideals would not only broaden the movement's political base but readily bolstered moral authority.¹¹ This Victorian outlook created a special niche for the Anglo-Jewish elite; as the most affluent, they had a singular obligation to act on behalf of the less fortunate and oppressed.

Appeals to Jewish fundamentalism or, in the case of Christian supporters, a pre-millennial eschatology, were greatly diminished in favor of a more secular orientation. This is not to suggest that apocalyptic beliefs had abated in England. To the contrary, despite the fact that much of the secular press as well as the more urbane politicians kept a discreet distance from "the fanatical and religious elements,"[12] pre-millennial evangelicalism actually made significant gains among the public at large and within the established church. Furthermore, the previous Philo-Judaean role was now taken up by the much larger London Society, an organization whose direction had shifted from a wholly conversionist stance to the incorporation of Christian Zionism and the promotion of a Jewish homeland in Palestine. Unlike their predecessors, the London Society did not cosponsor public meetings, but their leading members still played a critical behind-the-scenes role, lobbying government figures as well as the media in the promotion of movement goals.[13]

Also in contrast to 1827, a charge of ritual murder was leveled against Jews. It began as a notorious incident in the Middle East; shortly thereafter, certain elite factions, especially in France but also including England, used this slander to cast doubt on Jews as a whole.[14] Much effort was thus placed on discrediting allegations that deliberately undercut the resurgent movement's high moral ground. The timing of this affair was also disturbing because it surfaced during a period when the general standing of Jews had begun to increase both in Britain and on the Continent. The stigma of blood libel only served to buttress old hatreds. What is more, in France Jews felt dismayed by what they perceived as Prime Minister Thiers's grossly unprincipled and nonsupportive stance. The implicit bargain that had been in place since Napoleon—that Jews would be welcome citizens as long as they shed the vestiges of cultural and religious otherness—had become seriously undermined. Elsewhere in Europe, Moses Hess, a German proto-Zionist, admitted that the blood libel had stirred "a bitter feeling of agony" within him. "Then it dawned upon me for the first time," he recalled twenty years later, "that I belong to my unfortunate, slandered, despised, and dispersed people. And already, then, though I was greatly estranged from Judaism, I wanted to express my Jewish patriotic sentiment in a cry of anguish."[15] Repeated references to ritual murder certainly dominated the press and undoubtedly angered Hess as well as many other Jews.[16] But Hess's awakening to Judaism's political strength and unity also coincided with the wave of protest meetings that seemed to erupt spontaneously in cities throughout the Atlantic world and which drew mass attention to the profound injustices abroad. As the Central Consistory of French Jews emphasized to the minister of foreign affairs during the height of the Damascus affair, "The Israelites of all countries, whose ancient and holy beliefs seem incriminated, are protesting with energy. Generous men outside their faith have shared their indignation."[17] As part of this consciousness-raising, these transnational protests reinforced Jewish diaspora identity and imbued increasing numbers of Jews with a sense of empathic solidarity. Just as with the earlier mobilization, there was a belief in a common cause; individual fate became intertwined with the collective good.

RITUAL MURDER CHARGE

News regarding the bizarre "murder" of an obscure Catholic friar in Damascus, which cast blame on some eminent Jews of that city, first appeared in the *Sémaphore de Marseille* in mid-March 1840; another more detailed and graphically charged piece was published in the same paper the following month, at which time the article was reprinted throughout the European press.[18] "The crimes imputed to the Jews," as the London *Times* observed, "have produced an immense sensation on the continent."[19] The particulars of this extraordinary case (the friar's corpse was never located) evolved into a horrific account that maintained a façade of authenticity. Minute details of ritual homicide were in fact initially published in the papers as if this was legitimate news.[20] Both Adolphe Crémieux, a preeminent defense attorney and vice president of the Consistory of French Jews, and Anglo-Jewish leader Sir Moses Montefiore, recently knighted by the queen, based their response on the universal principles of humanity and justice and envisioned all Jews as a unified body. They denounced these charges not only as gross calumny but as a major threat to world Jewry that needed to be refuted in the most forceful manner possible.

This seminal event originated in Damascus, an ancient city of 100,000 and the administrative center of Egyptian-controlled greater Syria, and was sparked by the disappearance of a Capuchin friar named Père Thomas (Thomas de Camangiano).[21] For over three decades, the elderly cleric, a native of Sardinia, had vaccinated both Christian and Jewish children against smallpox and made his rounds amid the alleyways and densely populated residential quarters, always in the accompaniment of his Arab-Christian servant. Concern over the friar's welfare first arose after he missed a dinner engagement with a certain Dr. Massari, the Christian physician to Sherif Pasha, the Syrian governor. Père Thomas's charitable work notwithstanding, contemporary sources describe him as a quick-tempered and problematic character given to drinking. A day or so before his disappearance, for example, both he and his servant were involved in a fierce altercation with a Muslim muleteer, a row that so provoked the Muslim that he threatened the friar's life.[22] As with most pertinent evidence in this case, however, this incident was ignored by authorities. Be that as it may, it was not long after a search party failed to locate either Père Thomas or his assistant that a group of monks accused the city's Jews of ritual murder—an unprecedented allegation in Damascus. These monks then circulated antisemitic literature to justify their claims.[23] The usually discordant Arab-speaking Christians, a group that included Greek Orthodox, Maronite, Armenian, and

Syrian Catholic, were now unified in their condemnation; angry crowds demanded justice and indicted Jews of a hideous conspiracy. Complicating the matter even further was the fact that the affairs of the Capuchin order in the Middle East had traditionally been relegated under French auspices. While the newly appointed French consul, the Comte de Ratti-Menton, was obligated to investigate the friar's disappearance, the degree to which he was permitted to indict and harass the Jewish residents of Damascus was a most singular development.[24]

Père Thomas's unexplained absence was therefore interpreted through the peculiar political and ethnoreligious milieu of Damascus and, as we shall see, the broader political designs of the French consul. After consistent denial by the Jews of any knowledge or complicity in the cleric's disappearance, a nondescript member of the Jewish community, a barber by trade, was taken into custody, and, following this man's firm refutations, Ratti-Menton delivered him over to Sherif Pasha, whereupon the barber suffered severe beatings. Only afterward did the fine points of a hideous cabal begin to emerge. Among the measures that were brought to bear against the Jewish community, sixty-three school boys, some as young as four, were shackled, imprisoned, and given only scant portions of bread and water; an estimated seventy men, taken at random, were flogged, put in chains, and thrown into the same dank prison. As a result of several "confessions," seven leading merchants and three rabbis were charged with murder and subjected to systematic torture. The cruel measures that were employed by Sherif Pasha, with the full cooperation of Ratti-Menton, would shock many in the West. Techniques included prolonged use of the bastinado (blows to the feet), immersion in water, singeing beards and nostrils with fire, gouging eyes, protracted flogging, and pressure tourniquets brutally applied to the head. Several prisoners did not survive their ordeal.[25] A credible witness who could have exonerated these unfortunate victims, a young Jewish shopkeeper who observed Père Thomas and his servant departing the city gates precisely at the time they were purported to be within the Jewish quarter, was flogged to death after he gave his testimony before the pasha. In another development that would infuriate Western sensibilities, a Muslim astrologer came forward with a list of Jews whose culpability was supposedly determined by divination; as a result, an additional two men, both wealthy Jews, were captured and tortured.[26]

The Comte de Ratti-Menton, an old-school French aristocrat and royalist whose conduct would draw fierce criticism abroad, declared that the blood of the murdered Père Thomas was used in the manufacture of unleavened Passover bread. Sherif Pasha concurred in this judgment, and so even the slightest dissent was severely quashed. Some prisoners did in fact issue false confessions to end their torment. Satisfied, Ratti-Menton compiled copious documentation (sans any reference to torture) and, convinced that his narrative would be accepted by his superiors, sent the dossier to Paris.[27] This report was actually an odd variation of a centuries-old tale that would more typically incriminate Jews in the killing and bloodletting of a prepubescent Christian boy, an especially gruesome accusation that often provoked deadly retribution whenever it arose in medieval Europe. In these accounts, Jews were rendered as diabolical and therefore the most brutal acts of revenge could be rationalized. In an attempt to place such destructive tales into context, scholars have noted the obvious imagery of the paschal lamb as well as the Eucharistic symbols of the body and blood of Christ—particularly potent motifs that appear to have contributed to the construction of this virulent form of Christian folklore.[28]

Within the context of Damascus, allegations of Jewish ritual murder may well have been unparalleled, but such a charge nonetheless served an immediate utility because it easily assigned guilt upon the least numerous and most vulnerable ethnoreligious group. Following the takeover of Syria in 1831 by Mehmed Ali, the Egyptian viceroy, Jews were stripped of their former power as well as economic privileges as "court Jews." Local Christians—many of whom nourished protracted family grudges against the Jews—were selected to replace them. Damascene Jews were thus left in an exceedingly vulnerable position.[29] What is more, according to Middle East historian Mary C. Wilson, official documents of the trial proceedings and other evidence suggest that the skewed judgment of Ratti-Menton was quite deliberate as the consul's overriding aim was to bolster French (and thus Catholic) interests. By placing Jews as scapegoats and degrading their status in the region even more, Ratti-Menton expected to curry favor with the Christian populace. France, Wilson notes, was particularly keen to improve relations with the Maronite community in greater Syria; these were Eastern Rite Catholics whose affiliation with the French could be traced to the Crusades. Furthermore, as the Maronite stronghold was located in strategically important Mount Lebanon, then part of Syria, any favored relationship would aid in the expansion of the French-Catholic sphere of influence.[30]

From the perspective of Mehmed Ali and his son, Sherif Pasha, a more secure and less rebellious Maronite population would have countered the ambitions of Great Britain, whose policies favored the Ottomans and their desire to regain Syria. France was Mehmed Ali's sole ally among the great powers; without French backing, Egyptian rule could not stand very long in Syria. Furthermore, given Ratti-Menton's intimate involvement, Mehmed Ali initially claimed that Christians actually controlled the proceedings against the Jews and thus his government could not be held accountable.[31] As a result, Damascene Jews were deemed expendable by the main parties, and antisemitism—described by the Austrian consul in Damascus as the "blind and ignorant fanaticism of the Christians in this country"—served as a tool to achieve political, religious, and, in the case of the deep-seated commercial rivalry between local Christians and Jews, economic ends as well.[32] Of course, the use of torture against the Jews also had broad psychosocial ramifications. Pain was transformed into a symbolic act; it was a conscious attempt to obliterate the victim's voice and autonomy—indeed, his very personhood.³³ By extension, torture also became an act of negation toward all Jews. Within the context of the Middle East (and indeed far beyond), this entire ordeal would have been perceived as a grave threat not only to personal and collective honor but to the welfare of Jews as a whole.³⁴

During the first week of April 1840, Adolphe Crémieux, a secular Jew and an attorney with a high reputation at the bar, joined most other literate Parisians by reading multiple newspaper accounts of a sensational story that emanated from the Syrian capital. Macabre techniques were described with precision, procedures that were purported to be used in the ritualized slaying of a pious Catholic cleric by a sinister Jewish cabal. The "holy martyr Thomas," it was asserted, was brought into the home of an elite Jewish merchant and was forcibly held to the floor while a barber grabbed the friar's beard and coolly slit his throat. "As soon as the victim expired," the story continued, "he was hung up by his feet in order to collect the blood. The body was then shredded, the head and the bones crushed, and clothes torn to shreds after which the remains of the martyr were spread in the sewers of the city."³⁵ Most Parisians were blithely unaware of Jewish matters, let alone the history of medieval blood libel or the details of Mosaic Law, and so this article left many readers truly horrified. In fact, the deviant nature of the accusations aroused widespread anxiety.³⁶ In their eagerness to print these salacious stories, the press at first omitted any opportunity for rebuttal. By 8 April, however, Crémieux penned a lengthy and impassioned refutation and, among other cogent points, accused the press of forfeiting their sacred obligation to present facts and to spurn fictitious slander. His letter was published in the *Journal des Débats* and reprinted abroad.³⁷ Crémieux was soon joined by the Jewish scholar Joseph Salvador, whose writings on a much-idealized ancient Israel were actually read "by ladies of the highest rank" in Paris.³⁸ Salvador submitted a widely circulated letter to the same paper wherein he denounced "the odious insinuations." What is more, he noted a historical parallel with the early Christians. Sixteen centuries earlier, equally baseless allegations of ritual sacrifice were leveled against Christians by their "pagan" contemporaries. Given the falsity of the charges, Salvador expressed confidence that the press would soon pursue matters in better accord with "humanity and public reason."³⁹ Although the tenor of some papers moderated—*La Presse*, for example, freely conceded the absurdity of the claims following Crémieux's renunciation⁴⁰—the original allegation still cast doubt in many people's minds, even among the educated, and inflamed antisemitic invective, especially within right-wing Catholic circles. In contrast to Salvador, Crémieux urged a resolute Jewish protest, pursued "in the name of all the world's Jews," that would stand as a worthy rejoinder to such hideous defamation.⁴¹ As an *affaire d'honneur*, any insult to one's reputation had to be rigorously met in kind. But the question remained: was Jewish honor at odds with the honor of France? Prime Minister Thiers, when pressed on the dubious conduct of the Comte de Ratti-Menton in the Chamber of Deputies, declared that honor was the prerogative of those who served the interests of France, not the Jews. "You appeal in the name of the Jews, while I appeal in the name of a Frenchman [Ratti-Menton] who, thus far, has fulfilled his duties with honor and fidelity."[42] Thiers's oratory was warmly received in the chamber.[43] After several such incidents and following Crémieux's subsequent arrival in London, where he met with Anglo-Jewish leaders concerning the Damascus affair, it is hardly surprising that Crémieux emphatically declared to his British colleagues that "France is against us."[44]

LONDON RESPONDS

The initial reaction of the Board of Deputies toward the events in Syria included a remarkable attempt, especially in light of the Board's legacy of inaction, to ask the British government to intervene diplomatically on behalf of the Jews in Damascus. On 30 April, Joseph G. Henriques, then president of the Board, joined with other notables such as Sir Moses Montefiore, Isaac L. Goldsmid, and Baron Lionel de Rothschild in a meeting with Lord Palmerston, the Foreign Affairs secretary, at Downing Street. This high-level engagement, the details of which were reported in the London press, resulted in Palmerston's pledge to use the influence of the British consul at Alexandria, Egypt, to persuade Mehmed Ali to end the torture of the Jewish prisoners.[45] Furthermore, a similar incident of blood libel had surfaced on the island of Rhodes, then under Ottoman control, and the foreign office committed to alleviating that situation as well. Throughout May, however, articles originating in the French press—including a letter written by a certain Damascus friar (a colleague of Père Thomas) which defended Ratti-Menton, detailed, yet again, his fellow cleric's "horrible assassination" and claimed that Thomas's "bones" were now venerated by Christians and Muslims alike—were reprinted without qualification by the influential *Times*.[46] The *Times*, in a purported effort to remain neutral in what it deemed "one of the most important cases ever submitted to the notice of the civilized world, and upon which the very existence of the Jewish religion, and of the Jews as a separate class of the community, may be said to depend," actually succeeded in keeping the controversy alive.[47] Regardless of the paper's claims of impartiality, there was clearly no point, other than casting suspicion upon the Jews, in including most of this material—especially some blatantly antisemitic texts of dubious origin.[48] One of these, *Argument against the Jews upon Their Law and Customs* (1716) supposedly authored by a former rabbi and alleged to be an insider's look into the barbaric practice of ritual murder, was apparently a best-seller among monastic circles in Romania.[49] Extracts were published in the *Times*, and though the newspaper admitted the text's "intolerant spirit," the editors also asserted that such material was required in order for readers to arrive at an informed judgment—implying, of course, that the text possessed some legitimacy. It should be noted that as the Tory paper of record, the *Times* was opposed to the very Whig government that was enacting, among other policies, open support for the Jews of Damascus. The newspaper's deliberate ambiguity on this controversy only fed into public doubts and thus can be seen as a force of significant opposition toward the renascent Jewish rights movement. As another London paper sardonically remarked, "The *Times* has lately become the champion of religion, morality, and virtue, and besides that, it pretended to take on the cause of the Jews of Damascus, and in the spirit of kindness towards them . . . they took care to print every document that could possibly make them appear guilty."[50] The highly influential *Literary Gazette*, quite shockingly in the view of many educated Jews, also followed much the same policy as the *Times*.[51] All this occurred during a period when the voice of the British press was regularly compared to the power of Britain itself—"gigantic, all-pervading, extending to the utmost verge of the known world."[52] The blood libel became the focus of countless magazine and newspaper articles in Britain, and, augmented by the charges in Rhodes, the subject gained even more momentum on the Continent as well. It was becoming obvious to the Central Consistory, the Board of Deputies, as well as the influential Rothschild family in Paris, Vienna, and London that these escalating events necessitated a resolute response from the Jewish community. The Consistory opted to send Crémieux to Alexandria and Damascus, where he could act in the capacity of a high-level emissary; hopefully, it was thought, the British Deputies would coordinate their actions with the French and dispatch their own envoy—in all likelihood Moses Montefiore—in concert with Crémieux.

In parallel with these events and largely unknown in the West at the time, the London Society pursued its own brand of Middle East diplomacy. In March, following an urgent appeal from Jewish leaders in Jerusalem, the Society's mission director, John Nicolayson, sent George W. Pieritz, a missionary (and converted Jew) to Damascus with the aim of convincing Sherif Pasha of the falsehood of the blood ritual allegations.[53] Upon his arrival on 30 March, Pieritz undertook an in-depth review of the Jewish persecution (his investigative narrative was later published in London, to great effect). Pieritz was evidently warned against approaching the pasha; instead, Jewish leaders, all of whom were confined to the city, urged the missionary to advocate their cause and to submit a petition on their behalf directly to Mehmed Ali in Egypt—a weighty undertaking that Pieritz readily assented to. Through the intervention of the British consul-general in Alexandria, Pieritz pleaded the case for the Damascene prisoners before the viceroy on 16 May, whereupon Mehmed Ali ordered a reinvestigation of the charges. The viceroy, according to the missionary, also claimed that he had sent word to Sherif Pasha to "desist from tortures" and to treat the prisoners humanely "for the present."[54]

In addition to the London Society's efforts in the Middle East, the organization's leadership—which included Lord Ashley, the Bishop of Ripon, Sir Thomas Baring, and Sir George Rose—visited Downing Street in May to put additional pressure on Palmerston to seek redress on behalf of the Jews of Damascus and Rhodes. Afterward, the Society published a memorial that attested to the "unmerited and cruel torment . . . of the people of Israel" in the *Times*.[55] On his own initiative, Ashley made use of his personal access to Palmerston (both men were related by marriage), and in a succession of dinners and correspondence, Ashley not only promoted the cause of the Jews in Damascus but proposed the idea of a Jewish return to the Holy Land, wisely centering his arguments on the political and commercial advantages that would be gained rather than basing his case on biblical prophecy.[56] Remarkably, Palmerston conveyed his interest in this proposal. To be sure, the Damascus affair was becoming enmeshed in much broader international tensions. Britain would soon lead a military engagement against Egyptian forces in Syria during the fall, and Austria, Prussia, and Russia supported Palmerston's move to reinstate Ottoman control over Syria and the Holy Land—eventually forcing Mehmed Ali's withdrawal back to Egypt. As Jews were now publicly responding to the atrocities in Damascus, presenting a very damning view of Egyptian rule in Syria in the process, such negative publicity only bolstered Palmerston's foreign policy aims.[57] The activities of the London Society and the Jews themselves were therefore most welcome from the government's perspective. Such a favorable political climate boded well for a resurgent Jewish rights movement.

Details of Pieritz's journey to Alexandria and Damascus would not be known in England for several more weeks. London Jews, however, were much aware of the blood libel controversy that seemed to worsen each day. Increased demands were placed on the Board of Deputies, especially as the intentions of the Consistory were now made public. It was within this context that another gathering of Anglo-Jewish notables took place on 12 and 15 June in London. Compared with the earlier rise of the Jewish rights movement, these affairs were certainly far more hierarchical and subdued in nature. Yet these proceedings, which included Crémieux as well as many of the Cousinhood's inner sanctum, were enacted with a keen eye to their potential notice in the media. During the second such gathering held at Montefiore's Park Lane residence, a broadsheet was distributed to the media. This notice refuted the charges against the Jews at Damascus and stated the desire of the Board to enlist Montefiore to journey to the Middle East with Crémieux. It was now becoming apparent that these crisis meetings had become linked to a unified strategy and that a common goal was being set in place. In a key development and in noticeable contrast to the Consistory's emphasis on diplomatic initiatives, Montefiore, who, as president of the London Committee of Delegates, had long resisted sponsoring public meetings (at least when it concerned the topic of Anglo-Jewish political liberties), now consented to hold a "public meeting of the Jews" at London's Great Synagogue located at Dukes Place.[58] This occasion was certainly "a conspicuous development in the evolution of modern Jewish politics," as Jonathan Frankel has observed, but public meetings, as we now know, had already evolved as part of the contentious repertoire of London Jews.⁵⁹ Montefiore ordered a circular to be printed that requested the attendance of the "heads of all Jewish families in the metropolis"—remarkably without distinction between Ashkenazi or Sephardi congregations.⁶⁰ Approximately three months in the making, a remobilization of the Jewish rights movement had in effect been set in motion by the very group who had formerly avoided the earlier insurgence.

The speeches that were delivered during the Great Synagogue meeting of 23 June reflected intense communal concern over the Judeophobia that continued to make inroads across the Middle East and Europe.⁶¹ In addition, the meeting's presumption of acting as the de facto voice of world Jewry generated a fervent atmosphere more typical of a political campaign than a communal gathering. "The subject that has called us together is not one of ordinary importance," as Barnard Van Oven reminded the overflow crowd of nearly eight hundred.⁶² In fact, Van Oven observed, as they had chosen to meet "in the very temple of our faith," such a unique event was by itself striking evidence of the grievous and unusual threat that confronted them. A voracious "monster" of bigotry had emerged, he continued—a force that could do such injury that "the very name of a Jew shall be heard only with horror and disgust." The considerable progress that had been made on behalf of Jewish rights—indeed Jewish collective identity as a whole—appeared under siege. A "slanderous lie" was increasing and gaining credibility as a result of the absurd charges in the press. "It is not, then, merely for the sake of humanity—not only for the sake of our oppressed brethren that we are called on to act," Van Oven reasoned, "it is our own battle that we fight, though, thank HEAVEN, our own country is not the battlefield."⁶³ It is worth noting that Van Oven, physician to the poor of the Great Synagogue and a longtime liberal advocate, never questioned that Anglo-Jewry had an inherent obligation to take a leadership role in this escalating crisis.

Montefiore served as chairman, and he, along with the other speakers, stood on the bimah, a raised platform enclosed by an ornate wooden balustrade located at the center of the large, basilica-shaped chamber. The deliberations of the previous meetings of the Board of Deputies were recited by the meeting secretary, along with the rationale for the present assembly. Additionally, several letters written by the Jewish leaders of Damascus, Alexandria, and Constantinople were read aloud; these attested to the dire state of their imprisoned brethren as well as the grim fact that these unfortunates would be executed without a major reversal by the viceroy. The supportive actions of the British government and the considerable overtures of the Rothschilds in countering this escalating incident were also lauded.⁶⁴ Montefiore had not yet announced his intentions to act as the Anglo-Jewish emissary, and so this crucial detail was still in question as a succession of speakers approached the bimah, including David Salomons, a proprietor of the East India Company and the future lord mayor of London. More than any of those who spoke that evening, however, it was Montefiore—former sheriff of London, recently elected president of the Board of Deputies, and an observant Jew—who would infuse his oratory with a deeply felt humanitarian ethos. An individual of considerable wealth, Montefiore nonetheless spoke in the straightforward idiom of the enlightened bourgeoisie and intended his address to reach well beyond his immediate Jewish audience. With dramatic flair, he reminded those in attendance that the gravity of the situation did not allow for mere compliments on his behalf. As far as his proposed mission with Crémieux was concerned: "if the meeting deemed him a fitting person to undertake so important a trust he would cheerfully ... comply (loud cheers)." He felt the full measure of this mission with such intensity that, as the *Morning Chronicle* reported,

> The only relief to his anxiety was that M. Crémieux, a gentleman of the first eminence among the Jewish community in France, had been deputed to accompany him. They were going to assert the claims of outraged humanity, and to uplift the dark veil which hung over the diabolical accusations against their brethren, to bring their accusers to shame and contempt; to remove the stain cast upon the name of their nation by the bigotry, intolerance, fraud, and rapacity of their unprincipled oppressors. More than this, they want to induce a more liberal policy among the governors of the East; to prevail on them to abolish the use of torture and to make justice henceforth triumphant over uncurbed power. He had a confident hope that their mission would be attended with success and that they would be enabled to show that there was not a heart [that did not] beat in their cause.[65]

Just as many successful leaders, and not unlike Moses Levy, Montefiore possessed a natural talent for political theater. Thus, he selected that very moment to bid his farewell, thereby eliciting "great emotion" in the synagogue. Six feet three inches tall and often appearing in the flamboyant, gold-braided uniform of a lord lieutenant of the City of London—by all accounts Montefiore seemed to emanate a "knightly valor."[66] He knew the rules of Victorian pageantry and showmanship and was not averse to putting himself on display, especially in the service of Jewish rights. Modern historians have occasionally remarked upon Montefiore's supposed "pomposity and self-aggrandizement."[67] Geoffrey Alderman, for example, dismissed all of Montefiore's activities on behalf of world Jewry as motivated by personal aggrandizement and "productive of little concrete good."[68] Such hypercritical assessments are in stark contrast to the myriad hagiographic narratives written by many of Montefiore's well-intentioned contemporaries—"The cordial grasp of his hand, his benign mien, the kindness and good-humored wisdom of his conversation are beyond the aging touch of fashion."[69] Whatever one may think of Montefiore as a personality, there is no reason to doubt his integrity or his commitment to the resurgent movement. On the occasion of the Damascus affair, he was in full command of the romantic idiom, and he was at ease in expressing heartfelt sentiments;

70 *The Rise of Modern Jewish Politics*

indeed, communal pride, both in Montefiore as a person and in his accomplishments, would soon grow exponentially. As movement analysts note, there is an increased need for such charismatic figures during periods of crisis, especially when minority identities are under vigorous assault.[70] The self-confidence these leaders typically convey acts as an effective countermeasure to the politics of denigration. Montefiore's well-heeled manner and celebrated largesse projected a positive image to the press and certainly belied any notion of shame. [The buoyant, self-assured slogans of the 1960s social movements, such as "Black is beautiful" and "woman-power," served a similar function.[71]] Be that as it may, the affair at the Great Synagogue was not marred by the slightest dissent and was widely perceived as a successful demonstration of Jewish unity and thus a fitting rebuke to charges of ritual murder. The newspaper-reading public in Britain, continental Europe, the United States, and in the leading Caribbean colonies would take serious note of this dynamic protest and also looked favorably upon Montefiore and Crémieux's humanitarian mission to the Middle East.

The sense of crisis that was allowed expression at the Great Synagogue meeting is indicative of the degree to which this event had signaled a remobilization of the Jewish rights movement. Van Oven's "horror and disgust"

Figure 3.1 Even in old age, Sir Moses Montefiore easily conveyed the self-confidence that underpinned his status as the consummate Jewish rights advocate.

Source: *Illustrated London News*, 3 November 1882.

and Montefiore's desire to bring "shame and contempt" upon those who libeled the Jews is precisely the sort of emotive language that builds support for social movements and aids in sustaining unity and momentum. Activists often go to great lengths to disseminate their ideas to the largest possible audience and as quickly as possible, while simultaneously attempting to associate their cause with political legitimacy.[72] Thus, adhering to the precedent established in 1827, the affair at the Great Synagogue was followed two weeks later by a separate solidarity meeting sponsored by an elite group of Christian supporters. In this instance, however, the setting was Egyptian Hall, the magnificent meeting and banqueting hall at Mansion House, the lord mayor's town palace. Instead of an evangelical-led assembly, the meeting that took place on 3 July was held under the auspices of high-ranking city officials, some of whom were intimate business associates of Montefiore as well as other elite Jews. This particular advance made a positive impression in the media; it endowed the protest assembly and the movement itself with the prestigious imprimatur of the City of London (a feat not even the antislavery crusade managed to attain). While historians have briefly noted the high profile of Mansion House during the Damascus affair, scholars have yet to recognize how unusual this engagement by the City actually was. Thus, a more detailed understanding of this rarified institution (circa 1840) becomes a desideratum; indeed, as we shall see, it is essential to placing this event into accurate context.

4   Mansion House and Beyond

Located at the center of London's financial district, directly across from the Bank of England and the Royal Exchange, Mansion House symbolized the City's weighty economic and political power. The mayor's official residence certainly inhabited a privileged location that was virtually unmatched in Britain. Often perceived as the "greatest, grandest, and wealthiest city in the world," London at midcentury was imagined to have been excelled only by ancient Rome at its zenith.[1] Similarly, the one square mile that comprised the City was governed by so-called worthy citizens, some of whom rose to commercial prominence from rather humble origins.[2] The mayoralty was invested with significant powers: judicial and economic authority that was almost monarchical in scope. Selected for a one-year term from a pool of aldermen, each of whom was awarded a lifetime appointment, the lord mayor was regularly described as the "King of the City."[3] Indeed, this position came with a scepter and sword of state, a retinue of servants, sergeants and marshals, and a grand state carriage with powdered footmen. In addition to an impressive salary, the mayor had full use of an eighteenth-century palace with a marble-columned banqueting hall "in which to dispense the City hospitalities to the potentates of the earth who periodically come into our midst."[4] Among the lord mayor's special prerogatives was the power to bestow knighthoods and baronetcies (sheriffs and the mayors themselves were frequent beneficiaries).

During this period, the City "seemed oblivious to public duty," as one modern historian has commented, and appeared more intent on sponsoring elaborate entertainment, including extravagant state dinners, than attending to genuine public interest.[5] The London *Satirist*, never hesitant to cast barbs at vested interests, once suggested that the best indicator for success as an alderman was the ability to indulge in gluttony on a grand scale.[6] To be fair, occasional charitable and fund-raising events were held at Egyptian Hall, and individual "livery" companies in the City contributed to philanthropic causes.[7] These were, however, relatively modest efforts. In fact, it would be several more decades before Mansion House would establish itself as a venue for philanthropic or social movement activity, a public relations gesture that evolved only in response to escalating calls for reform.[8]

Adding to its reputation as a self-serving oligarchy, the City's everyday operations were held in rather splendid isolation, and details of its immense wealth were kept secure from outside scrutiny. What is more, the Corporation of London was protected from any legal challenges within its boundaries and possessed powers which extended beyond the City proper. Within its purview was a most lucrative "regulation of markets, coal dues and grain metages" throughout greater London.[9] All things considered, few institutions appeared to be farther removed from the broader culture of Victorian largesse, "improvement," democratization, and reform.

Given these circumstances, what could explain the uncharacteristic assembly at Mansion House on behalf of the Jewish minority in Damascus? The meeting itself offers substantive clues.[10] Not unexpectedly, Egyptian Hall was "crowded to excess" with an extensive cohort of eminent bankers and businessmen, members of Parliament, the inner circle of Jewish notables, a separate contingent of lesser-ranked but still prosperous Jewish merchants, as well as a "large number of ladies of respectability." On this occasion, however, there were few clergymen in attendance (members of the London Society were also absent from the platform). This was intended, after all, as "a meeting for the merchants," as Montefiore once phrased it.[11] At the onset, it was made clear that any form of debate would not be countenanced. "The large, numerous, and most respectable meeting," as the initial speaker, Alderman Thompson MP declared, "was not assembled for the purpose of discussing any question on which there was a probability of a difference of opinion."[12] As far as the judgment of the City was concerned, the allegation of ritual murder was fraudulent on its face; Jews had thus suffered the most "atrocious calumnies." The meeting's intention was to express sympathy for the "tyrannical persecutions" in Damascus with the expectation that their support would have an effect in the Middle East and thus forestall further suffering. Notably, Thompson did not dwell on the Damascus atrocities, leaving that function to the next speaker. He nonetheless made a special effort to emphasize the exemplary conduct of the Jews of London, especially their philanthropy toward the poor. "None of our fellow-citizens are more zealous in the spread of humanity, in aiding the poor and oppressed, in protecting the orphan and in promoting literature and knowledge as they are." Jewish charitable concerns had in fact progressed substantially from the time that Rabbi Crooll lamented the "deep sleep" of communal leaders.[13] Even so, and as the London reformers inevitably focused upon, the grandeur of the metropolis remained at odds with "the fearful masses of human misery" that existed just beyond the enclaves of high society[14] (an aspect of daily life that still included a very high proportion of Jewish poor). Yet the relative generosity of Jews attested to the fulfillment of their charitable obligations as elite males; and, as Thompson noted, these actions also extended well beyond communal concerns to include worthy Christian causes.[15] Benevolent acts were expected to transcend all religious denominations. Furthermore, Jewish financiers added immeasurably to London's financial prosperity and prestige: "He need only remind them of Rothschild, a name which will endure as long as the city of London itself (loud cheers)."[16] Surely the conduct of the prosperous Jews of the Middle East, Thompson reasoned, could not be that dissimilar from the entrepreneurs who, like David Salomons and Moses Montefiore seated before them, were awarded high honors by the Corporation through their former investitures as sheriffs.

Leading Jews had unquestionably made major strides since 1830. Although many had developed business ties with gentiles before this date, after the barrier of the freedom of the City had been removed, some Jews began to be welcomed into the Corporation's highest stratum. For both Salomons and Montefiore, this meant the privileges of City office; Jews were now seen in elaborate ceremonial finery, rode in luxurious state carriages, and further established intimate rapport with fellow financial elites. For these individuals at any rate, their former stigmatized identity as "stockjobbers" no longer applied. The entry of Jews as "freemen" altered exclusionary boundaries of long duration. Cultural capital—or "the high status cultural signals (attitudes, preferences, formal knowledge, behaviors, goods and credentials) used for social and cultural exclusion"[17]—had modified to include well-acculturated, "benevolent," and wealthy Jews. Both Mansion House and Guildhall certainly symbolized oligarchic privilege; yet, at least in this one respect, the Corporation actually renounced centuries of tradition. As Montefiore proudly made note after receiving his knighthood from Queen Victoria, his crest and arms—a banner inscribed in Hebrew with the word *Jerusalem* upon it—was now "floating proudly" among the other distinguished standards of Guildhall.[18] It was Montefiore's newly endowed cultural capital and not wealth alone that elevated him to this pivotal moment. Hence, one can readily appreciate the meeting as a gesture of solidarity on behalf of London's Jewish magnates, some of whom were now members of a quasi-royalty peculiar only to the metropolis. Furthermore, when viewed within the perspective of the nineteenth-century code of honor, the stigma of ritual murder, a bizarre allegation that undoubtedly evoked much anxiety, would also have been perceived as a grave assault to the reputation of the City itself.[19] The Mansion House meeting certainly embraced the spirit of British humanitarianism. Far more understated, however, was the City's defensive posture—a stance that was designed to reaffirm the honor, status, and social solidarity of the Corporation of London.

In keeping with the meeting's stated goal, Sir Robert Peel's condemnation of the Damascus persecution, delivered in the House of Commons a few weeks earlier, was read aloud by the meeting secretary. Peel's influential address included an extract taken from the recently arrived Pieritz report. This meticulous firsthand testimony vindicated the Jews of all charges and did so in a lawyerly, dispassionate tone that appeared quite credible. Among other matters, Pieritz specified the various forms of torture and plainly implicated the French consul in these ghastly proceedings—the overall effect was chilling.[20] Afterward, John Masterman, a director of the East India Company and MP for the City of London, rose to address the assembly and expressed "a desire common to all Englishmen of putting an end to oppression." Like Thompson before him, Masterman once again shifted his emphasis to "that liberal and influential portion of that people who resided" in England and singled out Montefiore for special praise ("no man was more respected for his virtues in public and in private life"). Following several more distinguished speakers with long-established ties to the East India trade, including Sir Charles Forbes and Lord Howden, a loud round of cheering ensued when Daniel O'Connell, the Irish MP and Jewish rights advocate, approached the podium. During his presentation, O'Connell drew an especially vivid connection between the worthy Jews of London and their Damascus brethren. "Let them suppose for a moment," he suggested,

> that the system of putting witnesses to the torture were applied in England, and let them think of the consequences to which such a practice would lead. Let them imagine that on evidence so extorted some of the *millionaires* then around him were loaded with fetters, and subjected to sufferings the most cruel—let them suppose these things, and he would ask if there was any one at that meeting who would not indignantly protest against proceedings so revolting? . . . I appeal to all Englishmen to raise their voices in defense of the victims of that shameful oppression. May the appeal go from one end of the British Isles to the other, and if the concurrence of an Irishman be wanting, here I am to testify to it.[21]

By evoking an image of the City's Jewish merchant princes as tortured and bound in the chains of a dismal Syrian dungeon, O'Connell adroitly linked the cause of Damascene Jews with the honor and dignity of the City. This imaginary rendering was intended to produce a "moral shock" by presenting the modern world as gone terribly awry.[22] Any sense of revulsion actually facilitated O'Connell's aim in placing the atrocities committed in a distant land within a more immediate and parochial framework. In marked contrast, however, Rev. Baptist Noel—chaplain to Queen Victoria and one of the few clergymen at the podium—differed in his orientation and stressed religious righteousness instead. In addition to the immense pain that had been inflicted upon the Jews by this "unfounded and malevolent" charge, the affair disparaged Christianity as well—a direct reference to the notorious conduct of the Comte de Ratti-Menton as well as the Catholic friars. To be sure, their actions had become a source of deep shame. "Christianity should be vindicated from such a crime," Noel declared. "The name of Jesus should not be held up to the world as capable of condoning such conduct." Noel's humanitarian mind-set, albeit one that was much under the sway of British nationalism, also allowed for a sincere empathy to be expressed for the Jews of Damascus. "It was their duty then to hasten to relieve their sorrows, and to spread the shield of British humanity over the defenseless."[23] Britain would not only come to the aid of the oppressed but would serve as a moral teacher as well.

A series of condemnatory resolutions were passed and, fully expecting that the three-hour meeting would "raise such a feeling in the country against the atrocities that had been committed against the Jews" that the actual perpetrators would be brought to justice, the assembly adjourned. A substantial fund was raised to assist in Montefiore's journey, and this was ultimately combined with donations previously collected at the Great Synagogue. Shortly thereafter, the lord mayor sent official copies of the Mansion House resolutions to Lord Palmerston and to all the foreign ambassadors in London. News of both public meetings was disseminated throughout the empire, and much of the world press—indeed, the front page of the *Journal des Débats* featured excerpts from the Mansion House speeches.[24] Published details would serve as a template for future protests. Comparable solidarity meetings took place in Manchester, Liverpool, Falmouth, and Dublin and also spread to Altona and Hamburg, the Caribbean (Jamaica, Barbados, and Curacao), and the United States (New York City, Philadelphia, Charleston, Richmond, Savannah, and Cincinnati).[25] In moving forward with the Great Synagogue meeting in June, Montefiore was astutely aware of what he had placed in motion. As he would later write to the Board of Deputies, "After all, it is London that must act upon the world, and through its press leave its imprint on civilization, its liberal feeling and humanity upon the East."[26] Even so, it is doubtful that either Montefiore or the Board could have anticipated the degree to which citizens in other countries would emulate what had taken place in the metropolis.

Cities which held meetings, either in tandem (i.e., Jewish and Christian), as in London, or in single instances of either religious denomination, possessed a vital, cosmopolitan Jewish merchant class with substantive links to the gentile community. Still, there were many locations in Europe, such as Marseille, Trieste, and Amsterdam, and the United States—Baltimore and New Orleans, for example—that met this standard and yet did not follow suit. The receptiveness of the local, national, or, in the case of the Caribbean, colonial government, as well as the leadership of the various Jewish and Christian congregations, was thus a substantial factor. What is more, with the exception of the twin cities of Hamburg and Altona and the multilingual port of Willemstad, Curacao, protests took place in English-speaking communities that traditionally held public meetings in high esteem.

Transnational human rights mobilizations were not without precedent at this time. For example, New York City's *Morning Herald* reminded readers that comparable affairs had taken place in America during the struggle for Greek independence (1821–1828). This substantial international philhellenic movement also took root in London and was in reaction to the persecution of the Greeks by the Ottoman Turks.[27] Large public meetings, consisting of "men of all parties and sects," made liberal donations to the cause.

The bond that united this fairly affluent and well-educated group consisted of a mutual sense of intellectual indebtedness to ancient Greek culture. But if this was true, the paper noted, "how much more do we not owe to the Hebrews?" The American moral code and legal foundation—even Christianity itself—were all indebted to the Jews. These points would in fact be brought up repeatedly throughout the meetings in the United States, and so the framing of these protests differed somewhat from Britain. [Paradoxically, and unknown to most people at the time, the Greek revolution also fomented anti-Jewish violence, and many Jews were massacred because they did not side with the insurgency.[28]] The *Herald* also stressed the ideal of religious freedom, a cherished tenet that united "good and humane men" of all denominations—"Baptists, Methodists, Catholics, Unitarians, Presbyterians, Quakers, and all others (for all have, in their day and generation, suffered their share of shameful persecution)." Now it was time, urged the paper, to boldly come forward and "express their sentiments against this sad persecution of the poor Jews of the East."[29]

REACTION IN THE UNITED STATES

Shortly after the Mansion House meeting, Montefiore and his entourage boarded a Royal Navy vessel and headed for France, where they would join Adolphe Crémieux in Paris. After an elaborate send-off in the French capital, Montefiore and Crémieux proceeded to Marseille, where they departed by ship for Alexandria, each man leading his own cadre of cultural, diplomatic, and linguistic advisors. By the time this Anglo-French delegation arrived in Egypt on 4 August, notice of this extraordinary undertaking as well as the London protests had been widely circulated. Despite the fact that steamships now transported the latest foreign newspapers across the Atlantic at increased speed, there was still a significant time lag reaching opposite shores. News of the Great Synagogue meeting, for example, would not be published in the United States until an entire month had elapsed, and the Mansion House proceedings took even longer.[30]

Social movements have often been compared with theatrical events because individual participants or "actors" draw upon a common repertoire of behavior that is strikingly similar to a public performance.[31] If these contentious episodes prove successful and manage to elicit media interest, then this winning scenario is often repeated, with variations, as the movement progresses. Analysts often refer to this tendency of social movements as "modular forms" of collective action.[32] That is, different participants in a variety of geographic locations have the option to adopt and slightly modify a proven contentious formula and in doing so transcend existing parochial limitations with comparative ease.[33] This innovation coincided with the fact that various social movements had already become national or transnational in scope. The public protests that burst upon the American scene in 1840 did in fact mirror the initial London event. With the exception of Charleston and Savannah, and despite the encouragement of the *Herald*, these gatherings were mostly held under Jewish auspices, however. In each instance, meeting secretaries stepped forward to present evidence of torture and atrocities as well as document the innocence of the Jews (the Pieritz report was particularly emphasized); resolutions were voted upon; and a succession of rousing and often eloquent speeches were rendered by communal figures and later published at length in the press. Donations were solicited on behalf of Montefiore's mission, and formal, authoritative statements were delivered to high-ranking government officials, urging action by the United States on behalf of Damascus Jews. Newspapers that supported the cause transcribed the proceedings in minute detail, sometimes in full-page spreads, displacing more conventional news—the kind of reverential consideration normally given to congressional debates of high national import. In at least two instances, again reflecting the political conventions of the day, these accounts were republished as pamphlets and distributed a second time.[34] Such social movement performances may have followed a set format, but meetings nevertheless evoked an insurgent reality—a level of contentiousness that not all synagogue communities were willing to embrace. For those that did, however, a cadre of well-educated, cosmopolitan Jews gathered in large numbers and not only expressed a lofty idealism but, most atypically, were more than willing to make emphatic demands, to express anger, and to hurl scathing criticism and rebuke at distant leaders.[35]

Contentious gatherings had never been part of the American Jewish experience. Until August 1840, Jews had indeed been a quiescent and insular group—notwithstanding Moses Levy's previous contributions abroad. Mordecai Noah's reputation as an orator and journalist in New York City, by then a substantial city of 313,000, helped to establish him as one of the best known Jews of his generation. Noah's fellow Jews, however, were far too entrenched in local concerns to allow a single individual to speak for all. Furthermore, there was no central organizational body, and many Jews would have abhorred the concept of a religious hierarchy, especially as manifested by the office of a chief rabbi. Instead, as historian Leon Jick has stated, a kind of "institutional anarchy" prevailed.[36] Pious Jews with some advanced knowledge of Hebrew but lacking formal rabbinical education served as "ministers" or *hazzans*. The country was similarly devoid of a Jewish oligarchy or Cousinhood that dominated communal affairs on a national level, and so the kind of procedural developments that led to the London meetings could not be duplicated in the United States. The decision to hold public protests was the exclusive choice of each synagogue. There may have been self-proclaimed "Israelites" of New York, Virginia, South Carolina, and so on, but these associational networks had more to do with reinforcing ethnopolitical identity than anything else. Ties of kinship, especially among the native-born elite and their widely dispersed relatives, also served as kind of unifying force. Jews, however, represented a minute fraction of a mostly rural populace of seventeen million, despite an increase in immigration during the previous decade which boosted the Jewish population threefold (to fifteen thousand).[37] The Damascus affair certainly thrust modern Jewish politics into the international arena, but in the United States it also provided a powerful cohesive force that had been missing up to that time. "We have *associated* ourselves, our feelings, and our sympathies, and have, all of us, spoken with one voice," claimed an incredulous young attorney, Henry M. Phillips, following the Philadelphia meeting.[38] In New York, Mordecai Noah also asserted the theme of unity: "The cause of one is the cause of all—the sufferings of one portion cannot be unfelt by the rest . . . and if the time has not arrived when the strong arm of Israel can once more be uplifted in the defense of the nation and its rights, we can yet raise our voice against the injustice of oppression."[39]

Such rare expressions of diaspora unity and collective demands for justice would surely have delighted Moses Levy. His initial inspiration for a Jewish rights movement, one that evolved from his participation in abolitionism, had in fact been vindicated. Levy knew full well that the culture of social reform and the influence of public opinion transcended national boundaries and that Anglo-American networks would be instrumental to future success.[40] The goals of the "extraordinary movement" had indeed crossed the Atlantic *and* under the initial impetus of Great Britain. But the leadership had long since passed to others. As it happened, Levy now resided in modest circumstances in St. Augustine, Florida, suffering through the economic downturn caused by the Second Seminole War.[41] Given the absence of any personal correspondence from this period, Levy's thoughts concerning the burgeoning Jewish rights movement in America can only be conjectured. In any case, there was no question that increasing numbers of Jews had committed themselves to a novel means of public expression, the same brand of identity politics that Levy forged years earlier.

The first protest meeting in the United States, sponsored by the Israelites of the State of Virginia, was held at the Hebrew Sunday School in Richmond on 16 August and chaired by the prominent attorney and city council member, Gustavus A. Myers.[42] In addition to a series of condemnatory resolutions, a special note of gratitude was given for the "laudable and liberal efforts made by our Christian brethren" in London—news of the Mansion House proceedings had in fact only recently arrived on the scene. A committee of correspondence was formed in order to unite with any likeminded organizations in the United States and elsewhere to pursue the cause of "general emancipation." Three days earlier in New York, however, the elders of Shearith Israel synagogue, America's preeminent Sephardic congregation, declined to permit "the use of the synagogue for a public meeting of Israelites," deeming that "no benefit can arise from such a course."[43] This negative decision resulted in a delay of the New York meeting and attests to the fact that more traditionalist Jews were still disinclined to enter the political public sphere. The elders continued to interpret such activism as a risk to the communal welfare. Stigmatization and powerlessness, at least within this time-worn perspective, was best negated by avoiding the public sphere.[44]

On 19 August, however, the Ashkenazi Congregation B'nai Jeshurun, following Richmond's lead, broke away from the quietist mold to take on the cause of Jewish rights in New York City. A large protest meeting was held in which Mordecai Noah figured prominently (a move that actually resulted in Noah's removal from the board of Shearith Israel). Afterward, a formal letter, signed by the meeting's officers, Israel B. Kursheedt and Theodore Seixas, was delivered to President Martin Van Buren—a New York Democrat—urging every possible effort to alleviate the suffering of Damascus Jews. This exchange, much more than the actual public addresses by Noah and others, would mark the New York meeting as being especially influential. A reply by Van Buren's secretary of state, John Forsyth, included a letter to the U.S. consul in Alexandria which affirmed that "the President *fully participates in the public feeling*" and instructed the consul to employ every reasonable effort to ensure "that justice and humanity may be extended to these persecuted people."[45] The date of the letter preceded the Richmond meeting by two days, and so this statement referred to the movement that had arisen as a whole. In so doing, Van Buren disregarded customary diplomatic reticence and permitted his secretary of state to identify him as an advocate of a burgeoning pro-Jewish movement—a position unmatched by any other Western head of government. Forsyth then made a conspicuous effort to publicize the administration's stance within the American Jewish community and the public at large. After the success of B'nai Jeshurun's letter, the Richmond and Philadelphia activists repeated the same strategy, and each received a similar response from Forsyth. This engagement by the administration was even more remarkable given the fact that the Damascus affair did not involve American citizens or directly impinge on U.S. commercial interests. Yet, other issues may have been at stake. Armed border clashes with Canada, for example, had escalated during Van Buren's tenure; siding with Britain in this high-minded cause in the Middle East may have been a means to ease tensions between the two nations. Electioneering may also have come into play. Van Buren was in the midst of a bitter reelection campaign against his Whig opponent (and ultimate victor), William Henry Harrison. Even the relatively small bloc of Jewish voters would have certainly been welcome. The president, on the other hand, curried no favor with Mordecai Noah, a conservative Whig and long-time New York political adversary who, according to biographer Jonathan Sarna, "hated Van Buren with a passion."[46] Whatever might have contributed to his stance, Van Buren obviously considered Jewish interests as part of his "universe of obligation"; that is, a body "toward whom obligations are owed, to whom the rules apply, and whose injuries call for expiation by the community."[47] The Van Buren administration's formal espousal of universal Jewish rights was unprecedented. Indeed, the particulars of the New York meeting as well as the official government correspondence were widely disseminated in the national press and eventually published abroad, including the London *Times*, the *Morning Chronicle*, and the *Journal des Débats*, adding still more legitimacy and weight to an already exceptional international response.[48]

On 27 August, Philadelphia's Congregation Mikveh Israel held another mass meeting on behalf of the Damascene Jews. Ironically, Rev. Isaac Leeser (1806–1868), a German Jewish émigré and the synagogue's *hazzan*, first moved into national prominence through a series of articulate newspaper articles that he authored in response to an essay by Joseph Wolff in the London *Quarterly Review* in 1828. Wolff's anti-Jewish polemic, written in the manner of a self-acknowledged "expert," may have been ignored by the majority of Jews in the United States, but Leeser felt especially obligated to issue a substantial reply.[49] By 1840 Leeser—an Orthodox Jew who remained unencumbered by any quietist tradition—was one of the country's leading communal figures. As keynote speaker, Leeser applied the same clear logic in the defense of Judaism and the Jewish people that he pursued earlier. But on this occasion, his rhetorical focus was solidly fixed on the emotional bonds of Jewish solidarity. Leeser was certainly no firebrand, but he still exhibited a persuasive ardor of conviction. While he admitted that, "as citizens, we belong to the country we live in," there was nevertheless a transcendent identity that marked all Jews as members of a distinct nation. His emphasis on Jewish "patriotism" was in fact a fairly radical stance for the time, especially in the context of a public forum where every word would be scrutinized by the media.

> Around me are those who assembled for no other purpose than to express in language not to be misunderstood, that they feel for their brothers who languish under the cruel bondage of oppression; that every cry of anguish uttered by their fellow believers elsewhere, touches a sympathetic chord in their own hearts. O, this is a soothing reflection! We have no country of our own; we have no longer a united government, under the shadow of which we can live securely; but we have a tie yet holier than a fatherland, a patriotism stronger than the community of one Government; our tie is a sincere brotherly love, our patriotism is the affection which unites the Israelites of one land to that of another. . . . [There] are no aliens among us, and we hail the Israelite as a brother, no matter if his home be the torrid zone, or where the poles encircle the earth with the impenetrable fetters of icy coldness.[50]

The Philadelphia meeting carried significant weight, especially given the fact that the city's major newspapers devoted an unprecedented level of coverage to the event. Much attention was given to the fact that local Christian ministers also participated in the cause and did so within the environs of the synagogue itself.

The next day in Charleston, the tenth largest city in the United States and a major cotton exporter to the textile mills of England, held the first of two public meetings. Charleston was the only city to strictly adhere to the London model; both a Jewish and a "city" meeting were held.[51] Charleston and London, as one Jewish observer noted, had become symbolically linked as "twin sisters in the great cause of suffering humanity."[52] Mayor Henry L. Pinckney insisted that the meeting was not called on behalf of purely religious grounds. The fact that the persecuted happened to be Jews was not in itself of primary concern. Rather "we come here," he explained, "as men, as patriots and philanthropists, as the free citizens of a free Republic, to express our united and unqualified abhorrence of religious persecution, by whomsoever it may be practiced, or upon whomsoever its dreadful tortures may be inflicted." Their present assembly was but one in a line of similar rallies held at the city hall: on behalf of Catholic emancipation in Britain, the November Uprising in Poland (1830–1831), and in concert with the Greek cause of independence. [Leeser also made similar allusions to the Greeks in his Philadelphia address.] Charleston interpreted its present role in light of its distinct cultural heritage and as a defender of liberty throughout the world.[53]

Other speakers begged to differ in one important matter. Rev. B. M. Palmer, a Presbyterian minister, asserted that the Damascus controversy was unlike any others that were held in the city. Rather, the events that gave rise to the day's assembly "form an obvious and important link in the chain of Providence." Persecuted Jews were "the seed of Abraham," and thus their oppression needed to be seen within a sacred framework. The minister also equated the "foul and bloody transactions" in the Middle East as a virtual act of war: "war with the spirit of the age—with the feelings of common humanity—with every tenet of religion." But guilt did not rest solely on the torturers overseas. "We have been in error on this subject," he insisted, "even in our liberal, enlightened, and highly favored land." If the "sword of persecution" was not literally wielded against the Jews, they had nevertheless partaken in hurtful social oppression.

> We have, in various ways, thought and felt and acted towards them, as though we scarcely regarded them as belonging to the same race as ourselves. True, this feeling, in some aspects and respects, has been mutual; existing on their part as well as on our own: prejudices from education, from habit, from a variety of causes, have created and continued a great social or rather anti-social gulph between us and them, wide and deep. It is time a bridge was thrown across it, opening the way to wider and more frequent and more profitable intercourse.[54]

Palmer was followed at the podium by the politician James S. Rhett, who referred to "a great moral movement now in progress throughout

Christendom" and affirmed that their meeting was "no common assembly." "The hand of the God of the Hebrews is visible in what we do, and it is his omnipotent voice which speaks to the hearts of the nations in behalf of his afflicted people." Stigmatization had not only been resisted, but in relying upon a Judeo-Christian perspective, the effects of the blood libel had been markedly weakened. Indeed, as Rev. William Brantly, president of the College of Charleston, dramatically asserted, "If in times past, I have been but too indifferent to the high destinies of this people, events such as that which has brought us together, are most effectual in producing a change in my feelings; under their influence I became a converted man, converted to better sympathies, better affections in every respect."

The following day, according to the *Charleston Courier*, the largest group of "Israelites" in the city's history met at the Hall of the Hebrew Orphan Society.[55] This unprecedented protest meeting was sponsored by Charleston's Reformed Society of Israelites—a liberal, splinter group who founded the first Reform congregation in the United States in 1825. Jacob C. Levy, an eminent merchant, chaired the proceedings. Many in the audience had also been in attendance at city hall; clearly, the words that were spoken on behalf of the Jews made an indelible impression among those who gathered at the hall. While this impressive sympathy movement had spread throughout the West, Levy observed, the potential for further oppression still loomed large. Beyond the horizon, in "semi-barbarous" countries, Jews were "treading on a spent, but smoking volcano, that might again rage with the fury of the middle ages—and at best it was a cold truce—unlike the warm alliance that progressively appeared to exist in countries enjoying free and popular governments." Nevertheless, the moral force of Europe and America would give "security of life, at least, to suffering and calumniated Israel," and most were in agreement that such horrors should be stopped. But the violence that Jews faced in such countries, he warned, could just as easily prove fatal to Christians in the future.[56] [Levy's observations would prove prophetic, as thousands of Damascene Christians were massacred by the Druze population twenty years later. The Catholic quarter was burned to the ground in the process.[57]]

The meetings in the United States continued to run their course and included Cincinnati as well as another "city meeting" in Savannah. Noting the movement's success in the United States, similar engagements took place in the Caribbean colonies during the following month. News of the eventual resolution of the Damascus crisis, however, resulted in a period of abeyance on both sides of the Atlantic. Given the regional diversity and fragmentation of Jewish communal life in America, the expression of an ancient diaspora unity or *Kelal Yisrael* that surfaced in the aftermath of the blood libel accusations was striking. As Leeser observed, "It awakened anew the spirit of brotherly love among us." In fact, some American Jewish historians have regarded the U.S. reaction to the Damascus affair as a crucial turning point—one that transformed the bond of world Jewry into one that also strengthened a distinctly American Jewry. Jacob R. Marcus went so far as to claim that Jews now thought of themselves "as a national American Jewish body."[58] This premise, however, seems premature. There is no doubt that the entry of Jews into the public political sphere, just as in England, was a seminal event that bolstered Jewish unity, greatly enhanced local Jewish-gentile relations, and improved the perception of Jews in the media. U.S. newspapers, in contrast with those in Britain and on the Continent, did not become active purveyors of the ritual murder accusations and were overwhelmingly supportive of the Jewish protest meetings. Even the president awarded his administration's imprimatur. Yet no single charismatic leader came to the fore. Indeed, there was no true national newspaper of record that could have significantly advanced the cause of Jewish rights. What is more, American Jews lacked the kind of organizational expertise that could have exploited the series of protests to maximum effect. And extensive interfaith coalitions and political networks were nonexistent. Many evangelicals still acted as aggressive proselytizers in the United States, a stance that created much animosity. And finally, American Jewry was not ready to concede local autonomy. Ten months following the Philadelphia meeting, for example, Leeser attempted to found a "union" of United States Jewry, which bore a certain similarity to the French Consistory system. But such a structured, authoritative approach would prove antithetical to the non-hierarchical sensibilities of Americans, and Leeser failed to bring his ambitious project to fruition. Moreover, some historians have expressed surprise as well as disappointment in the fact that American Jews did not respond to the Damascus crisis straight away.[59] But social movement mobilizations possess their own internal time frame and depend on complex variables that may not be easily discernible. Unlike in England, for instance, Jews in the United States did not possess any prior experience with public meetings or activism in general. This by itself was a difficult hurdle, especially given the dearth of national leadership or individual champions who could rise to the occasion (as Moses Levy did previously) and rally support. Nevertheless, a very significant Jewish response did emerge and, with the participation of a small cadre of influential Christians, established the foundation for future mobilizations.

MONTEFIORE AND CRÉMIEUX

Toward the end of August, negotiations with Mehmed Ali remained stalled as the Egyptian viceroy continued to withhold any concessions; he simply reiterated that the Jewish prisoners in Damascus were being treated "humanely." Complicating the proceedings was the news, just recently received, that the four European powers had arranged to force Egypt out of the Levant if Mehmed Ali did not withdraw on his own. Another factor that impeded progress was the fact that the Jewish delegation was restrained from following local custom and declined to offer anything of value that may have been construed as a bribe by the world press. Confronted with an exceedingly grim atmosphere at court, the mission withdrew its demand for the issuance of a *firman*—a formal decree that would have unequivocally renounced the blood libel allegation—in favor of the straightforward release of the surviving prisoners. Mehmed Ali unexpectedly granted this last request, apparently as a conciliatory gesture toward the threatening European alliance and as an effort to cast himself in a positive light. According to Jonathan Frankel, the pressure that Montefiore and Crémieux brought to bear against Mehmed Ali—a feat that these two Jewish notables accomplished despite the fact that their personal relationship had degraded into deep acrimony—functioned as the proverbial straw that broke the camel's back and resulted in a positive outcome.[60] Any attempt to view this situation within a purely diplomatic framework, however, is short-sighted. Of course, neither Montefiore nor Crémieux were actual diplomats, despite their courtly appearance and pretentions; nor were they recognized as such by Mehmed Ali. In essence, they were functioning as unorthodox political actors whose presence in Alexandria was far outside the mainstream. They were in fact social movement leaders and, as seen within current sociological understanding, transnational human rights activists. Their real constituency was nothing other than world Jewry. As it happened, Mehmed Ali's two attending physicians, both Europeans, came closest to acknowledging this distinction when, just prior to the viceroy's unexpected decision, they advanced the view that a favorable verdict would raise "the voice of six million Jews" in Mehmed Ali's favor.[61] The insurgent Jewish rights movement, in other words, endowed the mission with bargaining power perhaps far greater than either Montefiore or Crémieux realized. Because a militant Britain, Russia, Austria, and Prussia found it advantageous to align themselves with this escalating movement (the press had also become far more skeptical regarding the ritual murder allegation), Mehmed Ali's decision was made that much easier.

On 6 September, amid great cheers emanating throughout the Jewish quarter in Damascus, the nine remaining Jewish prisoners were liberated. This development proved embarrassing for the French and caught them off guard (Mehmed Ali failed to consult with his allies). The political clout that the Jewish rights movement attained in late summer 1840 actually reached a pinnacle of influence that would remain unequaled throughout the nineteenth century. This achievement, however, also provoked negative reactions from anti-Jewish factions; the French Catholic press, for example, became incensed. The *Univers*, in addition to its customary Judeophobic perspective, now claimed that the movement's ability to extract concessions in Egypt proved that "Judaism has reappeared as a power, as a nationality . . . and, as such, it has held all of Christianity in check."[62] At the same time, the fact that the viceroy failed to address the essential guilt or innocence of the Jews was also used to negate any achievements. Once more the theme of ritual murder was treated as a serious issue in France and in the conservative

British press as well—despite the fact that the prospects of an Anglo-French war increasingly dominated the headlines. Moreover, the Christian prelates in Syria began to reassert themselves and bitterly complained of suffering "vexations" by the Jews. No longer properly subservient, Jews from the surrounding areas gathered in Damascus—according to these clerics, at any rate—supposedly insulting and ill treating Christians and defaming their religion.[63] "We trust, after this," exclaimed the notoriously antisemitic *Age* (London), "we shall hear no more of the *persecution* of the *Jews* of Damascus."[64] The release of the Damascene prisoners may well have been "a day of joy for noble souls," to quote the Austrian consul,[65] but it also increased antipathy among those who no longer felt they held the upper hand.

After Mehmed Ali's decision to liberate the Jewish prisoners, Crémieux uncharacteristically diverted himself, at least temporarily, from the more pressing goals of the movement by focusing the remainder of his time in Egypt attempting to establish Jewish schools in Alexandria and Cairo, institutions that would follow a modern European standard. This was surely a worthy cause, but it also served to extricate the distinguished attorney from Montefiore, as the latter continued to infuriate Crémieux by his "arrogance" and "English vanity."[66] Montefiore, on the other hand, clung to his conviction that an official denunciation of the ritual murder charge, specifically in the form of a *firman*, remained a sine qua non. Hence the British contingent parted ways with Crémieux and headed toward Constantinople, where they had good reason to anticipate that Sultan Abdul-Mejid would favor their request for an official writ. Indeed, after Montefiore reached Constantinople on 5 October, he immediately found himself in good stead with Reshid Pasha, the minister of foreign affairs. [The sultanate's continued existence, it should be noted, was primarily due to the backing of the four powers.] In short order, Abdul-Mejid issued the *firman* that Montefiore so determinedly sought. This declaration not only regarded the blood libel as "nothing but pure calumny" but also granted that "the Jewish nation shall possess the same privileges" as all others in the empire and "shall be protected and defended."[67] This was a historic outcome not only in regard to the blood libel, but it ensured equal rights for the 300,000 Jews residing within the Ottoman Empire.

While Montefiore was negotiating in Constantinople, Crémieux and his entourage began a two-month journey home, stopping whenever they encountered a Jewish community to receive high accolades, gifts, and joyful recognition of the release of the Damascene Jews.[68] Once in Europe, perceptions of a triumphant return only escalated. A fleet of carriages met the French delegation as they disembarked at the port of Trieste; Crémieux now returned to France in a manner reminiscent of a victorious military hero. He met privately with distinguished leaders, including Prince Metternich, and delivered impassioned speeches, drawing great crowds along the way. Venice, Vienna, Frankfurt—Crémieux did not miss an opportunity to stage an event and gain maximum press recognition. Such a massive and

Mansion House and Beyond 87

Figure 4.1 Drawing of the imposing "Testimonial Monument in Silver" that was given to Montefiore by the Board of Deputies after his return to London.
Source: Illustrated London News, 27 February 1843.

spontaneous celebration on the part of European Jews was unprecedented; it became another novel means by which the struggle for Jewish rights would make significant strides in the public sphere.

In contrast, Montefiore's journey to England was mostly by sea and therefore lacked similar opportunities. Even so, his arrival in London in late February 1841 was not without fanfare. On 8 March, fitting receptions were given at the major synagogues, and sometime afterward, "a testimonial monument in silver,"[69] an elaborate commemorative centerpiece, three and a half feet in height and containing four panels that contrasted Montefiore's expedition with major biblical events, was awarded to the returning Anglo-Jewish champion. The need for such a memorial, of course, transcended traditional notions of gift giving, for it was primarily intended to influence public opinion. The artwork, commissioned by the Board of Deputies, not only demonstrated Montefiore's heroic stature, but it conveyed certain key achievements that needed to be reaffirmed in an elite cultural medium: the attainment of justice from foreign rulers, the entry of Jews as international players on the political stage, and the ultimate triumph of a distinctly Jewish humanitarianism. Atop the centerpiece was a neoclassical figure of David rescuing a lamb from a lion's jaws, and at each corner of the base were sphinxes which symbolized Jewish captivity in Egypt. The centerpiece's massive size belied any notion of Jewish quiescence or shame; its subtle execution—it was designed by George Hayter, the queen's portraitist—demanded attention and claimed cultural authority. The Jewish leadership had thus become adept at utilizing all manner of media to advance the dominant role of Anglo-Jewry in the campaign for Jewish rights.

On the appointed "Day of Thanksgiving," Rev. De Sola, rabbi of London's Spanish and Portuguese Jews' Synagogue, stressed that Montefiore's exultant homecoming and hero's welcome should be viewed in terms of his mission of peace—"he went to restore, not to take away liberty, and the only tears he had caused to be shed were those of joy."[70] As Montefiore and his wife Lady Judith departed the Sephardic synagogue after the service, a foreign correspondent was struck by the "earth-shattering" roar of the crowds as their carriage wound through the streets of London surrounded by an impromptu throng of several hundred ragged Jewish poor, as if Sir Moses was "a victor accompanied by chained prisoners."[71] The very word *Damascus* had become "the watchword of a new struggle for freedom," as another observer claimed; one that now linked foreign communal struggles directly to England.[72]

Part III
The Mortara Affair

5 "A Mighty Outcry Resounds"

One of the notable advances that followed the 1840 mobilization was the rapid proliferation of a Jewish press, a development that proved to be of central import in modern Jewish history.[1] This innovation reinforced bonds of solidarity and delineated mutual concerns within a purely Jewish perspective. In effect, the communal press functioned as an abeyance structure that assured movement continuity as participants withdrew from overt methods of protest.[2] By one count, fifty-three Jewish periodicals of varying formats and frequency were published during a six-year period that roughly coincided with the Damascus affair, including the influential *Archives Israelites de France* (1840), Isaac Leeser's *Occident and American Jewish Advocate* (1843), and England's *Jewish Chronicle* (1841).[3] The Damascus affair, notes historian David Cesarani, supplied the "immediate conditions which made it conceivable to launch a Jewish journal in England."[4] Indeed, the *Chronicle*, founded by Isaac Vallentine (one of the original 1827 activists), was designed as an "organ of self-defense" as well as a source of general information. The editorial biases and distortions of mainstream periodicals would, of course, continue, but now there would be an exclusively Jewish alternative that would serve a cohesive function and also provide a communal perspective to the "outside" press. To be sure, some European Jewish periodicals retained a traditionalist orientation and restricted content to religious matters only. Others, however, were under the direction of lay editors who opened their pages to a diverse range of secular topics and thereby served a political function that was quite unique in Jewish history. Individual articles or letters published in a foreign journal would frequently be translated and republished in another country; this facilitated a welcome sense of intercommunal communication. The *Jewish Chronicle* was certainly a leader in this type of clearinghouse role; indeed, the *Chronicle* of the nineteenth century has been described as "the leading Jewish newspaper in the world."[5] In 1858 the paper became a major force in the Jewish rights movement. The *Chronicle*'s editor/proprietor, Abraham Benisch (1811–1878)—a Bohemian-born Hebraist and journalist (and an early Jewish nationalist dating from his student days in Vienna)—initially took the lead in publicizing the Mortara incident and supplemented the public role of Moses Montefiore and the

92 *The Rise of Modern Jewish Politics*

Board of Deputies.[6] Various letters to the editor also allowed nonelite Jews to make a substantial impact on communal affairs.

The Mortara affair may at first seem to pale beside the deadly import and labyrinthine complexity of the Damascus blood libel, as the former involved a single Italian Jewish family and lacked widespread attempts at stigmatization. Upon closer examination, however, one can detect distinct parallels between these two major episodes. The theme of Jewish rights, for example, was once again placed on a philosophical fault line between two opposing forces: a nonmodern, hierarchical worldview upheld by an autocratic leader versus contemporary human rights values and an ascendant liberalism. During the summer and fall of 1858, much of the Western press began

Figure 5.1 The Papal States (center), Italian peninsula, and surrounding territories. Source: *Efter Stielers Hand-Atlas* (Stockholm, 1852).

to denounce the reactionary policies of Pope Pius IX, a pontiff who not only rejected such principles as religious toleration and the separation of church and state but opposed, by his own admission, "modern civilization" itself.[7] Pius was unable to deviate from the traditionalist norm and was bound to an unquestioned orthodoxy. But the pope's course of action during this period proved anathema to Napoleon III of France, whose soldiers, in addition to Austrian forces, assured the very existence of the Papal States. As we shall see, the Mortara affair undermined the spiritual and temporal authority of the papacy and became a crucial element in swaying public opinion in favor of Italian unification (*il Risorgimento*); it also amplified tensions between a tolerant and independent Piedmont (and its ally, Napoleon III) and Austrian-controlled Lombardy—a situation that ultimately led to the Second War of Italian Independence (1859). In retrospect, as the *Jewish Chronicle* justifiably claimed, "the most powerful auxiliary of the Italian movement . . . was the child Mortara."[8]

THEATER OF TEARS

In 1858 an incident involving a young Jewish boy in Bologna, the second largest city in the Papal States, and the Catholic Inquisition would grow into a media event of remarkable proportions. Details of this episode possessed a melodramatic flair and a heightened theatricality that was closely associated with popular novels that centered on social reform—a fact that definitely added to the media interest. Indeed, all the dramatis personae in this affair could easily have been lifted, with few alterations, from the pages of either Charles Dickens or Harriet Beecher Stowe. This point was used to disparage the movement by Catholic opponents, one of whom actually referred to the kidnapped boy as the "European Uncle Tom"—a mere fictive device "invented" by the pope's enemies.[9] Details of the affair, while subject to hyperbole, were in fact in general accordance with what actually transpired.

On 23 June, after church officials learned that a secret baptism had been performed at the home of Momolo and Marianna Mortara by the family's former domestic servant, Anna Morisi, the Bolognese Inquisitor ordered six-year-old Edgardo Mortara to be removed from his parental home. Several years earlier, Morisi, then only fourteen, believed an illness had placed the boy's life in jeopardy and so she allegedly performed a lay baptism (which she then kept hidden from the family). After news of this incident reached the local clergy and eventually the Holy Office in Rome, the disposition of the Mortara case was essentially a fait accompli. Following the law of the Papal States, Edgardo was declared a Christian; as such, he was required to be separated from his Jewish parents and educated in the Church. Secular newspapers in continental Europe, Britain, and the United States considered the boy's abduction from his home a gross violation of natural law and a shameful abuse of power. The London *Times* now found itself on the side of the Jews and considered the men who ordered the boy's removal not only guilty of "childstealing" but further declared that "the hand of every father, whatever his persuasion, should be raised against them."[10] A torrent of articles emphasized Edgardo's startling late-night seizure by the dreaded papal *carabinieri*—a veritable "theater of tears and affliction," as the papal official who witnessed the scene described it.[11] The same basic tale, although subject to minor distortions, was retold literally hundreds of times in the press. Ironically, as historian Bertram W. Korn once observed, "More interest was aroused over the little boy's fate than had been displayed in the lot of hundreds of thousands of suffering Jews in previous generations."[12]

On the infamous night in question, the police demanded that all eight of the Mortara children were to be roused from their beds. After Edgardo was identified, his parents were informed of the earlier baptism—at which point Marianna started shrieking, alerting the entire neighborhood to her torment. She held on to her boy and declared that they would have to kill her before she would let him go. Edgardo's brothers and sisters began to cry and tug at the *carabinieri*, begging them to leave their brother alone. But such pleas had no effect. The terrified child was "snatched up by the arms of the police" and placed in a waiting carriage that was surrounded by mounted troops. A large crowd gathered outside and cursed the "monstrous deed."[13] Momolo, apparently overtaken by shock and exhaustion, passed out completely after seeing his boy taken away.[14] Edgardo was transported directly to the House of Catechumens in Rome—a type of monastery, long held in infamy by Italian Jews, where converts (willing or otherwise) were kept in isolation from their families and friends and instructed in the tenets of Catholicism. "All the way from Bologna to Rome," claimed the *Corriere Mercantile* (Genoa), young Edgardo "did nothing but cry and beg them to take him back to his papa and mamma." During the journey an officer attempted to place prayer beads and a crucifix around the child's neck, "but the boy opposed it with all his little strength, refused to kiss it, and begged to give him instead a *muzuza*."[15] After word of the boy's abduction spread, a local correspondent observed that "all Bologna was horror-struck, even the supporters of the Papal Government and religion exclaimed against an act that violated the most sacred ties."[16]

The impassioned reaction of the Mortara family helped transform this account of forced conversion and sanctioned kidnapping, an event that still occurred with some frequency in the Papal States, into a genuine cause célèbre. The receptiveness of the press was integral to this notoriety; "childstealing" and other forms of blatant injustice suited the style of sensational journalism that was at its peak during the latter half of the nineteenth century, as newspapers continued to expand into a truly mass media.[17] Righteous passion, much more than reasoned argument, was what most appealed to the Victorian public. [This sentiment was reflected in Lord Shaftesbury's famous dictum, "Satan reigns in the intellect; God in the heart of man."[18]] Momolo and Marianna Mortara, together with their children, externalized their tragedy into an actual *teatro di pianto* (theater of tears). Not only did the family's emotionality lessen the barrier of Jewish otherness, but it also appeared more stereotypically Italian, and so this heartrending scene was filtered through a familiar European lens as well. The actions of this innocent Bolognese family, while spontaneous and genuine, was transfigured through the press into a form of passionate politics. Inquisitional intolerance resurfaced as if from another age; it had dared to assault cherished notions of hearth and home—sentiments that were revered within Victorian culture.[19] The middle-class home was not only envisioned as sacred and inviolate but was positioned as a bastion of respectability, a private fortress where deviance and crime were held at bay. The home, proclaimed the influential advocate of Victorian values, John Ruskin, was a "place of peace; the shelter, not only from all injury, but from all terror, doubt and division."[20] This institution served as an important counterbalance to the escalating pressures of social change, industrial capitalism, and the rigid dictates of evangelical culture.[21] As a result of the media frenzy surrounding the transgressions of the pope and his gendarmes, however, established rules were turned upside down—an unsettling scenario that was perceived as a serious threat by the public at large.

Unlike the counternarrative of the Damascus affair, which attempted to assign guilt to the Jewish victims themselves, the oppression suffered by the Mortaras remained clear and relatively unambiguous. During the previous mobilization of 1840, activists constructed individual narratives to inspire direct action; brief story lines that departed from the literal events in Damascus, whether it was Van Oven's voracious "monster" of bigotry, O'Connell's shackled London "millionaires," or Leeser's unity of all "Israelites."[22] In contrast, the movement that emerged during the Mortara kidnapping focused on a single straightforward account of unquestioned veracity; a story of arrogance and abuse. Antisemitism was shed of the dehumanizing cliché of the diabolical, money-obsessed Jew, and in its place appeared a credible account of a loving family that was torn asunder by an institution that not only objectified Jews and negated their humanity in the process but masked its intentions behind a morally suspect legal system. In effect, the parental rights and privacy of Jews were given no more credence than slave families in the American South. The incident became endowed with such moral standing that many European lay Catholics began to condemn the Church's treatment of the Mortara boy. The *Journal des Débats*, for example, surfaced as one of the leading critical voices during this period and repeatedly insisted that "canon law cannot impose rules that are in contradiction to natural law—that is to say, the law of God."[23] An editorialist in *La Presse* reaffirmed this stance: "Much as we pity and feel for the parents of this unfortunate little victim of Papal greed and despotism, the interests of the family are absorbed in the greater question of the interests of mankind."[24] The suffering of the Mortaras became linked with humanity writ large, and religious differences were subordinated. The only corrective to this threat, it seemed for many, was to join in protest.

In response to such claims, Pope Pius struck a self-consciously defiant pose and insisted that any disapproval by the "infidel" press only strengthened his resolve. His goal was to preserve the "immovable and indestructible principles of eternal justice."[25] The decision of the Inquisition (which Pius headed) was not only legitimate but an immutable duty, given the character and obligations of baptism. And, in a highly controversial move, the pope actually pronounced Edgardo as his own son. Inside Vatican circles, however, there was at least recognition that "the enemies of the [Catholic] Religion" had found fertile ground.[26] Defensive articles published in Church periodicals, however, tended to inflame the crisis. Most were reprinted as excerpts in the popular press and functioned like installments in a serialized novel, further piquing public interest. Columns in *L'Univers* (Paris) and *L'Armonia* (Turin) and other papers initially attested to Edgardo's sudden spiritual transformation, his attainment of "grace," and his calm, beatific desire to embrace the Church. After the secular press scoffed at this scenario as a convenient fabrication, a variety of arguments were utilized to dampen dissent. *Il Cattolico* (Genoa), for example, claimed that the pope had done the boy a good deed because he now benefited from educational and material benefits denied to Jews—a people, the paper insisted, who remain "infamous for the ugly stain with which the killers of Christ are marked."[27] Condemnation by the secular press was explained by the fact that a large number of "libertine" newspapers were owned by "Jewish bankers."[28] Edgardo's parents were then blamed for employing a Catholic housemaid, which was in fact a technical violation of the law, though seldom enforced. But any restriction based solely on religion appeared to be another example of the Church's assault on individual freedom. The *Tablet*, an organ of the Catholic Church in England, regarded "the affair Mortara" as a simple "question of the Catechism." This problem did not require "learning for its solution," the paper asserted; only humility and "a little grace to receive it as it ought to be received."

> But, unfortunately, that little grace is wanting to the *furious infidels* who create the disturbance, and darken a question as clear as the sun at noon. The child Mortara has acquired rights that no human power can take away, but by violence, and for the loss of which no government can ever make compensation. The act which made him a Christian is irrevocable, beyond the powers of any tribunal to annul, and by that act he *became as a dead child* to his Hebrew father . . . *as completely as if he died a natural death.*[29]

The curia not only failed to admit any injustice but remained curiously tone-deaf to its own inflammatory rhetoric. The Church's intrinsic anti-Judaism, its emphasis on legality and "catechism" over the Christian doctrine of love, and its constant affirmation of temporal power were all in opposition to mid-nineteenth-century liberalism. What was by then a massive public relations debacle continued to degenerate even more.

Beginning in late October, *L'Univers* resorted to antisemitic slurs in an effort to gain advantage. *L'Univers* was primarily intended for the lower-ranking clergy and the lay public and was under the direction of Louis Veuillot (1813–1883), an ultramontane lay Catholic and journalist.[30] Veuillot was certainly the most strident of the pope's journalistic defenders and initiated many of the arguments that were later used throughout a far-reaching network of Catholic periodicals. Anti-intellectual and combative, the self-educated Veuillot created powerful enemies as well as allies within the hierarchy. In 1853, for example, the archbishop of Paris accused him of "demagoguery" and banned *L'Univers* from the clergy. After rushing off to Rome, Veuillot quickly elicited the support of Pius IX, who then issued an encyclical that reversed the decision of the "Gallican" archbishop and resulted in the reinstatement of the defiant Veuillot. Pius in effect created a parallel power to the traditional French hierarchy—one that looked to the Vatican rather than the bishops for support.[31] By the time of the Mortara affair, *L'Univers* held a unique role in the country, and Veuillot was recognized as the secular head of an ultramontane countermovement that directed its energies at the forces of modernism itself. Veuillot's arguments in *L'Univers* were not only lambasted by the secular press, but a former professor of dogma, Abbé Vincent Delacouture, countered these claims in a series of critical articles in the *Journal des Débats*. The cleric not only mocked Veuillot for his deficiencies in "theological matters" but cited Aquinas, St. Paul, contemporary theologians, a host of papal rulings, and canon law to build a case against the abduction of any child from his natural parents, even in the case of baptism. Quoting from another learned authority, Delacouture asserted that "Baptism does not remove natural rights . . . the laws of the Church cannot prevail over the father's right." These popular articles were then combined and reprinted in pamphlet form.[32] *L'Ami de la Religion*, an influential, moderately liberal Catholic paper that was founded in clerical opposition to *L'Univers*, also disagreed with the actions of the Holy See and emphasized the spiritual rather than the temporal authority of the Church.[33]

Another threat to the Vatican's position surfaced at the same time: newly uncovered information that placed the validity of the baptism and the character of Anna Morisi, the former house servant, into contention. Notarized statements from a variety of reputable individuals, including the Mortara family doctor, attested to the fact that Edgardo's life had never been in mortal danger as an infant. Moreover, local (non-Jewish) citizens not only contested Morisi's baptism story but accused her of theft and noted her long record of sexual promiscuity. In fact, the girl's original dismissal from the Mortara household was due to her out-of-wedlock pregnancy and her scandalous behavior in the home. Such news seriously undermined the Church's story line that imbued the girl's character with saintly overtones. A dossier verifying the charges against Morisi was sent to the Vatican in early October; the contents then found their way to the press several weeks later.[34]

In reaction to these developments, a belligerent Veuillot evaded the central issues and reverted to defamation. *L'Univers* portrayed wealthy Jewish businessmen as an insidious cabal that aimed at world dominion; French Jews were cast as disloyal aliens undeserving of citizenship; and the Talmud was assailed as "monstrous" and irreconcilable with French civilization.[35] Such ideas were hardly new, but given Veuillot's favored position in the Vatican and the Church as a whole, one historian has placed him as "an important link between the incipient racist antisemitism of Voltaire and the full-blown Judeaophobia of [Édouard] Drumont," founder of the Antisemitic League of France (1889) and one of the leading players during the Dreyfus affair.[36] What most disturbed French Jewry at the time, however, was Veuillot's revival of the myth of ritual sacrifice and the supposed use of "the blood of a Christian child" during Passover.[37] This vile superstition was recycled once more from the Church's "antiquated arsenal," to paraphrase a contemporary observer.[38] Veuillot's use of such a grotesque allegation was a rather frantic attempt to reframe the issue and to regain the upper hand by casting all Jews as monstrous, with the intention of severing the Mortara family from a largely sympathetic public. This slander was received with justifiable outrage and united French Jews in furious opposition. Amid a stream of protests, a libel suit was lodged against *L'Univers* by the Central Consistory. Even though the case was permitted to proceed by government officials, Adolphe Crémieux, one of the attorneys in the suit, pleaded with the Consistory to use caution. "The entire press," Crémieux emphasized, had already "revealed the most noble and universal sympathy in favor of the sanctity of the home and the sacred right of paternal authority."[39] Any court proceeding would expose unnecessary risk and accomplish little by denouncing the blood libel. The Consistory reconsidered and ultimately withdrew its legal challenge.

Movement activists had ample cause to assume that public opinion was on their side, and they did not foresee any need to divert from the kidnapping narrative, other than for embellishment. This perception was shared on both sides of the Atlantic. As it happened, however, the most passionate expressions of outrage developed in the United States. "You have heard the shrieks of the mother," as Morris Raphall, now a New York City rabbi, declared before an overflowing Jewish protest rally in December. "You have heard the remonstrance of the father—that boy is mine, you have no claim to him, restore him to me," Raphall continued. "These anguished cries . . . have been re-echoed by tens and hundreds of thousands until the mighty outcry resounds throughout Europe, crosses the oceans, and everywhere arouses the sympathy of parents, the just indignation of men."[40]

THE MOVEMENT RESURFACES

In England the Mortara controversy coincided with the belated admission of Lionel de Rothschild, a duly elected Member of Parliament from the City of

London since 1847, to the Commons on 26 July 1858. This achievement was the culmination of an interfaith alliance forged between the Jewish elite—with their power base in the City of London—and Christian supporters who continued to press for the removal of Jewish political disabilities for three decades. "Honor and truth in the Baron [Rothschild] had at last had their effect," declared Barnard Van Oven at a large celebratory gathering at the London Tavern. "The point so ardently longed for had been gained, and the truth had triumphed."[41] The timing of this victory undoubtedly influenced the tactical repertoire that the Jewish leadership employed during the reemergence of the Jewish rights movement later that fall. Unlike the high-profile role that Montefiore and the Board of Deputies assumed in 1840, the leadership adopted a less confrontational posture that avoided protest meetings in favor of an insider strategy that consisted of lobbying government and Catholic Church leaders, issuing a call to action to Jewish congregations abroad, and Montefiore's attempt to influence the outcome by a high-profile trip to the Vatican in 1859.[42] Montefiore never explicitly stated his reasons for avoiding public meetings. It is likely, however, that he felt that success in Parliament dictated caution. Now that Jews were, ostensibly at any rate, incorporated into the body politic, some conservative power-holders may have interpreted public protests not only as bad form but as working against the national interest. Indeed, political emancipation was accomplished, rather incongruously, under a Conservative government headed by Lord Derby; a majority of the party had actually voted against the measure. In addition, Lord Malmesbury now led the Foreign Office. It became obvious that Malmesbury had no desire to alter the status quo in the Papal States and only wished to maintain British neutrality in the looming conflict between France and Austria.[43] The Derby ministry was in fact exceedingly cautious when it came to the pope and sought to maintain both his temporal and spiritual authority. Any inflammatory rhetoric that could have been interpreted as aiding Louis Napoleon's military ambitions was rigorously discouraged.[44] Nonetheless, Montefiore now headed a special committee of the Board of Deputies that was determined to elicit a united response with "foreign Jewish bodies" and did not hesitate to call on others to use whatever methods they deemed proper during this mobilization.[45] The Mortara case had "justly raised almost universal condemnation," Montefiore observed in his address to American Jewry dated 25 October. As he saw it, their goal was "the restoration of the child to its afflicted parents, and also the prevention of similar outrages for the future." He also emphasized what he believed to be the best manner of framing the insurgence: "this is a matter affecting not the Jews alone, *but also every other denomination of faith, except the Roman Catholic*; further, that it cannot be regarded exclusively under a religious aspect, but as placing in peril personal liberty, social relations, and the peace of families."[46]

Montefiore's ability to immediately take on the mantle of leadership—almost two decades following the onset of the Damascus affair—requires some clarification. During much of this time, Montefiore remained fairly conspicuous in the press. In 1846 a ukase issued by Tsar Nicholas I, which ordered the expulsion of the half million Jews that resided along the Austrian and Prussian border areas, sparked widespread indignation and concern. After a round of diplomatic initiatives, Montefiore and Lady Judith visited St. Petersburg, Russia, where Sir Moses succeeded in obtaining a personal audience with the tsar. Montefiore's visit, while cordial, did not result in the ukase being rescinded, however (it was subsequently unenforced after local officials objected to the economic consequences of such an exodus).[47] Montefiore and his entourage were then permitted to tour the Jewish communities in the Pale of Settlement and in the Kingdom of Poland, including the cities of Vilna and Warsaw.[48] Montefiore was soon besieged by thousands of his coreligionists, many of whom were destitute and who pleaded for aid, and was also awarded a hero's welcome from communal leaders. Montefiore's mere reception by the tsar was interpreted as a momentous event. While in Vilna, Lithuania's most celebrated rabbis waited upon him and sought his advice. The Jewish press was filled with hagiographic accounts of the "awe-inspiring" honors that were bestowed upon "the renowned defender of the Jewish people" and by Montefiore's inspirational acts of charity and benevolence. According to one correspondent, lectures that were given by Montefiore's learned companion and secretary, Louis Loewe, had a profound effect on the so-called new-fashioned Jews or "Berlinskys," many of whom reportedly abandoned their ways and became staunchly religious. Montefiore's orthodoxy was also hailed, for it was clear that he regularly fasted and "did not take the slightest nourishment until he had said his prayers."[49] Visits by Montefiore and his wife to synagogues, Talmud Torahs, and among the poor usually resulted in tearful scenes and in the giving of large sums to the needy. "His lady," the reporter continued, "had not a dry eye for weeping over the extreme distress she here beheld, as there are many of our poorer brethren who are almost perishing from starvation." Upon leaving Vilna for Warsaw, Montefiore was "escorted by multitudes" who all expected that such a benevolent man was truly God's "instrument to save us from much oppression."[50]

Montefiore's journey, which also included Berlin, Frankfurt, and the Grand Duchy of Posen as well as numerous towns and villages along the way, raised so much excitement among European Jewry that it could easily be compared to Crémieux's victorious return to Paris.[51] In exchange for permission to conduct this tour, Montefiore agreed to promote a certain number of the tsar's priorities, such as the adoption of agriculture and of Western-style clothing, and the instruction of secular subjects, including the Russian language, in the Talmud Torah schools.[52] Montefiore held a reasonable expectation that his cooperative posture might persuade the tsar to act more humanely toward his Jewish subjects. Unfortunately, despite the publicity that attended this mission, the tsar and his ministers did nothing to amend previous *ukazy*, such as the harsh taxation and military conscription decrees—leading some to conclude that their beloved Jewish knight had been deliberately mislead. Nevertheless, after his return to England, and upon the recommendation of Prime Minister Peel, Montefiore was rewarded for his efforts on behalf of Jewish rights with the title of baronet.

Unlike his previous missions, Montefiore's latest expedition did not escape criticism from other Jews. An anonymous writer in the *Allgemeine Zeitung des Judentums*, while much impressed with the cause of Jewish rights, particularly as it manifested itself during the Damascus affair, took Montefiore to task for acting as an independent agent. The previous heightened interest among the Jews of Europe and America "emanated from a concentrated unity of action and promised to achieve great things through the power that lies in every significant association." But now Montefiore was seen as carrying on without "the authority of the collective." Indeed, it was posited, the movement's "Holy flame" had been entirely diminished.[53] Such ideas were a distinct minority, however. As London's *Voice of Jacob* (the *Chronicle*'s one-time competitor) noted: "Public opinion has been with us . . . and as every disposition and energy increases in proportion as it is more frequently brought into exercise, so will this display strengthen and confirm the sympathy already enlisted on our behalf."[54] In other words, while Montefiore may not have ended Russian oppression, he nevertheless tapped into powerful feelings of Jewish solidarity wherever he traveled and further elicited compassionate understanding from the general public. The ramifications of his altruistic mission were therefore substantial. Unstated, however, was Sir Moses's intuitive grasp of the demands of a celebrity, a new type of public figure that first emerged during the nineteenth century. Individual prominence was no longer restricted to the nobility or to those who held high political office; fame could just as easily stem from the notice of the mass media alone and thus demanded constant renewal.[55] Yet Montefiore was not merely famous for being famous but was widely esteemed as a bona fide hero in an age that idolized gallant and selfless virtue. "Great Men," wrote Thomas Carlyle in 1840, serve as "a natural luminary shining by the gift of Heaven; a flowing light-fountain, as I say, of native original insight, of manhood and heroic nobleness; in whose radiance all souls feel that it is well with them."[56] Carlyle's influential treatise reconfigured a belief in heroes and hero worship, an ancient tradition dating to Aristotle, into the nineteenth-century Romantic idiom. Heroism merged perfectly with Victorian conceptions of manliness, since this ideal not only stressed physical rigor but also encompassed chivalric intent, benevolence, moral and political maturity, and independence—a virtuous equilibrium.[57] In this context, Sir Moses's continuance as a public personality, peripatetic risk taker, and international champion of Jewish liberties certainly strengthened his leadership and sustained the movement's cultural presence. Despite the inevitable abeyance of the Jewish rights movement, Montefiore upheld key goals and ensured the very survival of the flame by establishing a global network of supporters who could be relied upon during any future mobilization.

Montefiore's public profile was also reinforced by repeated visits to the Holy Land, where he held an abiding interest in the region's struggling Jewish population. In 1854 a devastating famine in Palestine resulted in the dramatic expansion of an international charity called the Holy Land Relief Fund. Montefiore, in conjunction with Britain's new chief rabbi, Nathan Adler, solicited nearly £20,000 for this fund. This charitable appeal was distinguished by reaching out to both Christians and Jews and by the utilization of both the press and modern fund-raising techniques.[58] Also in the 1850s, Montefiore succeeded in staving off a challenge to his leadership on the Board of Deputies by some of the younger, more reform-minded members of the Cousinhood and by Jews who resided outside of London and who resented Montefiore's often heavy-handed decision-making style. By the time of the Mortara controversy, Montefiore was in firm control, and his reputation as the consummate Jewish philanthropist remained intact.

The initial call for a resurgence of the Jewish rights movement came from the Jewish community in the Kingdom of Sardinia, which included Piedmont and its capital, Turin in northwestern Italy—the liberal center of the pro-unification movement. In August a memorial signed by representatives of the kingdom's principal congregations, twenty-one in total, was delivered to both the French Consistory and the British Board of Deputies and was also widely disseminated by the press. This document is remarkable for its confident manner as well as its blistering criticism of the Church. The Jews of Piedmont-Sardinia had enjoyed full citizenship for a decade, but they were also supported in their efforts during the Mortara affair by the prime minister, Count Camillo di Cavour, who was eager to employ the controversy as a propaganda tool against the Papal States. As the petitioners admitted, "the history of the past unfortunately records many cases similar to that of Mr. Mortara; but times have changed, and the civil and political conditions . . . permit us now at least to express our abhorrence of those deeds of cruelty." While it appeared only natural that they should have been the first to raise their voices against the "iniquitous act" in Bologna, these Jews also conceded that their actions would only cast temporary shame upon "the ignorant and fanatical ministers" who perpetrated the crime. More powerful agencies were required to lead the protest and to employ their influence within their national governments. In the meantime, following the precedent of previous mobilizations, the petition urged Jews to avail themselves "of the universal press to appeal to all mankind against acts which violate the most sacred rights of paternity in its dearest affections."[59]

The Central Consistory responded to this plea by formally requesting that Napoleon III intervene in the case—an especially cogent appeal since France served as the sole protector of the pope in Rome. The Consistory appealed to the emperor's reputation as a defender of the universal rights of man and argued that, although the abduction of the Mortara child involved foreigners, the fact that this scene played out in Rome "under the shadow of our glorious flag and before the eyes of our brave soldiers" strongly implicated France and indeed the emperor himself in this "odious" affair.[60] Unknown to the public, however, Louis Napoleon had already met in secret with Count Cavour at Plombières-les-Baines a month following the incident in Bologna. A treaty had been signed that committed France to join Piedmont-Sardinia in wresting control of a major portion of the Papal States and Lombardy from Austria, an action that would also result in the French annexation of the territories of Savoy and Nice. Armed conflict took place within a year. There is no doubt that the Mortara episode enraged the emperor's liberal disposition and reaffirmed his belief that the existence of the Papal States was a terrible anachronism. At the same time, however, the storm of controversy that resulted from the sanctioned kidnapping of the Mortara boy influenced world opinion in a manner that was favorable to the impending war.[61]

Despite the precarious position of the Papal States, Pius refused to concede to the pressure that was placed upon him by the French ambassador in the fall of 1858. The boy was to remain in Rome and, as the pope concluded, could never be returned to his parents. The futility of any diplomatic initiative was not lost on the British government. Following a meeting with Moses Montefiore on the subject of the Mortara abduction, Lord Malmesbury initially agreed to make the government's preferences known, but only through lower-ranking diplomats in Rome. The Foreign Office withdrew from engaging in even this tepid response, however, after Pius failed to buckle under French demands. "After the failure of Catholic Powers like France to influence the Papal government," the Foreign Office surmised, "it is manifest that the efforts of Her Majesty's government would be powerless to promote the praiseworthy object."[62] Prominent rabbis of Prussia, Holland, and the German states each sent petitions to Rome in the hope that their diplomatic appeals would dissuade Pius from his course of action. But none of these efforts, no matter how elegantly and respectfully phrased, made the slightest difference. "The opinion here is general and decided that nothing will induce the Pope to give up the lamb that has thus been juggled into the Romish fold," wrote the correspondent of the *Times* in Rome. "Pius IX," concluded the *Times*, "would as soon think of abandoning his tiara as of relinquishing the captured Jew."[63]

The most active Protestant organizational player in England during the Mortara affair was the Evangelical Alliance headed by Sir Culling Eardley. A few years earlier, Montefiore had joined Eardley in a business venture in Palestine, where they, along with other partners, had planned a railroad linking the cities of Jerusalem and Jaffa. Eardley, an ardent evangelical and a descendant of the legendary Jewish stockbroker Sir Sampson Gideon, was also quite brazen about his conversionist beliefs, as Montefiore eventually discovered. After Eardley rejoiced at length over the railroad's supposed role in facilitating the conversion of the Jews, Montefiore decided to part ways, and he calmly but very deliberately withdrew his support from the entire enterprise.[64] Upon his return to England, Montefiore had ample reason to politely decline Eardley's invitation to attend a protest meeting sponsored by the Evangelical Alliance in Liverpool—a center of Protestant anti-Catholic agitation—which was organized primarily in response to the Mortara controversy. "In the judgment of the committee of this board," Montefiore wrote, "the movements of the Christian world should be dissociated from those of the Jews; therefore, we trust that our declining to send a deputation to the Evangelical Alliance will be attributed to this cause, and we beg to assure you that we are not the less grateful for the kindness of the Alliance, nor the less mindful of the importance of their benevolent sympathy."[65] The meeting took place without Jewish participation; a sensible choice given that Eardley proceeded to interpret the injustice that was inflicted upon the Mortaras as an offense against "Christendom" and complained that the "inquisitors at Rome" had only succeeded in suppressing potential Jewish converts.[66] Hence, the Jewish rights movement in England remained uncharacteristically devoid of the type of strong political alliances that had proven so effective in the past.

The steady denunciation of the Mortara abduction by the French press was of course taken as a good sign. Yet, as the *Jewish Chronicle*'s Abraham Benisch reminded readers in late November, Napoleon III seemed satisfied with a policy of "gentle remonstrance" rather than forceful coercion. Furthermore, there was no guarantee that the French press would be allowed to continue "unchecked." [In fact, the French government was already in the process of imposing general press censorship regarding the subject of the Mortara kidnapping.] It was time, according to Benisch, for Jewish leaders to reevaluate their position. "It is a Jewish family upon which the outrage was committed; it is therefore the Jews to whom Providence has primarily assigned the task of vindicating humanity. We may rally around our banner as many auxiliaries as we can; the phalanx must be formed by ourselves."[67] Moreover, he declared that any "loud manifestation of feeling or open participation in a general demonstration" would prove impossible in any country that remained under the influence of Catholicism. Thus, the Jewish community in England would continue as "the natural centre of this agitation."[68] While Jews throughout the Anglophone world did indeed look to Montefiore and the Board of Deputies for leadership throughout much of the nineteenth century, Benisch failed to note that circumstances were not conducive for any "loud" demonstration in England either. Just as the Jews in the United States appeared to be on the verge of unleashing a robust response, the *Chronicle* appealed to the Board of Deputies and the lord mayor, David Wire—Montefiore's long-time associate who had accompanied him to the Middle East during the Damascus affair—to hold a protest meeting at Mansion House, similar to the one that was sponsored by the City in 1840.[69] "Fortified by the expression of sympathy resounding from a mighty empire," this meeting, Benisch asserted, would command universal respect. Despite the urging of the *Chronicle*, however, Montefiore avoided the subject. On this occasion, Mansion House meetings never became part of the protest repertoire. In a decision reached with other Board members, Sir Moses opted to travel to Rome instead, where he hoped to promote the cause of the Mortara family during a private audience with Pope Pius. This strategy may have been approved by the British Foreign Office, but when Malmesbury met with Montefiore before his departure in March 1859, the minister was clearly pessimistic about any chance of redeeming the Mortara boy,[70] a point of view that was also shared by the *Chronicle*. In fact, most of the paper's enthusiasm prior to Montefiore's trip had been focused on the unusual developments in the United States. Mass protest rallies condemning the actions of the pope began to surface, and the American Jewish community's first efforts to establish multicongregational alliances inspired great hope for the future. "Surely these results alone," Benisch asserted, "would be important enough in themselves to rescue the movement from the reproach of barrenness should it . . . be productive of no greater benefit."[71]

6   Toward Unity

AMERICAN PROTESTS

As we have seen, the image of the Mortaras as innocent victims aided in transforming the kidnapping of an obscure Italian Jewish boy into a human drama with universal appeal. Family-centered pathos combined with an often virulent anti-Catholic sentiment and allowed the movement narrative to span great distances. Compared to French Jews who had to contend with press censorship as well as communal reticence to engage in public protest meetings and Anglo-Jews who were constrained by governmental concerns over exacerbating the volatile situation throughout the Italian peninsula, Jews in the United States were free to demonstrate as they deemed appropriate. The events of 1840 had already established public protests as part of the communal repertoire. Yet the absence of national leadership was still quite apparent; even more so if one considers the number of Jewish arrivals in America. Immigrants had increased the national Jewish ranks to about 200,000.[1] In parallel with America's rapid rise as a leading industrial power, Jews also surfaced as major players. Even so, factionalism was the single most obvious characteristic of American Jewry: Polish, French, Dutch, Russian, Sephardic, Northern and Southern Germanic, and other cultural and linguistic traditions often divided Jewish newcomers into semi-warring factions. Quarrels between Reform and Orthodox were also rampant. Such choice obloquy as: "Haman, malicious slanderer, ignoramus of the first water, vile and venomous subject, Russian serf, a man vomiting poison and mad dog"[2] were unfortunately all too frequent in intrareligious disputes. Despite endemic infighting, the number of U.S. Jews was now larger than Britain's and roughly equivalent to that of France. But the receptiveness of the U.S. government to the goals of the Jewish rights movement had also shifted. Because of America's continued position as a major slave-holding country (with four million slaves, the United States was the world's leading slave power), national priorities were at odds with evolving international human rights standards. It would thus prove impossible for the Buchanan administration to follow Van Buren's enlightened precedent. Had Washington lodged any form of diplomatic complaint against the Vatican, such "intermeddling," as Secretary of State Lewis Cass put it, would have opened the door for embarrassing reproaches against the United States. The principle of state sovereignty therefore had to be upheld. Unspoken, however, was the fact that Catholics constituted one of the largest voting blocs within James Buchanan's Democratic Party; this detail alone did not augur well for government action.

The principal Jewish journals in the United States were Isaac Leeser's *Occident and American Jewish Advocate* (Philadelphia), Samuel M. Isaacs's *Jewish Messenger* (New York City), and Isaac M. Wise's *Israelite* (Cincinnati). All three were edited by rabbis and so their emphasis was usually more religious than political. As the Mortara affair evolved into an increasingly pressing issue, however, the subject soon dominated the content of these periodicals and inspired impassioned editorials. On 22 October the *Israelite* became the first Jewish paper to call for a united protest in America. "Religious liberty is set at naught by the fanaticism of the Roman Inquisition," declared the *Israelite*'s foreign affairs editor, Max Lilienthal. "Call meetings in your congregations! Address remonstrances and Petitions to our government in Washington. . . . We rise, not only for our cause but for one of the highest principles of our enlightened age, Religious Liberty, and no clerical inquisition!"[3] While this plea followed the broadly publicized proceedings of European Jews, it was exceptional that the *Israelite* took this stance before Moses Montefiore's official call to action. Many outspoken American Jews, it should be said, were highly educated European émigrés—like Lilienthal and Wise—who had been influenced by the failed revolutions of 1848 and were now at liberty to denounce an institution that not only willingly transgressed the basic rights of Jews but had become increasingly linked with repressive, monarchical regimes. In fact, mounting Catholic influence in the United States was often interpreted as a looming threat. The position advocated by Catholic papers, such as the *Freeman's Journal* (New York), the *Pilot* (Boston), *Catholic Mirror* (Baltimore), and the *Catholic Telegraph and Advocate* (Cincinnati) among others, was solidly in line with their European counterparts. This posture only increased feelings of Jewish distrust and humiliation. Isaac M. Wise (1819–1900), a leader of Reform Judaism in the United States, utilized his position with the *Israelite* to denounce the Catholic press with a vigor that would have met the approval of the most intemperate member of the anti-Catholic Know-Nothing Party: "The slaves of Rome, her clergy, editors, Jesuit leaders and agents in this country, have every spark of manhood so dragged out of themselves, have become so insolent and disreputable, are so much opposed to the liberties of free men, that they openly, boldly, avowedly advocate the kidnapping outrage of Bologna, and throw any amount of insult into the face of the Israelites of this country."[4] Leeser and Isaacs also unleashed their own brand of scathing commentary. The *Jewish Messenger* railed against the despicable actions of "the Roman Catholic soul-snatchers," and the *Occident* offered ample insights concerning "the ancient enemy of the Jews."[5] In the absence of a national organizational structure, the outcry of the Jewish press was pivotal in stoking the movement flame. Experience gained during the 1840 mobilization also offered an advantage; certain individuals, like Isaac Leeser, were now well versed in social movement dynamics. While the administration's unwillingness to press for the release of the Mortara boy did not initially impede momentum, the fact that the movement failed to modify Buchanan's rigid stance in any way was ultimately regarded as an embarrassing defeat by Jewish activists. Still, the Mortara mobilization was widespread and was sustained by an influential Jewish press and increased numbers of activists (both Jewish and Christian). An outpouring of highly emotive coverage from the mainstream media—the full impact of which reached "colossal dimensions,"[6] as the *New York Herald* noted—contributed toward this insurgence as well.[7] The press validated Jewish claims of injustice, cast the actions of the Vatican as existing outside acceptable norms, and continued to energize a growing activist segment in both the North and South, all during a period that was fraught with great political uncertainty.

Shortly after receiving Montefiore's written appeal, congregations in St. Louis, Philadelphia, Boston, Chicago, Indianapolis, Baltimore, and Savannah each drafted resolutions; petitioned the president and the secretary of state; posted their actions in the secular newspapers; and reported back to Moses Montefiore to keep him abreast of their activities.[8] On 18 November (Thanksgiving Day) in Philadelphia, Isaac Leeser organized a mass protest meeting representing six congregations (and also included Protestant ministers) which met at Leeser's newly established Beth El Emeth synagogue. A subcommittee was authorized to proceed to Washington, D.C., to urge U.S. officials to aid in the Mortara child's rightful return.[9] The Jews of Richmond and Charleston also conducted public protest meetings in a manner similar to those two decades earlier. On 24 November, Gustavus A. Myers once again chaired the Richmond meeting (this time at Beth Ahabah synagogue),[10] and Charleston Jews met at the city's Masonic Hall on 30 November. The Charleston protest was led by Samuel Hart, Sr., a local publisher and book seller, and the meeting included local rabbis as well as the city's leading Jewish businessmen. The assembly's resolutions, however, stood apart from most of the American Jewish community in that these proclamations bypassed any federal appeal and focused exclusively on public opinion instead. "The force of opinion" was envisioned as a great moral power: "It is the collective sense and feeling to which, in all similar cases, appeal must be made, and which, if it fails to redress present wrongs, may form a safeguard and defense in the future."[11] Historian Bertram W. Korn attributed the absence of any memorial to the federal government as a consequence of southern isolationism. This ethic placed greater value on local institutions and, as Korn stated, saw danger in "suggesting that the American government should remonstrate to another government about the application of its local laws."[12] [The Jews of New Orleans and Mobile also refrained from petitioning the government and kept their activities from the media during later meetings in December]. Of course, any questioning of state sovereignty, no matter where in the world it took place, would have unambiguous consequences in the South. Such sensitivities, however, did not deter Jewish protesters in Richmond or the petitioners in Savannah from setting their sights on Washington. Thus, it appears that some Jewish communities were more attuned to radical regional politics than their counterparts elsewhere in the South.

In New York City, Morris J. Raphall (1798–1868), former minister of the Birmingham synagogue in England and now rabbi of B'nai Jeshurun, planned a massive "Indignation Meeting" for early December. In preparation for this event, Raphall succeeded in organizing twelve of the city's congregations under the heading of the United Congregations of the Israelites of New York City, which in turn elected Raphall as permanent chairman. A pattern was beginning to develop: not only was there a notable increase in activism compared to 1840, but Jews began to band together in multicongregational efforts. When Abraham Benisch learned of these events, he was clearly elated; now that Montefiore's call for action had reached the United States, Benisch predicted that "the movement in America is likely to assume gigantic proportions."[13]

New York City (population 800,000) may have been the nation's leading metropolis and the residence of 40,000 Jews, but Jewish charitable and educational institutions were still limited and synagogues were fiercely independent of one another. "The worst part of it," lamented one contemporary observer, "is that our dignity is compromised and our position lowered in the eyes of the community by the attitude of congregations who complement each other with epithets."[14] The Mortara affair, however, functioned as a catalyst for unification, and the protest rally that was held at Mozart Hall on 4 December became a compelling symbol of Jewish union.[15] "In spite of the extreme inclemency of the weather," wrote the Republican *New York Times*, "the large hall was densely packed with Jews and Christians—the number of the former, of course, largely preponderating." The crowd was estimated at 2,500—a massive turnout by anyone's reckoning and the largest Jewish rights protest thus far in America.[16] Newspaper reports were deferential and often included transcripts of the speeches. To place this kind of reportage into proper context, one should consider the treatment awarded to other social movement gatherings that were held in the city earlier that year. Both the National Woman's Rights Convention, which featured such figures as Ernestine Rose, and the annual meeting of William Lloyd Garrison's American Anti-Slavery Society also took place at Mozart Hall (although attended in fewer numbers). Aside from brief notices, the New York papers generally ignored the Woman's Rights Convention, and though the Anti-Slavery Society gained a little more attention, the reporting lacked seriousness and tended to marginalize attendees.[17] These movements were perceived as pernicious threats by many power-holders in the United States and so coverage by the mainstream media, or the lack thereof, was in keeping with the reformers' liminal status. [In other cities in the North, Garrison was sometimes compelled to flee for his life.] The Jewish rights movement, however, was held on a far different and vastly more favorable plane. The struggle for Jewish civil equality in the Papal States simply did not impinge on the status quo in Protestant America, other than placing the Buchanan administration in an awkward diplomatic position. But the actions of the Inquisition, a sinister Old World archetype, transgressed esteemed virtues of religious freedom and fair play. The ill treatment of the Mortara family elicited sympathy, to be sure, but it also provoked outrage among those Protestants who met in protest with Jews in Philadelphia and New York. The "state of things in the old world," where, among other oddities, state churches still reigned, was perceived as dreadfully out of kilter with the values of enlightened America (the South's peculiar institution notwithstanding). Consequently, according to one New York state politician and newspaper editor, "it became Protestant to join Jew in the defense of religious freedom."[18] The movement also benefited from an upsurge in Protestant animosity toward Catholicism, a state of affairs exacerbated by the influx of millions of predominantly poor and unskilled Catholic immigrants into the major East Coast cities. This massive demographic shift contributed toward a volatile nativist or Know-Nothing movement that appealed to a significant faction of American-born Protestants.

As the first public demonstration by New York City Jews since the Damascus affair, the "immense assemblage" at Mozart Hall naturally attracted the attention of the city's major newspapers. The *Herald*, *Daily Tribune*, and the *Times* each reported on the event in full. The meeting was chaired by Jonas Phillips, former president of the city's Board of Common Councilmen. Aside from Phillips, the principal speakers included: rabbis Morris J. Raphall and Samuel M. Isaacs; Joseph Seligman, a prominent banker and financier; Raphael de Cordova, a respected humorist and lecturer; Alexander Levi, who represented the Jews of Montreal; and a select number of Christians such as Chauncey Shaffer, a noted trial lawyer and a leader of the American (Know-Nothing) Party. By this time it was clearly understood that the United States would not interfere in the Mortara case. Even so, the *Herald* predicted that the effect of such a numerous assembly, with its learned and compelling addresses, "will have its effect upon foreign governments, even though it should not reach them through the medium of the State Department at Washington."[19]

The oratory was in fact quite persuasive, and credibility was further enhanced by moderating anti-Catholic rhetoric. A conscious effort, for example, was made to distinguish between individual Catholics and the actions of the papacy. Addresses emphasized several recurrent themes that were embedded in the meeting's resolutions: (1) the kidnapping of Edgardo Mortara represented a barbarous regression in an otherwise progressive and civilized age and transgressed family rights and religious freedom, (2) condemnation had ensued from "the humane and enlightened of every creed" and from most of the European powers, (3) this persecution only served to unite Jews in defense of their coreligionists throughout the world, and (4) the movement that had resulted was not in any sense political or religious in motivation but had to be seen as "humanitarian."[20] Great care went into planning this event, and while such organization may have increased the appearance of movement unity and minimized any chance of embarrassment, it also decreased spontaneity. Even so, Mozart Hall was certainly the scene of passionate oratory (albeit written well in advance), and of course speakers made ample use of the core kidnapping narrative. Samuel Isaacs, for example, weaved a poignant scene in a rhetorical style that scarcely managed to rise above pure sentiment but was certain to make good reading in the penny press. "The wife of Mortara," Isaacs declared, "with the feeling characteristic of a mother in Israel, followed her child, until, failing from exhaustion, she could not pursue her journey.

> The child, in a tone of agony, called aloud from the carriage window, "Take me back to my dear mother." His sobs were stifled in the words, "You have no mother now but the church." Here then are the contestants. The "Holy Inquisition," so called, claims the child to be brought up and educated by its reputed parent, the church; whilst the brokenhearted and bereaved mother, with a strength almost superhuman, runs raving through the rugged streets of Bologna, wends her way to Rome, and, at her first interview with her Edgar, whilst the agents of the Inquisition look coldly on the proceedings, the parent and child are so bathed in tears that neither can utter a word. Now, sir, I ask you and this immense assemblage—Catholic, Protestant and Israelite—to whom does the child belong?[21]

Several speakers, including Isaacs and Raphall, compared the Vatican's treatment of the Mortaras to the mentality of the Dark Ages. Most pointed to the progress of liberal ideas, a product of the modern technological age, as the solution to this unfortunate regression. Raphael de Cordova utilized irreverent humor to turn the tables on the pope: "Suppose a band of armed Jews were to penetrate the Vatican and seize upon the Pope, and with a razor or some other sharp instrument (universal tittering) were to perform that operation (uproarious laughter), surely that would not make the Pope a Jew, any more than the sprinkling of water made a child of a Jew a Christian." Dark humor was certainly a movement innovation and, based on the audience reaction, appears to have been a popular one at that. One of the most effective speeches was reserved for the end. Benjamin W. Hart, a businessman and energetic member of B'nai Jeshurun, addressed those "friends of humanity" who were in attendance. "We conjure you, do not fail us," Hart pleaded.

> Do not fail yourselves, do not fail the common cause, do not lose the occasion. Support our efforts with all the means at your command.

Arouse your friends in this sacred cause, buckle your armor, fight the good fight; remember that the God of Israel is with us and will raise us up a champion. Be you that champion. Assemble together, meet, pass resolutions, as we have done tonight, that your mighty voices—the mighty voice of this great city—may be heard at Washington, whence it shall reverberate across the Atlantic and resound through the halls of the Vatican at Rome. (Loud cheers).[22]

Details of the New York City protest meeting spread rapidly in the United States; two weeks later, full coverage, taken from the *Herald*, was published in the *Jewish Chronicle*.[23] Ironically, it was during the high point of press exposure in America (winter 1858–1859) that Jewish leaders began to take note of the seeming ineffectiveness of their campaign. On 10 January, Isaac Leeser and other members of the Philadelphia committee met with President Buchanan and Secretary of State Cass in Washington, D.C. The meeting was cordial, but no breakthroughs were achieved. Despite the visit, as well as the numerous memorials, petitions, and resolutions that were received by the White House and State Department, and the mounting denunciation of the pope's actions by the newspapers, Buchanan and his cabinet stood resolutely opposed to any form of intervention. No matter how large and impressive the individual protest meetings—on 15 January, for example, a mixed protest of three thousand Jews and Christians met at San Francisco's Musical Hall—the fact remained that young Edgardo still resided under the control of the Catholic Church in Rome. Upon Leeser's return to Philadelphia, the reasons for the failure of his mission had become obvious. Had American Jewry acted in unison, as Leeser had hoped, and petitioned "the Executive in proper form," aided by delegates from across the country, reinforced with "tens of thousands of signatures, including governors of States, members of the Senate and House of Representatives, and the most influential names of the different congregations," the outcome would have surely been different, or so it seemed. The Philadelphia committee therefore passed a resolution that recommended that congregations from throughout the country consider "the propriety of electing delegates to represent them in the future, so as to form a body similar to the Board of Deputies of British Jews in London."[24] Unity in action was deemed paramount; otherwise all their efforts were misspent. In February, Isaac Wise also reached a similar conclusion. He reflected on the movement in the *Israelite* and admitted that American Jews "are a weak and distracted body, without the means to exercise that influence that we possess." This "failure" was ascribed to disunity. "Had we unitedly held a convention and acted in concert," Wise wrote, "the result would have been different."[25] Furthermore, while American Jews may have been proud to claim two U.S. senators as their own—Judah P. Benjamin of Louisiana and David L. Yulee of Florida (Moses Levy's estranged son)—Wise noted that both these individuals declined to take any action on behalf of the Mortara case, let alone advance Jewish interests in the United States.[26] "It appears those gentlemen," he declared in the *Israelite*, "do not like to interfere in matters and things of which no political capital can be made."[27] Jews had to confront reality and take charge of their affairs outside the mainstream political process.

The genesis of America's first national Jewish organization began in December 1858 during preparation for the Mozart Hall protest meeting and the formation of the United Congregations of Israelites of the City of New York. Four months after the meeting, and following a direct appeal from Benisch's *Chronicle* that urged U.S. Jews to form their own Board of Deputies, Samuel M. Isaacs acquired the backing of his congregation to initiate a national organization, and eventually nine New York congregations agreed to the idea of founding a "national Jewish defense organization."[28] It was decided to hold a general meeting beginning 25 November 1859. Although each synagogue in the country was invited to send two delegates to the New York gathering, less than 20 percent (twenty-four congregations) did so; indeed, only thirteen congregations from outside of New York City were represented. Despite Wise's previous statements, both he and his Reform colleague David Einhorn of Baltimore distrusted the intentions of the more conservative New Yorkers and declined to attend. Wise now appeared to contradict his former position. "Ah, if something wrong should be done to us, then the board will be our champion," he wrote facetiously.

> That is just the thing we do not want. The constitution and the spirit of liberty are our safeguard. If something should be done we as Jews dislike, we know well how to call public meetings, express our sentiment, and make ourselves heard and felt at the seat of government. Do we need agents or guardians in New York to demand redress in our name, if we consider ourselves wronged? Shame on such a juvenile idea! . . . We are no minors and need no guardians.[29]

Aside from the prickly Wise and the distrust exhibited by the reformers, the elite Sephardic synagogues, Mikveh Israel (Philadelphia) and Shearith Israel (New York) also refused to join. Isaac Leeser, however, took an active role in the proceedings and was elected vice president of the new Board of Delegates of American Israelites (1859–1878). Although a prime aspect of the Board's mission was to aid in the defense of Jewish rights both in the United States and abroad, a host of other causes included facilitating Jewish charitable and educational institutions and establishing uniform rabbinical standards.[30] Despite its flaws, the Board nonetheless filled an important niche; as the nation's sole representative Jewish body, it carried far more weight than any single congregation. Just as the previously moribund British Board of Deputies had metamorphosed into a vital social movement organization during the Damascus affair, similar centripetal pressures resulted in an organized (albeit imperfect) response from American Jews. Indeed, one of the most enduring features of the Mortara affair was the emergence of

Jewish rights organizations. As we shall see, the founding of the first Jewish transnational social movement organization, the Alliance Israélite Universelle (1860), was a direct result of the resurgence of 1858–1859 and arose from a sense of dissatisfaction with the existing social movement repertoire.

THE FINAL PHASE

Expectations for any significant resolution to the Mortara kidnapping were at low ebb when Montefiore arrived in Rome with his wife Judith and a small entourage on 5 April 1859. Not only was war very much on the horizon, but Montefiore's arrival in the holy city during Easter season proved exceedingly inopportune. The sense of ill timing was underscored by the presence of irate crowds in the city yelling "Long Live Independence!" while throngs of lay pilgrims and robed clerics of every description assembled to mark the passion and resurrection of the Savior.[31] This surreal conjuncture must have been unsettling for the renowned "champion of Israel" who had set out on an undertaking that many deemed futile and in a country where British influence was minimal. "I have not heard from any person since I left London that there was the slightest hope of success of my mission," Montefiore confided in his diary.[32] Any reasonable expectation for a papal audience was soon dashed; Montefiore then had to settle for an interview with Cardinal Antonelli, the papal secretary of state. During the meeting between Antonelli and Montefiore—the British attaché, Odo Russell, was also present—the cardinal accepted the Board's "memorial" that requested the release of Edgardo Mortara and promised to pass the document on to the pope. But Antonelli declined to discuss the matter of the baptism and considered the case closed.[33] "It was a bitter pill for poor Sir Moses to swallow," as the correspondent for the *Times* phrased it, "for he was full of hope; but the Cardinal gilded it as well as he could."[34]

Montefiore would certainly have been justified to view this meeting as an offensive snub; yet he continued to wait in the city for what he hoped would be an eventual papal audience. Montefiore's famed persistence would prove futile, however. The Vatican's intransigence could not have been entirely unexpected, however. Immediately following Montefiore's departure from England, a remarkable editorial by Abraham Benisch appeared in the *Chronicle* that reduced expectations for any breakthrough but still managed to frame Montefiore's Roman mission as a "sacred duty." Based on the evidence, few could expect that Pius would ever release the Mortara boy. Yet, as Benisch explained, such a loss, painful as it was, was still likely to prove beneficial for Jews as a whole. There were thus two "great objects" to be attained by Montefiore's journey. First, Montefiore's very presence in Rome would serve as a symbolic triumph; it would affirm to the office of the Inquisition that Jews were now to be regarded as part of the human family. The broad indignation that arose in response to the Mortara kidnapping "showed that human progress has at last reached the point on which man recognizes in man an equal and a brother, whatever his race or creed." Montefiore's mere presence would thus operate as a warning that "civilization will no longer tolerate such inequities." The next by-product of this undertaking would be to stimulate "the internal life of the Jewish community." Benisch proceeded to place the history of the Jewish rights movement into a suitably modern perspective (including allusions to the recently harnessed forces of electricity, a metaphor that many others also used throughout the nineteenth century). The reaction to the Mortara affair was not just an isolated incident but the product of waves of contention. And, just as Moses Levy described the nascent movement three decades earlier, Benisch likened the Jewish people to a single body. "Never before have the dispersed of Israel received within one and the same generation such powerful impulses for co-operation as in our time," he declared.

> Never before has the sentiment of oneness been so quickened within them as in our age. Each time they are called upon to combine for a national purpose, a portion of the feeling of isolation, which formerly rendered them so helpless in emergencies, is rubbed away by the contact, and self-dependence and confidence are generated and sustained; and no event within the community has in modern time stirred up such large masses of co-religionists and put them into communication with each other as this very Mortara affair. In America it has given rise to a movement which we fervently trust will result in a permanent organization of the large Jewish populations now spread all over the union. The Mortara atrocity may, in this respect, be compared to an electric shock applied to a strongly built but torpid limb. It brings new life to it. . . . The mission of Sir Moses Montefiore is the visible effect of this intensified feeling of Jewish oneness, bringing it clearly and distinctly to the consciousness of all members, and must, like every manifestation of an energy, strengthen it, and render its exertion more easy, whilst also contributing towards the formation of the habit itself. The grove within which the communal power slides has, by the fresh exercise, been still more deepened and smoothed. Every movement must in the future become safer, quicker, and more powerful.[35]

Benisch thus shifted the emphasis from the individual to the collective. No matter what happened during Montefiore's journey, the movement would continue in ever more "powerful" manifestations in the future. Once Jews became cognizant of this social movement perspective, they would see that they actually held the upper hand. Because the Vatican remained stationary amid universal progress, the pope and his subordinates had become the real outcasts in the modern world.

Although the *Chronicle* may have overstated Montefiore's position, the editorial nevertheless made real strides in expressing vital social movement concepts to a broad Jewish readership. Of course, Montefiore's trip fell dramatically short of expectations. By this time so much weight was placed on the anticipated audience with the pope that the subsequent rebuff cast a pall of defeat over the entire enterprise. The individual had overshadowed the collective, to paraphrase Benisch, and the outcome needlessly bolstered the perception of papal authority. Montefiore's refusal to call on the French ambassador for assistance and his earlier avoidance of a protest meeting in Paris initiated by the Evangelical Alliance began to alter public opinion of the Jewish "champion," especially among French Jews, who tended to regard Sir Moses as too Anglocentric and detached from the broader imperatives of the international movement. Montefiore had in fact journeyed through France on his way to Rome, and, unlike his cooperative stance during the Damascus crisis, he did not deem it necessary to meet with and discuss his mission with Jewish leaders, a decision that offended many in the community. Furthermore, in the view of a small but growing number of French Jews (including Isidore Cahen, editor of *Archives Israélites*), the failure of the Vatican undertaking accentuated the need for a new autonomous organization—one that was separate from older communal institutions like the Board and the Central Consistory (which was actually directly tied to the French government).

When Montefiore left Rome, war between Austria and Franco-Piedmontese forces had broken out, and in a few months Lombardy and Romagna (which included Bologna) fell to Piedmont. Shortly afterward in London, Cullen Eardley led a delegation of high-ranking evangelicals in a formal meeting with the new British foreign secretary, Lord John Russell, which was held in the hope of taking advantage of the altered political situation on the Italian peninsula and the pope's declining power. But Eardley's rather convoluted rationale for British intervention in the Mortara case was politely rejected by Russell. The following year, the process of Italian unification continued; provinces in central Italy fell under the control of Victor Emmanuel II of Piedmont-Sardinia. A revolution in southern Italy led by Garibaldi further placed the remaining Papal States in jeopardy, and by 1870—following Napoleon III's recall of the French garrison—Rome itself fell to the Italian army. While the forces of liberalism and "progress" were gaining momentum in Italy (despite the now powerless opposition of Pius IX), the fate of Edgardo Mortara, indeed the question of Jewish rights in general, had become intertwined in the affairs of a newly emergent, modern Europe. And while Edgardo would never be freed from his religious captors—he was later ordained a priest and remained an unwavering convert throughout his life—many of Benisch's opinions that had surfaced on behalf of the movement remained valid. The Mortara affair had exceeded the Damascus mobilization in the volume of Jewish protestors, and these activists had the added advantage of communicating via an international Jewish press. Jews had once again been jolted into action; a new self-confidence and common bond had resulted. Although Jews had reasserted themselves on the world political scene, the current insurgence also highlighted major dissatisfaction with the leadership. The two primary communal institutions that had served such a central function in 1840 now appeared overly cautious and conservative and were too concerned with their own national priorities. Moreover, the accommodating attitude of both the Board and the Consistory failed to stir any reciprocal governmental response. Despite massive and unprecedented support from the mainstream press, political opportunities were actually diminished throughout this particular mobilization. Jews were also cognizant of Protestant organizational development. Both the Evangelical Alliance and the Protestant Alliance, for example, had begun to assume

PAPAL ALLOCUTION.—SNUFFING OUT MODERN CIVILISATION.

Figure 6.1 The Mortara Affair seriously undermined the spiritual and temporal authority of Pius IX. It led many commentators—especially in Britain—to deem the papacy as an anachronism and to mock the pope's continued interference in the affairs of Europe.

Source: *Punch*, 13 April 1861.

transnational aspects. Christians had "numerous associations" of this type, as the *Univers Israélite* noted; such operations extended "over the whole face of the earth, making their religion everywhere respected."[36]

Convinced of the necessity of a new authority that would complement rather than diminish the traditional role of both the Central Consistory and the Board of Deputies—which were still deemed "necessary links between Judaism and the political authorities"[37]—in 1860 six young Jewish intellectuals, professionals, and businessmen (Aristide Astruc, Isidore Cahen, Jules Carvallo, Narcisse Leven, Eugene Manuel, and Charles Netter) founded the Alliance Israélite Universelle in Paris. The precepts of this transnational social movement organization included a call "to defend the honor of the Jewish name whenever it is attacked . . .

> To combat, where necessary, the ignorance and vice engendered by oppression; to work, by the power of persuasion and by all the moral influences at our command, for the emancipation of our brethren who still suffer under the burden of exceptional legislation; to hasten and solidify complete enfranchisement by the intellectual and moral regeneration of our brethren:—such, in its chief aspects, is the work to which the *Alliance Israélite Universelle* hereby consecrates itself.[38]

Aside from its rapid initial success in attracting affiliate groups and paid subscribers in various European countries, the *Alliance* represented a turning point in the Jewish rights movement, because its founders placed ultimate value on a new specialized and permanent organizational structure rather than on spontaneous and independent protests that only surfaced during contentious cycles. The *Alliance* also added political emancipation to the movement agenda. As we have seen, however, the call for a more centralized approach was already gaining ground throughout the Mortara episode. The *Alliance*, of course, has been a subject of much import in the historiography. While such scholars as Aron Rodrigue have recognized the organization's import as "the very incarnation of the reforming impulse of Western Jewry,"[39] until now its founding has never been placed within the context of the Jewish rights movement.

While a new generation of Jewish activists remained focused on paving the way for movement institutionalization toward the later phase of the Mortara affair, most of these individuals neglected any serious consideration of the issue of state sovereignty. The previous Damascus crisis was unique in that human rights principles *appeared* to trump state sovereignty. More accurately, the Damascus affair, as far as it related to individual governments, could easily be interpreted as an exercise in realpolitik. Britain's open support for Montefiore's Middle East mission represented a unique set of circumstances that would not be duplicated again in the century. The interests of Britain's European allies were aligned in such a manner that human rights merely became an opportune issue that could be exploited to further bolster the case for military action. The fact that the human rights transgressor was a Muslim also aided in what was essentially a type of public relations sleight of hand. In the Mortara case, Britain's national interests were best served by neutrality. There was no benefit to be gained by questioning any European nation's sovereignty, especially one that was headed by the leader of the Roman Catholic Church. Even France recognized the precariousness of such a stance. While the concept of human rights remained constant, the insurgences of 1840 and 1858 each involved entirely different sets of international and regional priorities. The successful conclusion of the Damascus affair therefore tended to raise unrealistic expectations during the onset of the Mortara affair. But as subsequent events would demonstrate, the foremost difficulty facing the movement was not the dearth of specialized organizational structures but deeply entrenched notions of national sovereignty. It was not until the middle of the twentieth century that this issue was addressed in an appropriate forum. The horrors of the Holocaust and of World War II coincided with the establishment of the United Nations to inspire the Universal Declaration of Human Rights in 1948—the foundational document of international human rights law.

Part IV
Romanian Pogroms

7 "A Scandal to Civilization"

The decades that followed the Mortara affair were marked by an escalation in antisemitic violence. Jews now routinely expressed outrage against mistreatment, no matter where in the world such events transpired, and the support of major Western powers as well as the press assured that the Jewish rights movement would not drift into abeyance. An expanding Jewish activism, both in the form of professional institutions like the Alliance Israélite Universelle—now under the leadership of Adolphe Crémieux—and, beginning in 1871, the Anglo-Jewish Association, to be followed in two years by the Israelitische Allianz zu Wien, as well as the continued exertions of Moses Montefiore and the Board of Deputies, sustained the movement over a considerable period. It also signaled internal divisions over tactics and strategy and a jockeying for power and control that surfaced after the Franco-Prussian War. Such intramovement rivalry, however, remains a fairly constant feature of social movements.[1] A much better organized American Jewish leadership began to contribute in the international arena, but this move was also subject to particular criticism. Despite a strong element of factionalism, the emergence of an enduring, high-profile organizational elite represented an important new phase of the movement.[2] Crémieux and Montefiore remained key leaders, but their influence was beginning to wane. A more conservative organizational structure surfaced—one that emphasized elite consensus and restraint over the older model of individual Jewish "champions."

Montefiore's 1864 journey to Marrakesh, Morocco, was one of the last of his foreign missions. In the short term at least, this episode was interpreted as another brilliant success. Concerned by reports of the torture and abuse of Jews, and given the prominent backing of the British Foreign Office, Montefiore's arrival in North Africa resulted in a fairly rapid response by Sultan Sidi Muhammad. A *dahir*, or official decree, written in the florid style of the Moroccan court, was interpreted as holding great promise, because it commanded that Jews were to be held in "perfect equality with all other people" and guaranteed "more security than heretofore."[3] The wording went to great lengths to assure Montefiore that "not even a fractional portion of the smallest imaginable particle of injustice shall reach any one of [the Jews]." Satisfied with his personal meeting with the sultan and with *dahir* in hand, Montefiore claimed success and returned to England. Afterward, however, the sultan began to interpret this document far less benevolently, actually stipulating that the decree applied to "virtuous Jews" only.[4] Nonetheless, Moroccan Jewry took the original statement on face value; thereafter, they were far less willing to accept their traditionally defined subaltern status. In this respect Montefiore's mission held long-term consequences for Morocco's half-million Jews. It also represented a public relations coup for the aging "knight"; the mission's initial flush of success rekindled Montefiore's position as a transnational social movement entrepreneur par excellence, and favorable press notice inspired thousands of congratulatory letters that flowed in to his London address from all parts of the globe.

In contrast to the relatively short-lived affair in Morocco, the crisis that emerged in Romania—also known as the United Principalities—appeared far more complex and intransigent. Indeed, the problems confronting Romanian Jewry became the primary focus of the Jewish rights movement from the mid-1860s to the 1870s. In 1866, a military coup added yet another element of instability to Romania, a remote Balkan country—brutally dominated in the past by both Russians and Turks—that barely managed to function as a coherent state and was rife with internal ethnic divisions.[5] Prince Carol (Karl von Hohenzollern), a German noble, was selected to replace the liberal Romanian Prince Cuza after the latter's forced abdication. In conjunction with this governmental flux, a rise in antisemitism also emerged, a sinister trend that was advanced by the country's intelligentsia.[6] Economic, ethnic, and religious tensions were exacerbated by an influx of Eastern European Jewish immigrants during the first half of the nineteenth century. Newcomers often denigrated Romanian culture and language and retained their distinctive, traditional garb from Russia and Galicia.[7] The majority of Jews in fact only spoke Yiddish, and their Hasidic-style "pendulous hair and fur caps" and other signs of an unassimilated demeanor further stoked enmity. Even so, there were an unusually high percentage of craftsmen and artisans among the Romanian Jews, especially in the province of Moldavia. Their overall numbers in the cities were also in far greater proportions than most locales in Western Europe. Antisemitism had been nurtured by the Orthodox Church for centuries, but a more virulent form of intolerance surfaced at this time. Jews were deemed the "lepers" of Europe, according to one influential clerical paper, and represented "everything that is hideous, repulsive, and bad."[8] A powerful faction of xenophobic Romanian nationalists used this intrinsic antisemitism to purposely stoke hatred and divisiveness.

During the drafting of a new constitution by the parliament, an article that would have bestowed citizenship to Jews resulted in fierce rioting in the country. Homes and businesses were targeted and Jews suffered massive losses. In June, Crémieux, acting in his capacity as president of the

Alliance, applied as much pressure as he could muster and journeyed to Bucharest, where he addressed the Assembly of Deputies to demand full political liberties. Former American slaves were accorded far more freedom, he declared, than the Jews of Romania.[9] Many of the nation's elite were educated in France, and a certain number admired Crémieux for his past affiliation with the French revolutionary government (1848). And so the celebrated attorney was given a polite, albeit limited, reception by these Francophiles. [Fifty deputies were in attendance when he spoke; the most strident opponents of emancipation were absent.[10]] Any residue of lofty idealism was short-lived, however, and the exigencies of local politics rapidly took center stage. The Romanian press, for instance, viciously caricatured Crémieux.[11] After his departure, rioters did not waste time in launching an assault on the Jewish quarter in Bucharest, where they also destroyed the ornate, newly constructed synagogue. Throngs surrounded the parliament building in order to intimidate politicians into revoking any move toward Jewish emancipation. Acceding to mob pressure, the offending article in the constitution was rewritten to exclude Jews; a militant backlash had thereby quashed any hope for equality.

News of arrests, expulsions, and continued brutality began to circulate in the media. Interior Minister Ion Brătianu (1821–1891) emerged as a major player in the antisemitic campaign and was the person most responsible for the pogromist mentalité that persisted throughout Romania for years. Men, women, and children were rounded up by police, shackled, and then deported to the Ottoman territory opposite the Danube River on the spurious charge of "vagrancy."[12] Hundreds of families were traumatized and faced financial ruin, while some men drowned after being thrown into the Danube while in chains. "This sad spectacle," wrote one observer, "accompanied on the one hand by the jeers and laughter of the populace, and on the other by the screams of distress of the women and children of our unfortunate coreligionists, is repeated every instant in the streets."[13] Various government and political party leaders, many believed, were deliberately inciting these measures for their own political advancement. Scores of Jews, "hunted down by all sides," feared a wholesale massacre unless the major European powers intervened.

Pleas for aid arrived in the Jewish communities of Paris, Berlin, and London. When the chief rabbi of Jassy (Moldavia) penned a heartfelt appeal to Montefiore—whom the rabbi praised as Israel's "lion"—and urged him to come to the rescue of his distressed brethren in Romania, it was precisely the type of request that the eighty-three-year-old found most difficult to refuse; indeed, he considered it "an imperative duty."[14] The forces of antisemitism in the United Principalities had become notorious throughout the media; Montefiore's application to the Board to proceed to Romania was thus readily sanctioned. When the *Jewish Chronicle*, still under the editorship of Abraham Benisch, heard of Sir Moses's intentions, Benisch lauded the mission while also demonstrating great affection and concern for the welfare of this octogenarian. Ultimately, "men like Sir Moses Montefiore are Providential," and as "God's chosen instruments," such individuals follow "a star of their own."[15] As a true champion and hero, Montefiore's undertakings were beyond mere human understanding. "Go forth," Benisch declared, and "smite the Goliath of Roumania." Implicit amid this hyperbole was the fact that the image of chivalrous heroes was beginning to fade and to be rendered quaint. Among the rising generation of Jewish leaders, among whom Benisch had started to establish himself, businesslike organizational structure was believed to be far superior to risk-filled, solitary ventures. Even so, Benisch's *Chronicle* had no intention of criticizing Montefiore or diminishing his celebrity and felt it was better to give him due respect and to offer hope for his safe return.

At first glance Montefiore's mission during the summer of 1867 may appear similar to his other trips abroad. Rather than deal with the legislature or make eloquent public demands, as Crémieux did earlier, Montefiore relied on face-to-face encounters with the reigning sovereign, Prince Carol; focused on the issues of basic human rights and religious tolerance rather than political emancipation; and arrived well-supplied with declarations from the European powers: Britain, Austria, France, Italy, Prussia, and Russia all officially sanctioned his mission. A politically stable Romania was felt to be in Europe's best interest, and these were the precise nations that were signatories of the Paris Convention of 1858, which gave them, in theory at least, supervisory status over Romania. In his petition to the prince dated 27 August, Montefiore emphasized that he not only represented Anglo-Jewry but was acting on behalf of Jews worldwide. He entreated Carol "to warn all evil disposed persons not to molest the Jews in any manner" and to assure that his Jewish subjects "shall enjoy perfect protection in all which concerns the safety of their persons and their property."[16] The local British consul, John Green, made certain that Montefiore would be well received by the prince, and a formal dinner reception at the palace was given in the visitor's honor. Following this official welcome, a reply to Sir Moses's petition arrived wherein Carol declared his government's commitment to religious liberty and the basic rights and protection of Romanian Jews—thus acknowledging, at least superficially, the requirements that had been previously set by the Paris Convention. In reality, however, the sovereign's authority was limited, and many Jews had reason to doubt his veracity. The document also included a disquieting assertion: it labeled past antisemitic acts as isolated events. And most troubling was Carol's denial that there was any substantive problem of religious persecution in the country. Yet Montefiore decided to make the best of the situation and later highlighted this document, just as he did with the *dahir*, as a tangible sign of success.

There was a far more sinister side to Montefiore's stay in Bucharest, however. In contradistinction to the cordial dealings with the prince, the mood among the general populace in the capital had become threatening. Rumors of a devious Jewish "conspiracy" began to circulate. Wealthy Jewish foreigners, with Montefiore supposedly at the vanguard, were seen as intent on acquiring all the best land in the country. Fears were deliberately stoked, and many assumed that Romania would "become a Palestine" and fall into the hands of "Hebrew bloodsuckers."[17] Anonymous death threats arrived at Montefiore's hotel suite, and one newspaper editor, aware of the growing menace, gravely urged the departure of the British visitors, "as the people were now going to kill Sir Moses." Such a threatening scenario had never presented itself during the history of the movement; there had always been a modicum of security in past dealings with foreign nations. Nevertheless, the inherent dangers of this mission were apparent well before Montefiore's departure from England (the Bucharest branch of the Alliance Israélite, for example, strongly advised against any visit). Sir Moses's nephew Arthur Cohen, a barrister, while initially accompanying his uncle on the journey, received a telegram from his family while en route to Bucharest that insisted that he withdraw from the undertaking precisely because of the high risks involved.[18]

The gravity of this situation was best expressed in a firsthand account written by Montefiore's trusted long-time companion, Louis Loewe, two decades later. In this narrative, Loewe described a gathering crowd located directly outside Montefiore's suite on the second floor of the Hotel Otettaliano. This dramatic scene, long ignored by historians, nevertheless captured Montefiore's role as a social movement leader during a period of great personal risk. Thousands assembled outside the hotel at the instigation of the journal, Naţiunea Română (Romanian Nation). A petition intended to save the country "from the lacerating claws of the Hebrews" surfaced in this periodical and demanded that Jews be barred from settling in the country or buying any state land and called for their deportation to "the land from whence they have come."[19] The petition also served as a call to action; it focused on the negation of Jewish rights (as personified by Montefiore) and was an effort to guard traditional socioeconomic interests. The massive turnout thus acquired characteristics of an embryonic, reactionary countermovement.[20] Scholars have in fact identified this period as the beginning of the government's long-term antisemitic campaign.[21] Throngs of people gathered, ostensibly to sign the petition, although, according to Loewe, many started to advance "towards the windows in a most threatening attitude."

> Some persons from the hotel then suddenly entered the room occupied by Sir Moses, terror-stricken at what they had seen and heard in the streets, calling his attention to the crowds at his window, and saying, "They want to take your life."
>
> Most persons in Sir Moses' position would have manifested great fear and excitement, but this was not the case with him. He went to the window facing the enraged populace, opened both wings, and placed himself right in front of it, and I had the privilege of being permitted to place myself at his side.

128 *The Rise of Modern Jewish Politics*

"Fire away," he said, "if you like. I came here in the name of justice and humanity to plead the cause of innocent sufferers." They stared at him at first for a few minutes. Then the shouting and tumult increased, but he still did not move.

Ultimately the crowd, threatening and shouting, dispersed. In the evening, Mr. Halfon, the banker [and head of the local branch of the Alliance] called. With tears in his eyes, he cried, "We shall all be massacred."[22]

Rather than taking precautions, Montefiore startled the mob by his extreme bravado, thereby gaining at least temporary advantage. [It is significant that on this occasion, Lady Judith, who passed away five years earlier, was no longer by Montefiore's side.[23]] The crowd may have dissipated, but by nightfall there was, as Halfon demonstrated, much lingering uncertainty and fear. Then in another bold move, Montefiore once again confronted the source of intimidation head on. As Loewe recalled, Sir Moses ordered an open carriage to be readied and requested that two lanterns be fully lit "so that his person might be seen by everybody" when he drove through the principal streets of the city. Halfon became even more panic-stricken upon hearing this. "Are you afraid?" Montefiore asked point blank. Without

Figure 7.1 Moses Montefiore addresses an angry crowd assembled outside his Bucharest hotel room.

Source: Diaries of Sir Moses and Lady Montefiore, ed. L. Loewe, vol. 2 (Chicago, 1890).

waiting for a reply and after asserting his own faith in the "holy cause" and in God's ultimate protection, Sir Moses, along with Loewe, took part in a two-hour tour of Bucharest in an open, well-lit carriage, as if nothing of significance had occurred. Word quickly circulated, and onlookers gathered alongside the streets to gaze upon the "*tres vénérable Baronett*," as Carol had addressed him earlier. This act was, of course, rife with symbolism. It surely emphasized Montefiore's celebrity standing within a remote European capital that relished all displays of gallantry and pomp. As a major iconic figure, any danger to Montefiore actually accentuated the ultimate importance of Jewish rights. The movement, as Montefiore stated, was a "holy cause" and a goal as vital as life itself. Fortunately, no one became a martyr to the cause on this occasion, and both individuals returned to the hotel unharmed and without incident. Given the high risks and Montefiore's bravado, this scene could have easily achieved legendary status, but any note of danger was purposely suppressed in favor of promoting the positive aspects of Prince Carol's declaration.

Once word of the intimidating crowd and death threats reached the prince, a contingent of armed guards was rapidly dispatched and stationed throughout the hotel. When Montefiore took his leave at the palace a few days later, a substantial cavalry unit escorted him and his entourage safely out of the country. Subsequent to Montefiore's departure, however, in a scene redolent of Crémieux's previous effort, Jewish expulsions again escalated. Hundreds endured public humiliation and forced deportation from the country. Synagogues were desecrated, men were dragged in the streets by their beards and hair and women stripped of their clothes. Dispossessed families wandered as refugees, their homes confiscated. Crémieux, Montefiore, and the Rothchilds exerted as much influence as they could with the European powers, and the Jewish MPs—Lionel de Rothchild and Francis Goldsmid—lobbied Parliament. It was obvious, however, that the major powers were not going to interfere on behalf of Romania's 200,000 Jews. Pogroms continued in a sporadic fashion for years afterward. Isaac Leeser, commenting in the *Occident*, sadly noted the limitations of the movement's tactics: documents signed by monarchs, no matter how grandiloquent, "fail to procure immunity from persecution." Leeser only hoped that future efforts would be "crowned hereafter with more success than they appear to have been just now."[24]

CONSUL PEIXOTTO

Attempts to alleviate the lingering Romanian crisis started anew in 1870, largely through the efforts of American Jewry. Beginning in early June, stories of a large-scale massacre, supposedly causing the deaths of thousands of Romanian Jews, began to circulate in several Midwestern cities. In a few days, mass Jewish protest meetings took place in Cincinnati, Memphis, and

Indianapolis, and a flurry of telegrams were sent to congressmen, senators, and the White House.[25] Initial reports soon proved to be an exaggeration (a mistake that was blamed on a regional wire service), and many assumed that the entire affair was a shocking hoax. Nonetheless, further investigation revealed, as the *New York Herald* confirmed in July, that there had actually been a serious outbreak of mob violence in Romania. In what was colloquially termed a "Jew hunt," hundreds of victims in the town of Botuscani, including very young children and the elderly, were ferociously clubbed and beaten by mobs of students and "street rowdies." Once again, homes, businesses, and a synagogue were pillaged and destroyed. The police generally stood idle and advanced only against those Jews who dared to band together to defend themselves.[26] Both the American Board of Delegates (now comprised of thirty congregations and societies) and B'nai B'rith (a fraternal and Jewish rights advocacy organization founded in 1843) pressured the administration of Ulysses S. Grant to condemn the atrocities. These same organizations then implemented an innovative plan to alleviate the still-festering situation.[27] This strategy resulted in the appointment of Benjamin F. Peixotto (1834–1890), a thirty-six-year-old New York City native, attorney, and former B'nai B'rith president, as the U.S. consul to Romania. Mild mannered and of slight build, Peixotto was nonetheless an untiring worker, a proven administrator, and a highly polished public speaker. Following confirmation by the Senate, Peixotto received the open support of President Grant, who acknowledged that he expected the consul would be solely engaged in "missionary work" on behalf of Romanian Jewry.[28] The cost of this unsalaried position as well as the consular staff and associated expenses would be borne solely by American Jewish contributors.[29] Such an extraordinary arrangement not only attested to the president's personal commitment to Jewish rights but also appears to have been an act of political atonement for the former Union general's notorious conduct during the Civil War. [In 1862 Grant ordered all civilian Jews under his jurisdiction in the Tennessee district to be expelled within twenty-four hours' notice, allegedly for trading in black market cotton. This order stirred a massive outcry from Jewish citizens and resulted in its revocation by Abraham Lincoln.[30]] Following Grant's election as president, the former general continued on close terms with the international Jewish financier, Joseph Seligman,[31] one of the principal Mozart Hall speakers who now headed the recently formed American Roumania Committee and had personally lobbied the president on behalf of the consular position.

Upon his arrival in Bucharest, Peixotto, very much an American outsider, became the primary Jewish rights advocate in the hotbed of Eastern European antisemitism—a noteworthy achievement and one that carried substantial risk. *Ha-Maggid*, a widely circulated Hebrew weekly published in Lyck, Prussia, aptly noted that the reason previous Jewish missions to Romania failed to produce any lasting effect was due to their "transitory" nature. Peixotto, on the other hand, arrived in the capital as the full-time "accredited representative of his country."[32] Indeed, after a few months, Peixotto was better able to assess the situation and concluded that the violence was not only "systematic" but stemmed largely from economic rivalry and the belief that Jewish merchants held an unfair business advantage. He also noted a contingent of demagogues who pandered to the "worst passions of their constituents" and utilized violent outbreaks to drive out Jewish competitors and to further their own political advancement.[33] These observations were mostly accurate. According to the philosophical musings of Ion Brătianu, a nation conquered by conventional weaponry still retained its right to liberty, but if it were "conquered by economic means," as he accused the Jews of doing, "it is destroyed forever."[34] Hence, Jews were considered the archenemies of an emergent, modern Romania; their mere existence was a problem of major proportions. Some historians believe the impetus behind nineteenth-century Romanian antisemitism largely stemmed from this peculiar political-economic thesis, much more than racialist or religious prejudices alone.[35]

Peixotto was not intent on being the mere eyes and ears of the movement; nor was he about to restrict himself to traditional consular duties. Rather, this cosmopolitan individual adopted an unusually energetic and persistent approach on behalf of his coreligionists, much as his American patrons had expected, and Peixotto's background as an attorney and newspaper editor as well as his Sephardic or "Portuguese" Jewish lineage (which was seen locally as far superior to the Polish or Ashkenazi Jews[36]) helped in pursuing his goals. Largely through his influence with Prince Carol and others in the government, local prefects who had formerly encouraged anti-Jewish rioting were removed, and additional repressive laws were averted. The consul bravely shunned bodyguards supplied by the prince while visiting remote Jewish communities; advocated the use of firearms as a legal means of self-defense (a first for the movement); founded the Zion Society, a Romanian Jewish fraternal organization, later affiliated with B'nai B'rith, which focused on Jewish unity and the establishment of schools; and founded a semiweekly, dual language (Romanian and German) newspaper, the *Rumänische Post* to counter the local antisemitic press and to promote movement objectives.[37] In addition to his official correspondence, the consul maintained close communications with distinguished Jewish leaders in London, Paris, Vienna, and Berlin.

One year after his arrival, Peixotto was taken aback by reports of a new wave of pogroms, this time in the two former Russian territories of Cahul and Ismail. These were counties within greater Bessarabia that had been ceded to Romania after Russia's defeat in the Crimean War. Peixotto's subsequent accounts relating to this obscure corner of the world assumed special credence, as newspapers in Europe and America published his detailed and highly emotive reports verbatim. In January, according to his correspondence to Jewish leaders in England, the Jews in Bessarabia were abruptly set upon and "for three days beaten, wounded, plundered, and driven out of their homes, which were battered to ruins." The reason behind this outburst, which the British consul claimed was entirely orchestrated by officials across the border in Russia, was the theft of some gold coins and a silver-gilt cross and coffer from a church in Ismail.[38] The thief, Jenkel Silbermann, was not only a stranger to the region but a Christian convert and a deserter from the Russian army. When apprehended and tortured under custody, he began to name five leading Jews in the town, including the rabbi, elders, and president of the congregation, as his supposed accomplices.[39] The accused were arrested and tortured severely. News regarding the church robbery spread rapidly to the populace, and rioting ensued. Peixotto described a scene of utter barbarism: streets were stained with blood, heads split open, arms broken, beards pulled out by the roots, hair torn from the scalp, and women raped. Some did not live through their ordeal. Sixty houses were destroyed and two synagogues were ransacked and used as privies. "But few Christians came to the relief of the starving women and children," he wrote.

> Relief only came on the third day, and then the Christians who did come wept when they beheld the misery that had been wrought ... hundreds are lying on straw in ruined houses. They say there is scarcely a village in the whole of Bessarabian Roumania where there have not been frightful scenes. The misery is dreadful. Help is needed immediately. I pray you, call a mass meeting of the Israelites of London, or of citizens without distinction to religion, to protest, in the name of humanity, against these frightful scenes, which threaten, as Passover approaches, to become still more dreadful. ... I cannot write more tonight. Try to make out this scrawl, blinded with my tears, and written with a hand trembling with indignation.[40]

As a result of this poignant appeal, members of the recently formed London Roumanian Committee, an independent body that was organized to counter the pogroms and included such figures as Sir Francis Goldsmid, Sir David Salomons, Abraham Benisch (retired since 1868 as the editor of the *Chronicle*[41]), Lionel L. Cohen, and L. M. Rothschild, were actually in a position to call a public meeting, with or without the approval of the Board of Deputies. The committee agreed with Peixotto that it was indeed time to look to "public opinion" rather than continue with more conventional tactics. "Sir Moses Montefiore had moved Courts and Cabinets," Cohen observed, and "Sir Francis Goldsmid has elicited the voice of Parliament: all in vain." It was then voted upon "to hold, as soon as practicable, a public meeting at the Mansion House" in order to express indignation at the outrages and to take steps to prevent them from occurring again.[42]

The 30th of May was "a red letter day in the annals of the Anglo-Jewish community," as the *Chronicle* described it.[43] Thirty-two years had elapsed since the last protest meeting in London; any public expression of indignation was therefore a rare and significant occurrence and was not to be taken lightly. The lord mayor, the earl of Shaftesbury, and the bishop of Gloucester were joined by forty MPs and a host of other eminent individuals of diverse religious backgrounds, including a contingent of the Cousinhood. Members of the Cohen, Mocatta, Rothschild, Sassoon, Goldsmid, Salomons, and Montefiore families were all present (significantly, however, Moses Montefiore chose not to attend). Mansion House meetings of course held immense symbolic significance, and news of this event was widespread.[44] Yet, unlike the Damascus affair, there was no call to action that resulted in an upsurge of protest meetings, and Moses Montefiore's absence surely did not aid in this regard. Aside from the publicity it generated, another significant contribution was its interdenominational composition. "Here were Low Church and High Church vying with non-conformity in declaring the outbreaks in Roumania a stain on Christianity," as New York City's *Jewish Messenger* observed.

> On the same platform stood Lord Bishop and Chief Rabbi, while Jewish and Christian members of Parliament mingled in the body of the house ... and through a council of men representing every shade of Christianity, acknowledged the right of the Jew to the title of man and to manly treatment. It was not charity which dictated the utterances at the meeting; it was religion unshackled by the limitations, prejudices, and inconsistencies of sects, and appearing in the garb of universal brotherhood, crowned with the Divine grace and radiant with the Divine blessing.[45]

The worldwide attention that the consul garnered in reaction to the Bessarabian pogroms proved particularly irksome to the Romanian government. The details that emerged were, considering their source, especially difficult to refute. Yet when Romanian ministers and diplomats were forced to confront these charges, they either minimized them as minor disturbances or denied them outright. The wealthiest Jews in the capital also began to resent the publicity that Peixotto had generated and appeared more committed to the status quo than to meaningful change. During the end of August, an opportunity arose that gave the consul's enemies substantial leverage and would thrust the enterprising American into significant controversy. In a letter to the Romanian ministry, Peixotto stated that he had been approached by a certain emigration society that desired to transport a number of Jews to the United States. He asked what the government's reaction would be to such a plan. What was intended as a simple query was pushed to a much higher level by the government. In an abrupt and unlikely show of magnanimity, the foreign affairs minister volunteered to issue an unlimited number of passports free to all Jews who wished "to leave the country to establish themselves elsewhere."[46] Emigration was an expensive and thus a limited option, even under the best of circumstances, and within the Jewish rights movement the subject was very controversial. Such a move, it was commonly thought, would divert attention away from governmental reforms and, ultimately, the attainment of Jewish rights (such was the original dilemma that confronted Moses Levy in 1827). Moreover, if Jews did not rush en masse to accept this opportunity, it would be seen as an indication that their lives were clearly not as unbearable as Peixotto had claimed. An intricate contest began to unfold, and the government, for once, began to undermine the consul's efforts.

Despite the furor that ensued, Peixotto would not disassociate himself from the emigration proposal. Quite the opposite, after the government played its hand, Peixotto began to actively promote the idea. In so doing, he believed that he could at least "rescue *some* and possibly promote the safety of all."[47] Given Romania's endemic antisemitism and a constant vituperative press, the ideal of political emancipation became a virtual chimera, or so the consul thought. As a result, Peixotto had become radicalized by his tenure in the country. Most of his time had been spent in staving off wholesale massacres or otherwise shielding the vulnerable Jewish population (actions that had heretofore eluded Bucharest's Jewish notables). Some form of rescue effort, certainly not gentle persuasion, appeared to be the only viable path. Political pressure from abroad was one of the few tools available for alleviating suffering, even if it meant that the consul would keep the political world "in a continual state of ferment," as the Romanian finance minister once complained.[48] Such an energetic and "undiplomatic" Jewish rights advocate had never appeared on the international scene before. But despite rumors that Peixotto kept a pistol and bowie knife on his person for self-defense, the consul was certainly not the unsophisticated provincial American that his enemies sometimes accused him of being. The consul's efforts, it should also be noted, were consistently backed by U.S. Secretary of State Hamilton Fish.[49]

With few exceptions, including several leading Romanian rabbis and Zvi Hirsch Kalischer, the well-known Zionist forerunner from Prussian Poland, most Jewish leaders, including the "Roumanian Committees" which Peixotto advocated and which now operated in New York, London, Berlin, Vienna, and elsewhere, vehemently opposed any emigration scheme, whether it was to America, Palestine, or any other locale.[50] Perhaps the most irate of all were the small faction of affluent Romanian Jews, the majority of whom were quite livid at Peixotto's unilateral decisions. Reportedly, thousands of Jews began to register at the American consulate for what they assumed would be free transport to the United States. Such a scene threatened to entirely undermine whatever sense of control Jewish leaders held. Heightened dissent within the movement coincided with a call emanating from the Berlin Roumanian Committee, headed by Gerson J. Bleichroder, Bismarck's personal banker, for an international conference of Jews to be held in Brussels. Delegates representing Britain, Germany, France, the United States, Austria, Holland, Belgium, and Romania met in private session on 28 and 29 October. Such a global assembly, chaired by Adolphe Crémieux and attended by Peixotto (Montefiore was again conspicuous by his absence), set a new organizational standard for the Jewish rights campaign. While organized by the Berlin faction, the "noble idea," unprecedented in modern times, actually originated with Peixotto.[51] The conference's stated objective was to establish a unified Jewish response to the situation in Romania.[52]

There were certainly no diplomatic or political breakthroughs that emanated from the International Roumanian Conference, as the event was referred to in the *Chronicle* (now a far more conservative publication). A great deal of the assembly's significance, like that of the Mansion House meeting, rested in its potent symbolism. But unlike the latter, which was primarily an interfaith protest that was fervently British in tone, the upcoming event held the promise of being a real-world demonstration of *Kelal Yisrael*. Peixotto's expectations were thus quite high: "the best men [were] drawn from all lands to deliberate for the emancipation of the downtrodden masses in Roumania."[53] The Brussels proceeding, however, consisted of approximately forty delegates and was held behind closed doors (an aspect that disappointed many) at the private residence of banker Raphael Bischoffsheim; the direction of the Jewish rights movement was at stake and confidentiality was considered paramount. Peixotto's hopes were soon dashed when two members of the Romanian delegation, Anton Levy and Emile Hirsch, long-time adversaries who were aligned with the Bucharest elite, were given prominent roles. As the conference attendees ultimately followed Levy and Hirsch's approach in dealing with the Romanian government, Peixotto was effectively sidelined. The consul was also excluded from a subcommittee (headquartered in Vienna) that was expected to submit a petition for Jewish political equality to the Romanian legislature. In a final blow, delegates unanimously rejected any attempt at emigration, and individuals did not hesitate to make their displeasure known to Peixotto personally. "About my ears," the consul confided to a close friend, "came noises enough to crush an ordinary mortal."[54] Exceedingly cautious of generating an anti-Jewish backlash, delegates were intent on "directing the course of public opinion" by demonstrating moderation and showing "the Jewish love of order and reverence for authority" as well as their "devoted attachment to the land of their adoption."[55] The Jewish establishment continued to regard national affiliation, patriotism, education, and assimilation as the proper values that should be inculcated. Any talk of a mass exodus was quashed.

"The Emigration Scheme would cut and not untie the Gordian knot," as the *Chronicle*'s Brussels correspondent asserted. "The constitution of Roumania would not be humanized, whilst fanaticism would secure another triumph." If Romanian Jews emigrated, the reporter continued, they "would be severing themselves from all they loved, without having the supreme satisfaction of knowing that their self-sacrifice had advanced the cause of liberty and civilization."[56] The prominence of social reform in general was being usurped by a political philosophy that held self-reliance and personal discipline as sacrosanct. "It is the individual mind and conscience," as Britain's Prime Minister William Gladstone famously declared, "on which mainly human happiness or misery depends."[57] A "minimal state" combined with individual effort, and not the misguided interference of outside agencies, was considered as the optimal path for society. Moreover, nationalism was especially ascendant in a newly unified Germany, and any concept that framed Jews, foreign or domestic, as anything less than fully patriotic was anathema. Complicating the political horizon even more was the specter of socialism, anarchism, and Marxism—as personified by the revolutionary Paris Commune of 1871. This tragic and short-lived experiment surfaced after the downfall of Louis Bonaparte's Second Empire (1851–1870) and was largely the result of a power vacuum that followed in the wake of France's defeat during the Franco-Prussian War.[58] Most of the privileged classes of Europe felt a common bond when confronted with such radical threats. "The class hatred and desperation released in the spring of 1871," as one historian has noted, "signaled to some the collapse of civilization itself."[59] Passionate rhetoric that was hostile to any form of governmental oppression had, quite frankly, become suspect throughout Europe. The *Chronicle*'s new editor, Michael Henry, thus considered it a special duty to recognize the sobriety and restraint of the Brussels delegates, all of whom, as Henry observed, "Did not allow themselves to be carried away by passion which so often animates those who take part in any social or political movement."[60] Curiously, not even "the recital of unmerited wrongs and sufferings" was allowed "to disturb the almost judicial calmness" that, at least according to this version of events, pervaded the proceedings.[61]

Despite the predominant view held in Brussels, no one could deny that a deeply troubling force had taken place in Romania, and there was no indication that brutal and deadly attacks would ever cease. But the financiers, intellectuals, and other eminent factions at the conference nevertheless regarded Peixotto's innovations as unacceptable. Extreme caution had taken hold. The Romanian delegates stressed their special status as insiders, their knowledge of local politics, and the advantages to be accrued by following restraint—a dispassionate approach that appealed to a new upper echelon of European Jewry. This antiemigration mind-set would change during the next decade, but as far as the present mobilization was concerned, the conference served as a deliberate rebuke to the American consul and, for all intents and purposes, spelled the end of the contentious phase of the movement.[62] Ironically, the leadership used this first international assembly to opt for restraint in the public sphere rather than press for united action.

During the remainder of Peixotto's tenure in Romania, he continued to be in close contact with the Jewish leadership in Europe and America, but the events in Brussels had altered the dynamics of the movement and lessened his international prestige. Despite the criticism in Brussels and the open hostility of the privileged Bucharest faction, much evidence attests to the fact that the majority of Romanian Jews regarded Peixotto in the highest esteem and with great fondness. According to the Jewish community of Galatz, for example, the consul's rigorous efforts resulted in a marked improvement in their daily lives: "open persecutions have ceased, a more tolerant spirit prevails, and our social and political position begins to grow better and brighter."⁶³ Furthermore, owing to Peixotto's actions on behalf of Romanian Jewry, Prince Carol exonerated (not simply pardoned) the five communal leaders who suffered torture and who were jailed during the outbreak in Bessarabia—a decision that provoked outcries from the Romanian press and elicited profound gratitude from the nation's Jews. While laws that prohibited Jews from dealing in tobacco and alcohol were passed, they were not enacted, also due to the consul's influence—a significant boon to the numerous Jewish tavern keepers. Not only did Jews enjoy comparative immunity from "violence and robbery," but, to cite a Romanian Jewish correspondent, "a new Civil Code, and the revised Municipal Law have secured them in their persons and property, and extended under certain conditions municipal franchise."

> Nor is this all. By the institution of the Society 'Zion,' schools have been founded in all the principal towns and the cause of education greatly promoted. Indeed a new era has dawned for our brethren which must continue to develop until the full light of moral, social, and political emancipation shall place the Roumanian Jew on the same level with those of France, England and America.⁶⁴

Less successfully, Peixotto's continued support for emigration failed to result in the kind of large-scale exodus that he envisioned. He still maintained, despite significant opposition, that fifty thousand Jews could be reasonably situated in the United States, a view also supported by his friend and fellow B'nai B'rith member Isaac Wise. American steamship companies in 1873 sent a representative named Leon Horowitz to Romania, where, with Peixotto's help, he toured the country, organizing "mutual emigration societies" in various towns, urging that people reap the rich harvest of life in America. Inexplicably, however, Horowitz failed to follow through on his promises and was no longer heard from.⁶⁵ Also that year, at the behest of the Roumanian Emigration Society headquartered in New York City, 150 Jewish emigrants arrived in America, although, as the society's president, Leopold Bamberger complained, "90% came as paupers and became a burden to our society from the very day they landed on our shores."⁶⁶ Other than a mere handful of additional Romanian Jews who arrived in Nebraska as farmers, emigration to America at this date proved entirely disappointing.

Only the most sanguine would expect that Peixotto's "new spirit of progress" in Romania would continue indefinitely once he left the country. But his term as consul was only assured for five years. The first indication of potential trouble surfaced during the spring and summer of 1874, when Peixotto left the damp Romanian climate for Saxony, where he recovered from an illness with his wife and family. The government took advantage of his absence by enacting the previously "dead letter" liquor law. In addition, hundreds of families became destitute after having their businesses forfeited in the rural district of Bacau. Peixotto sprang into action as soon as he learned of this repression and threatened Romanian ministers with "foreign intervention."

These individuals backed down and promised to ignore those Jews who operated businesses under fictitious Christian ownership and pledged to refrain from implementing the liquor prohibition.[67]

Peixotto faced a severe financial shortfall in 1875. His overseas Jewish patrons were regrettably sluggish in their promised support, and the expenses of maintaining a consulate in Bucharest were very high. Confronted with a humiliating lack of funds, he had no other recourse than to pay his debts and return to the United States before his term expired. Peixotto was granted six months leave from the State Department and departed Romania during the summer of 1875, leaving his wife and eight children in Dresden, where he could send for them once his finances improved. Upon Peixotto's arrival in London, however, Francis Goldsmid and other members of the Roumanian Committee prevailed upon him to return to Romania, apparently providing him with the necessary monetary resources to do so. Armed conflict had erupted between Montenegro and the Ottoman Empire, and this in turn sparked hostilities in Bulgaria; Russian intervention in the Balkans was deemed inevitable—a situation that was perceived as a grave menace to the stability of Romania. Because the United States would retain its neutrality if violence began to escalate, Peixotto was thought to be the best possible safeguard for the Jews. Fortunately, war managed to bypass Romania during Peixotto's additional stay, and this period proved comparatively uneventful.

Peixotto finally left Romania in June 1876 and arrived in New York City one month later. He began an extensive lecture tour and eventually regained some economic stability. The following year, President Rutherford B. Hayes appointed him as the U.S. consul in Lyons, a relatively undemanding but nevertheless fully paid post where he remained for eight years, having been reunited with his family. True to form, soon after Peixotto left Bucharest, the Romanian government, headed once more by Brătianu, began to invoke the liquor prohibition and the laws against "vagabondage," a euphemism for Jews, in the rural districts.[68] Eight Jews were reported murdered and eleven wounded in the town of Giurgevo some months later, an incident that aroused international condemnation. Shortly thereafter, an additional three persons were killed and 150 homes plundered and destroyed in the small town of Dorobani.[69] Fear of reprisals prevented a full accounting of the massacres that followed in the wake of Peixotto's departure. The Russo-Turkish War (1877–1878) interrupted anti-Jewish violence for a time, as did the intense international scrutiny that came about as a result of the Treaty of Berlin (1878) and subsequent recognition of Romania as a new independent state under the sovereignty of King Carol. Unfortunately, the Romanian atrocities would be superseded by an even more extensive set of pogroms in Russia beginning in the early 1880s, a period that held major consequences for the Jewish rights struggle and the Jewish people as a whole.

Part V
Russian Crises

8 "A Crisis in Jewish History"

Throughout the nineteenth century, most Russian Jews were restricted to the Pale of Settlement and were subjected to a continual process of social experimentation under the tsars. The Pale was thus a central component in this large-scale social engineering scheme. This vast region extended from the Baltic at its uppermost border to the Black Sea and Crimea to the south. The Jews who lived within confines of the Pale (Lithuania, Belorussia, Ukraine, Bessarabia, and New Russia) comprised an ethnoreligious minority of approximately three million people or 12.5 percent of the total population and were often the focus, as has been shown, of various *ukazy*. As in Romania, the "native" gentile majority or peasantry was adjudged by the government as requiring special legal advantages that would counter the so-called exploitative tendencies of Jews, especially as it related to the manufacture and sale of distilled spirits. Jews were regarded as the ultimate other. Even relatively enlightened Russian bureaucrats viewed them as "a large tribe completely alien to the native population by virtue of its morals, habits, and character, its faith and language."[1] An additional one million Jews were located within the Kingdom of Poland, a separate jurisdiction that was not subject to the restrictions of the Pale. By the 1880s, authorities had allowed a privileged faction of 54,000 to reside in the Eastern provinces of ethnic Russia—what was usually referred to as the "interior." These comparative few earned their living in such cities as St. Petersburg and Moscow and were admitted on the basis of being eminent merchants, highly credentialed artisans—expert tailors, metalsmiths, and shoemakers—university graduates, or military veterans.[2] An undefined number also crossed into this region illegally. One estimate places the total population of Russian Jews (circa 1881) at 4,086,650.[3] There is no question that this body constituted the largest Jewish community in the world, vastly exceeding all others.

In the two decades prior to the first wave of pogroms, the Pale had undergone significant social and economic changes. The development of a national railway system, for example, had a negative impact on traditional Jewish occupations. Those who had previously worked as teamsters, itinerant peddlers, or petty merchants found it increasingly difficult to sustain a livelihood. A hypercompetitive market developed, and Christian contemporaries often accused Jews of price fixing, collusion, and the production of shoddy merchandise.[4] These tensions also coincided with the emancipation of the serfs in 1861, a seminal event that actually placed new burdens on the peasantry. Many were required to pay inflated prices to the nobles for land the former serfs considered theirs by divine right.[5] Illiterate peasants no longer held the protection of the local nobility and remained as a segregated class that was saddled with debt and limited credit. The demise of serfdom, an institution that endured for two centuries, was thus not without major drawbacks and social turmoil.[6] This period also marked the economic decline of the landed nobles; many abandoned agricultural pursuits altogether and moved to the cities. Moreover, a rise in Pan-Slavism, nihilism, socialism, and a revolutionary underground intent on the overthrow of Tsar Alexander II (1818–1881) further added to socioeconomic and political uncertainty. Given such an unstable and weakened state structure, vulnerable citizenries, such as the Jews, were at a much greater risk of violence.[7] In this instance, the most obvious trigger that helped set anti-Jewish violence into motion was the assassination of Alexander II in March 1881, a deeply unsettling and destabilizing episode in Russian history. Indeed, research indicates that pogroms are far more likely to occur when state authority has suffered a loss of power during periods of political conflict and crisis.[8]

The initial pogrom took place on 15 April (Easter week) in Elisavetgrad, an important Ukrainian city of 43,000 located in the southern Pale. This was not simply an isolated and spontaneous attack but an event that was intimately linked to the political and social currents of the country. Rumors surfaced throughout Russia that blamed Jews for the regicide and avoided any notice of the radical revolutionaries (Narodnaia Volia) who were the actual perpetrators. Furthermore, newspapers located in the cities of St. Petersburg, Vilna, Kiev, and Odessa published a series of anti-Jewish articles that contributed to an atmosphere of hatred. Stoking this situation even more, false reports claimed that the new Tsar Alexander III (1845–1894) had issued a "spoliation ukase" that ordered the Russian people to avenge the former tsar's murder by attacking the Jews and their property.[9] There was ample reason to expect that violence would eventually break out somewhere in the Pale, especially since Easter typically marked the high point of enmity toward Jews. Most were unprepared, however, not only for the level of brutality and devastation that took place but the widespread nature of the pogroms and their ability to endure over time.

In Elisavetgrad an argument between a Jewish tavern owner and a gentile patron provoked an intensity of mob brutality that had never been witnessed before in this provincial center. Like the previous Romanian pogroms, destruction of property was systematically carried out; many Jews were beaten and suffered severe injuries, reports of rape were widespread (although, it appears, this particular claim may have been overstated by the media[10]), and several died as a result of these attacks. A general state of ruin and homelessness engulfed the city's substantial Jewish community of thirteen thousand. "A cry of rage and grief is raised from this unhappy district," declared an anonymous Christian informant.

> The town looks as if it had been devastated by the elements. Whole streets have been literally razed. Almost all the Jews' houses are sacked and all shops plundered. Bonds have been stolen and even destroyed. People but yesterday rich, or at least comfortably well off, are now beggars. Thousands of Jews are homeless and living on public charity. Many are seriously and others slightly wounded, several were killed. Do not imagine I am exaggerating; the picture is, alas! far below the reality.[11]

Some Jews had obviously flourished in cities such as Elisavetgrad. Despite the severe impoverishment of most of their brethren in the Pale, a minority had managed to adapt to the changing economy and prospered in business. An affluent and primarily urban Jewish merchant class had evolved, and it is significant that this group had become the first target of the rioters. After destroying the myriad shops and warehouses, the mob proceeded to enter Jewish homes, pillaging and wrecking the buildings and sacking the synagogues. Attempts by the police and military to quell the violence proved ineffectual.[12] After this massive assault, eyewitnesses described the heaps of broken furniture and scattered personal effects that clogged the streets. In what would become an iconic image of all the riots, massive piles of feathers from ripped pillows and bedding carpeted the scene. Whatever the initial mob failed to destroy or carry away, a second wave consisting of peasants from a nearby village eagerly finished off in their own quest for "Jewish loot."[13] During the two days of this rampage, hundreds of houses were destroyed, and losses were placed in the millions of rubles. Similar attacks spread beyond Elisavetgrad and terrorized a wide swath of the Pale. The London *Times*, in an influential and provocative series of articles, later reported that a cadre of professional ringleaders or agents provocateurs was often at the center of these events; printed placards were later discovered that falsely proclaimed that the tsar had awarded Jewish property to Christians.[14] The total number of pogroms in 1881–1882 alone has been placed at 259.[15] This figure, however, just as the number of victims and the total financial losses, is at best a broad estimate.[16] Nevertheless, it is quite clear that the waves of anti-Jewish riots dwarfed the Romanian atrocities and represented a degree of systematic violence that was unparalleled in modern Europe. Another factor in this brutal insurgence was the participation of unemployed transients, many of whom were former soldiers who were recently mustered out of the army following the Russo-Turkish War.[17] These men traveled to Ukraine and other parts of the Pale (via recently completed railroads) from ethnic Russia in a mostly futile search for jobs. Landless and out-of-work peasants were also included in the so-called barefoot brigade that had formed part of the mob.[18] Lack of appropriate police response throughout the duration of these outbreaks, a portion of which directly coincided with Christian religious holidays, only encouraged additional cases of "riot, rapine, murder and spoliation."[19] The government blamed revolutionaries for fomenting the pogroms; others assigned culpability to the Pan-Slavists (it still remains uncertain if there was a concerted effort by any one group). Despite this lack of accountability, waves of rioting and destruction resulted in thousands of homeless, injured, and impoverished families and were a significant factor in the eventual mass exodus of Jews.

Another look at the precipitating event in Elisavetgrad—the dispute between tavern owner and patron—adds some understanding as to why these Jews became the targets of such unprecedented animosity. For social theorists who interpret collective violence through the lens of social control, the quarrel itself becomes especially illustrative.[20] A typical publican held a position of power as this individual routinely extended or denied credit and inevitably enforced a code of proper conduct over a primarily lower-class clientele.[21] By virtue of their occupation, Jewish tavern keepers were also most visibly associated with the problem of peasant drunkenness. The fact that this incident triggered such massive retaliation was therefore indicative of a much deeper grievance in the community. Unilateral aggression usually serves as a method of righting a wrong, at least in the minds of those perpetrating the violence, by reestablishing traditional social parameters and control. In other words, any Jew, whether in the role of tavern keeper, store owner, or aspiring agriculturalist, would inevitably cross behavioral boundaries; since all displays of autonomy or authority on the part of Jews threatened the social hierarchy, resentment festered. It is perhaps unsurprising that the most successful pogromist rallying cry was: "The Jews will rule over us."[22] A Russian official summarized this situation with typical pessimism: "In all spheres of public life, the Jews are a sinister force directed against the Russian people and the existing order of things, a force against which, in the eyes of the people, neither individuals nor the state can prevail."[23]

Jonathan Frankel touched upon this issue in his well-known study of this period. In his explanation of the views of Moshe Lilienblum, a prominent Russian Jewish advocate of Palestinian immigration, Frankel notes that Lilienblum not only "cast doubt on the central assumption which had motivated two generations of maskilim in Russia" but had entirely reversed these preconceptions. Previously it was thought that the more "useful" Jews were to society, the more they would gain approval. "Now Lilienblum argued that the opposite was true," notes Frankel. "To be useful at any level meant to be successful, and success was dangerous." So dangerous, in fact, that it appeared to Lilienblum and others that the horrors of the "Middle Ages" had returned.[24] For increasing numbers of Jews, therefore, massive antisemitic attacks were seen as inevitable; the only recourse was to emigrate.

In contrast to lynching, where violence is directed at individuals, certain social theorists look upon rioting as a method of enforcing a concept of collective liability; men, women, children, and the elderly are thus all subject to the most egregious attacks. Normal controls and restraints are suspended under such circumstances. In this case, the fabrication of tsarist approval was certainly a convenient method of sanctioning brutality. The most severe forms of collective violence tend to occur whenever functional independence, interpersonal and cultural distance, as well as inequality are strongest between contested groups.[25] While there were certainly no ghetto walls or gates, most Jews resided in separate quarters in the towns and cities and were not entirely integrated into the social milieu. Jewish merchants traded and interacted with gentiles, but they frequently relied on business networks that were unconnected to their gentile contemporaries. On a cultural level—and quite distinct from the financial elites who served as "court Jews" to the tsars in St. Petersburg—the Jews of the Pale stood as a pariah group: "a large tribe completely alien to the native population." Not unlike the situation between blacks and whites in the postbellum American South, the "best" individuals in each camp kept their social distance from one another; they stood as mutual outsiders and were markedly unequal in status.[26] They remained, according to historian John Klier, "a compact, culturally distinct population"—a true "people apart."[27] Hence, contrary to Lilienblum's assumptions, some Jews may have enjoyed the outward trappings and status of economic success, but they were hardly assimilationists in the full sense of this term. Another contributing factor to the rioting, according to theory, was the composition of various "barefoot brigades"—the proverbial outside agitators. As many of these persons were strangers from well beyond community borders, violence became even more likely. All these factors constituted a very high degree of social polarization and thus are directly related to the probability of violent behavior. Most significantly, the level of polarization also increased the odds that brutal force would be employed against all Jews (collective liability) and for an extended period of time.[28]

As a form of contentious politics, collective violence, no matter how abhorrent, stakes some sort of claim upon the government. Charges of exploitation, real or imagined, frequently enter the political arena.[29] Following the initial wave of attacks, the Russian government, in an act that left many liberal Europeans utterly perplexed, sided with the pogromists in their complaints of an unequal playing field. Instead of making attempts at restitution toward the injured and severely distressed Jews, Interior Minister Nikolai Ignatiev (1832–1908), a noted Judeophobe who used the findings of the commissions of inquiry that were established as a cover for his own prejudiced views, attributed the rioting and devastation (what he labeled as "protests") to "Jewish exploitation."[30] The so-called May Laws then placed a new set of limitations on Jewish commerce and on where Jews could reside. While there is no indication that either the tsar or the central government were directly involved in the pogroms, the legislative concession to those who perpetrated these crimes delivered a substantial rebuke to Russian Jewry and seemed to give "Imperial sanction" for the continuation of hostilities.[31] It is small wonder that this era produced such depths of disillusionment within the Russian Jewish intelligentsia. "They had not rejected Russia," as Frankel emphasized, "Russia had rejected them."[32] It was at this time that Leo Pinsker (1821–1891), the Russian Jewish author of *Auto-Emancipation*, presented his pessimistic appraisal of the Jewish position in gentile society and proposed a radical solution to the recurrent suffering—that of Jewish nationalism and the establishment of a separate homeland.

> The Jews in the Occident have again learned to endure the cry of "Hep, hep!" as their fathers did in days gone by. The flaming outburst of indignation at the disgrace endured has turned into a rain of ashes which is gradually covering the soil. Close your eyes and hide your heads in ostrich-fashion as you will, if you do not take advantage of the fleeting moment of repose, and devise remedies more radical than those palliatives with which incompetents have for centuries vainly tried to relieve our unhappy people, lasting peace is impossible for you.[33]

BRITAIN AND AMERICA RESPOND

Despite the proliferation of Jewish social movement organizations in the major European capitals and in America, London was still regarded as the activist center of the movement in the 1880s. Throughout the past half-century, calls for Jewish protests had first emanated from the metropolis, but after months of news regarding the pogroms, the London leadership remained uncommonly silent. Aside from sending a large delegation to discuss the Russian persecutions with Foreign Secretary Lord Granville in May 1881 and a formal memorial that was fashioned seven months later that never reached the tsar (the Russian ambassador refused to transmit the document), the leadership kept a low profile.[34] For his part, Prime Minister Gladstone was disinclined to interfere in the matter. It should be noted that most of the earlier Jewish leaders in England, such as Francis Goldsmid and Abraham Benisch, had passed away (Adolphe Crémieux had also died two years earlier). Moses Montefiore was the exception; although at ninety-seven he was no longer part of the active organizational elite. The Anglo-Jewish Association, the Board of Deputies, and the newly formed Russo-Jewish Committee continued to adhere to the cautious "insider" approach that had gained the upper hand during the Romanian crises. The situation in the Pale was so massive and volatile that the bankers and financiers who were now in the movement's front ranks did not want to risk exacerbating matters by utilizing the more aggressive techniques of the past. This position was maintained despite the universal condemnation of Russia by the major press of England. As one Jewish editorialist noted incredulously, "On what other subject could it even be fancied that the *Times, Daily News, Standard, Telegraph, Morning Post, Pall Mall Gazette, Saturday Review,* and *Spectator* would join in one sentiment with one voice?"[35] Nevertheless, by January 1882, after additional mob attacks were reported in an outbreak in Warsaw on Christmas Day, and the fact that a Mansion House protest was scheduled for the first time without the active support of the Jewish community, Sir Nathaniel de Rothschild, chairman of the Russo-Jewish Committee, actually conceded that "the position of the Jews would be considerably strengthened if the movement was allowed to emanate from Christians."[36]

Asher Myers (1848–1902), the new editor of the *Jewish Chronicle* and Benisch's former assistant, took passionate exception to the committee's withdrawal from the political public sphere. In an unusually fiery editorial, Myers lamented that England no longer had "a Sir Francis Goldsmid to act with energy and decision in the midst of aimlessness and lethargy." If London Jews failed to speak up for their persecuted brethren in Russia and refused "to lead the movement," Myers concluded that such a relinquishment of responsibility would "ruin the cause irretrievably." "If the Jews are not moved by these events, no other class of men need apologize for being lukewarm or indifferent."[37] Similarly, a full-page article in the *Chronicle*

Figure 8.1 Coverage of the Russian pogroms by the British press was remarkably sympathetic toward the Jews, and newspaper accounts inevitably stressed the senseless mob brutality that was inflicted upon an innocent population.

Source: *Illustrated London News*, 4 June 1881.

authored by the pseudonymous "Jurisconsultus" excoriated the Jewish establishment in the harshest terms and saw their refusal to sponsor a protest meeting as nothing less than "*a crisis in Jewish history*" and a betrayal of all that had been gained in the past. "If they do not see and act upon this principle," the author declared, "the world might soon ask why they were ever let out of the ghetto at all, and perhaps talk of sending them back there."[38]

Such heated expressions of defiance toward the communal notables had not occurred since the initial movement of 1827, at least not to the degree that managed to rise to the level of public scrutiny. Myers's editorials, articles by Jurisconsultus, and the public support of Sir Francis Goldsmid's widow, Lady Louisa Goldsmid, a leader in the women's suffrage movement, managed to rouse the provincial leadership to take action on their own.[39] "The voice of the multitude" was first raised at a protest meeting at the Hebrew Congregation of Birmingham on 22 January. Speakers not only roundly condemned the Russian atrocities, but in a manner analogous to Moses Levy's rebuke of the communal elite, they ridiculed the London leadership for being "too much rocked in the cradle of luxury" and proclaimed that Birmingham Jews stood proudly apart from such indifference.[40] This volley was followed by similar protests in Brighton and at the Anglo-Jewish Association chapters in Manchester and Liverpool.[41] Stung by recriminations that the wealthy Jews of London were unable to "accurately perceive what such emergencies require," Chief Rabbi Hermann Adler defended the decisions of the communal leadership as maintaining the best possible course, given that "the present crisis is altogether of a different complexion" from previous outrages and thus required far more restraint in the public sphere.[42] Undeterred, the *Chronicle* increasingly featured the activities within the provinces rather than center all attention on the now staid London establishment. While these efforts hardly succeeded in wrenching control from the metropolis, at least some action had been taken by Jews before the much-anticipated Mansion House affair on 1 February.

As expected, the Mansion House meeting generated much excitement in London and drew worldwide press notice. Aside from the lord mayor, the earl of Shaftesbury, and the bishops of London and Oxford, for the first time a Roman Catholic prelate, Cardinal Manning (1808–1892)—a noted convert from Anglicanism and the head of the Catholic Church in England—took his place among the speakers. As it happened, Jewish communal leaders ultimately decided that attendance was mandatory; Sir Nathaniel de Rothschild, Sir Albert Sassoon, Sir Julian Goldsmid, Alfred de Rothschild, Lionel Cohen, and others were seated in the hall, although none were speakers. The entire list of Christian and Jewish luminaries, a virtual inventory of London's high society, was posted in the *Times* along with transcripts of all the speeches.[43] Unlike the 1840 assembly, this latest manifestation at Egyptian Hall was not skewed toward the London merchants but was intended as a display of philanthropic unity among a broad cross-section of the elite class, both secular and religious. Despite the presence of the elderly Shaftesbury, the spirit of evangelical fervor was no longer ascendant in England, and, as a whole, society was less predisposed to expressions of religious zeal and Romantic sentiment.[44] Despite this altered environment, the meeting included a celebrity endorsement from England's poet laureate Alfred Tennyson, which was read from the podium, and statements of other notables who were unable (or unwilling) to attend in person, such as the chief rabbi, were read aloud by the lord mayor. Each was greeted with loud applause. After introductory remarks, the main speakers went to some length to assure the public that their protest was well above the tumult of party politics. They had no intention of entering the political fray by criticizing the current British government or imputing the internal affairs of Russia. Deference "toward his Imperial Majesty of Russia" was awarded unusual priority, and it was stressed that "human sympathy and human justice" was what motivated their efforts, not politics. While the resolutions did not hesitate to pass judgment on the actions of the Russian government or its "laws that tend to degrade [Jews] in the eyes of the Christian population" and expose them "to the outbreaks of fanatical ignorance," the tenor was in a lower key than previous efforts.[45] Of all the orators, Cardinal Manning excoriated the actions of Interior Minister Ignatiev to the fullest, and also made the strongest case for "laws larger than any Russian legislation—the laws of humanity and of God, which are the foundation of all other laws."[46] In effect, Manning postulated a view of natural law that had been previously denounced by the Vatican during the Mortara affair. In the end, a special Mansion House fund was established for the Jewish relief agencies, such as the Alliance Israélite Universelle, to aid in an ongoing emigration movement to the United States—a cause that had now entered mainstream acceptance. Hermann Adler, now convinced that the only appropriate course to follow was emigration, pronounced it "the duty of every Jewish resident in the British Empire to contribute, according to his means" to the Mansion House fund.[47] In two weeks, the amount reached £42,550.

The London meeting was planned to coincide with a similar event in New York City held at Chickering Hall (also on 1 February) chaired by Mayor William R. Grace, a millionaire philanthropist and the city's first Irish American Catholic mayor. Many of New York's eminent citizens attended, and the spacious hall was filled beyond capacity, including a considerable number of Jews. Among the speakers was the popular New York politician William M. Evarts, recently retired as U.S. secretary of state, as well as several prominent Fifth Avenue pastors. Similar in tone to the Mansion House proceedings, speakers condemned Russia's pogroms in relatively restrained terms.[48] One individual proved to be the exception to the rule: Rev. Dr. Howard Crosby, a Presbyterian minister and chancellor of New York University, openly balked at the prevailing diplomatic tone. He insisted that he "could not stand there and compliment or say nothing antagonistic to the Russian Empire."

> He did not believe in the remedy suggested by Judge Davis [a previous speaker] for he had lived too long in New York to believe that law was effective (great applause) unless backed up by a strong, healthy public opinion. (Applause.) What Russia wanted was not law, but change of heart. Russia was barbaric, no matter how courteous we might want to be! (Applause.) The marks of her barbarism were in the two extremes of her society, Nihilism and Czarism, the first the legitimate child of the last.... God's vengeance would yet overtake those who oppressed [the Jews], and it was the glory of America that it had welcomed the Israelites and found in them the purest and best elements of her republican strength and liberty.[49]

Crosby's remarks (actually omitted by some New York papers) remain as one of the few critiques to emerge in the media. Not only had Christians taken the lead in the public sphere, as Nathaniel de Rothschild preferred, but there is no doubt that emotional restraint dominated. The event at Chickering Hall, according to the *New York Times* headlines, constituted a "sympathy meeting"—no longer was "indignation" an appropriate descriptor. "Tame and genteel" was the negative reaction of Isaac Wise to both meetings—he even suggested in the *Israelite* that the first resolution of these gatherings should have read: "Resolved, That Count Ignatiev [whom Wise believed orchestrated the pogroms] ought to be hanged as high as Haman."[50] Calmer minds prevailed among the movement leaders, however, and provocation was minimized—ostensibly from a desire to minimize the risk of reprisals against Russian Jewry. Indeed, immediately following the sympathy meetings and amid rumors that Britain would lodge some form of diplomatic complaint against the atrocities, Russia issued a thinly veiled threat in St. Petersburg that declared that it would not abide any form of interference in its internal affairs. Among other things, warned the government, such behavior "would create discontent and irritation among the Russian masses, and injure the position of the Jews."[51] Furthermore, these assemblies coincided with an insurgent "Anti-Semitic movement" (*Judenhetze*) that had surfaced in Germany a few years earlier, a movement that stirred hatred of Jews based on theories of racial supremacy rather than religion alone (the forerunner of Nazi antisemitism). The development of such blatant intolerance was mentioned with increasing frequency by the liberal press, and in fact the antisemitic movement was singled out for condemnation by Cardinal Manning at Mansion House as it was widely assumed that this insurgence had sparked the diabolical behavior in Russia.[52] Despite the objections that were lodged in the *Israelite*, the New York and London meetings nevertheless made important claims in the public sphere—messages that were aimed at supporters, adversaries, numerous world governments, and the public at large—and the resulting publicity inspired an intense flurry of meetings that followed in their wake. The most forceful mobilizations occurred in the British provinces: town hall meetings in support of the Russian Jews were presided over by mayors in Liverpool, Birmingham, Hull, Leicester, Falmouth, Bristol, Ramsgate, Portsmouth, Southampton, Sunderland, Wolverhampton, Sheffield, Brighton, Coventry, Swansea, Cambridge, and Oxford as well as the cities of Edinburgh, Glasgow, and Dublin.[53] The remarkable response in the United Kingdom, therefore, far exceeded the protests during the Damascus affair. "England, the mother of free peoples, has spoken," declared the now ecstatic Myers in the *Chronicle*. The fact that this was primarily a Christian movement no longer appeared as problematic as once feared. "It is a hearty and almost universal demonstration of the right feeling of this great people of whom we are proud to form not the least loyal part."[54] In the United States, the number of city-sponsored protests was not as numerous. Following Chickering Hall, mass meetings, usually featuring state and local politicians as well as mainstream Protestant and Catholic clergy, took place in Brooklyn, Philadelphia, and New Orleans. These assemblies each formulated resolutions and called upon Congress and President Chester A. Arthur to present official protests to the Russian government.[55]

While there were no protest meetings in France, the Russian pogroms did unleash a flurry of indignation from the French press.[56] In addition, author Victor Hugo published a poignant denunciation of the Russian barbarities in the Paris papers, an article that was translated and reprinted throughout the world.[57] Hugo also chaired the Committee for the Relief of the Russian Jews that was established in Paris specifically for soliciting funds for humanitarian relief. Newspapers such as the *Journal du Jura* and *Quatorze Juillet* joined in the fund-raising, and significant sums arrived even from provinces with little or no Jewish population. The combined efforts of Hugo and a separate fund headed by financier Alphonse de Rothschild amounted to an impressive 800,000 francs.[58]

EMIGRATION MOVEMENT

News of the protest mobilization in the United Kingdom and the meetings in the United States made a deep impression among Russian Jews. Moreover, the *Chronicle*'s public scolding of the London elite did not escape the attention of an influential cohort of Russian Jewish writers and journalists. Indeed, as John Klier has noted, the "Jewish newspapers in London play[ed] as vital a role as the press in the Russian capital."[59] All the leading Jewish periodicals were widely circulated among the editorial offices of the Jewish press, and outside articles were often selected for translation and republication. The editors of the Russian Jewish papers, such as *Razsvet* (Dawn) and the more conservative *Russkii evrei* (Russian Jew) in St. Petersburg were thus cognizant of the accusations that were cast against Anglo-Jewish leaders. Such incendiary views, so freely expressed, were antithetical to the more conservative communal status quo in Russia. The wealthy St. Petersburg notables led by Baron Goratsii Gintsburg (1833–1909) were largely immune from any questioning of their authority. Criticism aimed at the inaction of communal leaders in England thus spoke directly to Russian Jews, as the ravages in the Pale hardly inspired Gintsburg and his fellow elites to abandon their discreet, privileged roles within the corridors of power in favor of lodging protests in the public sphere. The Russian Jewish press, however, had long maintained the accepted protocol and had not yet criticized the notables, even though an increasingly condemnatory tone regarding the pogroms had emerged in the pages of *Razsvet*; indeed, the topic of emigration was even breeched.[60] In January 1882, coinciding with the *Chronicle*'s repudiation of the London magnates, another shift took hold among the *Razsvet* staff. Unlike in England, where the tradition of public protest meetings had long been a sine quo non, the single most contentious issue for Jews in Russia at this date—and the subject that would fracture the hold of the oligarchs on communal affairs—was the burgeoning emigration movement. In the face of all that had transpired, Gintsburg's circle remained loyal to the assimilationist ideal and thereby opposed the emigration proposals that had first been presented by Western agencies some months earlier. In a series of editorials, *Razsvet* declared it was time to come to terms both with the severity of the crisis and the changing nature of Russian society. The paper then bypassed traditional channels by publishing the results of an interview with Count Ignatiev entirely on their own authority, an act that constituted a grave breach of protocol in the eyes of the oligarchs.[61] Yet the newspaper staff—consisting of Illiel Orshanksy, Mordekhay Ha-Cohen, and Iakov Rozenfeld—continued on their populist path and advocated free and unfettered emigration and declared that the Russian community as a whole, not a foreign agency such as the Alliance, should select candidates for emigration.[62] Provincial leaders in the Pale were also urged to take responsibility for the emigration problem and to ignore the presumptive authority of the St. Petersburg oligarchs. A campaign was launched by the elite to undermine the credibility of *Razsvet*, and a divisive period of "agitation" that included meetings, petitions, letters to the editor, and even occasional death threats ensued. By February and March, most Russian Jews were not only separated into pro- and antiemigration camps, but among the former, the focus of settlement was further divided into Palestinian (*Palestintsy*) and American (*Amerikantsy*) factions. A key attribute of social movements—the appearance of an insurgent reality—therefore became more pronounced among Russian Jews than any other Jewish community at this time. What had evolved into a transnational humanitarian movement among Christians and Jews in the West turned into a highly contentious social movement in Russia. In both cases, the emigration movement assumed a distinct identity and can thus be conceived as a spin-off from the Jewish rights movement. In Russia this mobilization influenced other movements, including Zionism, but the initial period of contention among Jewish writers and journalists began with the issue of emigration and then progressed into a revolt against the "Petersburg millionaires."[63]

Emigration as a tangible issue first came to the fore in July 1881, as the Alliance in Paris initially attempted to deal with the pogroms, a crisis that—more than any other subject—defined its very existence: the defense of worldwide Jewry.[64] The Alliance decided to act on two fronts: to send representatives to Russia to report on the situation firsthand and to reexamine the subject of a mass departure from Russia. Ironically, given the Peixotto incident in Brussels, the Alliance agreed that the United States, "a vast, rich and free land," rather than Palestine or any other locale, would be the best choice for any migration scheme.[65] Despite the tentative nature of these plans, rumors began to spread, and by late August approximately five hundred desperate Russian Jewish refugees, all of whom assumed that their transport and expenses to America would be paid for and arranged by the Alliance, became stranded in pitiable condition in the Galician town of Brody located a few miles from the Russian border in Austro-Hungary [Brody would become a staging area for thousands of future emigrants, headed primarily for the United States, for several decades]. Nevertheless, the prospect of leaving Russia for new beginnings elsewhere captured the attention of Russian Jews by offering hope and deliverance for one segment of the community, while it simultaneously provoked other factions by its failure to face Russian society on its own terms and its attraction to the young, who seemed all too ready to depart the homeland and to embrace quick answers to complex problems. The cause nonetheless drew support from a variety of Jewish provincial newspapers in Vilna, Odessa, Grodno, Kiev, and Warsaw. As one might expect, the center of support was in the Pale, while those who were opposed were generally located farthest from scenes of collective violence.

The Hebrew Emigrant Aid Society (founded in November 1881 in New York City in response to the first influx of Russian Jewish immigrants) began to coordinate full-scale emigration with affiliates throughout the United States and with both the Mansion House Committee in London and the Alliance in Paris.[66] In April 1882 an international conference met in Berlin to further define and streamline the technical operations of this mass exodus.[67] After being first approved by a committee in Vienna, emigrants were sent on to Berlin, London, and then once more by ship to New York City, where their final destinations in the United States were ultimately carried out.[68] Within a span of several months, eight thousand Russian Jews arrived in America in this first large-scale international Jewish relief effort. [Between 1880 and 1920, more than two million Eastern European Jews—one-third of the population—left the Old World for the United States, radically impacting communal life in America.[69]] By no means can this massive influx be attributed to trauma of the pogroms alone. Indeed, there were profound social and economic factors at play, for both Jews and non-Jews.[70] And it should be noted that Jewish migration was not without significant instances of inter- and intracommunal strife. Even so, there is little question that without the preexisting organizational networks set in place by the Jewish rights movement, such an enormous demographic shift would have been considerably impeded.

MODERN JEWISH POLITICS IN RUSSIA

The astonishing rise in Jewish consciousness and political action that ensued during and after the Russian pogroms of 1881–1882 has been a topic of considerable scholarly interest. While it is not the intention of the present study to offer a detailed historiographical analysis, it is nevertheless important to note that many of the themes expressed in the current chapter bear a direct relationship to Eli Lederhendler's influential monograph, *The Road to Modern Jewish Politics* (1989).[71] In this work Lederhendler explored the evolving Jewish political sphere of pre-1881 Russia and found that a significant foundation existed prior to the upsurge in emigration-centered politics. Contrary to an earlier view held by Jonathan Frankel, who believed that this point in history represented nothing less than a "revolution in modern Jewish politics,"[72] Lederhendler, in a thesis that still resonates today, argued that Russian Jewry had already transitioned from the isolation of the traditional *kahal*—the executive communal body that formerly oversaw communal life in Russia and Poland and which had been abolished by the Russian state in 1844. Hence, not only were the Jews of the Pale no strangers to the political sphere, but the disintegration of the *kahal* system apparently accelerated a drive toward modernity.[73] Integral to this transformation, according to Lederhendler, was the increasing influence of a group of prominent and outspoken *maskilim* (adherents of the *Haskalah* or Jewish Enlightenment) between the decades of 1830 and 1870.[74] These Europeanized individuals filled the political vacuum that existed after the termination of the *kahal*. The time-worn role of the *shtadlanim* was eventually co-opted by politically well-connected *maskilim* who supported attempts by ranking government bureaucrats to bring Russian Jewry into the modern orbit. The function of a Jewish press—both as an arena of conflict as well as the primary means with which to influence public opinion (*da'at hakahal*)—was also crucial to the development of a distinct Russian Jewish political sphere.[75]

Lederhendler has been lauded for presenting a detailed and nuanced view of Russian Jewish political life before 1881. The author offers tangible insights, not the least of which is placing the mass disillusionment and ideological reconstruction that emerged into more complete context. On the other hand, it is hardly surprising—given the dearth of research into the subject—that Lederhendler omitted any mention of a Jewish rights movement, even when emphasizing the impact that the leading movement personalities, such as Moses Montefiore and Adolphe Crémieux, had upon the Russian *maskilim*, newspaper editors, and rabbis. This group not only looked to the *Haskalah* movement for inspiration during the pre-Crisis years, but, as Lederhendler actually suggests, the various campaigns that spanned the Atlantic on behalf of persecuted foreign Jews also made a deep impression on Russian Jewry.

If the *maskilim* were playing leadership roles in Russian Jewish politics by 1881, it was only attributable, as Lederhendler states, to a distinct behavioral change. Despite their previous position on the "extreme periphery of Jewish life," over the course of two decades the *maskilim* attained a "beachhead of considerable strategic advantage."[76] Lederhendler viewed the *maskilim*'s appropriation and redefinition of the traditional role of the *shtadlan*, which now included a public component—that of social critic and Jewish defender—as decisive. Interlaced throughout the book, however, are repeated references to the Damascus and Mortara affairs. As the author posits, Western Jewish rights leaders constituted a new model for Russian Jews to emulate.[77] The result was a distinct amalgam; a reinvention of the *shtadlanut* that combined the broad goals, values, and public function of noted Jewish rights figures with the regional political agenda and sensibility that was specific to the Russian *maskilim*. Unfortunately, Lederhendler does not adequately underscore this topic's significance and instead emphasizes "underlying structural changes" in the political life of Russian Jews.[78]

An excellent case in point is the stance taken by Mordecai Gunzberg. This nineteenth-century scholar and *maskil* was quite precise in relaying what had been gained by the Damascus blood libel and the Mortara affair. "Our foes come against us with force, and we fortify our position with truth," Gunzberg wrote in 1859. As a result, Western Jews "no longer, as they had of old, took their shame quietly." Instead of fasting, "wailing and mourning," and trusting only in Divine Providence, these modern Jews had armed themselves with the "truth" and many had entered the public sphere by editorializing in leading newspapers. Not only had they taken up the pen, but Moses Montefiore, who Gunzberg esteemed, used direct political leverage against the viceroy of Egypt on behalf of all his brethren. The traditional ideals of wealth and learning no longer sufficed. Instead, courage, valor, and decisive action had become mandatory.[79] The learned *maskil* had actually defined the kind of identity politics that had first supplanted the "mask of quietism" in 1827 London and attained eminence thereafter.

In the view of an anonymous contributor to *Ha-Maggid* (1863), not only was there a need for "men of wise heart and courage who fight God's battles in debating their enemies," but among "the saviors" of an era that the author envisioned as a proud new age, there also happened to be splendid organizations such as the Alliance Israélite Universelle as well as a plethora of "Jewish newspapers and their writers and supporters" who communicated tirelessly, not only in Hebrew but in most of the major languages.[80] Following the Mortara kidnapping, Eliezer Silbermann, publisher of *Ha-Maggid*, echoed many of the same sentiments as Abraham Benisch in the *Chronicle*. Similar to Benisch before him, Silbermann compared the power of public opinion to a force greater than any army.[81] Clearly, then, the Pale of Settlement did not exist in isolation from the rest of Europe, and it was through the newspaper medium that the ideals and actions of Jewish rights proponents became known to the world's largest Jewish community.

Lederhendler thus makes a solid case, albeit unintentionally, for two primary ways that the campaign for Jewish rights impacted Russian Jewish politics.

First, by adopting the forthright and principled stance of Jewish rights leaders, the *maskilim* were able to achieve far more credibility than relying on the *Haskalah* movement alone. Consequently, this heretofore marginalized and despised minority achieved the sort of political power that had previously eluded them. Second, the practical utilization of the Jewish press by a cohort of "enlightened" editors and writers, along with their appeal to public opinion, can now be seen as directly linked to the steady growth of Jewish rights activism and its intrinsic reliance on the press. As in Western Europe, Britain, and America, ideas were openly contested and rigorously debated in the Jewish press, and the revolutionary concept of the "voice of the people" became a force of political cohesion. In short, it was not only the abolition of the *kahal* and the inspiration of the *Haskalah* that accelerated the drive toward modernity in Russia. Amid the heady mix of novel concepts that flourished during the nineteenth century, one has to award due credit to the power and sway of the transnational Jewish rights campaign.

FIN DE SIÈCLE

For the most part, Jewish protest mobilizations in the West went into a period of abeyance during the last two decades of the nineteenth century, a phase that corresponded with a reduction of violence in Russia. Activity thus centered on the emigration movement instead. Banker and philanthropist Baron Maurice de Hirsch, for example, founded the Jewish Colonization Association in London (1891) and provided enormous sums for Russian Jewish agricultural colonies in North and South America. In marked contrast, public protests remained the primary responsibility of Christians. On 10 December 1890 in London, over two thousand people attended what was billed as the "Great Public Meeting at Guildhall"—the tradition of grand Mansion House–style meetings thereby continued, albeit in a different City venue. On this occasion, protests by eminent Christians against the threatened enforcement of anti-Jewish laws proved more forceful than in 1882.[82] The combined effect of the forthcoming resolutions and oratory, what the British ambassador in St. Petersburg referred to as "a volume of furious irritation," gained broad publicity.[83] In this instance, the Russian government was even more defiant than before, asserting that "if the whole of Europe were turned into a pro-Jewish meeting, Russia would still remain self-contained and independent."[84] In an act that seemed to confirm people's worst fears, a ukase was issued in March 1891 that nullified previous measures that admitted Jewish "artisans, craftsmen and workmen" to the city of Moscow—an estimated twenty thousand Jews were uprooted and ordered to abandon their homes and livelihoods and then forcibly transported by railroad to the Pale.[85] [A scene that was reminiscent of the concerns of 1827.]

"A Crisis in Jewish History" 157

Figure 8.2 The Bishop of Ripon delivers a stirring oration on behalf of the Jews of Russia before an audience of two thousand at the "Great Public Meeting at Guildhall," one of the last of the elite-style protest meetings in London.
Source: Illustrated London News, 20 December 1890.

Even while Judeophobia continued its hold in Russia and the German antisemitic movement gained force, many Jews still adhered to a confident worldview. Despite the presence of powerful enemies, Jews had made outstanding gains; it appeared that adversities had only made them stronger and more unified. A much more vital and dynamic sense of peoplehood had indeed surfaced, whereas just a few generations earlier Jews were widely dispersed and manifested a decidedly insular outlook. Rev. Dr. Henry Pereira Mendes, a respected author, graduate of University College London, former British rabbi, a medical doctor, Zionist, and now minister of New York's Shearith Israel congregation, exemplified this positivist mind-set in a popular sermon, "Is a New Era Before Judaism?" which was featured in the *New York Herald* in late December 1890. At the beginning of the nineteenth century, noted Pereira Mendes, "we were small, scattered communities, each a little world to itself, with no friction, with current thought, ideas, life itself almost, confined to the synagogue and the duties of religion." Now, toward the end of the century, a great and "miraculous" change had occurred.

> Thanks to our enemies, we have learned our strength. The theft of the Mortara boy and his forced conversion created our Alliance Universelle, with its branches today from Syria to America. . . . The outrages in Russia against the Jews eight years ago . . . gave the impetus to international Jewish conferences. We are thus united. We find we have become a living nation. . . . We stand today equipped with virile strength for self-government; with intellect matured and world recognized; with powers strong to guard and promote the holiest interests of human progress and civilization. . . . Organization also vindicates our claims to human justice and by enlightening the public with facts, make it impossible for a Russia to mock at resolutions condemning her un-Christian policy, such as have been passed by England's noblest prelates and peers, such as have been offered in the Congress of this great land.[86]

Despite the optimistic exhortations of Pereira Mendes, the final decade of the nineteenth century proved especially difficult for Jews. Xenophobic European nationalism and antisemitic fervor flourished. The German Conservative Party, for example, declared that Jews were a "corrosive" element in society, and antisemitism was incorporated into the party platform in 1892 in an attempt to widen electoral appeal. A few years later, the right-wing politician, Karl Lueger, an ardent antisemite, was elected mayor of Vienna. Beginning in 1894, Alfred Dreyfus, a French Jewish army officer, was falsely accused of espionage. This notorious incident aroused condemnatory articles in the press, public protests erupted, and each stage of the Dreyfus trial was followed in minute detail by the media. A "whirlwind of passions swept over France"[87] as well as most of the Western world, and the affair resulted in an extraordinary militancy between Dreyfus supporters and adversaries. The episode nevertheless failed to elicit a significant response from the Consistory or Alliance, the Anglo-Jewish magnates, or even the masses of newly settled Russian Jewish immigrants.[88] Hence, the movement that emerged in reaction to the Dreyfus incident, following an overall trend, consisted mostly of non-Jews. Prominent within the anti-Dreyfus camp was the virulent antisemitic journalist Édouard Drumont and the fanatic Catholic newspaper *La Croix*.[89] The affair has been characterized as a bitter contest for the soul of France, a Manichean struggle played out against a courtroom setting: Truth and Justice, as personified by the Dreyfusards, and the anti-Dreyfusard ideals of Honor and Tradition. The feverish press coverage proved remarkably influential. The Austro-Hungarian journalist, Theodor Herzl, for example, following much the same reasoning as Leo Pinsker before him, concluded (apparently independently) that assimilation was a mere chimera since Jews would, in the final analysis, be regarded as perpetual strangers within gentile nations. The modern political Zionist movement that Herzl led can thus be traced to the feelings of increased alienation that arose at this time.[90] As far as the Jewish rights movement is concerned, however, the dearth of any sustained Jewish protests places the Dreyfus episode on a different trajectory. Although a "monster demonstration" at London's Hyde Park—comprising as many as eighty thousand Dreyfus supporters—briefly surfaced after the second guilty verdict in 1898, this upsurge quickly subsided after a pardon was issued shortly thereafter.[91] The Dreyfusard solidarity campaign, while an extremely influential countermeasure to the mounting forces of European antisemitism, can thus be appreciated as yet another major spin-off from the core Jewish rights movement.[92]

9   The Kishinev Massacre

> *A crime has been committed so black that it casts a shadow upon the sunlight. When the world shall hear what has happened, humanity will sicken at heart, civilization will despair, liberty will vow vengeance. . . . No fire, no plague, no earthquake, could have wrought such havoc as the madness of these Russian monsters.*
>
> Anonymous Kishinev survivor (1903)[1]

> *The Kishinev pogrom was the reply of czarist Russia to the cry of freedom of its Jewish subjects. We knew intuitively that it was not to be the last [pogrom], but rather the signal for a whole series.*
>
> Chaim Weizmann (1949)[2]

Ironically, while the Kishinev massacre of 1903 elicits little recognition outside scholarly circles today, this tragic event was once considered among "the most noted of the *causes célèbre* of the world's history"[3] and generated more mass protests than the Damascus and Mortara affairs combined. The atrocities committed in Kishinev, located in southern Bessarabia (present-day Chisinau, Moldova), became the first humanitarian crisis of the twentieth century to be documented by on-location news photography—gruesome images of distorted corpses were published in myriad newspapers and magazines. Kishinev's persuasive power was thus quite significant.[4] Hayim Nahman Bialik's famous "City of Slaughter," a profoundly moving epic poem now regarded as a classic work of modern Hebrew literature, was written shortly after the massacre and influenced scores of Jews from both inside and outside Russia. Bialik's poem may not have been overtly Zionist, but as one author has aptly noted, the work became "an extended wail on behalf of the Jewish exile as a whole" and a powerful abnegation of diaspora life.[5] In conjunction with other literary and artistic forms, including essays, plays, as well as graphic art, the creative and intellectual by-products of this horrific chapter were emblematic of an intensity of indignation—accentuated by the mass media—which swayed public opinion to a marked degree.

The Kishinev Massacre   161

Details of the collective violence in Kishinev, capital city of Bessarabia, were strikingly similar to the 1881–1882 pogroms. Rumors once again claimed that the tsar—this time Nicholas II—had sanctioned anti-Jewish attacks. As in Elisavetgrad, the Jews in Kishinev constituted a significant segment of the population; in this case, almost half of the city's 110,000 residents.[6] Kishinev also experienced rapid economic expansion and population growth. In a comparatively short time frame, Jews became the city's largest ethnic minority and dominated commerce—a state of affairs that was perceived as a grave threat by the Moldavian and Russian populace.[7] The rioting lasted three days, and, similar to earlier incidents, violence and destruction were tolerated, indeed even promoted, by the local police. The most damage and the majority of the killings occurred in the southeastern section of the city, where relatively affluent, middle-class Jews resided.[8] Also fitting the earlier framework was the fact that the atrocities took place during Easter; included agents provocateurs who, among other acts, disseminated incendiary leaflets well ahead of the actual mob attacks; and was carried out by a group of outsiders as well as locals.[9] The violent frenzy resulted in murder, hundreds of injured and maimed, and the indiscriminate destruction or theft of property valued in the millions of rubles. In a final gesture of humiliation—as if adhering to a well-known, macabre script—the Kishinev mob covered their dead victims, even entire streets in the Jewish quarters, with masses of white feathers in a type of shaming ritual.[10]

The pogrom also took a cue from the past and employed the blood libel. For many months *Bessarabets*, an antisemitic tabloid that was sanctioned by authorities as the city's sole local newspaper, published a relentless series of anti-Jewish diatribes. In February the body of a teenaged Christian boy was found with multiple stab wounds in a nearby town. Despite local police reports that denied any Jewish connection to this killing, the government-subsidized *Bessarabets* accused Jews of ritual murder and featured inflammatory rhetoric and hate-filled headlines as part of a campaign to incite violence. Leaflets were also distributed, and their purpose was quite explicit: "Let us join on Easter Day in the cry 'Down with the Jews!' Let us massacre these sanguinary monsters who slake their thirst with Russian blood!"[11] Incitement thus appeared highly organized. Given that the region suffered from a financial downturn, which was then exacerbated by drought and crop failure, the preconditions for hostile action were firmly set. Prior to the mob attacks, Christian houses were chalk-marked with white crosses in order to spare them from destruction. According to some reports, the local Orthodox bishop was hardly a disinterested observer, and in a surreal scene he extended his holiday blessings upon the mob during his Easter carriage ride through the city.[12] Seminarians from the local religious colleges also joined in the fray and were observed with crowbars and axes in hand. What most distinguished Kishinev from other pogroms, however, were the increased number of killings and the routine use of mutilation and sadism. "In the midst of this mad inferno," wrote journalist Vladimir Korolenko, "the thirst for blood awoke."[13] Indeed, Kishinev became notorious for its gruesome savagery. Numerous eyewitness accounts claimed that spikes were hammered into the heads of Jewish victims, eyes gouged out, tongues severed, children beaten and casually tossed off roof tops, and women raped. Between fifteen hundred and two thousand persons partook in the carnage and did so without much concern for police interference or even public shame.[14] Forty-seven people died, including two babies, and nearly five hundred were wounded.[15] The Central Relief Committee at Kishinev determined that 123 children were left as orphans.[16] Any straightforward tally, however, hardly does justice to the shocking horrors and the terrible physical and psychic injuries that were inflicted upon the Jews of Kishinev on the holiest days of the Christian calendar.

Reports of the mass carnage in Russia appeared in the New York Jewish press on 27 April, eight days after the initial rioting; intensive and sympathetic coverage was adopted by much of the mainstream press and continued for weeks thereafter.[17] [In London the *Jewish Chronicle* published initial reports on 1 May.[18]] The Lower East Side was now home to over half a million Eastern European Jews; the city had thus been transformed into a center of world Jewry. Numbers of the dead and wounded in the press greatly surpassed more objective accounts that appeared later, and horrendous claims from Kishinev were frequently published with scant regard for journalistic accuracy.[19] Newspapers thus played a major role in advancing

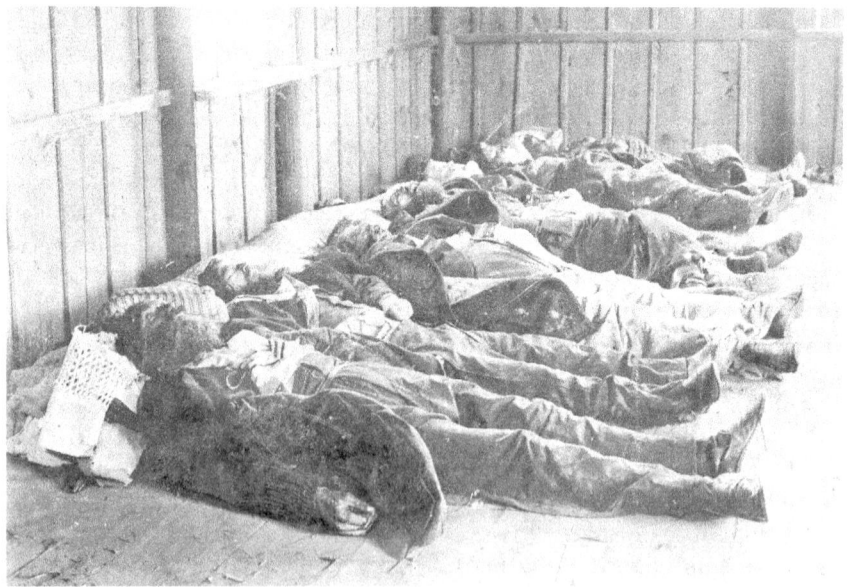

Figure 9.1 Assembled corpses of Kishinev victims.
Source: *Kishinevskii Pogrom* (Stuttgart, 1903).

highly inflamed rhetoric, just as in previous insurgences, and tended to focus on the most grotesque and dehumanized aspects of the pogrom. The use of shocking imagery functioned as much more than a technique to increase newspaper sales, however. Depictions of extreme violence and suffering actually aided the cause of previous movements—such as antislavery, antilynching, and child labor agitation—and the resultant moral shock that was elicited among the public often proved crucial in recruiting activists and in influencing public opinion.[20] Just as in previous insurgences, heightened emotions helped transform sympathetic bystanders into engaged partisans.

Shortly after news regarding Kishinev reached the United States, the boards of B'nai B'rith and the Union of American Hebrew Congregations contacted Secretary of State John Hay (1838–1905) to inform him of the Russian outrages and stated their intention to send emergency relief supplies to the Kishinev survivors. Crowds packed outside newspaper offices eagerly awaiting further information; irate speakers gave full vent to their feelings on street corners; and there was an upsurge of impromptu protest gatherings.[21] Six hundred Jewish veterans of the Spanish-American War met at the Hebrew Young Men's Benevolent Association and, under the leadership of former regimental commander, Colonel Maurice Simmons, petitioned President Theodore Roosevelt to demand prosecution of the culprits "in order to prevent a recurrence of the orgy of assassination."[22] Melodramatic plays based on the massacre were hurriedly written and performed throughout the city in a successful fund-raising drive, and multiple protest meetings were arranged in short order. The *New York Times* reported that in one instance, during the performance of a tune called "The Song of the Suffering Jews," the tally of all the coins and small bills that were thrown onto the stage of a Lower East Side theater amounted to an impressive $500.[23] Many of these working-class contributors were either former refugees from the 1881–1882 pogroms or their descendants. In a first for the movement, the Chinese immigrant community became active supporters and sponsored performances and solicited contributions as well.[24] Protests quickly gained momentum and spread beyond New York City to encompass a broad cross-section of the United States. By June, in response to a request from the Alliance in Paris, American Jews led by Jacob H. Schiff, Oscar S. Straus, and Cyrus L. Sulzberger collected a relief fund of $100,000 (a sum roughly equivalent to $2,000,000), a considerable portion of which consisted of small individual donations.

In striking contrast and despite a torrent of sensational articles in the London papers, Anglo-Jewish leaders adhered to their long-standing retreat from the public sphere. Any impassioned remark, even within the context of closed-door sessions, was held suspect by many members of the Board of Deputies. The Board was now chaired by David L. Alexander, an individual who preferred the time-worn stratagem of behind-the-scenes lobbying and who deferred to the wishes of Baron Gintsburg and the St. Petersburg magnates in this matter. This was also the approach taken by Sir Samuel Montagu, a London banker and chairman of the mostly dormant Russo-Jewish Committee. Protest meetings, it was assumed, would only attract radical elements and worsen the crisis. A single "heedless word dropped at a public meeting," Alexander believed, might have dire consequences in Russia and "be responsible for the loss of hundreds of lives."[25] Fund-raising activities were also dramatically curtailed. To complicate this scenario, the ultimate decision regarding the policy of Anglo-Jewry rested in the hands of a special Conjoint Foreign Committee of British Jews (1878), an amalgamation of the original Board and the Anglo-Jewish Association, headed by the noted journalist and anti-Zionist, Lucien Wolf (1857–1930). Wolf was in accord with Alexander and Montagu, and so the policy of noncontention appeared firmly entrenched. Even so, this situation did not exclude internal debate among various Board members, especially in light of the escalating American protests which were gaining extensive notice. The Board's protest faction included some of England's leading Zionists: Herbert Bentwich, Joseph Prag, and London's chief Sephardic rabbi, Dr. Moses Gaster.[26] Bentwich (1856–1932), an attorney and owner-editor of the prestigious *Law Journal*, reminded the Board that the present objections to public meetings were "the same raised in 1827, 1872, 1881, and 1890," and that despite similar dire warnings in the past, successful meetings were held nonetheless.[27] "The persecutions had been stopped by the public meetings held in previous generations, and it was for this generation to do its duty in the same way." In positing this argument, Bentwich not only linked the current state of affairs to the initiator movement of 1827, but he also placed all prior London protests as part of a movement continuum.[28] This viewpoint was shared by the *Chronicle*, which advised the leadership not to be too "chicken hearted" in regard to protests (to no effect).[29] Despite such comments, the paper kept a much lower profile than in the 1880s.

The majority of Anglo-Jewish notables were aligned with a new mainstream attitude that not only held reason and moderation as sacrosanct but went even further by denouncing the once-revered public meeting as a dangerous anachronism. This could not have been further removed from the situation in the United States. Americans actually witnessed one of the largest series of mass protest meetings in the nation's history. This resurgence marked a high point in the Jewish rights movement, and its massive scale was a sure sign that the contentious center of the Jewish rights movement had shifted—at least in this instance—to the New World. Beginning 2 May and continuing for two months, seventy-seven public protest meetings (Jewish, Christian, or a combination thereof) took place in fifty towns and cities. The magnitude of this mobilization was so unprecedented that the Jewish Publication Society of America, realizing its historic import, took great pains to document the entire episode.[30] This effort was headed by Dr. Cyrus Adler, one of the founders of the society and librarian of the Smithsonian Institution. Among other findings, Adler recorded 363 individual speeches pertaining to the Kishinev massacre; speakers included a former U.S. president (Grover Cleveland), two senators, nine congressmen, three governors, twenty-nine mayors, three college presidents, fifty-six rabbis, and fifty-five Protestant and Catholic clergymen. Moreover, 151 editorials in eighty newspapers, ranging from the major cities of New York, Chicago, Philadelphia, Boston, St. Louis, Baltimore, Cincinnati, and San Francisco to a plethora of smaller towns, condemned the Kishinev pogrom in no uncertain terms.[31]

The most prestigious mass meeting was held on 27 May at New York's Carnegie Hall, where a capacity audience of 3,500 enthusiastically received former president Grover Cleveland, Mayor Seth Low, and other eminent speakers.[32] Details of this "wildly enthusiastic" meeting were awarded front-page status by such prominent papers as the *New York Daily Tribune*. What appealed even more than the celebrity orators, according to the *Tribune*, were any patriotic references made to America "as a haven for the Jews." Whereupon, "the vast assemblage surged to its feet, stamping, clapping hands and shouting, while women in the boxes waved handkerchiefs as enthusiastically as their sisters in the topmost galleries."[33] Dominated by Christian sympathizers, this mass meeting actually took place at the request of prominent Jewish New Yorkers such as Jacob Schiff who trusted that such "indignation and protest . . . would not fail to make an impression upon the Russian government."[34] Carnegie Hall may have gained the most publicity in the United States and abroad, but there were vast numbers of meetings that also had significant impact. Clarence Darrow and the future Nobel Peace Prize winner Jane Addams certainly attracted large numbers at Chicago's Star Theatre, but lesser known personalities were generally the rule. At Boston's Faneuil Hall, for example, rabbis, local politicians, and Protestant clergymen spoke before a mass audience (using far more forceful language than the speakers at Carnegie Hall) to denounce "one of the blackest crimes of the age." Rev. Zvi Hirsch Masliansky, a native of Belorussia and a renowned Zionist, was keynote speaker and addressed the meeting in Yiddish. "What irony!" he exclaimed in a mocking tone. "The Czar, the peacemaker of Europe and the butcher of his own subjects, turning a whole city into a butcher shop!"[35] Another speaker, a Unitarian minister, used the opportunity to excoriate religious hypocrisy in general. "I am tired and sick of the religion that does not restrain human vice and hatred . . . that rolls its eyes to heaven and doesn't care who it steps on down here . . . that does not know God from the devil." Like virtually every other protest meeting in the country, the Boston meeting ended with a series of solemn resolutions that deplored the Russian atrocities and appealed to the U.S. government for diplomatic action. The massacre was, after all, "a most direct and flagrant violation of those sacred principles of life, liberty and the pursuit of happiness." Even though the lives of American citizens were not at stake, it was still the duty of government to oppose these crimes against humanity and to "intercede on behalf of our Russian brothers."[36]

One of the patterns that emerged during this protest surge was the increased visibility and participation among American Zionists—a group that was previously regarded as far removed from the Jewish establishment.

The Jewish rights campaign, just as it aided the cause of emancipation in Great Britain, invigorated Zionists, who now showed a remarkable willingness to participate in a movement that was actually dominated by a privileged group of assimilationist financiers (largely of German Jewish descent).[37] Zionists, primarily from New York, spoke before packed audiences of Russian Jewish immigrants in venues throughout the eastern seaboard. Leaders such as Richard Gottheil, Jacob de Haas, Jacob Miller, and the popular Rev. Masliansky drew enthusiastic crowds. When de Haas, a featured speaker at Philadelphia's Peuel Zedek Synagogue, stressed Jewish self-defense and described how Russian Jews were in the process of arming themselves against future attacks, the *Philadelphia Inquirer* remarked how "the enthusiasm of his listeners burst its bounds" and flooded the synagogue with loud, prolonged applause.[38] Gottheil, also in Philadelphia, reminded everyone that Zionists had long predicted that deadly persecutions would continue to reoccur. Nevertheless, he maintained that "It is unworthy of us as Americans, if we do not take advantage of our American privileges to do something for those of our race who walk in darkness.

> Terrible as were the horrors of Kishineff, the blood of the Jewish martyrs will not have flowed in vain if thereby we are called to our duties. The cries of the unfortunate victims have echoed and re-echoed throughout the world and the Hebrews have been united by a common bond. We cannot read of the terrible cruelties and withhold our help from the only cause that leads to peace for our brethren. We should give the Zionist movement such an impetus that it will roll on and on, gathering force until it finally culminates in the land of Palestine.[39]

Zionist participation was part of a general willingness to suspend the factionalism that usually pervaded communal ranks—miscellaneous groups of trade unionists, socialists, Zionists, Territorialists, Reform Jews, Sephardim, and Orthodox Ashkenazim—in order to respond to the gravity of the crisis as a unified body. The awakening of diaspora loyalty lessened, although certainly did not eliminate, the disdain that many affluent Americanized Jews felt toward their newly arrived Eastern brethren and, like previous insurgences, group cohesion was intensified. Highly acculturated German American Jews even started to attend Zionist meetings. One startled observer noted that "the most cultured specimens of German Jewry" began to participate in meetings and sat alongside the less sophisticated and bearded Russian Jews. "Was it Zionism that wrought this miracle or Kishinev? Chiefly the latter, I think."[40]

After months of fervent national protest, voluminous newspaper articles and editorials, and an onslaught of formal resolutions that arrived in Washington from various parts of the country, and after consulting with scores of American Jewish leaders, a once-reticent President Theodore Roosevelt (1858–1919) became convinced that some sort of diplomatic action was necessary: "I have never in my experience in this country known of a more immediate or a deeper expression of sympathy for the victims and of horror over the appalling calamity that has occurred."[41] In an unparalleled move by any head of state, on 14 July Roosevelt instructed Secretary of State Hay to deliver a respectfully worded but studiously "undiplomatic" protest petition authored by B'nai B'rith president Leo N. Levi and addressed to Tsar Nicholas II, knowing in advance that Russia would summarily reject any pro-Jewish appeal. Russia could also easily condemn the United States for its own legacy of race riots and lynching. Nevertheless, Roosevelt considered the symbolic and moral weight of the Kishinev petition as offsetting any negative repercussions that might arise. By this single act, as one New York newspaper phrased it, "Roosevelt has made this government the avenue of communication by which the popular protest in this country against the Kishinev massacres will reach the Czar's government."[42] Despite its formal rejection, many still believed that its contents had reached high-ranking ministers and was thus related to the tsar. The scale of cooperation between movement and government leaders in the United States became somewhat analogous to that of Montefiore and the Board of Deputies and the British Foreign Office in previous decades.

The position of Roosevelt and Hay was defined by Oscar Straus (1850–1926), a prominent New York Jewish businessman, U.S. diplomat, and Roosevelt's future secretary of commerce and labor (1906–1909), as "the diplomacy of humanity."[43] "The right of intercession, to protest against action or contemplated action . . . to express sympathy for the suffering," was justified if this diplomacy was based on humanitarian principles that were entirely detached from "national ambition." Roosevelt reasoned that public disapproval became a "manifest duty" if the crimes committed were of so vast a scale and such peculiar horror that protest was deemed a moral imperative.[44] In effect, the Roosevelt administration—like Van Buren's and Grant's—became active participants in the movement. All things considered, however, no prior social movement, including abolitionism, women's rights, or temperance, could have equaled the full scope and impact of the U.S. response to the Kishinev massacre. "The entire movement," Leo Levi observed, "made it apparent to the world that the 80,000,000 people who make up the citizenship of the United States had expressed through the President of the United States, the Secretary of State, the signers of the petition, their solemn protest against persecution on account of race or religion."[45]

The United States had therefore positioned itself as the most powerful player in the struggle for Jewish rights. This occurred not only during a time when masses of Russian Jews had established themselves in the United States, but it coincided with the nation's emergence as a world power following the Spanish-American War. This latter theme was frequently mentioned during the public protests. According to this thinking, acknowledgment as a military and political power also carried with it substantial obligations to uphold humanitarian values—a position originally forged by Great Britain.

This assumption of moral supremacy was, of course, fraught with serious contradictions (as U.S. behavior in the Philippines made manifestly clear to certain segments of the public). Yet, as the *Jewish Chronicle* noted, the countless "pamphlets, magazine articles, poems, newspaper letters," combined with the "rousing eloquence" of the protest meetings, editorials, and the Kishinev petition itself constituted a vast "moral tidal wave" that swept the entire country and threw "into gloomy contrast the inaction of our own community [in England]."

> A new force has arisen which has to be reckoned with on every relapse by a European Power into barbarism. . . . The new world with its million and more of enfranchised Jewry, has been called in to redress the moral balance of the old. That is the outstanding feature of the American protest.[46]

MOVEMENT TRANSFORMATION

The *Chronicle*'s lament over the state of the Jewish rights movement in England was echoed by other contemporary observers. "Is there no one in English Jewry who will follow the example of the late Sir Moses Montefiore?" asked Montefiore's former rabbi from Ramsgate, Herman Shandel. "Had these Kishinev massacres happened during Sir Moses' lifetime," continued Shandel, "iron chains would not have held him back from journeying to Russia."[47] He elaborated on past achievements and victories, extolling Crémieux, Goldsmid, Salomons, and other revered figures of the past; heroic personalities of a movement that no longer appeared to resonate in twentieth-century England. The claim that "liberty loving England is dead-silent" may have been a common motif during the spring and summer of 1903,[48] but despite these concerns the movement was far from dormant; it merely assumed a radically different form. To be sure, most elite Anglo-Jews withdrew from collective protest—a tendency thirty years in the making—and by this time neither evangelical nor mainstream Protestants lobbied parliament or sponsored meetings at Mansion House or Guildhall on behalf of persecuted Jews (primarily because Jewish notables no longer enlisted their help in the public sphere). More marginal groups gladly joined in the cause of Jewish rights, however. On 26 June the East End (Jewish) branch of the Social Democratic Federation—Britain's first socialist political party, together with an organization known as the Russian Democratic Circle (composed of Russian revolutionaries in exile), and the British affiliate of the Jewish Bund, sponsored a large protest meeting at the Great Assembly Hall in the East End—the nexus of London's working class. While the number of Jewish socialists was quite small in proportion to the greater community of 130,000,[49] the hall was filled to capacity (about six thousand) with mostly Russian Jewish immigrants and trade unionists.[50] This assembly was chaired by H. Frederick Green of the International Peace and Arbitration Association, and speakers ranged from the celebrated union leader Ben Tillett to the Russian nihilist Felix Volkhofsky. This protest was followed later by a street march composed of various Jewish trade unions, each holding their respective banners and signs—an innovation that would have been considered beyond the bounds of propriety in Montefiore's day. This peaceful procession began at Whitechapel and terminated at Hyde Park, where speakers addressed a large crowd estimated at "several thousands" (again mostly Jewish immigrants) on three strategically located platforms. While not among the speakers, several eminent Zionists, including Israel Zangwill and Herbert Bentwich, were present and freely mingled among the crowd. Most Jewish leaders were certainly uncomfortable with the Hyde Park rhetoric (one example: "Jewish capitalists in Russia and England exploit the misery of the Jewish working man.") Complaints did in fact surface at the Board of Deputies, and these affairs stood as obvious examples of what all Jews should steadfastly avoid. Even so, the mass protest meeting, street procession, and Hyde Park rally were deemed an unqualified success by the organizers.[51]

Inspired by these efforts, the English Zionist Federation arranged its own meeting at Great Assembly Hall on 6 July. Instead of advertising the assembly as a protest or indignation meeting, the occasion surfaced as a "Memorial Service." Over six thousand Jewish men, women, and children assembled to hear Dr. Herman Gollancz, professor of Hebrew at University College London, Rabbi Moses Gaster, and others amid an atmosphere of high reverence for the dead of Kishinev. Speakers went to some length "to keep down any harsh word that might change the character of a memorial service into an inflammatory meeting" and were anxious to avoid being castigated as "Howlers" by the London Jewish establishment. Yet it quickly became apparent that feelings could not be easily suppressed. As Gollancz admitted, they could hardly be responsible if some "sharp or unkind expression, though true and well-deserved, escaped their lips in the bitterness of their hearts, inflaming their words with the fire of their feelings." And so it was, although the memorial maintained a properly respectful tone, moving speeches were given free vent, along with loud cheering and applause. To meet together and bewail the atrocities inflicted on the Kishinev Jews would follow the tradition of the Prophets, Gollancz insisted. "It was the duty of every Jew to feel the pain and affliction of their brethren." Other addresses were delivered in Yiddish, and, according to the *Chronicle*, "the service concluded as impressively as it began with the recital of Kaddish and the singing of Yigdal . . . followed by the National Anthem, in which the vast concourse of men, women, and children heartily joined."[52]

The street march and mass demonstration, together with the meetings at Great Assembly Hall, constituted almost the entire public response to the Kishinev massacre in England.[53] [Elsewhere in the world, additional protest meetings took place in Melbourne and Sydney, Australia; meetings in Rome and Paris were organized by socialists; and a single protest in Amsterdam was sponsored by the Zionist Federation.[54] Although dwarfed by the magnitude of the U.S. protests and lacking any support from the Jewish establishment, the utilization of street marches and multiple platform speakers—modern tactics used by suffragettes, trade unionists, and temperance societies—proved very influential. In the future, large crowds would no longer be turned away, restricted by the space limitations of buildings, and a more militant protest style would also alter movement dynamics. After seventy-six years, the contentious repertoire of the Jewish rights campaign had begun to move beyond the restraints and highly dignified posture of an exclusive nineteenth-century meeting hall. Nonelite Jews took up what the Anglo-Jewish notables had forfeited and began to reinterpret the movement in a much more vital, egalitarian, and aggressive form (one that was actually closer in spirit to 1827) that would continue throughout the twentieth century.

Epilogue

Unfortunately, the Russian pogroms did not end with the Kishinev massacre but continued on an even worse scale for years to come. In 1904 there were forty-three pogroms, many of which were directly exacerbated by Russia's humiliating conduct of the Russo-Japanese War.[1] The following year, amid the unfolding chaos and anarchy of the Russian revolution, the world witnessed an even more deadly version of pogrom violence. Jews continued to be seen as "parasitic" exploiters of the peasants, and because a relatively small percentage had become active revolutionaries, all Jews were additionally branded as subversives. During the Russo-Japanese War, the antisemitic press claimed that Jews aided the enemy by providing funding, arms, and intelligence information and by desertion from the army (despite significant evidence to the contrary).[2] Jews were blamed for Russia's military failures as well as the revolutionary turmoil that began to envelope the collapsing tsarist regime.

By the time of the 1905 Revolution, approximately 100,000 Russian Jews were members of some kind of left-wing group (the Bund, Poale Zion or "Workers of Zion," Social Democrats, etc.).[3] Jewish participation in many of these organizations can be traced to the radicalization that took hold after the first wave of pogroms in 1881. Yet Jews never constituted the nucleus of revolutionary activity. On the other side of the Russian political spectrum was an amalgamation of right-wing, antisemitic, paramilitary groups known at the Black Hundreds who saw themselves as upholders of tsarist rule and the Russian Orthodox Church.[4] As a result of a nationwide labor strike and ongoing internal turmoil, Nicholas was forced into significant concessions. By signing the October Manifesto, the tsar agreed to the formation of a constitutional monarchy and the expansion of civil liberties. An elected legislative body called the Duma was also formed. Such a radical turnaround, however, caused a violent backlash from the right wing—including forces within the government. The months following the Manifesto witnessed a severe period of pogrom violence; within the first two weeks alone, 674 pogroms erupted on a shocking scale. Most incidents occurred in the southern regions of the Pale, where armed members of the Bund, organized as part of a self-defense network, were the least prevalent.

Arson and pillaging were rampant, and more than three thousand men, women, and children perished.

Details of these atrocities appeared in the leading papers of Britain and the United States; consequently, calls for public protests were widespread on both sides of the Atlantic. The American response differed dramatically from 1903. Street demonstrations were common throughout the major cities, the most important being the "Mourning March" in New York City. On 4 December 1905, 125,000 Jews, mostly Russian immigrants (including a contingent of 30,000 women), took to the streets in an orderly and well-orchestrated procession. Altogether, 350,000 people either participated directly in the march or gathered alongside as spectators.[5] By virtue of its size and somber authority, the march from the Lower East Side to Union Square was, according to the *New York Daily Tribune*, "the greatest of its character" to take place in New York.[6] Much of the city's business was suspended, and impersonal public thoroughfares were transformed (at least for an afternoon) into a deeply moving performance space for contesting Russian brutality and memorializing the dead.[7] Singing had become integrated into the movement's repertoire, and in combination with "the sounds of muffled drums and funeral marches played by numerous bands," a heightened sense of theatricality added to the demonstration's success.[8] "There were in line nearly one hundred organizations," according to the *Daily Tribune*, "labor, charitable, socialistic and Zionist, some of them wearing uniforms." Organized by the newly formed Jewish Defense Association (which had raised one million dollars in relief funds) and headed by Grand Marshall Joseph Barondess, a major figure in the Jewish labor movement (and a former aspiring actor), the procession proved to be an effective display of stagecraft. "The tears, the lamentations, the hysteria of a funeral cortege were all in evidence," observed the *Tribune*.[9] At the end of the march, Barondess addressed the crowd that had reached Union Square and read a series of resolutions that denounced the "powers of darkness and hatred, the Russian mob, the Russian rulers, which have brought back the cruelty of the Dark Ages."[10]

In England, as might be expected, the response from the Board of Deputies was at first muted. Increased numbers of Russian Jewish newcomers, most of whom were impoverished and unassimilated *Ostjuden*, had caused an anti-immigrant backlash in England (as evidenced by the Aliens Bill of 1905), and overt expressions of antisemitism began to be far more common. [Similar forces caused a corresponding increase in antisemitism in the United States during the early twentieth century.] Zionists were anxious to respond to the Russian atrocities, but they were deeply divided between two main groups: the English Zionist Federation, which included Messrs. Bentwich, Prag, and Gaster, and the Jewish Territorial Organization (ITO) headed by Israel Zangwill.[11] In mid-November both entities held separate public meetings in London, which followed the general procedure established through the years, including the reading of statements from prominent Christians.[12] The bitter antagonism between the Zionists and the ITO, however, overshadowed the very purpose of the proceedings, and any sense of unity and common purpose was greatly diminished.

In January 1906, after much delay, the Board of Deputies and the Anglo-Jewish Association finally relented to communal pressure and sponsored a public meeting "to express indignation and horror at the massacres." Very much in the tradition of Mansion House, members of the Jewish and Christian establishment met at the magnificent Queen's Hall in Central London and effectively revived the legacy of Judeo-Christian protests. Addresses by Lord Rothschild, the Bishop of Ripon, the Archbishop of Westminster, and others renewed a spirit of cooperation and indignation that was a constant hallmark of an earlier era.[13] Myriad protests and memorial meetings, composed of both Jews and Christians, also took place throughout England, Wales, Scotland, and Ireland.

Atrocities increased during the chaotic period of the Russian Civil War—an especially tragic time for Ukrainian Jewry (1919–1921) and one that featured Cossacks as the primary perpetrators of violence. An accurate accounting of all the dead may never be known; estimates range from a low of 35,000 to a high mark of 200,000.[14] As it happened, however, antisemitic atrocities in Poland reached the press well ahead of the Ukrainian devastation. Reports regarding Polish pogroms, coming at the end of World War I, touched off a virtual maelstrom of indignation in Britain and the United States. On 21 May 1919, hundreds of thousands marched in New York City and fifteen thousand eventually made their way to a protest rally at Madison Square Garden, where Charles Evans Hughes and Rabbi Stephen S. Wise delivered stirring orations.[15] Virtually every large city in the Northeast and Midwest followed New York's lead and held similar marches and protests. In England, a national "Day of Mourning" was observed on June 26, and a street march that met at Hyde Park was said to have attracted a crowd of 100,000.[16] In November the horrors of the Ukrainian pogroms became known in the media, and this touched off yet another round of demonstrations in both the United Kingdom and the United States.

A new pattern had thus formed in the twentieth century: contentious displays were steadily moving away from elite control and now incorporated increasing numbers of middle- and working-class Jews, many of whom had direct ties to the scene of violence abroad or were themselves actual survivors of previous attacks. More often than not, American Jews reacted first to the crisis, but both the United States and Britain now included massive numbers of participants and were less inclined to adhere to formal procedure and stately venues than in the past.

The Jewish rights movement continued in this more egalitarian vein during the 1933 anti-Nazi boycott. Organizations such as the Board of Deputies, the American Jewish Committee, and the Alliance Israélite Universelle (which had long been dominated by the European Jewish elite) all followed the wishes of the German Jewish leadership and disapproved of the boycott.

Even B'nai B'rith—which had taken such forceful stands in the past—cautioned Jews to adopt "dignified silence."[17] Nevertheless, Jewish merchants, Zionists, socialists, war veterans, and large numbers of women worked closely with such groups as the International League against antisemitism (Paris), the American Jewish Congress, and the British Anti-War Council and enacted a worldwide embargo of German products. In March 1933 an estimated one million people in more than eighty cities in the United States, including many non-Jewish supporters, remonstrated against the antisemitic policies of Nazi Germany.[18] Once more Madison Square Garden, this time under the auspices of the American Jewish Congress (whose membership mostly consisted of Eastern European Jews) and broadcast via national radio, served as the venue for what the *Jewish Chronicle*'s correspondent called "the most impressive protest ever held."[19]

The American Jewish Congress, under the leadership of Stephen Wise, also took the lead in an organized boycott of the 1936 Berlin Olympics. Wise succeeded in enlisting the support of the *New York Times*, a group of influential governors and congressmen, forty-one college presidents, the Federal Council of Churches, Catholic War Veterans, and the National Association for the Advancement of Colored People. This anti-Nazi campaign, while unable to move the Olympics from Berlin or to stop U.S. participation, did succeed in sponsoring a Jewish Olympiad in New York and joined in a separate People's Olympics in Spain (six thousand athletes registered for these games, but the outbreak of the Spanish Civil War quickly put an end to them). It should also be noted that Mayor Fiorello LaGuardia of New York became a vociferous supporter of the Jewish rights and frequently lashed out at the Nazi regime at this time.[20]

Ultimately, of course, the mounting violence toward Jews that had first appeared in Romania during the 1860s and then increased in intensity during a forty-year span in Russia finally culminated in the state-sanctioned genocide of six million Jews during the Holocaust—a crime of almost incomprehensible dimensions. The formation of the United Nations after World War II and the founding of Israel dramatically altered the political status of international Jewry, and the specter of the Holocaust became a potent symbol in the continuing efforts to quell antisemitism.

After the war, the Soviet Union appeared on the horizon as the main perpetrator of antisemitic violence and discrimination. Beginning in 1948, Stalin began a campaign that was focused on eliminating all traces of Jewish culture and distinctiveness. Even highly assimilated Jews were purged from universities and from politics—indeed any significant sphere of influence. Leading journalists, writers, and intellectuals were executed for supposed crimes against the state. The first public meeting that protested Soviet actions met in New York City in 1952 under the auspices of the Jewish Labor Committee.[21] The American Zionist Council then brought together a national meeting of thirty-four Jewish organizations whereupon it was urged to establish "an intensive mobilization of world public opinion against

Soviet antisemitism."[22] American Jews began to protest at the Soviet Mission at the United Nations and publicly urged Soviet Jews to immigrate to Israel. Stalin's death in 1953 and the rise of Nikita Khrushchev did not deter the Soviets from their policy of selective harassment, imprisonment, and intolerance based on a supposed "international Zionist conspiracy." Sporadic protests from the American Jewish community continued throughout the 1950s, but these efforts failed to spark a significant resurgence of the Jewish rights movement.

In the early 1960s, escalating numbers of Soviet Jews were accused of "economic crimes," and in one instance ninety-one were given death sentences. Most synagogues were closed down, the Hebrew language was forbidden, and any expression of Zionism was outlawed. After Israel's success in the Six-Day War (1967) and the severance of diplomatic relations with the Soviets, Israel no longer felt inhibited in regard to protesting the antisemitic policies of the Soviet Union, and a new sense of empowerment and pride came into play among world Jewry. Profoundly influenced by a plethora of 1960s social movements and revitalized by a new generation of American Jews who were determined to counteract what they saw as excessive Jewish passivity during the Holocaust, the Jewish rights campaign adapted to this altered environment by the employment of a new tactical and strategic repertoire. Israel was seen as the rightful home for persecuted Soviet Jews, and because the Soviet Union forbade any emigration, a highly contentious movement developed.

Organizations such as the Student Struggle for Soviet Jewry (SSSJ) and the Union of Councils for Soviet Jews (UCSJ) grew in popularity and offered a more activist alternative to mainstream Jewish organizations. A militant faction surfaced in 1968 with the appearance of the Jewish Defense League (JDL), founded by the highly controversial Brooklyn rabbi Meir Kahane.[23] "Free Soviet Jews" became a ubiquitous form of graffiti in New York City, and the harassment of Soviet diplomats and disruptions of performances by visiting Soviet artists, such as the Bolshoi Ballet, by the JDL attracted press headlines. Kahane's tactics escalated in violence, and as a result of the bombing of Soviet offices in Washington, D.C., the JDL was deemed a terrorist organization by the FBI. Needless to say, the JDL remained well outside acceptable parameters of the emerging movement. However, some Jews, just as civil rights activists in the South, pursued peaceful means of civil disobedience and were willing to be jailed for the cause; 1,300, for example, were arrested at a mass rally in Washington in March 1971.[24] The movement on behalf of Soviet Jewry increased in numbers and political influence and incorporated a highly diverse group of Orthodox, Conservative, and Reform Jews—the majority favored nonviolent protests. The Soviets began to release more Jews each year: 1,000 in 1970, 15,000 in 1971, and 25,000 in 1972. Buoyed by this success, an annual "Solidarity Sunday for Soviet Jewry," a mass march in midtown Manhattan, began in 1972 and routinely attracted between 200,000 and 300,000 protestors by the 1980s.[25]

In Washington, D.C., intensive congressional lobbying resulted in the passage of the Jackson-Vanik Amendment (1974), which denied most favored nation status to certain countries that restricted free emigration—one of the most notable legislative victories of the movement. By the mid-1980s, another shift in tactics occurred, and more activists adopted civil disobedience as a moral imperative; increased numbers of Jews began to participate in sit-down protests at Soviet consulates or United Nations headquarters (and even included prominent members of the New York Board of Rabbis). National boycotts against U.S. companies that engaged in business in the Soviet Union were widespread. The movement gained momentum as the number of Soviet Jews who were granted permission to leave the country escalated during the Gorbachev era.

In England groups such as Concerned Jewish Youth and the Women's Campaign for Soviet Jewry utilized many of the tactics pioneered in the United States, and the tradition of Hyde Park protests also continued during the 1980s. In general, however, disruptive scenes were deemed less acceptable in England than in America at this time.[26] Following more conventional tactics, the Jewish ex-Servicemen's Legion played a major role in lobbying Parliament. Jewish organizations in Israel, Canada, and Continental Europe all made notable contributions and sustained significant pressure on the Soviets; the protest slogan "Never Again!" resounded throughout the world press.

The movement for Soviet Jews resulted in the immigration of 1.3 million Jews to Israel, the United States, and other countries and was certainly one of the most remarkable periods in modern Jewish history. Its success was due in large part to the merging of Jewish interests with that of cold-war politics and the strategic interests of the United States, Britain, and other Western countries. Negative publicity in the world press and broad sympathy for such high-profile dissidents as Andrei Sakharov and Anatoly Shcharansky seriously damaged the image of the Soviets in a new post-Holocaust environment—a world that was much more cognizant of the primacy of human rights than ever before.[27]

The current situation is certainly not devoid of the continuing specter of antisemitism. The Middle East, according to historian Robert S. Wistrich, has become awash in a "culture of hatred" reminiscent of the worst excesses of Nazi Germany. A fervent anti-Americanism has merged with a striking dehumanization of Jews (as well as Holocaust denials) that has become quite worrisome. "Uncle Sam," Wistrich continues, "has coalesced with Shylock into a terrifying specter of globalization" that is perceived as a threat to the very foundation of Islamic society.[28] Lest anyone be lulled into a sense of complacency—based on notions of technological and moral progress—the lessons of the past can only point to the maintenance of vigilance in regard to Jewish rights and indeed human rights in general.

Conclusions

> *Sometimes the united voice of the Jewish people is heard, as it was heard in the Damascus Affair of 1840. . . . Sometimes it is ignored. But always the voice of our people must be raised in defense of justice and humanity.*
>
> Israel Goldstein (1955)[1]

A new form of Jewish political power emerged in the early nineteenth century, one that directly countered notions of Jewish powerlessness and was linked to innovative public performances. Predating Marxist and socialist ideologies, Jews opened up behavioral expression that had been culturally bounded for centuries. The ensuing struggle constituted one of the most enduring social movements in modern history. From its early origins in London in 1827, to Montefiore's gallant style of leadership in the Middle East, to the rise of the "Mourning March" and street processions of the early twentieth century, and then on to the civil disobedience of the 1980s, the campaign for Jewish rights evolved, shifted its contentious center from England to the United States, and adapted to a dramatically altered post-Holocaust environment. But like most significant movements, this collective enterprise was certainly not devoid of internal division and dissent. In what could have spelled its demise, the struggle for Jewish rights survived a generation of leaders who denigrated protesters as "Howlers" and believed that the best method for dealing with anti-Jewish oppression was "dignified silence" (an attempt to resurrect the mask of quietism). Even the ravishes of the Nazi regime did not dissuade another wave of international contention from surfacing during the 1970s and 1980s, however. "Never Again!" served as an impassioned call to action and a warning that silence would no longer be countenanced.

Despite the movement's remarkable influence and achievements and its intensive media coverage through the years, modern Jewish historians have yet to come to terms with any sense of continuity. Instead, each mobilization has been interpreted as a discrete and temporary event, and the concept of an ongoing movement that was so much a part of nineteenth-century protest has been lost. Even within this skewed perspective, major chapters have often been ignored, such as the unparalleled protest insurgence in America after the Kishinev massacre. Historians not only tend to avoid the swirl of passionate politics that envelope social movements, but if noted at all these collective endeavors are often held to unrealistic standards of "success." Certainly the Jewish rights struggle ran the gamut between stirring accomplishments and mobilizations that fell short of expectations. Any attempt to view the lengthy series of international protests as a steady progression of liberality and advancement would be at odds with a far more ambiguous reality. The Russian pogroms continued to take their deadly toll for decades; young Edgardo Mortara was never freed from the Vatican; and the anti-Nazi boycott did not deter German atrocities. Nevertheless, as one historian suggested in connection with the boycott endeavor, it actually defies common sense to consign "a movement of such large dimensions" to historical oblivion because it failed to halt the Nazi onslaught.[2]

Given such a background of neglect and misunderstanding of what constitutes any social movement's success or failure, some clarification is certainly warranted. To be sure, a more realistic set of criteria should be adopted in analyzing movements that focus on human rights. For example, one may legitimately ask whether constituents found themselves in an improved political and economic situation and experienced increased societal acceptance as a result of the movement. Indeed, one of the primary issues to be considered, according to social theorist William A. Gamson, is whether *new advantages* came into being during any movement's active phase.[3] Popular support is another key factor. Did movement goals cross over and expand to include larger segments of society as a whole? Longevity is yet another indication of a movement's impact, and if these collective enterprises are fortunate enough to attract a transnational following, then they are truly in a very select group. Most social movements, it should be said, are either ignored entirely by the media or rigidly suppressed by governments. Scholars have also begun to replace the terminology of "success" and "failure" with the more generic "outcomes," because this wording more accurately reflects the range of unintended consequences social movements frequently bring in their wake. Outcomes may also differ significantly when placed in short- and long-term perspectives. Enduring movements often contribute to new ways of thinking about the world and so determining their precise outcome is made especially difficult. Social movements have personal consequences, such as the assumption of activist identities. These effects, according to analysts Jeff Goodwin and James M. Jasper, "are perhaps the hardest movement impacts to study, yet they may be some of the most profound and longest-lasting outcomes."[4]

It also is helpful to review what the activists themselves thought about the Jewish rights campaign as well as their place in it. Abraham Benisch frequently referred to the movement using allusions to classical Greek military history. Protest surges became known as "phalanxes." "We may rally round our banner as many auxiliaries as we can [referring to Christian supporters]; the phalanx must be ourselves." Imagining the Jewish response to the Mortara affair in such terminology was itself an attempt to gain at least a psychological advantage. No matter what the outcome, the Jews could hold their heads erect because they united and rallied against a merciless foe. "It is a Jewish family upon which the outrage was committed; it is therefore the Jews to whom Providence has primarily assigned the task of vindicating the cause of humanity."[5] Each manifestation of the movement, as Benisch interpreted the process, only made the Jewish community stronger. By the time of the Kishinev massacre, the military motif became even more pronounced. The Mourning March in New York City, for example, proceeded to the rhythm of muffled drums and was composed of large contingents of Jewish veterans from the Spanish-American War as well as armed and specially uniformed "Zion Guards." Benisch's phalanx was thereby made manifest on the streets of New York, and in doing so, honor could be more readily redeemed.

The more cynical may point to the steady advancement of antisemitic violence in the nineteenth century and the horrors of the Holocaust in the twentieth as proof of the ultimate failure of the Jewish rights struggle. The most realistic approach, I believe, is to be willing to look at the movement in microcosm as well as the broad picture, to recognize its accomplishments and shortfalls, and to realize that social movements, as potentially powerful as they may be, cannot be expected to end all human misery and prejudice. Clearly, the women's rights struggle remains one of the most influential social movements of the modern era; however, no one can claim that it managed to end sexism or discrimination. Yet the feminist surge of the 1960s and 1970s helped set in motion a quantum shift in viewing women's roles in society and dramatically improved political opportunities. Similarly, as we have seen, England's "extraordinary movement" greatly accelerated Jewish assimilation, and its initial flush of success in the media provided the impetus for Jews to enter the political arena and to lobby for emancipation. Taking on the cause of their suffering brethren abroad may not have altered the day-to-day lives of Russian Jews, but selfless and philanthropic motives were perfectly in tune with the culture of reform in England and counteracted the clichéd image of Anglo-Jewry as selfish stockjobbers and uncouth old-clothes men. The passage to high respectability was not easily accomplished—as the reviled stereotype of London Jewry that Joseph Wolf employed in 1827 as well as the flippant remarks by Coleridge and Macaulay attest. Without a doubt, however, the standing of Anglo-Jewry made dramatic strides in a relatively short time frame. As the *Jewish Chronicle* proudly declared in 1871, "We cannot fail to be struck with a sense of grateful appreciation of the vast progress we have made and the eminence we have attained." In a span of just a few decades, as the *Chronicle* interpreted events, Anglo-Jews were no longer deemed "the political and social Pariahs of the country." The legislature, the professions, and schools, indeed the country's very "heart," as the paper further emphasized, "are open to us."[6] There is little question that the abandonment of the quietist mindset, the avid adoption of interfaith philanthropy and transnational activism, and the appearance of Jews as active players in the political public sphere were vital components in this turnaround. The Jews of England were certainly "members of a great and powerful nation," as London's *Voice of Jacob* noted in 1841. But national power was tempered by "natural generosity and sympathy for all that is just and good." Similarly, Jews had become, at least in the public mind, "champions for the rights of their brethren everywhere." It was in this fashion that they showed themselves worthy of being citizens. "The exertions for the interests of Judaism will here find its centre, and hence will they diverge to a circle that will embrace the whole earth."[7] Anglo-Jewry's continued position as Jewish rights champions was perceived as integral in attaining ultimate acceptance in British society.

The Damascus affair was surely one of the high points in the Jewish rights movement and inspired the surge of patriotism and pride of leadership that was embodied in the *Voice of Jacob*. For the first time concrete improvements could be seen in the lives of foreign Jews as well. Not only were the Jewish prisoners released in Damascus but the sultan's decree in Constantinople awarded significant rights to Jews residing in the Ottoman Empire. The success of Montefiore's efforts abroad placed the movement on a very firm footing; it presaged a high level of cooperation with the British Foreign Office; and helped sustain hope for similar achievements for years to come. Even the lack of a positive result in the case of Edgardo Mortara was not without major and mostly constructive outcomes for Jews. Most of the world press had become united in a collective outcry against the actions of the pope; the plight of the Mortara family became linked with Victorian sentiment and the middle-class reverence for hearth and home, and so the stigma associated simply by being Jewish was therefore mitigated. Evaluated solely within the perspective of a public relations campaign, the Vatican and its ultramontane advocates suffered substantial losses during the Mortara affair.

The Romanian pogroms may at first seem like one of the Jewish rights movement's lowest ebbs, but this episode still proved vital to the movement's development. Certainly, visits to Bucharest by Montefiore and Crémieux appeared to inflame the crisis; yet there is little doubt that Benjamin Peixotto's approach, together with his standing as United States consul, actually alleviated the suffering of Romanian Jewry and provided a new sense of unity and empowerment. Peixotto's efforts to establish emigration as a means to rectify the situation in Romania helped lay the foundation for the subsequent emigration movement of the 1880s. Hundreds of thousands of Russian Jews, many of whom had their Atlantic passages arranged and paid for by Jewish largesse, arrived in the New World—an impressive demonstration of communal philanthropy. The newly arrived Eastern Jews dramatically changed the complexion of American Jewry, and New York City now claimed the largest Jewish population in the world. By the early twentieth century, myriad factions within the larger immigrant community in both London and New York became the leading lights of the Jewish rights struggle and quickly took on the responsibilities that had been vacated by the communal magnates. This transition in leadership set the stage for the anti-Nazi rallies and the campaign for Soviet Jewry later on. These insurgences strengthened Jewish participation in the public sphere and further defined a public political culture that had first emerged a century before—a kind of identity politics that was so deeply felt and "infused with transcendental significance," as one recent scholar has put it, that by the 1970s the movement was beginning to be defined as a quasi-civil religion.[8] All things considered, few social movements can claim such a powerful and extensive record of accomplishment.

Throughout the nineteenth century, the campaign for Jewish rights was primarily an Anglophone concern—despite significant contributions by Crémieux and others. Several factors account for this. First, the movement's beginning phase was heavily dependent on the protest meeting, which incorporated a revered formula—perfected during the abolitionist crusade—that consisted of formal parliamentary conduct, stately venues, the appointment of aristocrats as presiding chairmen, and of course heartfelt oratory that was directed toward the benefit of the oppressed. The same basic formula was repeated in the British Caribbean colonies and in the United States (albeit with a far less formalistic approach and a notable lack of aristocratic pretensions). This type of self-conscious dramaturgy was not viewed with much favor on the Continent, however. Second, both the French Consistory and their German-speaking organizational equivalents, unlike the Board of Deputies in England and certainly the fragmented but highly independent Jewish leadership in the United States, were closely allied with their respective governments, and so the type of institutional independence that is so necessary for a contentious movement did not yet exist on the Continent. The founding of the Alliance in Paris promised much at the start, but it was not long before this organization was dominated by the more conservative Jewish oligarchs. Interests became skewed toward Jewish educational projects in North Africa and the Middle East rather than contentious Jewish rights issues. With the rise of the Jewish immigrant community at the turn of the century, movement dynamics changed drastically. Socialists and Zionists were far less concerned with presenting a refined image to the world, and a more egalitarian campaign surfaced with greater participation on the Continent (although the increasingly hostile pre–World War II era curtailed much of this initial activity).

The concepts of Jewish power and powerlessness are intrinsic to any study of Jewish history and are especially useful in a discussion of the campaign for Jewish rights. "When I speak of 'Jewish Power,'" writes historian

David Biale, "I have in mind the attempt to exercise strength and authority within a collective framework, informed by conscious political goals."[9] This statement actually summarizes the Jewish rights struggle rather well, although Biale had quite different intentions in formulating this conception. Contrary to the opinion of many historians, as Biale and others have noted, Jews were hardly the passive victims that have been previously imagined. Jews did not avoid political action for two thousand years but instead found effective methods to negotiate with the gentile world using significant forms of political negotiation—albeit often within the traditional confines of the *Kahal*. As we have seen, however, a new form of political power surfaced in the early nineteenth century, one that was linked to groundbreaking public protests and their respective coverage in the media. The struggle for Jewish rights directly countered notions of Jewish political powerlessness—the "slave" mentality of nonengagement in the political public sphere that Moses Levy attacked so forcefully—and helped redefine the roles of Jews in modern society. The movement represented a structural emancipation of Jewish politics, a radical change that the communal notables took advantage of during their drive for emancipation. Much later, the adherents of Zionism and socialism found the movement to their mutual advantage and helped to redefine an increasingly out of date contentious repertoire. The core values of the early nineteenth century nevertheless remained intact: Jews had a fundamental obligation to rise in defense of their coreligionists no matter where in the world they might suffer persecution; and collective protest, regardless of the form it assumed, had to take place in the public sphere. Protests were deemed critical, but the leadership also employed traditional lobbying techniques with government entities, were keenly attuned to the newspaper press, and welcomed well-placed Christian supporters—thereby increasing chances of meaningful change. The movement was founded in reaction to various "moral shocks," events considered so repellent and contrary to natural law that a collective sense of outrage helped participants engage in active protest and usually garnered the heightened attention of the media.[10] The adoption of the social movement by masses of Jews represented a sense of cognitive liberation and self-empowerment that may be difficult to fully comprehend today. Once embraced, Jews could not abandon it, even when the elite eventually turned their backs on the movement. When the Anglo-Jewish leadership appeared to divest themselves from all forms of public protest, this decision was not only interpreted as a heartless betrayal but as nothing less than a "crisis in Jewish history" and a regression toward a ghetto mentality.[11]

Ironically, the cyclical nature of the Jewish rights movement may strike some scholars as both intrinsically Jewish and at odds with customary historical practice. "The historian," as Biale and most others view the profession, "does not see the past as recurring but rather as made up of unique events, each to be understood in its own context. For the historian, the connection between past and present, so intuitive to the traditional Jew, is not at all obvious."[12] Yet, while it is abundantly clear that each movement phase discussed here was distinctive in its own right, the connection between past and present is crucial to fully understanding these historical processes. Without the willingness to engage in a cyclical view, historians will not only lose sight of a once "extraordinary movement" but the subsequent mobilizations that followed suit.

Notes

INTRODUCTION

1. Moses E. Levy ["Midrash," pseudo.], "To the Jewish Community on the Necessity of Better Educating Their Children in a Knowledge of Hebrew," *World* (London), 19 December 1827.
2. Levy's London years have been previously examined in C. S. Monaco, *Moses Levy of Florida: Jewish Utopian and Antebellum Reformer* (Baton Rouge, LA, 2005). Recently uncovered evidence has allowed these events to be greatly expanded and reinterpreted in a social movement framework; see Monaco, "'The Extraordinary Movement of the Jews of Great Britain': 1827–1831," *Journal of Modern Jewish Studies* 8 (November, 2009): 337–59.
3. For a comparison with other contentious events of the era, see John Boyd, R. A. Schweitzer and Charles Tilly, "British Contentious Gatherings of 1828," (working paper, Center for Research on Social Organization, University of Michigan, 1978). This particular study focused solely on 1828 and limited itself to a few select periodicals; hence, the significance of the meetings of the Jews was entirely missed.
4. This apt term was first used by Eli Lederhendler, *The Road to Modern Jewish Politics: Political Tradition and Political Reconstruction in the Jewish Community of Tsarist Russia* (New York, 1989), 58.
5. For a definition of abeyance, see Verta Taylor, "Social Movement Continuity: The Women's Movement in Abeyance," *American Sociological Review* 54 (October 1989): 761–75; see also Paul Bagguley, "Contemporary British Feminism: A Social Movement in Abeyance?" *Social Movement Studies* 1 (October 2002): 169–85; Traci M. Sawyers and David S. Meyer, "Missed Opportunities: Social Movement Abeyance and Public Policy," *Social Problems* 46 (1999): 187–206.
6. Jonathan Frankel, *The Damascus Affair: "Ritual Murder," Politics, and the Jews in 1840* (Cambridge, 1997), 224.
7. "Indignation Meetings of the Jews," *Jewish Chronicle*, 10 December 1858.
8. Adler quoted in "Persecution of the Jews in Russia," *Times* (London), 2 February 1882.
9. Jonathan Frankel was especially keen to link these events as examples of a united response to "crisis," but he was greatly hindered by the lack of a social movement framework; see Frankel, "Crisis as a Factor in Modern Jewish Politics, 1840 and 1881–82," in *Living with Antisemitism: Modern Jewish Responses*, ed. Jehuda Reinharz (Hanover, NH, 1987), 42–58.
10. That is to say, older scholarship of the 1960s often saw the "birth" of a particular movement as seemingly emerging "out of nowhere" and—apparently

uninfluenced by previous endeavors—presented an abrupt shift from a quiescent mode to public activism; Taylor, "Social Movement Continuity," 761.
11. For an excellent and highly accessible review of the antislavery movement, see Adam Hochschild, *Bury the Chains: Prophets and Rebels in the Fight to Free an Empire's Slaves* (New York, 2005).
12. Taylor, "Social Movement Continuity," 761–75; Doug McAdam, "Initiator and Spin-Off Movements: Diffusion Processes in Protest Cycles," in *Repertoires and Cycles of Collective Action*, ed. Mark Traugott (Durham, NC, 1995), 217–39; Nancy Whittier, "The Consequences of Social Movements for Each Other," in *Blackwell Companion to Social Movements*, eds. David A. Snow, Sarah A. Soule, and Hanspeter Kriesi (Malden, MA, 2004), 531–51.
13. "Board of Deputies," *Jewish Chronicle*, 3 July 1903.
14. H. Shandel, "Sir Moses Montefiore's Missions and the Kishinev Massacres," *Jewish Chronicle*, 29 May 1903.
15. "What Are the British Jews? And What May They Become?" *Voice of Jacob*, 16 September 1841.
16. Jonathan Haidt, *The Righteous Mind: Why Good People Are Divided by Politics and Religion* (New York, 2012).
17. "The Crisis in Jewish History," *Jewish Chronicle*, 20 January 1882.
18. David Biale, *Power and Powerlessness in Jewish History* (New York, 1986), 8–9.
19. Michael Brenner, *Prophets of the Past: Interpreters of Jewish History*, trans. Steven Rendall (Princeton, NJ, 2010), 198.
20. Barbara H. Rosenwein, "Worrying About Emotions in History," *American Historical Review* 107, no.3 (June 2002) <http://www.historycooperative.org/journals/ahr/107.3/ah0302000821.html> (accessed 21 September 2009); see also Jeff Goodwin and James M. Jasper, "Emotions and Social Movements," in *Handbook of the Sociology of Emotions*, eds. Jan E. Stets and Jonathan H. Turner (New York, 2007), 611–35.
21. For a concise overview, see Brenner, *Prophets of the Past*, 121–36.
22. Until comparatively recently, social theorists have also ignored the emotional turmoil that inevitably surrounds the political sphere and have stressed rationalistic models and structural analyses instead. See Jeff Goodwin, James M. Jasper, and Francesca Polletta, "Why Emotions Matter," in *Passionate Politics: Emotions and Social Movements,* eds. Jasper Goodwin Francesca and Polletta (Chicago, 2001), 1–26.
23. Carole Fink, *Defending the Rights of Others: The Great Powers, the Jews, and International Minority Protection, 1878–1938* (New York, 2004), 15; William D. Rubinstein and Hilary L. Rubinstein, *Philosemitism: Admiration and Support in the English-Speaking World for Jews, 1840–1939* (New York, 1999); Abigail Green, *Moses Montefiore: Jewish Liberator, Imperial Hero* (Cambridge, MA, 2010), 369.
24. Fink, *Defending the Rights of Others*, 15; Rubinstein, *Philosemitism*; Green, *Moses Montefiore*, 369.
25. Abigail Green, "The British Empire and the Jews: An Imperialism of Human Rights?" *Past and Present* 199 (May 2008): 175–205.
26. Donatella della Porta and Mario Diani, *Social Movements: An Introduction* (Malden, MA, 2006), 95; Taylor, "Social Movement Continuity," 761.
27. Taylor, "Social Movement Continuity," 762.
28. McAdam, "Initiator and Spin-Off Movements," 230.
29. For a complete listing, see Chapter 2.
30. "Großbritannien," *Allgemeine Zeitung*, 24 December 1827. American papers include *Philadelphia Gazette and Daily Advertiser*, 15 February 1828;

"Interesting Meeting of the Jews in London," *American Baptist Magazine* 7 (July 1828): 215. This last article was reprinted from *New York Observer*. See also "Interesting Meeting of the Jews in London," *Christian Secretary* (Hartford, Conn.), 29 March 1828; *Christian Watchman* (Boston), 14 March 1828; *Albion, A Journal of News, Politics, and Literature* (New York), 9 February 1828.
31. Monaco, *Moses Levy of Florida*.
32. John Lofland, *Social Movement Organizations: Guide to Research on Insurgent Realities* (New York, 1996), 311.
33. David Katz, "The Marginalization of Early Modern Anglo-Jewish History," in *The Jewish Heritage in British History: Englishness and Jewishness*, ed. Tony Kushner (London, 1992), 60–62; Mitchell B. Hart, "The Unbearable Lightness of Britain: Anglo-Jewish Historiography and the Anxiety of Success," *Journal of Modern Jewish Studies* 6 (July 2007): 146–52; Todd M. Endelman, "Writing English Jewish History," *Albion* 27 (Winter 1995): 627.
34. Jürgen Habermas, *The Structural Transformation of the Public Sphere: An Inquiry into a Category of Bourgeois Society*, trans. Thomas Burger (Cambridge, MA, 1989), 29.
35. See, for example, Eli Lederhendler, *The Road to Modern Jewish Politics: Political Tradition and Political Reconstruction in the Jewish Community of Tsarist Russia* (New York, 1989), 156.
36. Della Porta and Diani, *Social Movements*, 92–93, 97.
37. Lederhendler, *Road to Modern Jewish Politics*, 155; Jonathan Frankel, *Prophecy and Politics: Socialism, Nationalism, and the Russian Jews, 1862–1917* (Cambridge, 1984), 49.
38. Frankel, *Prophecy and Politics*, 49.
39. David Vital, *The Origins of Zionism* (Oxford, 1975), 154.
40. David Biale, *Power and Powerlessness*, 124.
41. "Report of the Proceedings of the late Public Meeting of the Jews," in *Second Annual Report of the Philo-Judaean Society* (London, 1828), 42.
42. Monaco, *Moses Levy of Florida*.
43. Moses E. Levy, "The Jews," *World*, 6 June 1827.
44. Leo Pinsker, *Auto-Emancipation*, trans. D. S. Blondheim (New York, 1906), 9.
45. "Meeting of the Jews," *Times*, 5 December 1827.
46. See, for example, Jacob Katz, *Jewish Emancipation and Self-Emancipation* (Philadelphia, 1986), 110–14; Lederhendler, *Road to Modern Jewish Politics*, 3–4, 155; Biale, *Power and Powerlessness*, 124–36.
47. W. Goodwin to Hon. Zabdiel Sampson, 17 February 1820, HR16A-G17.2, Record Group 233, Records of the U.S. House of Representatives, National Archives, Washington, D.C.
48. For a definition of a modern transnational activist, see Sidney Tarrow, *The New Transnational Activism* (Cambridge, 2008), 29.
49. Charles Tilly, *Popular Contention in Great Britain, 1758–1834* (Boulder, CO, 2005), 37.
50. Dermot Keogh, *Jews in Twentieth-Century Ireland: Refugees, Anti-Semitism and the Holocaust* (Cork, Ireland, 1998), 7; Ursula Henriques, *Religious Toleration in England, 1787–1833* (Toronto, 1961), 190.
51. McAdam, "Initiator and Spin-Off Movements," 217–39.
52. "Meeting of the Jews," *World*, 26 December 1827.
53. Quoted in Lisa Moses Leff, "Jewish Solidarity in Nineteenth-Century France: The Evolution of a Concept," *Journal of Modern History* 74 (March 2002): 54–55.
54. Della Porta and Diani, *Social Movements*, 157.

55. Endelman, "Writing," 624–25.
56. Ibid., 624.
57. Israel Finestein, "Jewish Emancipationists in Victorian England: Self-Imposed Limits to Assimilation," in *Assimilation and Community: The Jews in Nineteenth-Century Europe*, eds. Jonathan Frankel and Steven J. Zipperstein (Cambridge, 1992), 41.
58. Michael Clark, *Albion and Jerusalem: The Anglo-Jewish Community in the Post-Emancipation Era, 1858–1887* (Oxford, 2009), 28.
59. David Feldman, *Englishmen and Jews: Social Relations and Political Culture, 1840–1914* (New Haven, CT, 1995), 380.
60. Ibid., 382.
61. Anne F. Janowitz, "'Wild Outcasts of Society': The Transit of the Gypsies in Romantic Period Poetry," in *The Country and the City Revisited: England and the Politics of Culture, 1550–1850*, eds. Gerald Maclean, Donna Landry, Joseph P. Ward (Cambridge, 1999), 213–14, 222–23.
62. See, for example, *Eclectic Review* (December 1829): 521; S. T. Coleridge to Daniel Stuart, 12 October 1827, in *Collected Letters of Samuel Taylor Coleridge*, vol. 6, ed. Earl Leslie Griggs (Oxford, 2000), 704.
63. Levy quoted in "Appendix D: Brief Report of the Proceedings of the First General Meeting of the Philo-Judaean Society," *First Annual Report of the Philo-Judaean Society* (London, 1827), 42.
64. Ibid., 39, 42.
65. *Third Annual Report of the Philo-Judaean Society* (London, 1829), 13.
66. Robin Blackburn, *The American Crucible: Slavery, Emancipation and Human Rights* (London, 2011), 281. For their loss of "property," British slaveholders, much to the disappointment of abolitionists, received just under £20 million after the passage of emancipation.
67. Eric Foner, review of *The American Crucible: Slavery, Emancipation and Human Rights*, by Robin Blackburn, *The Nation*, 29 August–5 September 2011.
68. Christopher Leslie Brown, *Moral Capital: Foundations of British Abolitionism* (Chapel Hill, NC, 2006), 2–3.
69. [M. E. Levy], *A Plan for the Abolition of Slavery, Consistently with the Interests of All Parties Concerned* (London, 1828). Levy published this pamphlet anonymously, a factor that contributed to its subsequent historical neglect. For background, see Monaco, *Moses Levy of Florida*, 131–38.
70. Gertrude Himmelfarb, "The Idea of Compassion: The British versus the French Enlightenment," *Public Interest* 145 (Fall 2001): 11.
71. D. W. Bebbington, *Evangelicalism in Modern Britain: A History from the 1730s to the 1980s* (London, 1993), 82, 91–97; Boyd Hilton, *The Age of Atonement: The Influence of Evangelicalism on Social and Economic Thought, 1785–1865* (Oxford, 1991), 10–26.
72. "The Newspaper Press," in *The Extractor; Or, Universal Repertorium of Literature, Science and the Arts; Comprehending, Under One General Arrangement, the Whole of the Instructive and Amusing Articles from All the Reviews, Magazines, and Journals* (London, 1829), 578–87; David Turley, *The Culture of English Antislavery, 1780–1860* (London, 1991), 48. For a discussion of print culture and its relationship to other aspects of radical endeavor, such as mass meetings, petitions, and boycotts, see Kevin Gilmartin, *Print Politics: The Press and Radical Opposition in Early Nineteenth-Century England* (Cambridge, 1996).
73. Boyd Hilton, *A Mad, Bad, and Dangerous People? England 1783–1846* (Oxford, 2006), 20.
74. *World*, 9 July 1828.

75. M. E. Levy, letter to the editor, *World*, 12 December 1827.
76. Jacob Katz (1904–1998) may have made frequent use of sociological theory, but his research preceded the significant insights gained by social movement theorists in the last two decades, a body of work that the present volume makes ample use of. Katz first examined the applicability of historical sociology in his essay, "The Concept of Social History and Its Possible Use in Jewish Historical Research," *Scripta Hierosolymitana* 3 (1955): 292–312 and then made more intensive use of this concept in his landmark study, *Tradition and Crisis: Jewish Society at the End of the Middle Ages* (New York, 1961). For insight on Katz and this author's reliance on such seminal figures as Weber, Durkheim, and Mannheim, see Laurence J. Silberstein, "Historical Sociology and Jewish Historiography: A Review Essay," *Journal of the American Academy of Religion* 42, no. 4 (1974): 692–98; see also Simon Dubnow, "The Sociological View of Jewish History," in *Ideas of Jewish History*, ed. Michael A. Meyer (Detroit, 1987), 259–72.
77. See, for example, Peter Burke, *History and Social Theory*, 2nd ed. (Ithaca, NY, 2005), 1–16.
78. Ibid., 3. For additional discussion on this topic, see John Lukacs, "The Evolving Relationship of History and Sociology," *International Journal of Politics, Culture and Society* 1 (1987): 79–88; Theda Skocpol, "Sociology's Historical Imagination," in *Vision and Method in Historical Sociology*, ed. T. Skocpol (New York, 1985).
79. Charles Tilly and Sidney Tarrow, *Contentious Politics* (Boulder, CO, 2007); Sidney G. Tarrow, *Power in Movement: Social Movements and Contentious Politics*, 2nd ed. (Cambridge, 1998); Jeff Goodwin, James M. Jasper, and Francesca Polletta, eds., *Passionate Politics: Emotions in Social Movements* (Chicago, 2001).
80. Tilly, *Popular Contention*, 371.
81. Hank Johnston, "Verification and Proof in Frame and Discourse Analysis," in *Methods of Social Movement Research*, eds. Bert Klandermans and Suzanne Staggenborg (Minneapolis, 2002), 73–75.
82. Florence Passy, "Political Altruism and the Solidarity Movement," in *Political Altruism? Solidarity Movements in International Perspective*, eds. Marco Guigni and F. Passy (Lanham, MD, 2001), 3–25.
83. Bar Yohai quoted in Jonathan Sacks, *To Heal a Fractured World: The Ethics of Responsibility* (New York, 2007), 84. This mandate appears in the Talmud: "All Jews are responsible for each other" (*Kol Yisrael arevim zeh bazeh*).
84. "The Anti-Jewish Movement in Russia," *Manchester Times*, 18 June 1881.
85. "Persecution of the Jews: The Meeting in Philadelphia," *National Gazette* (Philadelphia), 3 September 1840.
86. This view is exemplified in the "Diary for the Month of December," *London Magazine* 10 (January 1828): 81–82. For working-class antagonism to the movement, see "The Jews," *Cobbett's Weekly Political Register*, 5 January 1828.
87. "The Mortara Abduction," *New York Herald*, 5 December 1858.
88. *Daily Inter-Ocean* (Chicago), 2 February 1882.

CHAPTER 1

1. Ruud Koopmans, "Protest in Time and Space: The Evolution of Waves of Contention," in *The Blackwell Companion to Social Movements*, eds. David A. Snow, Sarah A. Soule, and Hanspeter Kriesi (Malden, MA, 2004), 19.

2. Boyd Hilton, *A Mad, Bad, and Dangerous People? England 1783–1846* (Oxford, 2006), 372–437; see also David Cannadine, *The Rise and Fall of Class in Britain* (New York, 1999), 61–62.
3. Thomas Carlyle to Lady Ashburton, 4 March 1854, Carlyle Letters Online [CLO], <http://carlyleletters.org> (accessed 1 December 2007).
4. Clyde J. Lewis, "The Disintegration of the Tory-Anglican Alliance in the Struggle for Catholic Emancipation," *Church History* 29 (March 1960): 25.
5. Koopmans, "Protest in Time and Space," 24; Manochehr Dorraj, "The Crisis of Modernity and Religious Revivalism: A Comparative Study of Islamic Fundamentalism, Jewish Fundamentalism and Liberation Theology," *Social Compass* 46 (1999): 228.
6. "On the State of Religious Parties in England," *Monthly Repository of Theology and General Literature* 1 (January 1827): 1.
7. Hilton, *A Mad, Bad, and Dangerous People*, 176. The influence of the apocalyptic faction would escalate throughout Britain, and within two decades over half of evangelicals would identify with the premillennial schema; see Grayson Carter, *Anglican Evangelicals: Protestant Secessions from the Via Media, c. 1800–1850* (Oxford, 2001), 155.
8. Mark Patterson and Andrew Walker, "'Our Unspeakable Comfort,' Irving, Albury, and the Origins of the Pre-Tribulation Rapture," in *Christian Millenarianism: From the Early Church to Waco*, ed. Stephen Hunt (Bloomington, IN, 2001), 114.
9. Henry Mayhew, *London Labour and the London Poor: A Cyclopedia of the Condition and Earnings of Those That Will Work, Those That Cannot Work, and Those That Will Not Work*, 3 vols. (London, 1861), 2: 118.
10. Todd M. Endelman, *The Jews of Georgian England, 1714–1840: Tradition and Change in a Liberal Society* (Philadelphia, 1979), 192–226.
11. Thomas Carlyle to Jean Carlyle Aitken, 26 October 1853, Carlyle Letters Online [CLO], <http://carlyleletters.org> (accessed 1 December 2007).
12. S.T. Coleridge to John Murray [August 1820], *Collected Letters of Samuel Taylor Coleridge: 1820–1825*, ed. Early Leslie Griggs (Oxford, 1971), 5:91.
13. Mitchell B. Hart, "The Unbearable Lightness of Britain: Anglo-Jewish Historiography and the Anxiety of Success," *Journal of Modern Jewish Studies* 6 (July 2007): 150.
14. Haim Bermant, *The Cousinhood: The Anglo-Jewish Gentry* (London, 1971).
15. "Review of *Brief Memoir of the Jews, in Relation to Their Civil and Municipal Disabilities*, by Apsley Pellatt," *Eclectic Review* (December 1829): 521.
16. S.T. Coleridge to Daniel Stuart, 12 October 1827, in *Collected Letters of Samuel Taylor Coleridge*, ed. Earl Leslie Griggs, 6 vols. (Oxford, 2000), 6:704.
17. Thomas Babington Macaulay to Hannah Macaulay, 31 May 1831, in *The Letters of Thomas Babington Macaulay*, ed. Thomas Pinney (Cambridge, 2008), 2: 24; James Boswell, "The Journal of a Tour to the Hebrides with Samuel Johnson, LL.D.," 1 September 1773, *Boswell's Life of Johnson Including Boswell's Journal of a Tour of Hibrides and Johnson's Diary of a Journey into North Wales*, ed. George Birbeck Hill (New York, 1891), 5: 164–65.
18. "Review of *Brief Memoir of the Jews*," *Eclectic Review* (December 1829): 521; Endelman, *Jews of Georgian England*, 22.
19. Werner Sombart, *Jews and Modern Capitalism* (New York, 1913), 90; Frank Felsenstein, *Anti-Semitic Stereotypes: A Paradigm of Otherness in English Popular Culture, 1660–1830* (Baltimore, 1995), 166.
20. Goldwin Smith, "The Jewish Question," *Eclectic Magazine of Foreign Literature, Science, and Art* 34 (December 1881): 820.

21. David Hume, "Essay IX: Of Public Credit," in *Philosophical Works of David Hume* (Edinburgh, 1828), 3: 398.
22. *Eclectic Review* (December 1829): 522.
23. Pierre Bourdieu, *The Field of Cultural Production: Essays on Art and Literature*, ed. Randal Johnson (New York, 1993), 8, 46.
24. Mordechai Rozin, *The Rich and the Poor: Jewish Philanthropy and Social Control in Nineteenth-Century London* (Brighton, UK, 1999), 65–86.
25. Todd M. Endelman, *The Jews of Britain, 1656–2000* (Berkeley, 2002), 85.
26. [Joseph] Crooll, "The Jews," *World*, 2 July 1828.
27. Endelman, *Jews of Georgian England*, 119.
28. See C. S. Monaco, *Moses Levy of Florida: Jewish Utopian and Antebellum Reformer* (Baton Rouge, 2005).
29. Ibid., 95–114.
30. Ibid., 41, 105–6.
31. Jacob Toury, "M. E. Levy's Plan for a Jewish Colony in Florida—1825," in *Michael: On the History of the Jew in the Diaspora*, ed. Lloyd P. Gartner (Tel Aviv, 1975).
32. Jonathan D. Sarna, *Jacksonian Jew: The Two Worlds of Mordecai Noah* (New York, 1981), 61–75.
33. Henry Samuel Morais, *Eminent Israelites of the Nineteenth Century* (Philadelphia, 1880), 252–55.
34. "Selig Newman," in *Cyclopaedia of Biblical, Theological, and Ecclesiastical Literature* (New York, 1894), 7: 20–21. See also Selig Newman, *The Challenge Accepted: A Dialogue Between a Jew and a Christian* (New York, 1850); Jonathan D. Sarna, "The American Jewish Response to Nineteenth-Century Jewish Missions," *Journal of American History* 68 (June 1981): 39–40. Newman has often been labeled as orthodox, but it is clear that he actually held a middle-ground between what he referred to as "immovable orthodoxy on the one hand, and the frenzied rashness of reform on the other"; see S[elig] Newman, "The Necessity of Union," *Occident and American Jewish Advocate* 8 (March 1851): 603.
35. Ibid., 599.
36. The ranking "Jewish champion" at the time was the fighter Barney Aaron; see "Barney Aaron and Frank Redman," *Bell's Life in London and Sporting Chronicle*, 19 August 1827.
37. "An Hebrew" [pseudo.], "The Jews," *Morning Chronicle*, 19 July 1827.
38. Although largely hagiographical, key incidents in Wolff's extremely idiosyncratic life are presented in W. T. Gidney, *The History of the London Society for the Promotion of Christianity Amongst the Jews, from 1809–1908* (London, 1908), 101–11. For a far less reverent and thoroughly amusing description of Wolff's later years, see Joseph Leech, *The Church Goer: Rural Rides; or, Calls at Country Churches* (London, 1847), 232–41.
39. Details of this incident are related in "Philo-Judaean Society," *Times*, 9 March 1827. For more on the perception of unruliness with the mob, see Charles Tilly, *Popular Contention in Great Britain, 1758–1834* (Boulder, CO, 2005), 153. On the threatening character of religious apostates in general, see Martin E. Marty, *When Faiths Collide* (Malden, MA, 2005), 34–35, 101–2.
40. "An Hebrew" [pseudo.], "The Jews," *Morning Chronicle*, 19 July 1827.
41. Endelman, *Jews of Georgian England*, 78.
42. These leaders included George Vernon, president; J. J. Strutt, and Viscount Mandeville, co–vice presidents; Henry Drummond, treasurer; John Aq. Brown, secretary; and Rev. Hugh McNeile; see Philo-Judaean Society, *First Annual Report of the Philo-Judaean Society* (London, 1827).

43. See Philo-Judaean Society, *First* and *Second Annual Report of the Philo-Judaean Society.*
44. Historians have assumed that both Bexley and Grant were Philo-Judaeans; for example, see Abigail Green, "The British Empire and the Jews: An Imperialism of Human Rights?" *Past and Present* 199 (May 2008): n. 67, 189. Nevertheless, neither Bexley nor Grant is listed in the membership roles of this organization nor did they contribute to Philo-Judaean meetings. They functioned instead as political allies. See the *First, Second,* and *Third Annual Reports of the Philo-Judaean Society* (London, 1827–1829).
45. Brown, *The Jew: The Master-Key of the Apocalypse* (London, 1827).
46. Most Philo-Judaean officers attended the first Albury conference. For a list of attendees, see Columba Graham Flegg, *"'Gathered Under Apostles,' A Study of the Catholic Apostolic Church* (Oxford, 1992), 37–38; see also, Carter, *Anglican Evangelicals,* 177–79.
47. Yet the society was certainly not immune from a deeply ingrained conversionist culture; for background, see Mel Scult, *Millennial Expectations and Jewish Liberties: A Study of the Efforts to Convert the Jews in Britain, up to the Mid-Nineteenth Century* (Leiden, 1978), 132–33.
48. Viscount Mandeville quoted in the *World,* 23 May 1827.
49. Judith W. Page, *Imperfect Sympathies: Jews and Judaism in British Romantic Literature and Culture* (New York, 2004), 167.
50. Church historian Wolfram Kinzig has distinguished between two forms of philo-Semitism: primary and secondary. *Primary philo-Semitism,* according to Kinzig, has occurred throughout history, mostly in relation to millenarian or end-times movements in Christianity. The secondary form, in contrast, does not stem from a positive view of either Jews or Judaism but is subordinate to such impulses as conversionism. For a discussion of Kinzig and other authors on this topic, see Stephen G. Burnett, "Philosemitism and Christian Hebraism in the Reformation Era," in *Geliebter Feind Gehasster Freund: Antisemitismus und Philosemitismus und Geschichte und Gegenwart: Festschrift zum 65. Geburtstag Von Julius Schoeps,* eds. Irene A. Diekmann and Elke-Vera Kotowski (Berlin, 2009), 135–46. See also, Wolfram Kinzig, "Philosemitism," in *Dictionary of Jewish-Christian Relations,* eds. Edward Kessler and Neil Wenborn (Cambridge, 2005), 342–43.
51. Brown's competing Abrahamic Association was merged into the Philo-Judaean Society; see William Brooks, letter to the editor, *World,* 5 December 1827 and "Philo-Judaean Society," *World,* 23 May 1827.
52. Both Drummond and McNeile, for example, assumed leadership positions in the Surrey Anti-Slavery Society; see *World,* 31 October and 7 November 1827.
53. Drummond quoted in Hilton, *Mad, Bad, and Dangerous People,* 405
54. Joseph Wolff, "Mr. Wolff and the Jews of London," *Morning Chronicle,* 22 June 1827.
55. Wolff's invective reached the United States under the heading, "The Jews of London"; see, for example, *Boston Recorder and Religious Telegraph,* 28 December 1827; *Western Luminary,* 21 November 1827; and *The Religious Intelligencer* (New Haven, CT), 5 January 1828.
56. "Diary for the Month of July," *London Magazine,* 1 August 1827, 462.
57. Martin E. Marty, *When Faiths Collide* (Malden, MA, 2005), 35.
58. See, for example, the letters published in the *Morning Chronicle* on 25 and 28 June and 7 and 21 July 1827.
59. Coincidentally, Wolff's vitriolic publications were also noticed in the United States by Isaac Leeser, a young German Jewish immigrant and future *hazzan*

at Philadelphia's Mikve Israel Synagogue. Leeser's indignation inspired a series of articles in defense of Judaism that established the newcomer's reputation in America; see Lance J. Sussman, *Isaac Leeser and the Making of American Judaism* (Detroit, 1995), 42–45.
60. John Tosh, "Gentlemanly Politeness and Manly Simplicity in Victorian England," *Transactions of the Royal Historical Society* 12 (2002): 455–72.
61. Augustus Pugin and John Britton, *Illustrations of the Public Buildings of London* (London, 1838), 2: 246.
62. "Anti-Slavery Society," *World*, 7 May 1828.
63. *First Report*, 35.
64. Eli Lederhendler, *Jewish Responses to Modernity: New Voices in America and Europe* (New York, 1994), 24.
65. "Continuation of Mr. Levy's Letter," *World*, 20 June 1827. Levy's address was subject to errors of editing and transcription when it first appeared in the *World* newspaper and later in the *First Report of the Philo-Judaean Society*. Levy succeeded, however, in having the *World* reprint his entire speech, based on his own manuscript; see the Appendix.
66. Owen Whooley, "Masterframes and Movement Trajectory: A Case Study of the American Abolitionist Movement," paper presented at the annual meeting of the American Sociological Association, San Francisco, 2004.
67. Mario Diani, "Leaders or Brokers? Positions and Influence in Social Movement Networks," in *Social Movements and Networks: Relational Approaches to Collective Action* (Oxford, 2003), 107.
68. Eugene Stock, *The History of the Church Missionary Society* (London, 1899), 1: 147.
69. McNeile quoted in "The Philo-Judaean Society," *World*, 23 May 1827.
70. R. W. Dale, *History of English Congregationalism* (New York, 1907), 688; H. R. Fox Bourne, *English Newspapers: Chapters in the History of Journalism* (London, 1887), 2:45.
71. Bourne later served as a Magistrate in Jamaica and kept up with his relationship to Holland; see B. W. Higman, "To Begin the World Again," in *Jamaica in Slavery and Freedom: History, Heritage and Culture*, eds. Kathleen E. A. Monteith and Glenn Richards (Kingston, Jamaica, 2002), 295.
72. *World*, 19 May 1828.
73. Sidney G. Tarrow, "States and Opportunities: The Political Structuring of Social Movements," in *Comparative Perspectives on Social Movements: Political Opportunities, Mobilizing Structures, and Cultural Framing*, eds. Doug McAdams, John D. McCarthy, and Mayer Zald (Cambridge, 1996), 60.
74. For the origins of the early women's rights movement, see Blanche Glassman Hersh, "'Am I Not a Woman and a Sister?' Abolitionist Beginnings of Nineteenth-Century Feminism," in *Antislavery Reconsidered: New Perspectives on the Abolitionists*, eds. Lewis Perry and Michael Fellman (Baton Rouge, LA, 1979), 252–83; Helen LaKelly, "Abolitionist Feminists of the Anti-Slavery Convention of American Women of 1837: The Role of Theological Vision and the Ethic of Sympathy" (PhD diss., Union Theological Seminary, 2003); Nell Irvin Painter, *Sojourner Truth: A Life, A Symbol* (New York, 1997); Sandra F. VanBurkleo, *"Belonging to the World," Women's Rights and American Constitutional Culture* (New York, 2001), 103–24.
75. Boyd Hilton, *Age of Atonement, The Influence of Evangelicalism on Social and Economic Thought, 1785–1865* (Oxford, 1986), 209.
76. "Mortara Abduction" [Rev. Isaacs' Address], *New York Herald*, 5 December 1858.
77. Victor Hugo, "Les Juifs," *La Presse* (Paris), 19 June 1882.

CHAPTER 2

1. Details of this petition are found in J[ohn] A[quila] Brown, letter to the editor, *Morning Chronicle*, 3 July 1827.
2. Todd M. Endelman, *The Jews of Georgian England, 1714–1830: Tradition and Change in a Liberal Society* (Philadelphia, 1979), 79.
3. It is unclear whether the group at Salvador House was connected with the Society for the Investigation of Prophecy, founded in 1826 by Edward Irving, Lewis Way, and James Hatley Frere. Both groups shared the same basic theology; for background on the Irvingite organization, see Grayson Carter, *Anglican Evangelicals: Protestant Successions from the Via Media, c .1800–1850* (Oxford, 2001), 176; Columba Graham Flegg, *"Gathered Under Apostles," A Study of the Catholic Apostolic Church* (Oxford, 1992), 40. For an unfavorable and, according to Levy, grossly distorted view of his deliberations at Salvador House, see Abraham Jones Le Cras, letter to the editor, *New Jerusalem Magazine and Theological Inspector* (November 1827): 336–38. The intentions of the Salvador House prophetic group can be further gleaned from "Prophecies Investigated in 1827," *Midnight Cry* (New York), 9 December 1842.
4. M. E. Levy, letter to the editor, *World*, 31 October 1827.
5. "Society for Investigating the Prophecies," *World*, 3 October 1827.
6. This challenge appeared as an advertisement in the *World*, 7 November 1827. Examples of some of Gordon's intemperate rhetoric can be found in "The Jews," *World*, 14 November 1827.
7. On the evolution of these meetings as well as invaluable firsthand commentary, see "W.C.," letter to the editor, *World*, 6 August 1828.
8. "Discussion of the Oral Law Between Jews and Christians," *Morning Chronicle*, 19 January 1828.
9. "Meetings of the Jews," *Times*, 5, 24, and 31 December 1827; *Morning Chronicle*, 19 January 1828; "W.C.," letter to the editor, *World*, 6 August 1828.
10. See especially *Times*, 24 and 31 December 1827; *Morning Chronicle*, 19 January 1828; *World*, 2, 9, and 16 January 1827.
11. These names are gleaned from news reports and transcripts of the proceedings of the Jews that appeared in newspapers and periodicals (all of them cited herein). The Johnson surname may be connected to a well-known Jewish family from Devon; see Bernard Susser, "Social Acclimatization of Jews in Eighteenth and Nineteenth Century Devon," in *Exeter Papers in Economic History No. 3: Industry and Society in the South West* (Exeter, 1970), 60.
12. C.S. Monaco, *Moses Levy of Florida: Jewish Utopian and Antebellum Reformer* (Baton Rouge: LA), 125.
13. For a more detailed look at Levy's religious views, see Monaco, *Moses Levy of Florida*.
14. Nan Johnson, "The Popularization of Nineteenth-Century Rhetoric: Elocution and the Private Learner," in *Oratorical Culture in Nineteenth Century America: Transformations in the Theory and Practice of Rhetoric*, eds. Gregory Clark and S. Michael Halloran (Carbondale, IL, 1993), 139–57.
15. Gregory Clark and S. Michael Halloran, "Introduction: Transformations of Public Discourse in Nineteenth-Century America," in *Oratorical Culture in Nineteenth Century America*, 2. On the importance of Greek and Roman rhetoric in 1820s England, see "Inaugural Discourse of Mr. Brougham when elected Lord Rector of the University of Glasgow, Delivered April 6, 1825," in *Select British Eloquence: Embracing the Best Speeches Entire, of the Most Eminent Orators of Great Britain for the Last Two Centuries*, ed.

Chauncey A. Goodrich (New York, 1884), 937–47; see also Gilbert Highet, *The Classical Tradition: Greek and Roman Influences on Western Literature* (New York, 1985).
16. Iain McCalman, *Radical Underworld: Prophets, Revolutionaries, and Pornographers in London, 1795–1840* (Cambridge, 1988), 113–16.
17. Francesca Polletta and James M. Jasper, "Collective Identity and Social Movements," *Annual Review of Sociology* 27 (2001): 284.
18. Thomas Scott, Introduction to *The Restoration of Israel* by Joseph Crooll (London, 1814), v–vi.
19. "Ukase issued by Imperial Mandate for Regulating the Existing Laws Concerning the Residence of Jews," *World*, 31 October 1827.
20. Mikhail Beizer, *The Jews of St. Petersburg: Excursions Through a Noble Past* (Philadelphia, 1989), 6.
21. I am obliged to Professor Michael Stanislawski for offering his insight into this rarely noted ukase; Michael Stanislawski [mfs3@columbia.edu], "Ukase of 1827," private e-mail message to author, 1 February 2010.
22. "Meeting of the Jews," *Times*, 5 December 1827.
23. "Meeting of the Jews," *World*, 5 December 1827.
24. For more on this tradition, see John Klier, *Russians, Jews, and the Pogroms of 1881–1882* (Cambridge, 2011), 257–64.
25. "Meeting of the Jews," *World*, 5 December 1827.
26. Ibid.
27. M. E. Levy ["Midrash," pseudo.], "To the Jewish Community on the Necessity of Better Educating Their Children in a Knowledge of Hebrew," *World*, 19 December 1827.
28. John P. LeDonne, *The Russian Empire and the World, 1700–1917: The Geopolitics of Expansion and Containment* (New York, 1997), 308–16; John Howes Gleason, *The Genesis of Russophobia in Great Britain: A Study of the Interaction of Policy and Opinion* (Cambridge, 1950), 83.
29. "Judaism and the Jerusalem Bishoprick," *Christian Remembrancer* 12 (July–December 1846): 225.
30. "Public Meeting of the Jews," *World*, 12 December 1827.
31. Ibid.
32. See, for example, "Public Meeting of the Jews Respecting the Russian Persecution," *Morning Chronicle*, 21 December 1827; "Public Meeting of the Jews, *World*, 26 December 1827; "Interesting Meeting of the Jews in London," *American Baptist Magazine* 7 (July 1828): 215; "Public Meeting of the Jews," *Baptist Magazine* (January 1828): 35; "Interesting Meeting of the Jews in London," *Christian Secretary* (Hartford, Conn.), 29 March 1828; *Christian Watchman* (Boston), 14 March 1828; *The Albion, A Journal of News, Politics, and Literature* (New York), 9 February 1828.
33. "Interesting Meeting of the Jews in London," *American Baptist Magazine* 7 (July 1828): 215.
34. "Public Meeting of the Jews," *Baptist Magazine* (January 1828): 35.
35. Despite formal Jewish emancipation in 1790–1791, full political rights in France did not become a reality until the removal of corporate disabilities in 1830; discrimination in the professions continued well into the nineteenth century; see Lisa Moses Leff, *Sacred Bonds of Solidarity: The Rise of Jewish Internationalism in Nineteenth-Century France* (Stanford, CA, 2006), 6.
36. M. E. Levy, letter to the editor, *World*, 6 August 1828.
37. Ibid.
38. For a synthesis of previous work in this area, see Yosef Salmon, "The Historical Imagination of Jacob Katz: On the Origins of Jewish Nationalism," *Jewish Social Studies* 5 (1999): 161–76. The anti-assimilationist focus of

Ahad Ha'am or Asher Ginzberg (1856–1927), the so-called father of spiritual Zionism, bears resemblance to Levy's views. Ha'am's statement that political rights constituted "spiritual slavery under the veil of outward freedom" would have been in perfect accord with Levy's sentiments; see Ahad Ha'am, "Slavery in Freedom," in *Selected Essays*, trans. Leon Simon (Philadelphia, 1912), 177; see also Steven J. Zipperstein, "Ahad Ha'am and the Politics of Assimilation," in *Assimilation and Community: The Jews in Nineteenth-Century Europe*, eds. Jonathan Frankel and Steven J. Zipperstein (Cambridge, 1992), 344–63.

39. John Tosh, "Gentlemanly Politeness and Manly Simplicity in Victorian England," *Transactions of the Royal Historical Society* 12 (2002): 458.
40. James Eli Adams, *Dandies and Desert Saints: Styles of Victorian Masculinity* (Ithaca, NY, 1995), 61–63.
41. Israel quoted in the *World*, 26 December 1827.
42. Levy quoted in the *World*, 26 December 1827.
43. "Diary for the Month of December," *London Magazine* 10 (January 1828): 81–82.
44. "The Jews," *Cobbett's Weekly Political Register*, 5 January 1828.
45. Bourne quoted in "Public Meetings of the Jews, *World*, 26 December 1827.
46. Coverage in the *World*, *Times*, and *Morning Chronicle* can be found throughout November and December 1827. In addition, see "Jews," *New Times*, 7 December 1827; "Meeting of the Jews," *Courier* (London); "Russian Ukase," *Baldwin's London Weekly Journal*, 24 November 1827; "The Jews in Russia," *Trades' Free Press* (London), 4 November 1827; "The Jews," *Atlas* (London), 9 December 1827. UK periodicals include: "Persecution of the Jews in Russia," *Monthly Repository and Review of Theology and General Literature* 11 (January 1828): 139–40; "Public Meeting of the Jews," *Baptist Magazine* (January 1828): 30–35; *Church of England Bulwark and Clergyman's Protector* (January 1828): 32–33; "Foreign, Religious and Literary Intelligence," *Christian Examiner and Church of Ireland Magazine* (April 1828): 307–8; "Jews," *New Monthly Magazine and Literary Journal* (January 1828): 187. For the provincial press, see "Public Meeting of the Jews Respecting the Russian Persecution," *Bristol Mercury*, 24 December 1827; "London," *Hampshire Telegraph and Sussex Chronicle* (Portsmouth) 10 December 1827; "The Jews," *Ipswich Journal*, 1 December 1827; *Leeds Mercury*, 1 December 1827; "The Russian Ukase," *Hull Packet*, 6 November 1827; "Persecution of the Jews," *North Wales Chronicle* (Bangor), 27 December 1827; "The Jews," *Liverpool Mercury*, 11 January 1828; "Meetings of the Jews," *Sydney Gazette and New South Wales Advertiser*, 23 June 1828.
47. For German and Dutch coverage, see "Großbritannien," *Allgemeine Zeitung*, 24 December 1827 and "Groot-Brittannie," *Dagblad van's Gravenhage*, 2 January 1828. American papers include *Philadelphia Gazette and Daily Advertiser*, 15 February 1828; "Interesting Meeting of the Jews in London," *American Baptist Magazine* 7 (July 1828): 215. This last article was reprinted from the *New York Observer*. See also "Interesting Meeting of the Jews in London," *Christian Secretary* (Hartford, Conn.), 29 March 1828; *Christian Watchman* (Boston), 14 March 1828; *Albion, A Journal of News, Politics, and Literature* (New York), 9 February 1828.
48. John Lofland, *Social Movement Organizations: Guide to Research on Insurgent Realities* (New York, 1996), 322–23.
49. *Times* and *World*, 2 January 1828; *Morning Chronicle*, 3 January 1828.
50. For background on how social movements adapt to changing and less receptive political environments, see Verta Taylor, "Social Movement Continuity:

The Women's Movement in Abeyance," *American Sociological Review* 54 (October 1989): 761–75.
51. Wellington's opposition to Jewish civil rights and his intolerance toward Jews generally, see Arthur Wellesley, "The Jews' Right to Citizenship Denied," 1 August 1843, and "The Jews Have No Right to Civil Equality," 1 August 1833, in *Maxims and Opinions of Field-Marshall His Grace the Duke of Wellington, Selected from His Writings and Speeches During a Public Life of More Than Half a Century. With a Biographical Memoir by George Henry Francis, Esq.* (London, 1845), 334–38. See also J. H. Stocqueler, *The Life of Field Marshal the Duke of Wellington* (London, 1853), 2: 174, 186. In private correspondence, Wellington indulged in a medieval conception of Jews as devils (replete with tails); see Christopher Hibbert, *Wellington: A Personal History* (New York, 1997), 84.
52. Lionel G. Robinson, ed., *Letters of Dorothea, Princess Lieven, During Her Residence in London, 1812–1834* (London, 1902), 174.
53. Joe Foweraker, *Theorizing Social Movements* (London, 1995), 65; Lofland, *Social Movement Organizations*, 310–15.
54. Levy also published an influential antislavery pamphlet, *A Plan for the Abolition of Slavery, Consistently with the Interests of All Parties Concerned* (London, 1828) and coauthored a book, *Letters Concerning the Present Condition of the Jews: Being a Correspondence between Mr. Forster and Mr. Levy* (London, 1829).
55. M. E. Levy ["Midrash," pseudo.], "To the Jewish Community."
56. *Address to the Sons of Israel* (London, 1828); see also Endelman, *Jews of Georgian England*, 244.
57. Ibid.
58. Levy's stance against full political rights, as well as the discord this engendered among some coalition members, is summarized in Levy, "State of the Jews," *World*, 6 August 1828.
59. Philo-Judaean Society. *First Annual Report of the Philo-Judaean Society* (London), 16.
60. Bexley quoted in Philo-Judaean Society. *Second Annual Report of the Philo-Judaean Society* (London), 13–14.
61. Eldon quoted in "Parliamentary Intelligence," *Leeds Mercury*, 3 May 1828.
62. Wellington quoted in "Parliamentary Intelligence," *Leeds Mercury*, 3 May 1828.
63. Philo-Judaean Society. *Second Annual Report*, 14.
64. Mel Scult, *Millennial Expectations and Jewish Liberties: A Study of the Efforts to Convert the Jews in Britain, up to the Mid Nineteenth Century* (Leiden, 1978), 131; U.R.Q. Henriques, "The Jewish Emancipation Controversy in Nineteenth-Century Britain," *Past and Present* 40 (1968): 127.
65. M. Salbstein, *The Emancipation of the Jews in Britain: The Question of the Admission of the Jews to Parliament, 1828–1860* (Rutherford, NJ, 1982); A. Gilam, *The Emancipation of the Jews in England, 1830–1860* (New York, 1982); Henriques, "The Jewish Emancipation Controversy."
66. Francis H. Goldsmid, *Memoir of Sir Francis Henry Goldsmid*, 2nd ed. (London, 1882), 24.
67. Ibid.
68. Charles Tilly, *Popular Contention in Great Britain, 1758–1834* (Boulder, CO, 2005), 37.
69. "Parliamentary Intelligence," *Times*, 11 July 1828; see also "The Jews," *Hull Packet*, 26 August 1828; "The Jews," *Morning Chronicle*, 25 September 1828.
70. "Meeting of the Jews," *Morning Chronicle*, 19 August 1828.
71. "Meeting for the Relief of the Jews," *Times*, 27 August 1828.

72. Isaac L. Goldsmid to the Parnassim and Vestry of the Great Synagogue, 26 September 1836, Acc/3121/A/005/A (ff 33–45), Meetings of the Board of Deputies of British Jews, London Metropolitan Archives. I am grateful to Abigail Green for sharing her copy of this letter.
73. *Diaries of Sir Moses and Lady Montefiore*, ed. L. Loewe (Chicago, 1890), 1: 60.
74. Dermot Keough Keogh, *Jews in Twentieth-Century Ireland* (Cork, Ireland, 1998), 7.
75. Monaco, *Moses Levy of Florida*, 142–71.
76. Todd M. Endelman, *The Jews of Britain, 1656–2000* (Berkeley, CA, 2002), 106; for reference to public meetings, see Abigail Green, "Rethinking Sir Moses Montefiore: Religion, Nationhood, and International Philanthropy in the Nineteenth Century," *American Historical Review* 110 (June 2005): 651.
77. Just as Levy himself, it is certainly true that both Montefiore and Goldsmid had formed earlier business partnerships with prominent gentiles, some of whom became close friends; see Abigail Green, "The British Empire and the Jews: An Imperialism of Human Rights?" *Past and Present* 199 (May 2008): 189.
78. Philo-Judaean Society, *Third Annual Report*, 16; this benevolent society was founded in 1829; see Charles Henderson, *Modern Methods of Charity: An Account of the Systems of Relief, Public and Private in the Principal Countries Having Modern Methods* (New York, 1904), 662–63.
79. Philo-Judaean Society, *Third Annual Report*, 17.
80. Isaac L. Goldsmid to the Parnassim and Vestry of the Great Synagogue, 26 September 1836, Acc/3121/A/005/A (ff 33–45), Meetings of the Board of Deputies of British Jews, London Metropolitan Archives.
81. Hermann Gollancz, *Sermons and Addresses* (New York, 1909), 598.
82. "Petition in Favour of the Jews," *Hansards Parliamentary Debates*, vol. 24 (1830): 769–74.
83. Green, "Rethinking Sir Moses Montefiore," 651.
84. For reference to "the now defunct Philo-Judaean Society," see *Examiner* (London), 12 June 1831. After Drummond and others left the Church of England, loyal Anglicans, such as Rev. Hugh McNeile, maintained their distance from this rebellious faction (on this conflict, see Carter, *Anglican Evangelicals*, 185–86; Flegg, *"Gathered Under Apostles,"* 53. The death of John Aq. Brown in 1830 may also have contributed to the organization's demise.
85. *Oxford Dictionary of National Biography*, s.v. "Sir Isaac Lyon Goldsmid"; L. Abrahams, "Sir I. L. Goldsmid and the Admission of the Jews of England to Parliament," *Transactions of the Jewish Historical Society of England* 4 (1899–1901): 116–76.
86. Co-optation of social movement goals was and still remains a technique by which elites, consciously or otherwise, attempt to control movements by "manipulating the symbolic environment" in their favor without making any attempt to alter the basic hierarchical power structure; see Lofland, *Social Movement Organizations*, 310–11.

CHAPTER 3

1. David Brion Davis, "Slavery and Progress," in *Anti-Slavery, Religion, and Reform: Essays in Memory of Roger Anstey*, eds. Christine Bolt and Seymour Drescher (Folkstone, UK, 1980), 353.
2. F. David Roberts, *The Social Conscience of the Early Victorians* (Stanford, CA, 2002), 259.
3. Ibid., 311.

4. Charles Dickens, *A Christmas Carol. In Prose. Being a Ghost Story of Christmas* (London, 1843), 33.
5. Quoted in [John Dix], *Pen Pictures of Popular English Preachers* (London, 1852), 69; see also John Matthias Weylland, *Round the Tower, or, The Story of the London City Mission* (London, 1875), 18–19. For an assessment of Noel, see Grayson Carter, *Anglican Evangelicals: Protestant Secessions from the Via Media, c. 1800–1850* (Oxford, 2001), 312–55.
6. Roberts, *Social Conscience of the Early Victorians*, 258.
7. On the theme of humanitarianism, race, and antislavery, consider David Brion Davis, *The Problem of Slavery in the Age of Revolution 1770–1823* (Ithaca, NY, 1975); Catherine Hall, *Civilising Subjects. Metropole and Colony in the English Imagination 1830–1867* (Cambridge, 2002); Christine Bolt, *Victorian Attitudes to Race* (London, 1971); Douglas Lorrimer, *Victorians and Race* (London, 1975); David Turley, *The Culture of English Antislavery 1780–1860* (London, 1991); Seymour Drescher, *Capitalism and Antislavery* (Oxford, 1986).
8. Harry Stone, "Dickens and the Jews," *Victorian Studies* 2 (March 1959): 223–53. Decades later, a similar anti-Semitic bias arose among so-called progressives in the United States; see Donald Pizer, *American Naturalism and the Jews: Garland, Norris, Dreiser, Wharton and Cather* (Urbana, IL, 2008).
9. Simon Chesterman, *Just War or Just Peace? Humanitarian Intervention and International Law* (Oxford, 2001), 25, 41; Sean D. Murphy, *Humanitarian Intervention: The United Nations in an Evolving World Order* (Philadelphia, 1996), 52–53.
10. Chesterman, *Just War or Just Peace*, 32–33; Murphy, *Humanitarian Intervention*, 53–54.
11. For a discussion of this general tendency, see Bert Klandermans, "The Demand and Supply of Participation: Social-Psychological Correlates of Participation in Social Movements," in *Blackwell Companion to Social Movements*, eds. David A. Snow, Sarah A. Soule, and Hanspeter Kriesi (Malden, MA, 2004), 368.
12. Lady Palmerston to Princess Lieven, 13 November 1840, quoted in Donald M. Lewis, *The Origins of Christian Zionism: Lord Shaftesbury and Evangelical Support for a Jewish Homeland* (New York, 2010), 146.
13. For a recent overview of the contributions of London Society and Lord Shaftesbury during the Damascus affair, see Lewis, *Origins of Christian Zionism*, 175–89.
14. For the use of stigma as a tool to repress social movements, see Myra Marx Ferree, "Soft Repression: Ridicule, Stigma, and Silencing in Gender-Based Movements," in *Authority in Contention*, eds. Daniel J. Myers and Daniel M. Cress (Amsterdam, 2004), 91–93.
15. Moses Hess, *The Revival of Israel: Rome and Jerusalem, the Last Nationalist Question*, trans. Meyer Waxman (1943, reprint; Lincoln, NE, 1995), 67–68.
16. For background, see Kenneth Koltun-Fromm, "A Narrative Reading of Moses Hess's Return to Judaism," *Modern Judaism* 19 (February, 1999): 41–65.
17. Central Consistory to the Ministry of Foreign Affairs, 20 July 1840, quoted in Lisa Moses Leff, *Sacred Bonds of Solidarity: The Rise of Jewish Internationalism in Nineteenth-Century France* (Stanford, CA, 2006), 122.
18. Jonathan Frankel, *The Damascus Affair: "Ritual Murder," Politics, and the Jews in 1840* (New York, 1997), 74–77. The original article published in March reached the United States about a month later; see "A Singular Event," *North American and Daily Advertiser* (Philadelphia), 24 April 1840.

19. *Times*, 20 April 1840.
20. See, for example, *Journal des Débats*, 6 April 1840.
21. S. Posener, *Adolphe Crémieux: A Biography*, trans. Eugene Golob (Philadelphia, 1940), 89. The best overall historical treatment remains Frankel's *Damascus Affair*.
22. G.W. Pieritz, *Persecution of the Jews at Damascus* (London, 1840), 2–3; "Report of Mr. Merlato, the Austrian Consul at Damascus, addressed to M. Laurin, Consul-General for Austria at Alexandria, dated March 23, 1840," *The Era* (London), 17 May 1840.
23. For more on the unique character of the blood libel allegation within Damascus, see Najwa Al-Qattan, "Litigants and Neighbors: The Communal Topography of Ottoman Damascus," *Comparative Studies in Society and History* 44 (July 2002): 527, n. 1. The activities of the monks are related in "Report of Mr. Merlato," *The Era* (London), 17 May 1840. This report identifies an anti-Semitic text, *La prompta Bibliotheca*, as playing a role in promoting the blood libel; see also Frankel, *Damascus Affair*, 53; Ronald Florence, *Blood Libel: The Damascus Affair of 1840* (New York, 2006), 92.
24. Frankel, *Damascus Affair*, 17–64; Florence, *Blood Libel*, 3–39.
25. While Islamic law invalidated confessions that were elicited under torture, religious proscriptions were dramatically at odds with the legal code of the Ottoman Empire. Still, Ottoman law restricted torture only to suspects with lengthy criminal backgrounds, to cases with strong circumstantial evidence, or to those who gave contradictory evidence. Ostensibly, mere accusations—such as those that surfaced against the Damascene Jews—were usually not sufficient grounds for torture. See Edward Peters, *Torture* (Philadelphia, 1985), 92–93.
26. "Translation of a Hebrew Letter from the Jews of Damascus to the Elders of the Congregation at Constantinople" [27 March 1840], *Manchester Times and Gazette*, 25 July 1840.
27. Frankel, *Damascus Affair*, 20–25.
28. R. Po-Chia Hsia, *The Myth of Ritual Murder: Jews and Magic in Reformation Germany* (New Haven, CT, 1988), 1–13; Hermann L. Strack, *The Jews and Human Sacrifice* (London, 1909) 30–49; Alan Dundes, "The Ritual Murder or Blood Libel Legend: A Study of Anti-Semitic Victimization through Projective Inversion," in *The Blood Libel Legend, A Casebook in Anti-Semitic Folklore*, ed. Alan Dundes (Madison, WI, 1991), 336–78. For additional insight concerning the German folkloric tradition and blood libel tales (with reference to the Damascus affair), see Elliot Schreiber, "Tainted Sources: The Subversion of the Grimms' Ideology of the Folktale in Heinrich Heine's 'Der Rabbi von Bacherach,'" *The German Quarterly* 78 (Winter 2005): 29–32.
29. Thomas Philipp, "The Farhi Family and the Changing Position of the Jews of Syria, 1750–1860," *Middle Eastern Studies* 20 (October 1984): 37–52.
30. Mary C. Wilson, "The Damascus Affair and the Beginnings of France's Empire in the Middle East," in *Histories of the Modern Middle East: New Directions*, eds. Israel Gershoni, Hakan Erdem, and Ursula Wokock (Boulder, CO, 2002), 70–71.
31. See, for example, the account in the *Caledonian Mercury* (Edinburgh), 8 June 1840.
32. Austrian consul cited in "The Persecution of the Jews of Damascus," *Chambers Edinburgh Journal*, 4 July 1840. For background on the political and economic rivalries between the Christian and Jewish minorities, see Walter P. Zenner, "Middleman Minorities in the Syrian Mosaic: Trade, Conflict, and Image Management," *Sociological Perspectives* 30 (October 1987): 400–71.

33. Christopher J. Einolf, "The Fall and Rise of Torture: A Comparative and Historical Analysis," *Sociological Theory* 25 (June 2007): 105.
34. For additional background, see Yaron Ben-Naeh, "Honor and Its Meaning Among Ottoman Jews," *Jewish Social Studies* 11 (Winter 2005): 19–50.
35. *Journal des Débats Politiques et Littéraires*, 6 April 1840.
36. Frankel, *Damascus Affair*, 198–205.
37. See, for example, Ad[olphe] Crémieux, letter to the editor, *Journal des Débats*, 8 April 1840.
38. "Life of Joseph Salvador," *The Academy: A Weekly Review of Literature, Science, and Art* (London), 3 September 1881. Salvador's reputation rested in large part to his *Histoire des institutions de Moïse et du peuple hébreu*, 3 vols. (Paris, 1828).
39. Salvador's letter, dated 10 May 1840, was reprinted in its entirety in the *Times* (London), 18 May 1840.
40. *La Presse*, 12 April 1840.
41. Crémieux, letter to the editor, *Journal des Débats*, 8 April 1840.
42. Thiers quoted in Posener, *Adolphe Crémieux*, 104.
43. David Vital, *A People Apart: The Jews in Europe, 1789–1939* (Oxford, 1999), 241.
44. Cremieux quoted in Lucien Wolf, *Sir Moses Montefiore: A Centennial Biography with Selections from Letters and Journals* (New York, 1885), 88
45. *Times*, 2 May 1840.
46. "Father Thomas," *Times*, 18 May 1840.
47. *Times*, 25 June 1840.
48. See, for instance, "A Mystery Hitherto Concealed and Now Published for the First Time," *Times*, 25 June 1840.
49. Andrei Oisteanu, *Inventing the Jew: Antisemitic Stereotypes in Romanian and Other Central-East European Cultures* (Lincoln, NE, 2009), 409.
50. "The *Times*, the Jews, and the Bible," *Satirist; or, the Censor of the Times* (London), 11 October 1840.
51. The *Gazette*'s position is made clear in Barnard Van Oven, letter to the editor, *Literary Gazette and Journal of the Belles Lettres, Arts, Sciences, & c.* (9 May 1840): 295–96.
52. Van Oven, letter to the editor, *Literary Gazette* (9 May 1840): 295.
53. Lewis, *Christian Zionism*, 177–80.
54. Pieritz, *Persecution of the Jews*, 21.
55. "Persecution of the Jews of Damascus and Rhodes," *Times*, 2 June 1840.
56. Lewis, *Christian Zionism*, 181–89; Frankel, *Damascus Affair*, 308-10.
57. For background on Palmerston's position vis-à-vis Mehmed Ali, see Khaled Fahmy, *All the Pasha's Men: Mehmed Ali, His Army, and the Making of Modern Egypt* (Cambridge, 1997), 295–99; Richard Brown, *Church and State in Modern Britain, 1700–1850* (New York, 1991), 513.
58. Quoted in Frankel, *Damascus Affair*, 217.
59. Frankel, *Damascus Affair*, 219.
60. "The Jews at Damascus," *Times*, 25 June 1840.
61. For details of this meeting, see "Persecution of the Jews at Damascus," *Morning Chronicle*, 25 June 1840; *Caledonian Mercury* (Edinburgh), 29 June 1840.
62. Van Oven quoted in Frankel, *Damascus Affair*, 220. For the synagogue's normal seating capacity, see Carol Herselle Krinsky, *Synagogues of Europe: Architecture, History, Meaning* (Mineola, NY, 1996), 415.
63. *National Gazette* (Philadelphia), 27 August 1840.
64. "Persecution of the Jews at Damascus," *Morning Chronicle*, 25 June 1840.
65. Ibid.

66. Penina Moise, "On the Persecution of the Jews of Damascus," in *Sephardic-American Voices: Two Hundred Years of a Literary Legacy*, ed. Diane Matza (Hanover, NH, 1997), 22.
67. Frankel, *Damascus Affair*, 217.
68. Geoffrey Alderman, *Modern British Jewry* (Oxford, 1998), 46–47.
69. Wolf, *Sir Moses Montefiore*, 253.
70. Ray F. Baumeister, Karen L. Dale, and Mark Muraven, "Volition and Belongingness: Social Movements, Volition, Self-Esteem, and the Need to Belong," in *Self, Identity, and Social Movements*, eds. Sheldon Stryker, Timothy J. Owens, and Robert W. White (Minneapolis, 2000), 242–43.
71. Myra Marx Ferree, "Soft Repression: Ridicule, Stigma, and Silencing in Gender-Based Movements," in *Authority in Contention*, eds. Daniel J. Myers and Daniel M. Cress (Amsterdam, 2004), 92–93.
72. Donatella Della Porta and Mario Diani, *Social Movements: An Introduction* (Malden, MA, 2006), 233.

CHAPTER 4

1. T.C. Noble, *The Lord Mayor of London: A Sketch of the Origin, History and Antiquity of the Office, Reprinted from the City Press* (London, 1860), 9.
2. Quoted in Timothy B. Smith, "In Defense of Privilege: The City of London and the Challenge of Municipal Reform, 1875–1890," *Journal of Social History* 27 (Autumn 1993): 60.
3. Alexander Pulling, *The City of London Corporation Inquiry* (London, 1854), 40.
4. [William Torrens], *The Government of London* (1884), 7–8.
5. Smith, "In Defense of Privilege," 73.
6. "The Alderman in Trouble," *Satirist*, 29 November 1840.
7. W. Carew Hazlitt, *The Livery Companies of the City of London: Their Origin, Character, Development, and Social and Political Importance* (London, 1892), 88–89.
8. Smith, "In Defense of Privilege," 73.
9. Ibid., 61.
10. A full record of the proceedings was included in "Persecution of the Jews in Damascus—Great Meeting at the Mansion House," *Times*, 4 July 1840; "Persecution of the Jews," *Morning Chronicle*, 4 July 1840.
11. "Communication from Sir Moses Montefiore to the Lord Mayor," *Times*, 12 October 1840.
12. "Persecution of the Jews," *Morning Chronicle*, 4 July 1840.
13. By this time, in addition to a variety of widow's, orphan's, and old people's homes, almshouses and other charities, there were seven Jewish schools in London that taught a combined number of three thousand students—a marked improvement over the 1820s; see Henry Mayhew, *London Labour and the London Poor: A Cyclopaedia of the Condition and Earnings of Those That Will Work, Those That Cannot Work, and Those That Will Not Work* (London, 1862), 2: 128–29.
14. The Bishop of London quoted in *The Lancet* (November 1844): 181.
15. This interfaith standard was clearly stated by Barnard Van Oven: "Britons, although they may differ in faith and hope, unite in all offices of charity"; Van Oven, letter to the editor, *Literary Gazette* (9 May 1835): 295.
16. "Persecution of the Jews in Damascus—Great Meeting at the Mansion House," *Times*, 4 July 1840.
17. Quoted in Diana Elizabeth Kendall, *Members Only: Elite Clubs and the Process of Exclusion* (Lanham, MD, 2008), 53.

18. Moses Montefiore, *Diaries of Sir Moses and Lady Montefiore*, ed. L. Loewe (Chicago, 1890), 1: 122, 126.
19. For more on this topic, see John F. Dovidio, Brenda Major, and Jennifer Crocker, "Stigma: Introduction and Overview," in *The Social Psychology of Stigma*, eds. Todd F. Heatherton et al. (New York, 2000), 1–28.
20. Pieritz's account was soon published by the London Society and widely distributed. These efforts—so much at odds from the previous conduct of Joseph Wolff—even earned praise from Jews who normally scorned such "unfortunate apostates"; see Donald Lewis, *The Origins of Christian Zionism: Lord Shaftesbury and Evangelical Support for a Jewish Homeland* (Cambridge, 2010), 180.
21. "Persecution of the Jews," *Morning Chronicle*, 4 July 1840; portions of O'Connell's speech also cited in Heinrich Graetz, *History of the Jews* (Philadelphia, 1895), 657.
22. Drew Halfmann and Michael P. Young, "War Pictures: The Grotesque as a Mobilizing Tactic," *Mobilization: An International Quarterly* 15, no. 1 (2010): 1–24.
23. "Persecution of the Jews," *Morning Chronicle*, 4 July 1840.
24. "Grande-Bretagne," *Journal Des Débats*, 7 July 1840.
25. Jonathan Frankel, *The Damascus Affair: "Ritual Murder," Politics, and the Jews in 1840* (Cambridge, 1997), 224. For in-depth details on the Manchester meetings, see "Town's Meeting—Persecution of the Jews," *Manchester Guardian*, 25 July 1840; "Meeting of the Manchester Hebrew Association," *Manchester Times*, 4 July 1840.
26. Montefiore quoted in Frankel, *Damascus Affair*, 358.
27. *Morning Herald* (New York), 2 September 1840. For background on this movement, see Angelo Repousis, "'The Cause of the Greeks': Philadelphia and the Greek War for Independence, 1821–1828," *Pennsylvania Magazine of History and Biography* 123 (October 1999): 333–63; Virginia Penn, "Philhellenism in England (1821–1827)," *Slavonic and East European Review* 14 (January and April 1936): 363–71, 647–60.
28. Steven J. Zipperstein, *The Jews of Odessa: A Cultural History, 1794–1881* (Stanford, CA, 1986), 119.
29. *Morning Herald* (New York), 2 September 1840.
30. See, for example, "Persecution of the Jews of Damascus," *North American and Daily Advertiser* (Philadelphia), 23 July 1840; for news of Mansion House, see "Persecution of the Jews of Damascus," *Boston Daily Courier*, 13 August 1840.
31. This influential thesis was originally developed by Charles Tilly; see *Popular Contention in Great Britain, 1758–1834* (Boulder, CO, 2005), 43.
32. Sidney Tarrow, *Power in Movement: Social Movements and Contentious Politics*, 2nd ed. (Cambridge, 1998), 29–42.
33. Michael P. Young, *Bearing Witness Against Sin: The Evangelical Birth of the American Social Movement* (Chicago, 2006), 11–21.
34. City of Charleston, *Proceedings of a Public Meeting of the Citizens of Charleston Held at the City Hall, on the 28th August, 1840, in Relation to the Persecution of the Jews of the East. Also, the Proceedings of a Meeting of the Israelites of Charleston, Convened at the Hall of the Hebrew Orphan Society, on the Following Evening, in Reference to the Same Subject* (Charleston, 1840); *Persecution of the Jews of the East, Containing the Proceedings of a Meeting Held at the Synagogue Mikveh Israel, Philadelphia, on Thursday Evening, the 28th of Ab, 5600* [28 August 1840] (Philadelphia, 1840).
35. Details of these meetings were also sent abroad. See, for example, "Correspondence on the Subject of the Damascus Persecution," *Times* (London),

19 September 1840; *Times*, 21 September 1840; *Morning Chronicle* (London), 15 September 1840; *Bristol Mercury*, 19 September 1840.
36. Leon A. Jick, *The Americanization of the Synagogue, 1820–1870* (Hanover, NH, 1976), 68.
37. Appendix 1, "Growth of the American Jewish Population," in *The American Jewish Experience*, 2nd ed., ed. Jonathan D. Sarna (New York, 1997), 359.
38. Phillips quoted in "Persecution of the Jews: The Meeting at Philadelphia," *National Gazette* (Philadelphia), 3 September 1840.
39. *Morning Courier and New York Enquirer*, 21 August 1840.
40. For insights on Anglo-American social reform, see Amanda Claybaugh, "Toward a New Transatlanticism: Dickens in the United States," *Victorian Studies* 48 (Spring 2006): 439–60.
41. C. S. Monaco, *Moses Levy of Florida: Jewish Utopian and Antebellum Reformer* (Baton Rouge, LA, 2005), 162.
42. "Meeting of the Israelites," *United States Commercial and Statistical Register* (Philadelphia), 16 September 1840.
43. As quoted in William A. Rosenthall, "The Damascus Affair: Its Impact on the United States of America" (MA thesis, Hebrew Union College—Jewish Institute of Religion, 1956), 43.
44. For an overview of this tendency, see Helen Fine, "Explanations of the Origin and Evolution of Antisemitism," in *The Persisting Question: Sociological Perspectives and Social Contexts of Modern Antisemitism*, ed. Helen Fine (Berlin, 1987), 8.
45. John Forsyth to John Glidden, 14 August 1840, *Times* (London), 19 September 1840 [italics are mine]. This document is included in *The Jew in the American World: A Source Book*, ed. Jacob Rader Marcus (Detroit, 1996), 185. Forsyth, it should be emphasized, was hardly known as a civil liberties advocate, as he led the government's case in the Amistad affair.
46. Jonathan D. Sarna, *Jacksonian Jew: The Two Worlds of Mordecai Noah* (New York, 1981), 102.
47. Helen Fein, *Accounting for Genocide, National Responses and Jewish Victimization During the Holocaust* (New York, 1979), 33.
48. These documents were published in the *New York Herald*, 29 August 1840 and subsequently reprinted multiple times; see, for example, "Damascus Persecution," *Daily National Intelligencer* (Washington, D.C.), 2 September 1840; "Damascus Persecution," *Public Ledger* (Philadelphia), 31 August 1840; "Persecution of the Jews," *Floridian and Advocate* (Tallahassee), 24 October 1840. See also "The Charge Against the Jews in the East," *Morning Chronicle*, 22 September 1840; *Times*, 19 September 1840. The Forsyth dispatches appeared in the *Journal des Débats*, 22 September 1840.
49. Lance J. Sussman, *Isaac Leeser and the Making of American Judaism* (Detroit, 1995), 42–43. For more on this incident, see Isaac Leeser, *The Jews and the Mosaic Law* (Philadelphia, 1833).
50. "Persecution of the Jews: The Meeting in Philadelphia," *National Gazette* (Philadelphia), 3 September 1840.
51. The full transcripts of the Mansion House meeting were published in the *Charleston Courier*, 17 July 1840.
52. [City of Charleston], *Proceedings of a Public Meeting*, 3–5.
53. Ibid.
54. Ibid. See also, "Public Meeting of the Citizens of Charleston," *Charleston Courier*, 29 July 1840.
55. "Meeting of the Israelites of Charleston," *Charleston Courier*, 31 July 1840.
56. [City of Charleston], *Proceedings of a Public Meeting*, 19–20.
57. Ross Burns, *Damascus: A History* (New York, 2005), 251–53.

58. Jacob Rader Marcus, *United States Jewry, 1776–1985*, vol. 1 (Detroit, 1989), 660.
59. For an early example of this tendency, see Joseph Jacobs, "The Damascus Affair of 1840 and the Jews of America," *Publications of the American Jewish Historical Society* 10 (1902): 121; more recently, see Jonathan Sarna, *American Judaism* (New Haven, CT, 2004), 104. Moreover, Jacob R. Marcus makes special note of Shearith Israel's refusal to participate, interpreting this decision as both a failure of leadership and of moral authority; indeed, he considers this a "symbolic renunciation" of Sephardic authority in the United States [Marcus, *United States Jewry*, 679].
60. Frankel, *Damascus Affair*, 352–53.
61. These physicians, named Clot and Gaetani, were each paid ten thousand francs by Crémieux in order to influence Mehmed Ali; see Frankel, *Damascus Affair*, 372.
62. "Affaire de Damas," *Univers*, 8 October 1840.
63. "Vicar of the Greek Patriarch, et al to the Gentlemen Consuls" (Damascus), 4 January 1841, *Age* (London), 14 March 1841.
64. Ibid.
65. Merlato quoted in "Letter from A. Crémieux" [15 September 1840], *Times*, 10 October 1840.
66. Crémieux quoted in Frankel, *Damascus Affair*, 340.
67. Montefiore, *Diaries*, 279.
68. S. Posener, *Adolphe Crémieux: A Biography*, trans. Eugene Golob (Philadelphia, 1940), 119–21; Frankel, *Damascus Affair*, 372–74.
69. Lucien Wolf, *Sir Moses Montefiore: A Centennial Biography with Selections from Letters and Journals* (New York, 1885), 98.
70. De Sola quoted in "Jewish Festival," *Morning Chronicle*, 9 March 1841.
71. Quoted in Frankel, *Damascus Affair*, 384. see also, "Jewish Festival," *Morning Chronicle*, 9 March 1841.
72. Wolf, *Sir Moses Montefiore*, 99.

CHAPTER 5

1. Eli Lederhendler, *The Road to Modern Jewish Politics: Political Tradition and Political Reconstruction in the Jewish Community of Tsarist Russia* (New York, 1989), 84–157; David Cesarani, *The Jewish Chronicle and Anglo-Jewry, 1841–1991* (Cambridge, 1994), 31; Jonathan Frankel, "Jewish Politics and the Press: The 'Reception' of the *Alliance Israelite Universelle* (1860)," *Jewish History* 14 (2000): 29.
2. For background on abeyance structures, see Verta Taylor, "Social Movement Continuity: The Women's Movement in Abeyance," *American Sociological Review* 54 (October 1989): 762.
3. David Vital, *A People Apart: The Jews in Europe, 1789–1939* (Oxford, 1999), 234.
4. Cesarani, *Jewish Chronicle*, 9. Similar periodicals certainly existed in the years immediately preceding the Damascus affair, perhaps the most familiar being the *Allgemeine Zeitung des Judenthumes* (1837), but the idea of a Jewish press was still in its infancy.
5. Lloyd P. Gartner, "Emancipation, Social Change, and Communal Reconstruction in Anglo-Jewry, 1789–1881," *Proceedings of the American Academy for Jewish Research* 54 (1987): 99. Gartner excluded "Hebrew and Yiddish publications of general character" from consideration.
6. Cesarani, *Jewish Chronicle*, 42.

7. Frank J. Coppa, "Pio Nono and the Jews: From 'Reform' to 'Reaction,' 1846–1878," *Catholic Historical Review* 89 (October 2003): 692.
8. *Jewish Chronicle*, 14 December 1860.
9. Quoted in Bertram W. Korn, *The American Reaction to The Mortara Case: 1858–1859* (Philadelphia, 1957), 148.
10. "Foreign Intelligence," *Times*, 19 October 1858.
11. Quoted in David I. Kertzer, *The Kidnapping of Edgardo Mortara* (New York, 1997), 8.
12. Korn, *The Mortara Case*, 17.
13. "The Secret Baptism and Forcible Abduction of a Jewish Child," *Jewish Chronicle and Hebrew Observer*, 10 September 1858.
14. This is a composite view taken from a variety of sources; see, for example, "The Mortara Case," *Examiner* (London), 20 November 1858; "The Mortara Affair," *New York Herald*, 4 December 1858; *Daily News* (London), 13 November 1858. For the most authentic version, based on later court transcripts, see Kertzer, *Kidnapping of Edgardo Mortara*, 3–12, n. 1. This court testimony added details that were omitted from some newspapers; evidently, the family was allowed twenty-four hours to prepare themselves for the inevitable, a fact that better explains Signor Mortara's ultimate exhaustion and collapse.
15. *Corriere Mercantile* quoted in the *Daily News*, 13 November 1858. Court testimony differed substantially from this account; see Kertzer, *Kidnapping of Edgardo Mortara*, 53–54.
16. "The Mortara Case," *Examiner*, 20 November 1858.
17. Michael Diamond, *Victorian Sensation: Or the Spectacular, the Shocking and the Scandalous in Nineteenth-Century Britain* (London, 2003) 2–3; Matthew Rubery, *The Novelty of Newspapers: Victorian Fiction After the Invention of the News* (New York, 2009), 3–19; see also Dallas Liddle, "Anatomy of a 'Nine Days Wonder': Sensational Journalism in the Decade of the Sensational Novel," in *Victorian Crime, Madness, and Sensation*, eds. Andrew Maunder and Grace Moore (Hampshire, UK, 2004), 89–103; Alan J. Lee, *The Origins of the Popular Press in England, 1855–1914* (London, 1976), 21–41.
18. Lord Shaftesbury, 31 January 1871, in *The Life and Work of the Seventh Earl of Shaftesbury*, ed. Edwin Hodder (London, 1887), 2: 19.
19. Mike Hepworth, "Privacy, Security and Respectability: The Ideal Victorian Home," in *Ideal Homes? Social Change and Domestic Life*, eds. Tony Chapman and Jenny Hockey (London, 1999), 25–26.
20. Ruskin quoted in Lori Anne Loeb, *Consuming Angels: Advertising and Victorian Women* (New York, 1994), 19.
21. Ibid., 18.
22. For an analysis of social movement narratives, see Francesca Polletta, "Contending Stories: Narrative in Social Movements," *Qualitative Sociology* 21 (1998): 419–46.
23. *Journal des Débats*, 25 October 1858.
24. "The Mortara Case, From La Presse," *Living Age* 59 (November 1858): 719.
25. Quotation in Coppa, "Pio Nono and the Jews," 689.
26. Quotation in Ariella Lang, *Converting a Nation: A Modern Inquisition and the Unification of Italy* (New York, 2008), 160.
27. Quotation in Kertzer, *Kidnapping of Edgardo Mortara*, 135.
28. *L'Armonia* (Turin), 27 October 1858.
29. *Tablet* quotation (including italics) reprinted in the *Catholic Layman* (Dublin), 18 November 1858.

30. M. Patricia Dougherty, "The Rise and Fall of 'L'Ami de la Religion': History, Purpose, and Readership of a French Catholic Newspaper," *Catholic Historical Review* 77 (January 1991): 39.
31. Hervé Serry, "Littérature et religion catholique (1880–1914). Contribution à une socio-histoire de la croyance," *Cahiers d'histoire. Revue d'histoire critique* 87 (2002): 37–59. For more on Veuillot's antisemitism, see Pierre Pierrard, *Louis Veuillot* (Paris, 1998), 67–70.
32. Andre Vincent Delacouture, *Le droit canon et le droit natural dans l'affaire Mortara* (Paris, 1858), 23–27. Delacouture was censored by the Papal Nuncio, but the abbé's immediate superior, the archbishop of Paris, remained supportive; see "Archbishop of Paris and M. Veuillot," *Jewish Chronicle*, 7 January 1859.
33. "La Civiltà," *L'Ami de la religion, journal et revue ecclesiastique, politique et litteraire*, 27 November 1858, 494–500.
34. For a full account of this episode, see Kertzer, *Kidnapping of Edgardo Mortara*, 91–101. The Morisi scandal first appeared in the press during late October; see "The Mortara Case," *Morning Chronicle*, 28 October 1858.
35. Natalie Isser, *Antisemitism during the French Second Empire* (New York, 1991), 38–42.
36. Arnold Ages, "Veuillot and the Talmud," *Jewish Quarterly Review* 64 (January 1974): 230. For background on French antisemitism during this period, see Zosa Szajkowski, "The Jewish Saint-Simonians and Socialist Antisemites in France," *Jewish Social Studies* 9 (January 1947): 47–49.
37. *L'Univers*, 19 November 1858.
38. [Rev. Isaac M. Wise], "The Facts and Object," *Israelite* (Cincinnati), 7 January 1859.
39. Crémieux quoted in Isser, *Antisemitism*, 42.
40. *New York Herald*, 5 December 1858.
41. "Report of the Meeting of the Jewish Community at the London Tavern," *Israelite* (Cincinnati), 17 September 1858.
42. For more on *insider* and *outsider* tactics, see Felix Kolb, *Protest and Opportunities: The Political Outcomes of Social Movements* (Frankfurt/Main, 2007), 49–50; Verta Taylor and Nella Van Dyke, "'Get Up, Stand Up,' Tactical Repertoires of Social Movements,' in *Blackwell Companion to Social Movements*, eds. David A. Snow, Sarah A. Soule, and Hanspeter Kriesi (Malden, MA, 2004), 267.
43. Lord Malmesbury to Lord Cowley, 7 January 1859, in James Howard Harris, *Memoirs of an Ex-Minister* (London, 1885), 457.
44. Lord Malmesbury, diary entry, April 15 [1859], Malmesbury, *Memoirs*, 477. In addition, any stridently anti-Catholic position would have undoubtedly offended those Catholics who had long supported Anglo-Jewish political emancipation.
45. Lucien Wolf, *Sir Moses Montefiore: A Centennial Biography with Selections from Letters and Journals* (New York, 1885), 155.
46. Moses Montefiore, message from the President of the London Committee of Deputies for the Jews, 25 October 1858, in "The Mortara Case—Movement of the Jews," *New York Times*, 22 November 1858.
47. Abigail Green, *Moses Montefiore: Jewish Liberator, Imperial Hero* (Cambridge, MA, 2010), 197.
48. For Montefiore's diary entries regarding this trip, see *Diaries of Sir Moses and Lady Montefiore*, ed. L. Loewe (Chicago, 1890), 1: 335–58.
49. *Jewish Chronicle*, 26 June 1846.
50. Ibid.

51. *Diaries of Sir Moses and Lady Montefiore*, 335–58; Wolf, *Sir Moses Montefiore*, 133–36; Green, *Moses Montefiore*, 185–94.
52. Moses Montefiore to Hananel De Castro (Warsaw), 20 May 1846, in *Jewish Chronicle*, 12 June 1846.
53. "Aus dem Grossherzogthum Posen," *Allgemeine Zeitung des Judentums*, 6 July 1846, 406–7, quoted in Green, *Moses Montefiore*, 195.
54. "Mission of Sir Moses Montefiore to Russia," *Voice of Jacob*, 19 June 1846.
55. For the emergence of nineteenth-century celebrity, see Nicholas Dames, "Brushes with Fame: Thackeray and the Work of Celebrity," *Nineteenth-Century Literature* 56 (June 2001): 25–26; for additional insight, see Charles Kurzman et al., "Celebrity Status," *Sociological Theory* 25 (December 2007): 347–67.
56. Thomas Carlyle, *On Heroes, Hero-Worship, and the Heroic in History* (London, 1840), 4.
57. Norman Vance, *The Sinews of the Spirit: The Ideal of Christian Manliness in Victorian Literature and Religious Thought* (Cambridge, 1985), 2, 10, 17, 21.
58. Green, *Moses Montefiore*, 235.
59. Marco Foro to [Moses Montefiore], 19 August 1858, in "Forcible Abduction of a Jewish Child," *Morning Chronicle*, 10 September 1858.
60. Quoted in Kertzer, *Kidnapping of Edgardo Mortara*, 86.
61. According to a theory entertained by Lord Malmesbury, the emperor was driven to war from his intense fear of assassination by the Carbonari, a secret fraternity that Louis Napoleon had joined while a young man in Italy. Now that he was emperor, it was expected that he would force Austria from northern Italy, a primary goal of the Carbonari. See Malmesbury, 16 February 1859, *Memoirs of an Ex-Minister*, 466.
62. E. Hammond to the Earl of Shaftesbury, 11 December 1858, *Times*, 17 December 1858.
63. "The Roman States," *Times* (London), 22 November 1858.
64. Green, *Moses Montefiore*, 253–54.
65. Montefiore excerpt in the *Jewish Chronicle*, 12 November 1858; see also "December 17th [1858]," *Diaries of Sir Moses and Lady Montefiore*, 2: 122.
66. *Jewish Chronicle*, 12 November 1858.
67. "The Official Papal Reply," *Jewish Chronicle*, 26 November 1858.
68. Ibid.
69. [Abraham Benisch], "The Second Report to the Board of Deputies on the Bologna Case," *Jewish Chronicle*, 31 December 1858.
70. Kertzer, *Kidnapping of Edgardo Mortara*, 166–67.
71. [Benisch], *Jewish Chronicle*, 31 December 1858.

CHAPTER 6

1. Benisch noted the American Jewish population as 250,000. Recent historians, however, place the high-end estimate at 200,000 (ca. 1860); see "Appendix 1: The Growth of the American Jewish Population," in *The American Jewish Experience*, ed. Jonathan D. Sarna (New York, 1997), 359.
2. Allan Tarshish, "The Board of Delegates of American Israelites (1859–1878)," in *American Jewish History*, ed. Jeffrey S. Gurock (New York, 1998), 6: 189.
3. Lilienthal quoted in Bertram Wallace Korn, *The American Reaction to the Mortara Case: 1858–1859* (Cincinnati, 1957), 28.
4. [Isaac M. Wise], "The Catholic Press," *Israelite* (Cincinnati), 17 December 1858.
5. Isaacs and Leeser quoted in Korn, *Mortara Case*, 25–26.

6. *New York Herald* quoted in Korn, *Mortara Case*, 95.
7. For discussion on the role of newspapers in social movement diffusion, see Kenneth T. Andrews and Michael Biggs, "The Dynamics of Protest Diffusion: Movement Organization, Social Networks, and News Media in the 1960 Sit-Ins," *American Sociological Review* 71 (October 2006): 752–77; on the development of American newspapers, see Alfred McClung Lee, *The Daily Newspaper in America: The Evolution of a Social Instrument* (London, 2000).
8. Similar meetings were held in Mobile (19 December 1858) and Memphis (27 January 1859); see *Israelite*, 11 February 1858.
9. *Public Ledger* (Philadelphia), 19 November 1858.
10. Herbert T. Ezekiel and Gaston Lichtenstein, *The History of the Jews of Richmond from 1769 to 1917* (Richmond, 1917), 146–47.
11. "Meeting of the Israelites," *Charleston Mercury*, 1 December 1858.
12. Korn, *The Mortara Case*, 45.
13. [Abraham Benisch], "Indignation Meeting of the Jews," *Jewish Chronicle*, 10 December 1858.
14. Leo Merzbacher quoted in Leon A. Jick, *The Americanization of the Synagogue, 1820–1870* (Hanover, NH, 1976), 146.
15. In a prelude to Raphall's mass meeting, a smaller protest was held in Harlem on 1 December by a group of largely immigrant Jews at Eisner's Hall; see Korn, *The Mortara Case*, 45–46.
16. "The Mortara Case: Jewish Meeting in Mozart Hall," *New York Times*, 6 December 1858.
17. "Abolitionists in Council," *New York Herald*, 12 May 1858; see also "The American Anti-Slavery Society—Fanaticism Rampant," *Sun* (Baltimore), 13 May 1858.
18. H[enry] H. Van Dyck, "Religious Liberty Meeting," *Albany Evening Journal*, 24 December 1858. Despite the apparent goodwill generated toward the Jews during the Mortara incident, the United States was certainly not immune from antisemitism; see, for example, Robert Rockaway and Arnon Gutfeld, "Demonic Images of the Jew in the Nineteenth Century United States," *American Jewish History* 89 (December, 2001): 355–81.
19. "The Jewish Meeting at Mozart Hall," *New York Herald*, 6 December 1858.
20. "The Mortara Abduction: Indignation Meeting of the Jewish Residents of New York," *New York Herald*, 5 December 1858.
21. "The Mortara Abduction," *New York Herald*, 5 December 1858.
22. Address of B. M. Hart, *New York Herald*, 5 December 1858.
23. *Jewish Chronicle*, 24 December 1858.
24. Quoted in Korn, *The Mortara Case*, 67.
25. *Israelite*, 4 February 1859.
26. *Israelite*, 11 February 1859. David Levy adopted the "Yulee" surname shortly after his election to the Senate. This name was part of Moses Levy's full Moroccan family name, Ha-Levi ibn Yuli. David had long been estranged from Judaism and, like Judah P. Benjamin, married a Christian; see C. S. Monaco, *Moses Levy of Florida: Jewish Utopian and Antebellum Reformer* (Baton Rouge, LA), 4, 19, 164.
27. *Israelite*, 11 February 1859.
28. Lance J. Sussman, *Isaac Leeser and the Making of American Judaism* (Detroit, 1995), 217.
29. [Isaac Wise], "Board of Delegates of American Israelites," *Israelite*, 27 January 1860.
30. Tarshish, "Board of Delegates of American Israelites," 169.
31. Abigail Green, *Moses Montefiore: Jewish Liberator, Imperial Hero* (Cambridge, MA, 2010), 272.

32. Moses Montefiore, *Diaries of Sir Moses and Lady Montefiore*, ed. L. Loewe (Chicago, 1890), 2: 89.
33. Lucien Wolf, *Sir Moses Montefiore: A Centennial Biography with Extracts from Letters and Journals* (New York, 1885), 160–61.
34. "The Papal States," *Times*, 5 May 1859.
35. [Benisch], "Sir Moses Montefiore's Mission to Rome," *Jewish Chronicle*, 4 March 1859.
36. *Univers Israelite* excerpt in *Jewish Chronicle*, 30 March 1860.
37. *Bulletin de l'Alliance Israelite Universelle* (Paris, 1860), 14.
38. Ibid., 20–21.
39. Aron Rodrigue, "Abraham de Camondo of Istanbul; the Transformation of Jewish Philanthropy," in *Profiles in Diversity: Jews in a Changing Europe, 1750–1870*, eds. Frances Malino and David Sorkin (Detroit, 1998), 54.

CHAPTER 7

1. Theodore D. Kemper, "A Structural Approach to Social Movement Emotions," in *Passionate Politics: Emotions and Social Movements*, eds. Jeff Goodwin, James M. Jasper, and Francesca Polletta (Chicago, 2001), 72.
2. Some authors have remarked on the innovative nature of this new communal arrangement, albeit without placing this change within the context of the Jewish rights movement; see, for example, Carole Fink, *Defending the Rights of Others: The Great Powers, the Jews, and International Minority Protection, 1878-1938* (New York, 2004), 15; Abigail Green, *Moses Montefiore: Jewish Liberator, Imperial Hero* (Cambridge, MA, 2010), 369.
3. For an English translation of the *dahir*, see "Edict of the Emperor of Morocco," *Jewish Chronicle*, 4 March 1864.
4. Green, *Moses Montefiore*, 317.
5. Albert S. Lindeman, *Esau's Tears: Modern Anti-Semitism and the Rise of the Jews* (Cambridge, 1997), 310.
6. William O. Oldson, "Rationalizing Anti-Semitism: The Romanian Gambit," *Proceedings of the American Philosophical Society* 138 (March 1994): 26.
7. Lindeman, *Esau's Tears*, 313–14.
8. "Libels in a Rouman Paper," *Jewish Chronicle*, 14 September 1866. This article includes extracts from the *Trumpet*, an antisemitic clerical paper. For additional background, see Fritz Stern, *Gold and Iron: Bismarck, Bleichroder, and the Building of the German Empire* (New York, 1979), 354–55; I. C. Butnaru, *The Silent Holocaust: Romania and Its Jews* (New York, 1992), 2.
9. Green, *Moses Montefiore*, 343.
10. "Bucharest," *Jewish Chronicle*, 20 July 1866.
11. Butnaru, *Silent Holocaust*, 16.
12. Israel Davis, *The Jews in Roumania; A Short Statement of Their Recent History and Present Situation* (London, 1872), 12; Letter from Moldovia (1867), in Moses Montefiore, *Diaries of Sir Moses and Lady Montefiore*, ed. L. Loewe (Chicago, 1890), 2: 193–94.
13. "Persecution in the Danubian Principalities," *Jewish Chronicle*, 7 June 1867.
14. Montefore, *Diaries of Sir Moses*, 2:195.
15. "Mission to Roumania," *Jewish Chronicle*, 1 July 1867.
16. Montefiore, "To His Serene Highness Prince Charles I," 27 August 1867, in *Diaries of Sir Moses Montefiore*, 2: 199–200.
17. Excerpt from the Bucharest paper *Natinuea* in *Diaries of Sir Moses*, 2: 200–1.
18. Diary entry (Vienna), 16 August 1867, *Diaries of Sir Moses*, 2: 198.
19. *Natinuea* excerpt, in *Diaries of Sir Moses*, 2: 200.

20. For background on countermovements, see Mayer N. Zald and Bert Useem, "Movement and Countermovement Interaction: Mobilization, Tactics, and State Involvement," in *Social Movements in an Organizational Society: Collected Essays*, eds. Mayer N. Zald and John D. McCarthy (New Brunswick, NJ, 2003), 247–72; Victoria Johnson, "The Strategic Determinants of a Countermovement: The Emergence and Impact of Operation Rescue Blockades," in *Waves of Protest: Social Movements Since the Sixties*, eds. Jo Freeman and Victoria Johnson (Lanham, MD, 1999), 241–65.
21. Radu Ioanid, "The Holocaust in Romania: The Iasi Pogrom of June 1941," in *Holocaust: Critical Concepts in Historical Studies*, ed. David Cesarani (London, 2004), 3: 477.
22. Montefiore, *Diaries of Sir Moses*, 2: 204–5.
23. The "absence of personal constraints" is in fact a leading factor in adopting high-risk strategies; see Karl-Dieter Opp, *Theories of Political Protest and Social Movements: A Multidisciplinary Introduction, Critique, and Synthesis* (New York, 2009), 114.
24. Leeser quoted in Green, *Moses Montefiore*, 355.
25. "Massacre of Jews in Roumania," *Cincinnati Daily Gazette*, 3 June 1870; "Jewish Massacre in Roumania: Meeting of the Israelites Last Night," *Cincinnati Daily Enquirer*, 6 June 1870.
26. "Persecution of the Roumania Jews," *New York Herald*, 2 July 1870.
27. These organizations were buoyed by their earlier success in urging the Grant administration to condemn Russia's planned mass expulsion of Jews from the borderland with Romania the previous year; see Rafael Medoff, *Jewish Americans and Political Participation* (Santa Barbara, CA, 2002), 103; Ronald J. Jensen, "The Politics of Discrimination: America, Russia, and the Jewish Question," *American Jewish History* 75 (March 1986): 288–89.
28. U. S. Grant, letter of introduction, 8 December 1870, in Max J. Kohler and Simon Wolf, "Jewish Disabilities in the Balkan States: American Contributions Toward Their Removal with Particular Reference to the Congress of Berlin," *Publications of the American Jewish Historical Society* 24 (1916): 13. For more on Peixotto, see Lloyd P. Gartner, "Roumania, America, and World Jewry: Consul Peixotto in Bucharest, 1870–1876," *American Jewish Historical Quarterly* 58 (September 1968): 25–116.
29. An annual fund of $10,000 was raised; see "Jews of Roumania," *Jewish Chronicle*, 24 May 1872.
30. Bertram W. Korn, *American Jewry and the Civil War* (Marietta, GA, 1995), 122–55.
31. Ibid., 145, 280, n. 78. Grant formed a close friendship with Seligman's brother Jesse dating to 1843.
32. *Maggid* excerpt in *Jewish Chronicle*, 20 January 1871.
33. Peixotto excerpt in *Jewish Chronicle*, 19 May 1871.
34. Brătianu quoted in Diana Mishkova, "The Interesting Anomaly of Balkan Liberalism," in *Liberty and the Search for Identity: Liberal Nationalism and the Legacy of Empires*, ed. Iván Zoltán Dénes (Budapest, 2006), 450.
35. Ibid., 451–52.
36. Oldson, "Rationalizing Anti-Semitism," 28; Gartner, "Roumania, America, and World Jewry," 30.
37. Kohler and Wolf, "Jewish Disabilities," 23.
38. Gartner, "Roumania, America, and World Jewry," 68; stolen items are described in Davis, *The Jews in Roumania*, 14
39. Benjamin Peixotto to Mr. Hunter, 7 February 1872, in "Message of the President of the United States," S. Exec. Doc. 75, 42nd Congress, 2nd Sess., 14 May 1872, 3.

40. Benjamin Peixotto, "The Persecution of Jews in Roumania," *Birmingham Daily Post*, 23 March 1872; see also an earlier article, "Ill-Usage of the Jews in Roumania," *Daily News* (London), 23 February 1872.
41. Benisch retired due to an unspecified, painful illness. Michael Henry was then hired as the new editor; see Ascher I. Myers, "Jacob Franklin," *Jewish Chronicle*, 13 November 1891; David Cesarani, *The Jewish Chronicle and Anglo-Jewry: 1841–1991* (Cambridge, 1994), 49.
42. "The Roumanian Persecutions," *Jewish Chronicle*, 3 May 1872.
43. "The Jews of Roumania: Great Meeting at the Mansion House," *Jewish Chronicle*, 31 May 1872.
44. See, for example, "Bigotry in Roumania," *Times* (London), 31 May 1872; "Persecution of the Jews in Roumania," *Daily News* (London), 31 May 1872; *Journal des Débats* (Paris), 3 June 1872; "Jews of Roumania: Great Meeting at the Mansion House," *Israelite* (Cincinnati), 21 June 1872; "English Sympathy for the Suffering Jews of Roumania," *Times Picayune* (New Orleans), 31 May 1872.
45. *Jewish Messenger* excerpt in the *Cincinnati Daily Gazette*, 6 July 1872.
46. Quoted in Gartner, "Roumania, America, and World Jewry," 80.
47. Ibid., 98.
48. Ibid., 77.
49. Hamilton Fish to Benjamin Peixotto, 13 May 1872, in "Message of the President of the United States," S. Exec. Doc. 75, 42nd Congress, 2nd Sess., 14 May 1872, 14.
50. Gartner, "Roumania, America, and World Jewry," 81–82.
51. *Jewish Chronicle*, 14 July 1876.
52. The *Jewish Chronicle*, 22 November 1872, gave the following (unofficial) list of delegates: "London: Sir Francis Goldsmid, Mr. F. S. Mocatta; Paris: MM. Adolphe Crémieux, Isidor, Grand Rabbin; Albert Cohn, S. H. Goldschmidt, Michael Erlanger, Narcisse Leven, J. Rosenfeld; Berlin: Prof. Lazarus, Dr. Kristetter, B. Liebermann, F. Reichenheim, Meyer Cohen; Vienna: Dr. L. Kompert, S. Gottlieb; Amsterdam: J. Levy, Advocate; S. H. Goldschmidt of Leyden; New York: I. Seligman; Roumania: B. Peixotto, two Rabbis and four other Israelites; Brussels: Dr. Astruc, Chief Rabbi of Belgium; M. Louis Lassen, President of the Consistory; M. Bischoffshein, Senator; MM. Joseph Oppenheim, Jacques Errera, George Prins, Jacques Weiner, Dr. Hanael Didisheim, Secretary to the Belgian Consistory, was appointed Secretary to the Conference, MM. Samson Weiner, jun. and Leon Errera, jun., assistant Secretaries. M. Charles Netter of the Jaffa Agricultural School, attended the conference."
53. Peixotto quoted in Gartner, "Roumania, America, and World Jewry," 92.
54. Ibid., 93.
55. "The International Roumanian Conference," *Jewish Chronicle*, 15 November 1872.
56. Ibid.
57. Gladstone quote in David Bebbington, *The Mind of Gladstone: Religion, Homer, and Politics* (Oxford, 2004), 261.
58. Roger V. Gould, *Insurgent Identities: Class, Community, and Protest in Paris from 1848 to the Commune* (Chicago, 1995), 153–54.
59. Jerrold Seigel, *Bohemian Paris: Culture, Politics, and the Boundaries of Bourgeois Life, 1830–1930* (Baltimore, 1986), 181.
60. "The International Roumanian Conference," *Jewish Chronicle*, 15 November 1872.
61. Ibid.
62. Abraham Benisch remained an important exception to the rule and continued to advocate for a stronger activist stance vis-à-vis Romanian oppression; see Benisch's anonymous letter to the editor signed by "A Member of the Roumanian Committee," in *Jewish Chronicle*, 13 December 1872.

Notes 213

63. The Galatz petition was published in "Departure of Mr. Peixotto," *Jewish Chronicle*, 22 October 1872.
64. Ibid.
65. Gartner, "Roumania, America, and World Jewry," 98–99.
66. Bamberger quote in Kohler and Wolf, "Jewish Disabilities," 27.
67. Gartner, "Roumania, America, and World Jewry," 103–4.
68. "Further Persecution of the Jews in Roumania," *Jewish Chronicle*, 1 September 1876.
69. "Reported Massacre at Giurgevo" and "Outrages in Roumania," *Jewish Chronicle*, 25 May and 15 June 1877.

CHAPTER 8

1. Quoted in Benjamin Nathans, *Beyond the Pale: The Jewish Encounter with Late Imperial Russia* (Berkeley, CA, 2002), 66.
2. Ibid., 50–65.
3. John Klier, "Russian Jewry on the Eve of the Pogroms," in *Pogroms: Anti-Jewish Violence in Modern Russian History*, eds. John Klier and Shlomo Lambroza (Cambridge, 1992), 4–5, n. 6. Klier believed this number to be more accurate than the figure of five million that has often been cited.
4. Klier, "Russian Jewry," 6.
5. Geoffrey A. Hosking, *Russia and the Russians: A History* (Cambridge, MA, 2001), 289–90.
6. Alexander Polunov, *Russia in the Nineteenth-Century: Autocracy, Reform, and Social Change, 1814–1914*, eds. Thomas C. Owen and Larissa G. Zakharova, trans. Marshall S. Shatz (Armonk, NY, 2005), 106.
7. Rogers Brubaker and David D. Laitin, "Ethnic and Nationalist Violence," *Annual Review of Sociology* 24 (1998): 424. A similar point of view is expressed in I. Michael Aronson, "The Anti-Jewish Pogroms in Russia in 1881," in *Pogroms: Anti-Jewish Violence in Modern Russian History*, 47.
8. Werner Bergmann, "Ethnic Riots in Situations of Loss of Control: Revolution, Civil War, and Regime Change as Opportunity Structures for Anti-Jewish Violence in Nineteenth- and Twentieth-Century Europe," in *Control of Violence: Historical and International Perspective on Violence in Modern Societies*, eds. Wilhelm Heitmeyer, Heinz-Gerhard Haupt, Stefan Malthaner, and Andrea Kirschner (New York, 2011), 487.
9. Aronson, "Anti-Jewish Pogroms," 45–49. For more detail, see Aronson, *Troubled Waters: The Origins of the 1881 Anti-Jewish Pogroms in Russia* (Pittsburg, 1990).
10. John Klier, *Russians, Jews, and the Pogroms of 1881–1882* (Cambridge, 2011), 13.
11. Extract from a letter, *Times*, 11 May 1881.
12. Klier, *Russians, Jews, and the Pogroms*, 26–28.
13. Quoted in Shlomo Lambroza, "Jewish Responses to Pogroms in Late Imperial Russia," in *Living with Antisemitism: Modern Jewish Responses*, ed. Jehuda Reinharz (Hanover, NH, 1987), 256.
14. "Persecution of the Jews in Russia," *Times*, 11 January 1882.
15. Aronson, "Anti-Jewish Pogroms," 47.
16. Klier, *Russians, Jews, and the Pogroms*, 11.
17. Ibid., 51.
18. Aronson, "Anti-Jewish Pogroms," 47–48.
19. "Persecution of the Jews in Russia," *Times*, 11 January 1882.
20. For background on this interpretation, see Roberta Senechal de la Roche, "Collective Violence as Social Control," *Sociological Forum* 11, no.1 (1996): 97–128. For a recent study, see Bergmann, "Ethnic Riots," 487–516.

21. Glenn Dynner, "Legal Fictions: The Survival of Rural Jewish Tavernkeeping in the Kingdom of Poland," *Jewish Social Studies* 16 (Winter 2010): 32. Alcoholism was and still remains a major problem. During the nineteenth century, a typical Russian town of 25,000 possessed as many as thirty-six taverns and fifteen or so liquor shops and bars; see Walter G. Moss, *A History of Russia, Since 1855* (London, 2005), 120, 173.
22. Quoted in Heinz-Dietrich Löwe, "Pogroms in Russia: Explanations, Comparisons, Suggestions," *Jewish Social Studies* 11 (Autumn 2004): 20.
23. Quoted in Hans Rogger, "Government, Jews, Peasants, and Land in Post-Emancipation Russia: Two Specters: Peasant Violence and Jewish Exploitation," *Cahiers du Monde russe et soviétique* 17 (April–September 1976): 172.
24. Jonathan Frankel, *Prophecy and Politics: Socialism, Nationalism, and the Russian Jews, 1862–1917* (Cambridge, 1981), 86–87.
25. Senechal de la Roche, "Collective Violence," 106.
26. For a comparison of pogrom violence with riots in the United States, see Hans Rogger, "Conclusion and Overview," in *Pogroms: Anti-Jewish Violence in Modern Russian History*, 351–58. For more on the phenomenon of lynching, see W. Fitzhugh Brundage, *Lynching in the New South: Georgia and Virginia, 1880–1930* (Champaign, IL, 1993).
27. Klier, *Russians, Jews, and the Pogroms*, 2–3.
28. Senechal de la Roche, "Collective Violence," 116; Charles Tilly, *The Politics of Collective Violence* (Cambridge, 2003), 21–22.
29. Tilly, *Politics of Collective Violence*, 10–11; see also Christhard Hoffman, Werner Bergmann, and Helmut Walser Smith, "Introduction," in *Exclusionary Violence: Antisemitic Riots in Modern German History*, eds. Christhard Hoffman, Werner Bergmann, and Helmut Walser Smith (Ann Arbor, MI, 2002), 12.
30. Klier, *Russians, Jews, and the Pogroms*, 181.
31. "Persecution of the Jews in Russia, *Times*, 25 January 1882.
32. Frankel, *Prophecy and Politics*, 87.
33. Leo Pinsker, *Auto-Emancipation*, trans. D. S. Blondheim (New York, 1906), 1.
34. For a full account of the foreign office delegation, see "Jews in Russia," *Times*, 25 May 1881; for the memorial to the tsar, see "Persecution of the Jews in Russia," *Times*, 25 January 1882.
35. "The Crisis in Jewish History," *Jewish Chronicle*, 20 January 1882.
36. "Board of Deputies," *Jewish Chronicle*, 20 January 1882.
37. "The Next Step," *Jewish Chronicle*, 20 January 1882.
38. "The Crisis in Jewish History," *Jewish Chronicle*, 20 January 1882; for more on Myers and the *Chronicle*, see David Cesarani, *The Jewish Chronicle and Anglo-Jewry, 1841–1991* (Cambridge, 1994), 67–102.
39. Louisa L. Goldsmid, letter to the editor, *Jewish Chronicle*, 20 January 1882. For more on Lady Goldsmid, see Elizabeth Crawford, *The Women's Suffrage Movement: A Reference Guide* (London, 1999), 247.
40. Quoted in Frankel, *Prophecy and Politics*, 72.
41. "The Jews in Russia: Provincial Meetings," *Jewish Chronicle*, 27 January 1882.
42. Hermann Adler, "Abstract of a Sermon Delivered at the Western Synagogue on the 28th January, 1882, by the Rev. Dr. Hermann Adler," in *Jews as They Are*, ed. Charles Kensington Salaman (London, 1882), 309–10.
43. "Persecution of the Jews of London," *Times*, 2 February 1882.
44. For an insightful contemporary look at the declining state of evangelicalism and Shaftesbury's place in this altered environment (as well as the ambiguity with which Jews regarded Shaftesbury), see "The Death of Lord Shaftesbury," *Jewish Chronicle*, 9 October 1885.

45. "Persecution of the Jews of London," *Times*, 2 February 1882. Selective editing of these speeches by the press was another means by which contentiousness was muted. A more aggressive edge managed to surface in the unabridged version of the Mansion House oratory in the *Jewish Chronicle*, 3 February 1882.
46. Manning as quoted in the *Times*, 2 February 1882.
47. "Pastoral Circular of the Chief Rabbi," *Jewish Chronicle*, 10 February 1882.
48. "The Hebrews in Russia: New York's Sympathy for Them in Their Suffering," *New York Times*, 2 February 1882; "The Jews," *New York Herald*, 2 February 1882.
49. Crosby speech excerpt in *American Israelite*, 10 February 1882.
50. *American Israelite*, 10 February 1882.
51. "Official Declaration," *Jewish Chronicle*, 17 February 1882.
52. *Jewish Chronicle*, 3 February 1882.
53. "Provincial Meetings," *Jewish Chronicle*, 17 and 24 February 1882.
54. "The Russian Atrocities—Public Meetings, and Parliament," *Jewish Chronicle*, 10 February 1882.
55. "A Potent Protest," *Times-Picayune* (New Orleans), 18 March 1882. For coverage of the Philadelphia and Brooklyn meetings, see "Sympathy—Protest," *Philadelphia Inquirer*, 6 March 1882.
56. Zosa Szajkowski, "How the Mass Migration to America Began," *Jewish Social Studies* 4 (October, 1942): 291–92.
57. Victor Hugo, "Les Juifs," *La Presse* (Paris), 19 June 1882.
58. Frankel, *Prophets and Politics*, 72.
59. Klier, *Russians, Jews, and the Pogroms*, 296.
60. Steven Cassedy, "Russian-Jewish Intellectuals Confront the Pogroms of 1881: The Example of 'Razsvet,'" *Jewish Quarterly Review* 84 (October 1993 and January 1994): 148.
61. Klier, *Russians, Jews, and the Pogroms*, 301–2.
62. Frankel, *Prophets and Politics*, 75–76.
63. Ibid., 79.
64. *Razsvet*'s editorial shift to pro-emigration coincides with the *Alliance*'s new resolve. This took place 24 July 1881. See Cassedy, "Russian-Jewish Intellectuals," 148.
65. Frankel, *Prophets and Politics*, 59.
66. This organizational alliance was certainly not free from discord or petty politics; see Klier, *Russians, Jews, and the Pogroms*, 375–80.
67. George Osofsky, "The Hebrew Emigrant Aid Society of the United States (1881–1883)," in *Politics and the Immigrant*, ed. George E. Pozzetta (New York, 1991), 229.
68. Frankel, *Prophecy and Politics*, 73–74.
69. Gerald Sorin, *A Time for Building: The Third Migration, 1880–1920* (Baltimore, 1992), xv, 1; see also Ann E. Healy, "Tsarist Anti-Semitism and Russian-American Relations," *Slavic Review* 42 (Autumn 1983): 409.
70. Michael Stanislawski, *For Whom Do I Toil? Judah Leib Gordon and the Crisis of Russian Jewry* (New York, 1988), 146–47.
71. Eli Lederhendler, *The Road to Modern Jewish Politics: Political Tradition and Political Reconstruction in the Jewish Community of Tsarist Russia* (New York, 1989).
72. Frankel, *Prophecy and Politics*, 49.
73. Michael Stanislawski criticizes Lederhendler by observing that while this executive body was abolished, the autonomous legal authority of each Jewish community was left intact. Jewish communal operations were highly secretive, and thus no one today, according to Stanislawski, is truly familiar with the full scope of communal authority; see Stanislawski, review of *The Road*

216 Notes

to *Modern Jewish Politics: Political Tradition and Political Reconstruction in the Jewish Community of Tsarist Russia*, by Eli Lederhendler, *Slavic Review* 51 (Spring 1992): 173–74.
74. Lederhendler, *Road to Modern Jewish Politics*, 88.
75. Ibid., 130–33.
76. Ibid., 88.
77. Ibid., 108.
78. Ibid., 5.
79. M. Gunzberg, *Hamat damesek* (Konigsberg, 1859–1860), 39, 43–44, quoted in Lederhendler, *Road to Modern Jewish Politics*, 107–8.
80. *Ha-Maggid* 24 (1863) quoted in Lederhendler, *Road to Modern Jewish Politics*, 137.
81. Lederhendler, *Road to Modern Jewish Politics*, 131.
82. "Persecution of the Jews in Russia: Great Public Meeting in the Guildhall," *Jewish Chronicle*, 12 December 1890.
83. Sir Robert Morier to Lord Salisbury (St. Petersburg), 25 December 1890, in Moshe Perlmann, "The British Embassy in St. Petersburg on Russian Jewry, 1890–92," *Proceedings of the American Academy for Jewish Research* 48 (1981): 318–19.
84. Quoted in *Jewish Chronicle*, 19 December 1890.
85. Simon Dubnow, *History of the Jews in Russia and Poland* (Philadelphia, 1918), 408–9; Healy, "Tsarist Anti-Semitism," 414.
86. "Is a New Era Before Judaism? Dr. H. Pereira Mendes' Solution of the Jewish Problem," *New York Herald*, 28 December 1890.
87. "The Dreyfus Trial: The Speech for the Defence," *Times*, 9 September 1899.
88. On the lack of interest by the bulk of Jewish immigrants, many of whom regarded the affair as "trivial" compared to Russian persecution, see Karin Hofmeester, *Jewish Workers and the Labour Movement: A Comparative Study of Amsterdam, London, and Paris, 1870–1914* (Hants, UK, 2004), 233–42. According to Michael Burns, *France and the Dreyfus Affair: A Documentary History* (Boston, 1999), 151: "Jews, though clearly interested in the fate of their coreligionists and his affair, neither engineered nor dominated the protests."
89. For an overview of the Catholic component, see Vicki Caron, "Catholic Political Mobilization and Antisemitic Violence in Fin de Siècle France: The Case of the Union Nationale," *Journal of Modern History* 81 (June 2009): 294–346.
90. Although Herzl himself wrote "what made me a Zionist was the Dreyfus trial," some scholars have taken issue with this self-assessment. See, for example, Jacques Kornberg, *Theodor Herzl: From Assimilation to Zionism* (Bloomington, IN, 1993), 190–200.
91. "The Hyde Park Demonstration," *Jewish Chronicle*, 22 September 1898.
92. The details of the Dreyfus affair have been covered in depth by publications too numerous to be listed here. Nevertheless, in addition to the work already mentioned, I have found Ruth Harris, *Dreyfus: Politics, Emotion, and the Scandal of the Century* (New York, 2010) especially useful; see also Albert S. Lindemann, *The Jew Accused: Three Anti-Semitic Affairs (Dreyfus, Beilis, Frank), 1894–1915* (Cambridge, 1991), 94–128.

CHAPTER 9

1. This extract is from a letter written in Hebrew from a resident of Kishinev to a friend in Minneapolis. It was then translated and published in the *Minneapolis Journal*, 22 May 1903.

2. Chaim Weizmann, "Sokolow and the Kishinev Days," *Palestine Post*, 20 January 1949.
3. A. S. Solomons, "Israel's Tribute to John Hay," *New Era* (August 1905): 119.
4. Author Mikhal Dekel makes note of the media frenzy and the role of photography in "'From the Mouth of the Raped Woman Rivka Schiff,' Kishineff, 1903," *Women's Studies Quarterly* 36, no. 1–2 (2008): 199–207.
5. S. Daniel Breslauer, *Toward a Jewish (M)orality: Speaking of a Postmodern Jewish Ethics* (Westport, CT, 1998), 135.
6. Edward H. Judge, *Easter in Kishinev: Anatomy of a Pogrom* (New York, 1992), 26.
7. Ibid., 136.
8. Ibid., 58.
9. Shlomo Lambroza, "The Pogroms of 1903–1906," in *Pogroms: Anti-Jewish Violence in Modern Russian History*, eds. John D. Klier and Shlomo Lambroza (Cambridge, 1992), 200.
10. "Survivor Tells of Awful Sights at Kishineff," *Philadelphia Inquirer*, 27 May 1903; Statement of Ida Rahatnik, *New York Times*, 18 May 1903; Judge, *Easter in Kishinev*, 56–57; Monty Noam Penkower, "The Kishinev Pogrom of 1903: A Turning Point in Jewish History," *Modern Judaism* 24, no. 3 (2004): 187–88.
11. Quoted in E. Semenoff, *The Russian Government and the Massacres: A Page of the Russian Counter-Revolution* (London, 1907), 39.
12. Penkower, "The Kishinev Pogrom," 187; Judge, *Easter in Kishiniv*, 52. Author Michael Davitt denied any active role by the bishop; see Davitt, *Within the Pale: The True Story of Anti-Semitic Persecutions in Russia* (New York, 1903), 135–36.
13. Vladimir Korolenko, "Kishinev: The Medieval Outbreak Against the Jews," in *Great Events by Famous Historians*, eds. C. F. Horne, J. Russ, and J. Rossiter (1909), 20: 35–49.
14. Lambroza, "The Pogroms of 1903–1906," 201.
15. Ibid., 210.
16. "The Jewish Chautauqua," *Menorah* 35 (August 1903): 119.
17. Penkower, "Kishinev Pogrom," 190.
18. "Anti-Semitic Riots in Russia," *Jewish Chronicle*, 1 May 1903.
19. "Tells of Kishinev Horror," *Sun* (New York), 17 May 1903; "Helped Bury the Butchered," *New York Tribune*, 28 May 1903; "Letters from Survivors of Kisheneff Show Enormity of Offenses Committed," *St. Louis Republic*, 17 May 1903.
20. Drew Halfmann and Michael P. Young, "War Pictures: The Grotesque as a Mobilizing Tactic," *Mobilization: An International Quarterly* 15, no. 1 (2010): 1–2.
21. Taylor Stults, "Roosevelt, Russian Persecution of the Jews, and American Public Opinion," *Jewish Social Studies* 33 (January 1971): 16.
22. "Hebrew War Veterans Act," *Baltimore American*, 12 May 1903.
23. *New York Times*, 17 May 1903.
24. Philip Ernest Schoenberg, "The American Reaction to the Kishinev Pogrom of 1903," *American Jewish Historical Quarterly* 63 (March 1974): 265.
25. "Board of Deputies—The Kishineff Massacres," *Jewish Chronicle*, 29 May 1903.
26. For background on these individuals, see Eugene C. Black, "A Typological Study of English Zionists," *Jewish Social Studies* 9 (Spring–Summer 2003): 20–55.
27. "Board of Deputies," *Jewish Chronicle*, 3 July 1903.
28. Wolf also drew upon past examples of Jewish public protest in London, but in his case the former meetings only confirmed their irrelevance:

"The outrages of course ceased, but they ceased [in Wolf's estimation] before the meetings were held." Quoted in Eugene C. Black, *The Social Problems of Anglo-Jewry, 1880–1920* (Oxford, 1988), 305.
29. "Board of Deputies—The Kishineff Massacres," *Jewish Chronicle*, 29 May 1903.
30. *The Voice of America on Kishineff*, ed. Cyrus Adler (Philadelphia, 1904).
31. Ibid.
32. "Wild Over Cleveland," *New York Daily Tribune*, 28 May 1903.
33. Ibid.
34. Schiff quoted in Zosa Szajkowski, "Paul Nathan, Lucien Wolf, Jacob H. Schiff and the Jewish Revolutionary Movements in Eastern Europe 1903–1917," *Jewish Social Studies* 29 (January 1967): 15.
35. Masliansky quoted in Adler, *Voice of America*, 48.
36. Adler, *Voice of America*, 49.
37. Schoenberg, "The American Reaction," 267–68.
38. "Hebrews' Refuge from Ills Is Zion," *Philadelphia Inquirer*, 18 May 1903.
39. Ibid.
40. Quoted in Jonathan Frankel, *Prophecy and Politics: Socialism, Nationalism, and the Russian Jews, 1862–1917* (Cambridge, 1981), 475.
41. Roosevelt quoted in Adler, *Voice of America*, 472.
42. *Evening Mail and Express* (New York), 25 June 1903.
43. Oscar S. Straus, "Straus Defines Our Humane Diplomacy," *New York Times*, 27 April 1912; for a full exposition, see Straus, "Address of Honorable Oscar S. Straus on Humanitarian Diplomacy of the United States," in *Proceedings of the American Society of International Law at Its Sixth Annual Meeting Held at Washington, D.C. April 25–27, 1912* (Washington, DC, 1912), 45–54; see also Straus, "Israel's Tribute to Hay," *New Era* 7 (August 1905): 120. The Straus appointment was intended, as Roosevelt admitted, "to show Russia and some other countries what we think of Jews in this country"; quoted in Edmund Morris, *Colonel Roosevelt* (New York, 2010), 647, n. 220.
44. Roosevelt quoted in Straus, "Address of Honorable Oscar S. Straus," 52. Both Roosevelt and Straus seriously undermined their case by conflating U.S. intervention in Cuba with this new sense of humanitarian diplomacy.
45. Levi quoted in Israel Cowen, "Tribute to a Dead Leader," *Menorah* 36 (April 1904): 235.
46. "Two Books on Kishinev: America and the Russian Jews." *Jewish Chronicle*, 22 April 1904.
47. H. Shandel, "Sir Moses Montefiore's Missions and the Kishinev Massacres," *Jewish Chronicle*, 29 May 1903.
48. Sol M. Greenberg, letter to the editor, *Jewish Chronicle*, 19 June 1903.
49. Geoffrey Alderman, *London Jewry and London Politics, 1889–1986* (London, 1989), 76.
50. "Protest Meeting at Great Assembly Hall," *Jewish Chronicle*, 26 June 1903.
51. "The Hyde Park Demonstration," *Jewish Chronicle*, 26 June 1903.
52. "Memorial Service at the Assembly Hall," *Jewish Chronicle*, 10 July 1903; "The Kishinev Outrages," *Times*, 7 July 1903.
53. David Alexander and Claude Montefiore, president of the Anglo-Jewish Association, only managed to publish a joint letter of condemnation of the massacre in the London *Times*; see Alexander and Montefiore, letter to the editor, *Times*, 18 May 1903.
54. *Jewish Chronicle*, 12 June 1903.

EPILOGUE

1. Shlomo Lambroza, "The Pogroms of 1903–1906," in *Pogroms: Anti-Jewish Violence in Modern Jewish History*, eds. John D. Klier and Shlomo Lambroza (Cambridge, 1992), 213.
2. Ibid., 215, 218; Monty Noam Penkower, "The Kishinev Pogrom of 1903: A Turning Point in Jewish History," *Modern Judaism* 24, no. 3 (2004): 201.
3. Lambroza, "Pogroms of 1903–1906," 221.
4. Robert Weinberg, "The Russian Right Responds to 1905: Visual Depictions of Jews in Post Revolutionary Russia," in *The Revolution of 1905 and Russia's Jews*, eds. Stefanie Hofman and Ezra Mendelsohn (Philadelphia, 2008), 55–69; Hans Rogger, *Jewish Policies and Right-Wing Politics in Imperial Russia* (Berkeley, CA, 1986), 188–211, 212–32.
5. This number includes an estimated 100,000 spectators that assembled in Brooklyn.
6. "Jews March to Dirges: Mourn Massacred Dead," *New York Daily Tribune*, 5 December 1905.
7. For insight regarding street demonstrations and the public sphere, see Gabor Gyani, "Uses and Misuses of Public Space in Budapest: 1873–1914," in *Budapest and New York: Studies in Metropolitan Transformation, 1870–1930*, eds. Thomas Bender and Carl E. Schorske (New York, 1994), 99–101.
8. "Jews March to Dirges," *New York Daily Tribune*, 5 December 1905.
9. Ibid.
10. "Jews in Huge Parade, Mourn Dead in Russia," *New York Times*, 5 December 1905. For background on the utilization of parades for social movement protest, see Lee A. Smithy and Michael P. Young, "Parading Protest: Orange Parades in Northern Ireland and Temperance Parades in Antebellum America," *Social Movement Studies* 9 (November 2010): 393–410.
11. Todd M. Endelman, *The Jews of Britain, 1656–2000* (Berkeley, CA, 2002), 189; Eugene C. Black, *The Social Politics of Anglo-Jewry, 1880–1920* (Oxford, 1988), 29–30, 48, 217.
12. "The Massacres in Russia: Important Meetings of Protest," *Jewish Chronicle*, 17 November 1905.
13. "The Anti-Jewish Atrocities in Russia: Public Meeting at Queens Hall," *Jewish Chronicle*, 12 January 1906.
14. Peter Kenez, "Pogroms and White Ideology in the Russian Civil War," in *Pogroms: Anti-Jewish Violence*, 302.
15. "The Great Protest," *Jewish Daily News* (New York City), 23 May 1919; "Thousands Join in Parades and Big Madison Square Garden Meeting," *New York Tribune*, 22 May 1919.
16. "The Pogroms: A Day of Mourning," *Jewish Chronicle*, 27 June 1919; "Poland: The Day of Mourning and Protest," *Jewish Chronicle*, 4 July 1919; Norman Davies, "Great Britain and the Polish Jews, 1918–20," *Journal of Contemporary History* 8 (April 1973): 127–28.
17. Quoted in Rafael Medoff, *Jewish Americans and Political Participation* (Santa Barbara, CA, 2002), 109.
18. Norman H. Finkelstein, *American Jewish History* (Philadelphia, 2007), 133; apparently more than three hundred "communities" took part in this protest; see "Protestants, Catholics, Will Join Mass Meeting Here to Protest Nazi Abuse of Jews," *Trenton Evening Times* (New Jersey), 26 March 1933; "Treatment of Jews in Germany: American Protests," *Times* (London), 24 March 1933.
19. "American Wave of Disgust," *Jewish Chronicle*, 31 March 1933; Medoff, *Jewish Americans*, 107–9.

20. "Mayor LaGuardia Defies Hitler at Anti-Nazi Rally," *Palestine Post*, 17 March 1937.
21. Albert D. Chernin, "Making Soviet Jews an Issue: A History," in *A Second Exodus: The American Movement to Free Soviet Jews*, eds. Murray Friedman and A. Chernin (Hanover, NH, 1999), 20.
22. Quoted in Chernin, "Making Soviet Jews," 21.
23. For background on Kahane, see Mark Juergensmeyer, *Terror in the Mind of God: The Global Rise of Religious Violence*, 3rd ed. (Berkeley, CA, 2001), 53–60.
24. Medoff, *Jewish Americans*, 162.
25. "200,000 at Rally for Soviet Jewry," *New York Times*, 4 May 1987.
26. "Protestors Disrupt Soviet Concert," *Jewish Chronicle*, 1 May 1981; "Shcharansky Rally," *Jewish Chronicle*, 15 May 1981.
27. For more background, see Stuart Altshuler, *From Exodus to Freedom: A History of the Soviet Jewry Movement* (Lanham, MD, 2005).
28. Robert S. Wistrich, "The Old-New Anti-Semitism," in *Those Who Forget the Past: The Question of Anti-Semitism*, ed. Ron Rosenbaum (New York, 2004), 89.

CONCLUSIONS

1. Israel Goldstein, "Address Before the Culture Council of the Jewish Community of Paris, France, 31 January 1955," in Israel Goldstein, *American Jewry Comes of Age: Tercentenary Addresses* (New York, 1955), 74.
2. Sharon Gewirtz, "Anglo-Jewish Responses to Nazi Germany 1933–39: The Anti-Nazi Boycott and the Board of Deputies of British Jews," *Journal of Contemporary History* 26 (April 1991): 255.
3. William A. Gamson, "Defining Movement 'Success,'" in *The Social Movement Reader: Cases and Concepts*, eds. Jeff Goodwin and James M. Jasper (Malden, MA, 2009), 414.
4. Goodwin and Jasper, "Introduction: What Changes Do Social Movements Bring About?" in *The Social Movement Reader*, 412.
5. "The Official Papal Reply," *Jewish Chronicle*, 26 November 1858.
6. "Our Brethren at Home,' *Jewish Chronicle*, 3 November 1871.
7. "What Are the British Jews? And What May They Become?" *Voice of Jacob*, 16 September 1841.
8. Shaul Kelner, "Ritualized Protest and Redemptive Politics: Cultural Consequences of the American Mobilization to Free Soviet Jews," *Jewish Social Studies* 14 (Spring/Summer 2008): 2–3. See also Jonathan Woocher, "'Sacred Survival' Revisited: American Jewish Civil Religion in the New Millennium," in *Cambridge Companion to American Judaism*, ed. Dana Evan Kaplan (New York, 2005), 283–98. Woocher's chapter refers to the transition of the Soviet Jewry movement from insurgence to a state of abeyance, although he does not use this specific terminology.
9. David Biale, *Power and Powerlessness in Jewish History* (New York, 1986), 7.
10. For more on the "moral shocks" concept, see Jeff Goodwin, James M. Jasper, and Francesca Polletta, eds., *Passionate Politics: Emotions and Social Movements* (Chicago, 2001), 16–17, 106, 148–51.
11. "The Crisis in Jewish History," *Jewish Chronicle*, 20 January 1882.
12. Biale, *Power and Powerlessness*, 8–9.

Appendix

Address to the First General Meeting of the Philo-Judaean Society

Moses E. Levy

Freemasons' Hall,
Great Queens Street,
London, England
18 May 1827

The Right Hon. Lord Viscount Mandeville in the Chair.

The Report of the Society having been read, it was moved by Major-General Neville, seconded by John James Strutt,—and

Resolved, That the Report be received, and printed under the direction of the Committee, and that this Meeting concur in the following Resolutions, suggested by Moses Levy, Esq., a gentleman of the Hebrew nation, as the basis of conciliatory measures toward that people, viz.

1. That the persecutions which the house of Israel have endured for past generations are grievous, affecting their temporal as well as moral condition.
2. That it is the duty of all believers in Revelation to counteract, as much as lies in their power, these effects, and to remove the causes which have brought the people of Israel to the deteriorated state in which they now present themselves.
3. That as the continuation and existence of the people of Israel manifest to the world a miraculous living monument of the truth of Revelation, it is the duty of all believers to direct their aim and labour to raise that people from the moral turpitude into which our forefathers have contributed to plunge them.
4. That this duty we owe to humanity, as well as to ourselves, in order that we may atone for, and remedy, as much as possible, these wrongs; and, above all, to accelerate that period foretold in the Bible, when Jew and Gentile shall unite in one faith, and the world enjoy that state which from the beginning existed in the will of the Creator.

Mr. Levy expressed his concurrence with these Resolutions, and entered at large on the past sufferings and present condition of the Hebrew nation.

Were I to consider myself but as a mere Jew, I ought, perhaps, to express only gratitude to the Society for the Resolutions which have been just read, and the benefits they hold out to an Israelite. But, in considering myself a believer in Revelation, I naturally revert to its effects, and the great work it has achieved since its first promulgation: and, following the continued Divine interpositions, which God has vouchsafed to exert in behalf of degenerate man to recall him to himself, I am struck at the stupendous plan which Revelation presents.

Behold, on the one hand, the living testimony which the miraculous preservation of the house of Israel bears to the truth of Revelation; and on the other, the gradual diffusion of its influence through the active agency of the Christian world. My mind, under such an influence, soars above its capability of conception, and is forcibly directed to those great destinies of man, to which past events, and the wonderful signs of the present times, obviously tend. The joy therefore, which, as a mere member of the house of Israel, I feel at the dawning prospects which the Resolutions, just read hold forth, is lost in the consideration of the *still greater consequences they are capable of leading to*; namely, the great aim and end for which we were separated and constituted a peculiar people.

In this character, my Lord, I feel myself justified in common with all believers in Revelation, in taking part in the discussion on this most interesting occasion. The truth of the Resolutions just read is so evident, that no Christian with whom I have conversed for these twenty years, and they have been numerous indeed, ever denied the grievous treatment which my nation has experienced; and who did not wish that it were possible, by applying some efficacious remedy, to heal the desperate wounds it had occasioned. The Resolutions are so true, that no one present, I trust, can gainsay them; but, unfortunately, truth is often an enemy to itself, by the mere circumstance of its being too true. A discriminating writer very justly observes, "The most awful and interesting truths are often considered so true that they lose the power of truth, and lie bed-ridden in the dormitory of the soul, side by side, with the most exploded and despised of errors."

It is, therefore, necessary, my Lord, that the Resolutions should not receive a merely cold assent, but that they should be acted up to with energy, in order to rescue them from the paralyzing and deadly indifference to which the want of novelty exposes simple truth. My aim is to point out, first, that, the prostrate house of Israel loudly call for a remedy; secondly, that this remedy, when applied, must reach the Christian as well as the Jew; and, thirdly, how the resolutions will operate, if properly applied, on the Christian, the Jew, and the world at large.

But, before I proceed, I shall, in order to be better understood, make three distinct discriminations: first, that the *Christian* and the *Christian world*, are, in my estimation, widely different; the one, in endeavouring to be a true Christian as far as the other by his nominal Christianity will permit him, is, as he ought to be, a friend of Israel; whilst the other has been his most deadly enemy.

The second discrimination I make, is between an *Israelite* and the *house of Israel*; an Israelite is responsible, as an individual, for his actions, and must work his own salvation as a member of the human family, whereas, the house of Israel have an office to perform in the plan of the regeneration of man: hence, Israel, are, in reality, the property of mankind, for whose benefit we exist, and not for our peculiar and exclusive good; and, lastly, that whilst the conversion, which is in the spirit of Christianity, was in former ages enforced on the *individual* Israelite by the dagger on the one hand; so on the other, the house of Israel were persecuted by decrees on decrees, or by bulls on bulls, teeming with the utmost severity, and aiming at the very extinction of the nation. At present, however, the severe measures by which conversion was enforced upon us in former ages, has given way to the more persuasive language of love, which the London Society has used with the most unremitting exertions. But such a remedy, or even that which this Society offers in relieving the distressed and necessitous Israelite, can only reach individuals; but where—where, I ask, is the remedy for the house of Israel?—there is none. What means are there to counteract the direful effects of past edicts that were heaped on the proscribed nation? as yet, none have been adopted.

Now, my Lord, I will revert to the three considerations to which I wish to direct the attention of *the Christian*. Is there any Christian, who, in attending to his Bible, can turn aside from the duty which he owes to the people of Israel? Is there any *Christian* who can be regardless of the wrongs done to us by past generations, or deny that the desolate house of Israel demand a remedy? Yet, the urgency of a remedy is not felt, even by the major part of thinking believers; whether amongst Jews or Christians. That the question may be placed in its true light, I must be permitted to touch slightly on the past persecutions, not for the sake of making them at present a matter of reproach towards the, Christian, but merely to trace the direful effects resulting from them.

I need only revert to the fourteenth century, at which period persecution assumed a most cruel and destructive tendency, by directly aiming at the intellect. The Jews were first debarred from having any schools among them, and from exercising any of the liberal arts; most of the synagogues were taken from them and shut up, down to be old-clothes men and petty shop-keepers; and then, after thus brutalizing their minds by shutting out every thing that could expand or instruct, it was made a subject of reproach to them. They were accused of cupidity, but how could it be otherwise that they should not be over-reaching, when they saw themselves surrounded by misery on all sides, and left none but three of the most wretched trades to carry on their dealings in? How could it be wondered at that they would cheat the Christians, after being so unmercifully pillaged and persecuted by them? Is it to be wondered at, when, perhaps, there were times when, they had not so much as a piece of bread to put into the mouths of their wives and children?

But this was not enough to satisfy their persecutors. After this, they must be turned out, and hunted from place to place like savages. Barbary, Turkey, Poland, the wilds of Prussia, they tried them all, and every where found an enemy in man; and such had been the state of things generally, till within the last five and twenty, or thirty years. Since that time, the Christians have begun to feel the Revelations of God more strongly; but, unfortunately, while this sentiment has been expanding, the ancient prejudice has still prevailed. The question was still asked, 'Are they not over-reaching'? and piety is not ashamed to screen behind it the worst of feelings. It was true that the Jew was no longer persecuted with the faggot, but he was with contempt, which, to his feeling, was a worse persecution than that of the faggot; for whilst the latter only destroyed the body, the former ruined the soul. In short, in the words of the prophet Jeremiah, it might be said "Sion has spread forth her hands, and there is no one to comfort her; the Lord has delivered me into their hands from whom I am unable to rise up." And what is the consequence of such a state of things? Without a country,—without a field of action for intellect to expand, or for virtue to be exercised—without any food for reflection—the Israelite is compelled to centre all his comforts and the powers of his noble faculties, in his miserable self. And, while inhaling the moral pestilential atmosphere that surrounds his contracted sphere, he is made to drag the chain of servitude, and is prevented from soaring beyond himself. 'Where every man is his own end, (Bishop Hackett observes,) all things must come to a bad end.' Can an Israelite, who is daily made to exercise a state directly opposed to that which Revelation teaches, apply to his Bible and feel its spirit, or be alive to the aim and end to which it points? No, it is impossible! The full force of this, however, can only be felt by the practical believer in Revelation. No, the Book—the Sacred Book! is unhappily sealed from the very people who are constituted its special guardians and witnesses. Its precepts and its prophecies are to us now, in the language of Ezekiel, "but as a lovely song of one that hath a pleasant voice;" we hear the words, but we do them not.

But the Christians say, let the Jews embrace Christianity, and all these difficulties will be remedied. Let it be granted. But how is it possible that this can be done with a nation scattered up and down in all directions; some amongst Christians—some amongst Mahommedans—and some amongst Idolaters? If, indeed, the Jews must ultimately turn, the Almighty seems clearly, by their dispersion, to have placed it beyond the power of man to affect, who can at best only convert one here and there; the work he evidently reserves for himself. Clearly, then, this is but a subterfuge which the enemy of man puts into the mouth of the *soi-disant* believers, in order to keep alive that hatred towards the Jews; an effectual weapon, by which he still disputes the way of life with the spirit of Revelation.

I will now, my Lord, touch upon the second consideration; namely, that the Christian world likewise require a remedy, which can only be found at the hand of a true Christian. Let the most liberal person present repeat to himself, first "Christian," and then "Jew," and he will feel a difference in the sensation of his nerves as he pronounces the two words. It is too true, the weeds which necessarily arise in the heart from such a state of things, cannot but counteract the influence of Revelation, and nip the blossom in the bud of the fruit which its spirit is capable of bringing forth. In vain will the Christian of the present day attempt to get rid of this hatred, which preys upon the vital principle of Revelation. How can I shake off this prejudice, will he say, when the Jew is actuated by no sentiment of patriotism; his views are centred but in himself; piety and religion are but nominally and outwardly observed by him; how can I then, will the Christian say, sympathize with, or love such a being? But the Jew, on the other hand, with greater justice may say, how can I be a patriot, deprived of a country, or of sympathizing countrymen? How can I exist for any higher purpose, when I am compelled to live but for my miserable self? And how can I be alive to the spirit of the religion I profess, if the vices it condemns are the attendant consequences of my slavery? Thus, we see, my Lord, that sin begets sin, and becomes its own punishment: the persecuted and the persecutors have fallen in the net which their transgressions prepared for them. In vain will the thinking part of believers look for a remedy in any other means than such as Revelation points to; for now it is scarcely possible to distinguish between the effect and the cause; whether the prostrate state of the Jews be owing to the hatred of the Christians; or, the hatred of the Christians, the natural consequence of the prostrate state of the Jews. But what is the result of all this? Let the ravages which infidelity is making answer the question.

Having traced the impediments which intercept the rays of the light of revelation, and thereby prevent them from maturing those fruits which its spirit is calculated to produce in the breast of the believer, I will now attend to that grievous state of things under which the Christian, world is at present labouring; and which, in its tendency, is of a still more alarming and awful nature. It is a question of serious consideration to a believer in revelation, whether *the persecuted, or the persecutor, will eventually prove the worst off*. This is an awful side of the picture, my Lord! However merited may have been our punishment, the time must come, when the Almighty will say "enough" to our sorrows, for the Lord will not contend for ever, neither will He be always wroth. The period will arrive, when the merited cup of trembling will be drank up to its dregs, and the cup of the Lord's fury be taken from our hands, and given to those who delight in afflicting us; and will the Christian world, believers in revelation, be regardless of the consequences, with these judgments before them? Will they like to share the cup of trembling with the infidel oppressors? In vain may the Christian, as an individual, say, I am exempt, not being an actual persecutor of a Christian nation, and screen himself by saying, the laws of my country do not authorize persecution. But let it be recollected, that the past persecutions of the world have brought the children of Israel to such a state, that even the most pious and best of Christians, cannot, from the natural frailty of human nature, be free from prejudice against the Jew. What, then, may we expect from the mere nominal Christian? Can we hope for more forbearance and charity from him?

Allowing that oppressive persecution has ceased in Christendom, has it ceased in Africa and in Asia? Poor Israel! Is the Christian not bound to pity still? Can the Israelite of Europe and America say, that he can improve his moral condition, when the Jew of Barbary, Turkey, or elsewhere, operates either directly or indirectly as a drawback? But has the spirit of persecution ceased in Christendom indeed? Would to heavens it had! I will not notice the late edicts of the present pope, which, although operating on the minds of the greater part of the Christian world, bear, in my opinion, no comparison to the persecuting spirit of the other parts of Christendom. The Greeks, in their present struggle for liberty, treated the unfortunate Jews who fell in their way, with more cruelty than if they had been Turks; although, strictly speaking, they could only be regarded as mere loyal slaves to their late common master. I mention this, not with the view of prejudicing their cause; no! they are still believers in revelation, and are therefore objects of tenderness: all the blood that I could spare from the cause of my people, should willingly be offered for their emancipation, on which their regeneration principally depends. I merely cite this case, to shew how Satan turns every occurrence to his own ends, whilst the deluded nominal Christian is made to aggravate even retaliatory measures into unheard of inhumanity and cruelty, the mind being operated upon by the religious hatred to the Jew.

It may be said that the Greeks have for many ages been slaves, and that the, influence of revelation could not have made much progress. I will grant this. But let us turn to civilized Europe,—Christian,—Protestant Europe. The laws which existed, and still exist, in some parts of Germany, against the Jews, are in their nature so degrading, that did they not operate to debase the mind of the Israelite, they must recoil on the people with whom they originated, and serve to mark them as the most mischievous of inhuman hearts. I will not make any observations on the common mode of persecution in many parts of Germany: such as where the Jew must not dare to frequent different places of public resort; his being obliged to pay dearly for sleeping a night in certain towns, and the like; but will merely confine myself to the more aggravated species of persecutions: as, for instance, where the Jews are obliged to pay a toll in passing a particular gate. But a toll!! O! Christian, hear this, and blush for man. The Jew must pay a toll with swine!!! The printed card, or formula, on which the receipt is given, bears the words *Jew* and *Swine*; and a son of Abraham is handed this card, with the pen passed through the word *swine*, retaining the words, "The Jew has paid his toll." At Frankfort, scarcely more than two years back, an edict was passed, to restrain the Jews from having more than fifteen marriages a year, although there were more than a thousand families residing at the place. Virtuous daughters, and chaste matrons of England, drop a tear at this most accursed species of persecution, aimed at the daughters of Israel!—Shall the Lord hold his peace? Shall he be still silent? Shall he refrain from the vengeance due to such unparalleled refinement of human malice? Is there any parallel in history to an act so diabolical? Pharaoh's edict aimed at destroying the innocent babe, but here the dagger of the assassin is aimed at the destruction of the soul.

At such a picture, the most inveterate enemy to the house of Israel ought to relent. But can the Israelite expect to find pity in a people, or nation, when he is himself regardless of the state of his own brethren? This—this, my Lord, is the most painful—the most dismal side of the picture of fallen Israel: a picture that must excite compassion in the most obdurate heart. The persecutions have been so continued, so general, that the Israelite is himself insensible to the state of his nation. He hears—he sees—and experiences all these sufferings, without their arousing even a stifled sigh in his breast. All his feelings, alas! are absorbed in and devoted to the only pleasure persecution left him, namely, the acquirement of wealth, to enjoy eatables which he never raised, drink wines he never cultivated, and wear clothes which he does not manufacture. In this insensibility, we may trace the direful effects of the system of persecution; which refined malice directs against the noble faculties of the mind; here we see how preferable is the torture, the sword, or the faggot to the persecution of contempt.

What, my Lord, is to raise the house of Israel from such a torpor? Nothing but Divine assistance, for we cannot aid ourselves. And who can screen the Christian world from the vengeance due to such an unparalleled system of persecution, unless they seek shelter under the shadow of a merciful Creator, by timely repentance and contrition? Thus, we see, that the Jew has to contend internally and externally against obstacles that render it impossible for him to soar above himself, or receive benefit from that revelation, whose guardian he was constituted. In the like manner, the Christian, notwithstanding the advantages of nationality, has to contend, both internally and externally, with obstacles which deter him from bringing to maturity those fruits which the spirit of revelation is calculated to produce. He is compelled to live in the clouded and dense atmosphere created by the Christian world, which daily increases with the growth of infidelity; and while it multiplies the stumbling-blocks before a believer, it, at the same time, hurries on those consequences that must naturally result from such a state of things. Hence the Christian, as well as the Jew, requires a remedy; and such a remedy, as, when applied, will affect both parties equally: or, as I have already proved, the cause and effect are now so blended, that it would be impossible to distinguish the one from the other.

It is now necessary to ask, what remedy is there of a nature calculated to effect this? The answer, is simple—such as revelation points out; which will naturally lead us to the third consideration, viz. how the resolutions just proposed will operate, if properly applied, on the Christian, the Jew, and the world at large. As the resolutions contain simple truths, these truths would, if made the subject of reflection, and from reflection brought into action, be eventually restored to their native lustre. The soul then, under the quickening spirit of such an influence, will feel softened at the sorrows of persecuted Israel, and in condemning the cause from which they originated, a contrite spirit must necessarily ensue. If such a spirit be propagated by the pious Christian, and brought within the reach of every reader of the Bible, however simple he may be, he will feel its effect. A mind thus prepared in reading his Bible, cannot but associate with the subject, the miraculous preservation of the house of Israel, the testimony they bear to, the word of God, and the part, they act in the plan of the regeneration of man. Impressed with these interesting truths, the Bible will be read with profit; and by the light it affords, the heart cannot but participate in the scheme which revelation opens, to the mind. Instead, then, of reading the Bible for the salvation of his own soul, he will enter into its views, and will endeavour to become an instrument in the hands of Providence. Thus will his salvation be attained with more ease, as the consequence of doing the will of God, instead of being the principal object of pursuit.

By these means, the prejudice towards the Jew will be overcome, he will first pity, and ultimately love; for thus is the human heart acted upon—it knows no medium; when hatred cannot be indulged, love must; and when love is once roused, it necessarily will attract a corresponding sentiment. It is then, and only then, that the light which the spirit of revelation is capable of imparting, will shine in its full splendour. Love, by which the Omnipotent powers harmonized the creation, and to propagate which, man was made and created, is the only means by which the way of God is to be understood; to counteract which, has ever been the aim of the enemy of man, and therefore love is the only instrument by which a believer can effectually and successfully attack him. It therefore follows, my lord, that the resolutions before us, if acted upon with energy, will be of spiritual service to the Christian; and in raising the voice of justice and contrition, all generous hearts will naturally be attracted; the Word of God will be read with greater benefit; and the seeds of infidelity will be destroyed. At the magic sound of nationality, the hearts of all Israel, both far and near, will be moved, and the mind will necessarily soar above itself in the spirit of revelation; for to an Israelite, nationality and the Bible are synonymous; he will seek it with a proportionate degree of avidity, as the patriotic flame rages in his breast; he will attend to its whole structure, instead of its mere disjointed parts; he will be led to the knowledge of the importance of the office consigned to the house of Israel; his heart will sympathise with the love which the other believers have roused in him; and his newly-quickened mind will be alive to its sensibility. Then will the Bible, in its letter as well as its spirit, be sought after and attended to, to satisfy his daily growing thirst, (the only key that can effectually open the sinful heart); prayers dictated by a contrite heart must necessarily follow; a sure precursor of that spirit of supplication which God has promised by the hand of his prophets, leading to those great destinies prepared for happy man in the original will of the Creator, when He said, "Let there be light, and there was light."

But it may be asked, can all this be affected by such simple means, and through the agency of so few persons as are here present? Yes, my lord, with less, much less a number. The God of heaven delights in doing great works by small means. Look at Israel—a handful of men, compared to the mass of the human family, yet were they made the means of transmitting to man the revelation of God; and are, in their very captivity and dispersed state, the wonder and astonishment of mankind, serving as witnesses—living witnesses—to the truth of revelation. Yes! every one that has a Bible, or tenders one to reclaim or convert a sinner, feels, as it were, the spirit of the house of Israel, as forming a part of the sacred volume, and which seems to say, this book is true, for I am witness of its veracity. Again let us throw a glance at Great Britain, what was she one or two centuries ago? Her number did not amount to that of the children of Israel at the time of their Exodus from Egypt; and occupying a spot of ground scarcely distinguishable on the globe. Behold her now, the progenitor and head of mighty nations; look at the skeleton map, if I may so express myself, her sons have traced in the world, to be filled up by their future generations. Let us throw a bird's-eye view at the astonishing history she will present a century hence. Look at that gigantic nation, the people of the United States of America, speaking the same language and operated upon by the same habits; manners, and customs, and moved by the same spirit. Let us look forward to the time when her sons will have spread from sea to sea—when they coalesce with the happy islands of the Pacific, which have already begun to receive the light of civilisation and revelation at the hands of both mother and daughter. Look at those eighty millions of souls inhabiting the shores of British India; and lastly, consider Africa, which seems to promise that the period will soon arrive, when her benighted sons will lose both their slavery and idolatrous practices, and exchange the darkness that has hitherto warped their souls, for the cheering and vivifying light of revelation.

Thus we see, from a handful of men, occupying an insignificant spot on the earth, the British nation is made an instrument in the hands of God to propagate the light which revelation furnishes for the progressive civilisation to a great portion of the habitable world. Can any one say, that all this is the effect of mere chance? that it is not guided by Providence; a Providence that delights to do great works through the agency of small means? I therefore repeat, my lord, that I am not in the least discouraged at commencing the work by means however small; provided it be undertaken in the true spirit of the Bible, it will, it must, ultimately succeed. Let the standard be raised by pious persons, it will soon take root amongst the generous sons of Great Britain, and the voice of sympathy towards the fallen children of Israel will be echoed by their offspring, the people of the United States. Their condemnation of past persecutions will be sufficient to deter all tyrants from exercising the inhuman cruelties that so much degrade human nature: whether they be in Asia, Africa, or Europe, the mere fact of such acts having been condemned by the people of England and America, will, as it were, proclaim to the world the language of Isaiah, "Keep silence before me, O, isles! and let the people renew their strength, let them come near, and then let them speak."

I will now, my lord, close my address, by reiterating what I have tried to impress on the minds of the Christians, viz., *that the Christian world calls for a remedy, and that this remedy can only be obtained by attending to that of Israel.* It is time that the Christian world should look on a people with an eye of personal affection, whom they have so long persecuted and vilified. "There is none," in the language of Isaiah, "to guide her amongst all the sons whom she hath brought forth, neither is there any one that taketh her by the hand of all the sons that she hath brought up." Yes, my lord, it is a duty the Christian world owe to themselves and to the house of Israel, who have been in reality their parent, and that of the world. The Bible holds forth this language throughout. The true Christian, therefore, is urgently called upon to apply a remedy to the house of Israel, and to the Christian world, in the mere attempt of which, the work may be said to be effected, and bring about that time, when the hearts of the fathers will return unto their children, and the hearts of the children unto their fathers.

Source: Levy's address is combined here from two editions of the *World* newspaper: 6 and 20 June 1827.

Selected Bibliography

NEWSPAPERS AND PERIODICALS CONSULTED

Academy: A Weekly Review of Literature, Science, and Art (London)
Albany Evening Journal
Albion, A Journal of News, Politics, and Literature (New York)
Allgemeine Zeitung (Augsburg)
Allgemeine Zeitung des Judentums (Leipzig)
American Baptist Magazine (Boston)
Ami de la Religion (Paris)
Archives Israelites de France (Paris)
Armonia (Turin)
Baltimore American
Baptist Magazine
Bell's Life in London and Sporting Chronicle
Birmingham Daily Post
Bristol Mercury
Boston Daily Courier
Boston Recorder and Religious Telegraph
Caledonian Mercury (Edinburgh)
Catholic Layman (Dublin)
Chambers Edinburgh Journal
Charleston Mercury
Christian Examiner and Church of Ireland Magazine (Dublin)
Christian Remembrancer (London)
Christian Secretary (Hartford, Conn.)
Christian Watchman (Boston)
Church of England Bulwark and Clergyman's Protector
Cincinnati Daily Enquirer
Cincinnati Daily Gazette
Cobbett's Weekly Political Register (London)
Dagblad van's Gravenhage (The Hague)
Daily Inter-Ocean (Chicago)
Daily National Intelligencer (Washington, D.C.)
Daily News (London)
Eclectic Magazine of Foreign Literature, Science, and Art (London)
Eclectic Review (London)
Era (London)
Examiner (London)
Floridian and Advocate (Tallahassee)
Freeman's Journal (New York)

232 Selected Bibliography

Hampshire Telegraph and Sussex Chronicle (Portsmouth)
Hull Packet
Ipswich Journal
Israelite (Cincinnati)
Jewish Chronicle (London)
Jewish Daily News (New York)
Jewish Messenger (New York)
Journal des Débats (Paris)
Lancet (London)
Leeds Mercury
Literary Gazette and Journal of the Belles Lettres, Arts, Sciences, &c. (London)
Liverpool Mercury
London Magazine
Mail and Express (New York)
Manchester Guardian
Manchester Times
Midnight Cry (New York)
Morning Chronicle (London)
Morning Courier and New York Enquirer
Morning Herald (New York)
Morning Post (London)
Monthly Repository and Review of Theology and General Literature (London)
National Gazette (Philadelphia)
New Jerusalem Magazine and Theological Inspector
New Monthly Magazine and Literary Journal (London)
New York Observer
New York Times
New York Tribune
North American and Daily Advertiser (Philadelphia)
North Wales Chronicle (Bangor)
Occident and American Jewish Advocate
Palestine Post
Pall Mall Gazette (London)
Philadelphia Gazette and Daily Advertiser
Philadelphia Inquirer
Presse (Paris)
Public Ledger (Philadelphia)
Punch
Religious Intelligencer (New Haven)
San Francisco Call
Satirist; or, the Censor of the Times (London)
St. Louis Republic
Sydney Gazette and New South Wales Advertiser
Sun (Baltimore)
Sun (New York City)
Tablet (London)
Telegraph (London)
Times (London)
Times Picayune (New Orleans)
Trenton Evening Times (New Jersey)
United States Commercial & Statistical Register (Philadelphia)
Univers (Paris)
Univers Israelite (Paris)

Voice of Jacob (London)
World (London)

PRINTED PRIMARY SOURCES

Address to the Sons of Israel. London, 1828.
Adler, Cyrus, ed. *The Voice of America on Kishineff*. Philadelphia: Jewish Publication Society of America, 1904.
Adler, Hermann. "Abstract of a Sermon Delivered at the Western Synagogue on the 28th January, 1882, by the Rev. Dr. Hermann Adler." In *Jews As They Are*. Edited by Charles Kensington Salaman. London: Simpkin, Marshall, 1882.
Carlyle, Thomas. *On Heroes, Hero-Worship, and the Heroic in History*. London: Chapman and Hall, 1840.
City of Charleston. *Proceedings of a Public Meeting of the Citizens of Charleston Held at the City Hall, on the 28th August, 1840, in Relation to the Persecution of the Jews of the East. Also, the Proceedings of a Meeting of the Israelites of Charleston, Convened at the Hall of the Hebrew Orphan Society, on the Following Evening, in Reference to the Same Subject*. Charleston, 1840.
Brown, John Aq. *The Jew: The Master-Key of the Apocalypse*. London: Hatchard and Son, 1827.
Davis, Israel. *The Jews in Roumania: A Short Statement of Their Recent History and Present Situation*. London: Anglo-Jewish Association, 1872.
Davitt, Michael. *Within the Pale: The True Story of Anti-Semitic Persecutions in Russia*. New York: A. S. Barnes, 1903.
Delacouture, Andre Vincent. *Le droit canon et le droit natural dans l'affaire Mortara*. Paris, 1858.
Dix, John. *Pen Pictures of Popular English Preachers*. London: Partiridge and Oakey, 1852.
The Extractor, Or, Universal Repertorium of Literature, Science and the Arts; Comprehending, Under One General Arrangement, the Whole of the Instructive and Amusing Articles from All the Reviews, Magazines, and Journals. London, 1829.
Goldsmid, Francis H. *Memoir of Sir Francis Henry Goldsmid*. 2nd rev. ed. London: Kagan Paul, Trench, 1882.
Gollancz, Hermann. *Sermons and Addresses*. New York: Bloch, 1909.
Goodrich, Chauncey A., ed. *Select British Eloquence: Embracing the Best Speeches Entire, of the Most Eminent Orators of Great Britain for the Last Two Centuries*. New York: Harper and Brothers, 1884.
Griggs, Earl Leslie, ed. *Collected Letters of Samuel Taylor Coleridge: 1820–1825*. Vol. 5. Oxford: Clarendon Press, 2000.
Harris, James Howard. *Memoirs of an Ex-Minister*. London: Longmans, Green, 1885.
Hess, Moses. *The Revival of Israel: Rome and Jerusalem, the Last Nationalist Question*. Translated by Meyer Waxman. 1918. Reprint, Lincoln, NE: University of Nebraska Press, 1995.
Hodder, Edwin, ed. *The Life and Work of the Seventh Earl of Shaftesbury*. Vol. 2. London: Cassell, 1887.
Hume, David. *Philosophical Works of David Hume*. Vol. 3. Edinburgh: Black and Tate, 1828.
Kohler, Max J., and Simon Wolf. "Jewish Disabilities in the Balkan States: American Contributions Toward Their Removal with Particular Reference to the Congress of Berlin." *Publications of the American Jewish Historical Society* 24 (1916): 1–137.

Leech, Joseph. *The Church Goer: Rural Rides; or, Calls at Country Churches.* London: John Ridler, 1847.
Leeser, Isaac. *The Jews and the Mosaic Law.* Philadelphia, 1833.
Lieven, Dorothea. *Letters of Dorothea, Princess Lieven, During Her Residence in London, 1812–1834.* Edited by Lionel G. Robinson. London: Longmans, Green, 1902.
Mayhew, Henry. *London Labour and the London Poor: A Cyclopedia of the Condition and Earnings of Those That Will Work, Those That Cannot Work, and Those That Will Not Work.* Vol. 2. London: Charles Griffin, 1861.
McNeil, Hugh. *Anti-Slavery and Anti-Popery: A Letter Addressed to Edward Cropper.* London: Hatchard, 1838.
Moise, Penina. "On the Persecution of the Jews of Damascus." In *Sephardic-American Voices: Two Hundred Years of a Literary Legacy.* Edited by Diane Matza. Hanover, NH: University Press of New England, 1997.
Montefiore, Moses, and Judith Montefiore. *Diaries of Sir Moses and Lady Montefiore.* Edited by L. Loewe. 2 vols. Chicago: Belford Clarke, 1890.
Newman, Selig. *The Challenge Accepted: A Dialogue Between a Jew and a Christian.* New York, 1850.
———. "The Necessity of Union." *The Occident and American Jewish Advocate* 8 (March 1851).
Noble, T. C. *The Lord Mayor of London: A Sketch of the Origin, History and Antiquity of the Office, Reprinted from the City Press.* London, 1860.
Persecution of the Jews of the East, Containing the Proceedings of a Meeting Held at the Synagogue Mikveh Israel, Philadelphia, on Thursday Evening, the 28th of Ab, 5600. Philadelphia, 1840.
Philo-Judaean Society. *First Annual Report of the Philo-Judaean Society.* London, 1827.
———. *Second Annual Report of the Philo-Judaean Society.* London, 1828.
———. *Third Annual Report of the Philo-Judaean Society.* London, 1829.
Pieritz, G. W. *Persecution of the Jews at Damascus.* London: London Society for Promoting Christianity Among the Jews, 1840.
Pinsker, Leo. *Auto-Emancipation.* Translated by D. S. Blondheim. New York: Maccabaean, 1906.
Pulling, Alexander. *The City of London Corporation Inquiry.* London, 1854.
Scott, Thomas. Introduction to *The Restoration of Israel*, by Joseph Crooll. London, 1814.
Smith, Goldwin. "The Jewish Question." *Eclectic Magazine of Foreign Literature, Science, and Art*, December 1881.
Stockqueler, J. H. *The Life of Field Marshal the Duke of Wellington.* Vol. 2. London: Ingram, Cooke, 1853.
Straus, Oscar S. "Address of Honorable Oscar S. Straus on Humanitarian Diplomacy of the United States." In *Proceedings of the American Society of International Law at Its Sixth Annual Meeting Held at Washington, D.C. April 25–27, 1912.* Washington, D.C.: n.p., 1912.
Torrens, William. *The Government of London.* 1884.
Wellesley, Arthur. *Maxims and Opinions of Field-Marshall His Grace the Duke of Wellington, Selected from His Writings and Speeches During a Public Life of More Than Half a Century. With a Biographical Memoir by George Henry Francis, Esq.* Edited by George Henry Francis. London: Henry Colburn, 1845.
Weylland, John M. *Round the Tower, or, The Story of the London City Mission.* London: Partridge, 1875.
Wolf, Lucien. *Sir Moses Montefiore: A Centennial Biography with Selections from Letters and Journals.* New York: Harper & Brothers, 1885.

SECONDARY SOURCES

Abrahams, L. "Sir I. L. Goldsmid and the Admission of the Jews of England to Parliament." *Transactions of the Jewish Historical Society of England* 4 (1899–1901): 116–76.
Adams, James Eli. *Dandies and Desert Saints: Styles of Victorian Masculinity.* Ithaca, NY: Cornell University Press, 1995.
Ages, Arnold. "Veuillot and the Talmud." *Jewish Quarterly Review* 64 (January 1974): 229–60.
Alderman, Geoffrey. *London Jewry and London Politics, 1889–1986.* London: Routledge, 1989.
———. *Modern British Jewry.* Oxford: Oxford University Press, 1998.
Al-Qattan, Najwa. "Litigants and Neighbors: The Communal Topography of Ottoman Damascus." *Comparative Studies in Society and History* 44, no. 3 (July 2002): 511–33.
Altshuler, Stuart. *From Exodus to Freedom: A History of the Soviet Jewry Movement.* Lanham, MD: Rowman & Littlefield, 2005.
Andrews, Kenneth T., and Michael Biggs. "The Dynamics of Protest Diffusion: Movement Organization, Social Networks, and News Media in the 1960 Sit-Ins." *American Sociological Review* 71 (October 2006): 752–77.
Aronson, I. Michael. "The Anti-Jewish Pogroms in Russia in 1881." In *Pogroms: Anti-Jewish Violence in Modern Jewish History.* Edited by John D. Klier and Shlomo Lambroza, 44–61. Cambridge: Cambridge University Press, 1992.
———. *Troubled Waters: The Origins of the 1881 Anti-Jewish Pogroms in Russia.* Pittsburg, PA: University of Pittsburg Press, 1990.
Bartal, Israel. "The First Nationalist or a Belated Shtadlan? Thoughts on the Works of Moses Montefiore." In *The Age of Moses Montefiore: A Collection of Essays.* Jerusalem: Misgav Yerushayalim, 1987.
Baumeister, Ray F., Karen L. Dale, and Mark Muraven. "Volition and Belongingness: Social Movements, Volition, Self-Esteem, and the Need to Belong." In *Self, Identity, and Social Movements.* Edited by Sheldon Stryker, Timothy J. Owens, and Robert W. White. Minneapolis: University of Minnesota Press, 2000.
Bebbington, David. *The Mind of Gladstone: Religion, Homer, and Politics.* Oxford: Oxford University Press, 2004.
Bebbington, D. W. *Evangelicalism in Modern Britain: A History from the 1730s to the 1980s.* London: Routledge, 1993.
Beizer, Mikhail. *The Jews of St. Petersburg: Excursions Through a Noble Past.* Edited by Martin Gilbert. Translated by Michael Sherbourne. Philadelphia: Jewish Publication Society, 1989.
Ben-Naeh, Yaron. "Honor and Its Meaning Among Ottoman Jews." *Jewish Social Studies* 11 (Winter 2005): 19–50.
Bergmann, Werner. "Ethnic Riots in Situations of Loss of Control: Revolution, Civil War, and Regime Change as Opportunity Structures for Anti-Jewish Violence in Nineteenth- and Twentieth-Century Europe." In *Control of Violence: Historical and International Perspective on Violence in Modern Societies.* Edited by Wilhelm Heitmeyer, Heinz-Gerhard Haupt, Stefan Malthaner, and Andrea Kirschner. New York: Springer, 2011.
Bergmann, Werner, Christhard Hoffman, and Helmut Walser Smith. Introduction to *Exclusionary Violence: Antisemitic Riots in Modern German History.* Edited by Christhard Hoffman, Werner Bergmann, and Helmut Walser Smith. Ann Arbor: University of Michigan Press, 2002.
Berman, Aaron. *Nazism, the Jews and American Zionism, 1933–1948.* Detroit: Wayne State University Press, 1990.

Bermant, Haim. *The Cousinhood: The Anglo-Jewish Gentry*. London: Eyre and Spottiswoode, 1971.
Biale, David. *Power and Powerlessness in Jewish History*. New York: Schocken Books, 1986.
Bialik, Hayim Nahman. "City of the Killings." In *Songs from Bialik: Selected Poems of Hayim Nahman Bialik*. Edited and translated by Atar Hadari. Syracuse, NY: Syracuse University Press, 2000.
Black, Eugene C. "A Typological Study of English Zionists." *Jewish Social Studies* 9 (Spring–Summer 2003): 20–55.
———. *The Social Problems of Anglo-Jewry, 1880–1920*. Oxford: Basil Blackwell, 1988.
Blackburn, Robin. *The American Crucible: Slavery, Emancipation and Human Rights*. London: Verso, 2011.
Bourdieu, Pierre. *The Field of Cultural Production: Essays on Art and Literature*. Edited by Randal Johnson. New York: Columbia University Press, 1993.
Boyd, John, R. A. Schweitzer, and Charles Tilly. *British Contentious Gatherings of 1828*. Ann Arbor: Center for Research on Social Organization, University of Michigan, 1978.
Brenner, Michael. *Prophets of the Past: Interpreters of Jewish History*. Translated by Steven Rendall. Princeton, NJ: Princeton University Press, 2010.
Breslauer, S. Daniel. *Toward a Jewish (M)orality: Speaking of a Postmodern Jewish Ethics*. Westport, CT: Greenwood Press, 1998.
Brown, Christopher Leslie. *Moral Capital: Foundations of British Abolitionism*. Chapel Hill: University of North Carolina Press, 2006.
Brown, Richard. *Church and State in Modern Britain, 1700–1850*. London: Routledge, 1991.
Brubaker, Rogers, and David D. Laitin. "Ethnic and Nationalist Violence." *Annual Review of Sociology* 24 (August 1998): 423–52.
Brundage, W. Fitzhugh. *Lynching in the New South: Georgia and Virginia, 1880–1930*. Champaign: University of Illinois Press, 1993.
Burke, Peter. *History and Social Theory*. 2nd ed. Ithaca, NY: Cornell University Press, 2005.
Burns, Michael. *France and the Dreyfus Affair: A Documentary History*. Boston: Bedford/St. Martin's, 1999.
Burns, Ross. *Damascus: A History*. New York: Routledge, 2005.
Butnaru, I. C. *The Silent Holocaust: Romania and Its Jews*. Westport, CT: Greenwood Press, 1992.
Cannadine, David. *The Rise and Fall of Class in Britain*. New York: Columbia University Press, 1999.
Caron, Vicki. "Catholic Political Mobilization and Antisemitic Violence in Fin de Siècle France: The Case of the Union Nationale." *Journal of Modern History* 81 (June 2009): 294–346.
Carter, Grayson. *Anglican Evangelicals: Protestant Secessions from the Via Media, c. 1800–1850*. Oxford: Oxford University Press, 2001.
Cassedy, Steven. "Russian-Jewish Intellectuals Confront the Pogroms of 1881: The Example of 'Razsvet.'" *Jewish Quarterly Review* 84, no. 2–3 (October 1993 and 1994): 129–52.
Cesarani, David. *The Jewish Chronicle and Anglo-Jewry, 1841–1991*. Cambridge: Cambridge University Press, 1994.
Chernin, Albert D. "Making Soviet Jews an Issue: A History." In *A Second Exodus: The American Movement to Free Soviet Jews*. Edited by Murray Friedman and A. Chernin. Hanover, NH: Brandeis University Press, 1999.

Chesterman, Simon. *Just War or Just Peace? Humanitarian Intervention and International Law*. Oxford: Oxford University Press, 2001.
Clark, Gregory, and S. Michael Halloran. "Transformations of Public Discourse in Nineteenth-Century America." Introduction to *Oratorical Culture in Nineteenth Century America: Transformations in the Theory and Practice of Rhetoric*. Carbondale, IL: Southern Illinois University Press, 1993.
Clark, Michael. *Albion and Jerusalem: The Anglo-Jewish Community in the Post-Emancipation Era, 1858–1887*. Oxford: Oxford University Press, 2009.
Claybaugh, Amanda. "Toward a New Transatlanticism: Dickens in the United States." *Victorian Studies* 48 (Spring 2006): 439–60.
Coppa, Frank J. "Pio Nono and the Jews: From 'Reform' to 'Reaction,' 1846–1878." *Catholic Historical Review* 89, no. 4 (October 2003): 671–95.
Cowen, Anne, and Roger Cowen. *Victorian Jews Through British Eyes*. London: Vallentine Mitchell, 1998.
Cowen, Israel. "Tribute to a Dead Leader." *Menorah* 36 (April 1904): 230–37.
Crawford, Elizabeth. *The Women's Suffrage Movement: A Reference Guide, 1866–1928*. London: UCL Press, 1999.
Dale, R. W. *History of English Congregationalism*. New York: Armstrong and Son, 1907.
Dames, Nicholas. "Brushes with Fame: Thackeray and the Work of Celebrity." *Nineteenth-Century Literature* 56, no. 1 (June 2001): 23–51.
Davies, Norman. "Great Britain and the Polish Jews, 1918–20." *Journal of Contemporary History* 8, no. 2 (1973): 119–42.
Davis, David Brion. *The Problem of Slavery in Western Culture*. Ithaca, NY: Cornell University Press, 1966.
———. "Slavery and Progress." In *Anti-Slavery, Religion, and Reform: Essays in Memory of Roger Anstey*. Edited by Christine Bolt and Seymour Drescher. Folkestone, UK: W. Dawson, 1980.
Dekel, Mikhal. "'From the Mouth of the Raped Woman Rivka Schiff,' Kishineff, 1903." *Women's Studies Quarterly* 36, nos. 1 and 2 (Spring–Summer 2008): 199–207.
De la Roche, Roberta Senechal. "Collective Violence as Social Control." *Sociological Forum* 11 (1996): 97–128.
Della Porta, Donatella, and Mario Diani. *Social Movements: An Introduction*. 2nd ed. Malden, MA: Blackwell, 2006.
Diamond, Michael. *Victorian Sensation: Or the Spectacular, the Shocking and the Scandalous in Nineteenth-Century Britain*. London: Anthem Press, 2003.
Diani, Mario. "Leaders or Brokers? Positions and Influence in Social Movement Networks." In *Social Movements and Networks: Relational Approaches to Collective Action*. Edited by Mario Diani and Doug McAdam. Oxford: Oxford University Press, 2003.
Dorraj, Manochehr. "The Crisis of Modernity and Religious Revivalism: A Comparative Study of Islamic Fundamentalism, Jewish Fundamentalism and Liberation Theology." *Social Compass* 46, no. 2 (June 1999): 225–40.
Dougherty, M. Patricia. "The Rise and Fall of 'L'Ami de la Religion': History, Purpose, and Readership of a French Catholic Newspaper." *Catholic Historical Review* 77, no. 1 (January 1991): 21–41.
Dovidio, John F., Brenda Major, and Jennifer Crocker. "Stigma: Introduction and Overview." In *The Social Psychology of Stigma*. Edited by Todd F. Heatherton, Robert E. Kleck, Michelle R. Hebl, and Jay G. Hull, 1–28. New York: Guilford Press, 2000.
Dubnow, Simon. *History of the Jews in Russia and Poland*. Philadelphia: Jewish Publication Society of America, 1918.

———. "The Sociological View of Jewish History." In *Ideas of Jewish History*. Edited by Michael A. Meyer. Detroit: Wayne State University Press, 1987.
Dundes, Alan. "The Ritual Murder or Blood Libel Legend: A Study of Anti-Semitic Victimization through Projective Inversion." In *The Blood Libel Legend, A Casebook in Anti-Semitic Folklore*. Edited by Alan Dundes, 336–78. Madison: University of Wisconsin Press, 1991.
Dynner, Glenn. "Legal Fictions: The Survival of Rural Jewish Tavernkeeping in the Kingdom of Poland." *Jewish Social Studies* 16 (Winter 2010): 28–66.
Einolf, Christopher. "The Fall and Rise of Torture: A Comparative and Historical Analysis." *Sociological Theory* 25 (June 2007): 101–21.
Endelman, Todd M. "The Englishness of Jewish Modernity in England." In *Toward Modernity: The European Jewish Model*. Edited by Jacob Katz. New Brunswick, NJ: Transaction, 1987.
———. "German Jews in Victorian England." In *Assimilation and Community: The Jews in Nineteenth-Century Europe*. Edited by Jonathan Frankel and Steven J. Zipperstein, 57–87. Cambridge: Cambridge University Press, 1992.
———. *The Jews of Britain, 1656–2000*. Berkeley: University of California Press, 2002.
———. *The Jews of Georgian England: 1714–1830: Tradition and Change in a Liberal Society*. Philadelphia: Jewish Publication Society of America, 1979.
———. "Writing English Jewish History." *Albion: A Quarterly Journal Concerned with British Studies* 27, no. 4 (Winter 1995): 623–36.
Ezekiel, Herbert T., and Gaston Lichtenstein. *The History of the Jews of Richmond from 1769 to 1917*. Richmond: Herbert T. Ezekiel, 1917.
Fahmy, Khaled. *All the Pasha's Men: Mehmed Ali, His Army, and the Making of Modern Egypt*. Cambridge: Cambridge University Press, 1997.
Fein, Helen. *Accounting for Genocide, National Responses and Jewish Victimization During the Holocaust*. New York: Free Press, 1979.
Fein, Helen, ed. *The Persisting Question: Sociological Perspectives and Social Contexts of Modern Antisemitism*. Berlin: Walter de Gruyter, 1987.
Feldberg, Michael, ed. *Blessings of Freedom: Chapters in American Jewish History*. Hoboken, NJ: American Jewish Historical Society, 2002.
Feldman, David. *Englishmen and Jews: Social Relations and Political Culture, 1840–1913*. New Haven, CT: Yale University Press, 1994.
Felsenstein, Frank. *Anti-Semitic Stereotypes: A Paradigm of Otherness in English Popular Culture, 1660–1830*. Baltimore: Johns Hopkins University Press, 1995.
Ferree, Myra Marx. "Soft Repression: Ridicule, Stigma, and Silencing in Gender-Based Movements." In *Authority in Contention*. Edited by Daniel J. Myers and Daniel M. Cress. Research in Social Movements, Conflicts and Change. Amsterdam: Elsevier, 2004.
Finestein, Israel. "Jewish Emancipationists in Victorian England: Self-Imposed Limits to Assimilation." In *Assimilation and Community: The Jews in Nineteenth-Century Europe*. Edited by Jonathan Frankel and Steven J. Zipperstein, 38–56. Cambridge: Cambridge University Press, 1992.
Fink, Carole. *Defending the Rights of Others: The Great Powers, the Jews, and International Minority Protection, 1878–1938*. New York: Cambridge University Press, 2004.
Finkelstein, Norman H. *American Jewish History*. Philadelphia: Jewish Publication Society, 2007.
Flegg, Columba Graham. *"Gathered Under Apostles," A Study of the Catholic Apostolic Church*. Oxford: Oxford University Press, 1992.
Florence, Ronald. *Blood Libel: The Damascus Affair of 1840*. New York: Other Press, 2006.
Foweraker, Joe. *Theorizing Social Movements*. London: Pluto Press, 1995.

Fox Bourne, H. R. *English Newspapers: Chapters in the History of Journalism.* Vol. 2. London: Chatto & Windus, 1887.

Frankel, Jonathan. "Assimilation and the Jews in Nineteenth-Century Europe: Towards a New Historiography?" In *Assimilation and Community: The Jews in Nineteenth-Century Europe.* Edited by J. Frankel and Steven J. Zipperstein, 1–37. Cambridge: Cambridge University Press, 1992.

———. "Crisis as a Factor in Modern Jewish Politics, 1840 and 1881–82." In *Living with Antisemitism: Modern Jewish Responses.* Edited by Jehuda Reinharz. Hanover, NH: University Press of New England, 1987.

———. *The Damascus Affair: "Ritual Murder," Politics, and the Jews in 1840.* Cambridge: Cambridge University Press, 1997.

———. "Jewish Politics and the Press: The 'Reception' of the Alliance Israelite Universelle (1860)." *Jewish History* 14 (2000): 29–50.

———. *Prophecy and Politics: Socialism, Nationalism, and the Russian Jews, 1862–1917.* Cambridge: Cambridge University Press, 1981.

Gamson, William A. "Defining Movement 'Success.'" In *The Social Movement Reader: Cases and Concepts.* Edited by Jeff Goodwin and James M. Jasper. Malden, MA: Blackwell, 2003.

Gartner, Lloyd P. "Emancipation, Social Change, and Communal Reconstruction in Anglo-Jewry, 1789–1881." *Proceedings of the American Academy for Jewish Research* 54 (1987): 73–116.

———. "Roumania, America, and World Jewry: Consul Peixotto in Bucharest, 1870–1876." *American Jewish Historical Quarterly* 58, no. 1 (September 1968): 25–116.

Gewirtz, Sharon. "Anglo-Jewish Responses to Nazi Germany 1933–39: The Anti-Nazi Boycott and the Board of Deputies of British Jews." *Journal of Contemporary History* 26 (April 1991): 255–76.

Gidney, W. T. *The History of the London Society for the Promotion of Christianity Amongst the Jews, from 1809–1908.* London: n.p., 1908.

Gilam, Abraham. *The Emancipation of the Jews in England, 1830–1860.* New York: Garland, 1982.

Gilmartin, Kevin. *Print Politics: The Press and Radical Opposition in Early Nineteenth-Century England.* Cambridge: Cambridge University Press, 1996.

Gleason, John Howes. *The Genesis of Russophobia in Great Britain: A Study of the Interaction of Policy and Opinion.* Cambridge: Cambridge University Press, 1950.

Goldstein, Israel. *American Jewry Comes of Age: Tercentenary Addresses.* New York: Bloch, 1955.

Goodwin, Jeff, and James M. Jasper. "Emotions and Social Movements." In *Handbook of the Sociology of Emotions.* Edited by Jan E. Stets and Jonathan H. Turner, 611–35. New York: Springer, 2007.

Goodwin, Jeff, James M. Jasper, and Francesca Polletta. "Why Emotions Matter." Introduction to *Passionate Politics: Emotions and Social Movements.* Edited by Jeff Goodwin, James M. Jasper, and Francesca Polletta, 1–24. Chicago: University of Chicago Press, 2001.

Gottlieb, Moshe. *American Anti-Nazi Resistance, 1933–1941.* New York: Ktav, 1982.

Gould, Roger V. *Insurgent Identities: Class, Community, and Protest in Paris from 1848 to the Commune.* Chicago: University of Chicago Press, 1995.

Graetz, Heinrich. *History of the Jews.* Edited by Bella Lowy. Vol. 5. Philadelphia: Jewish Publication Society of America, 1895.

Green, Abigail. "The British Empire and the Jews: An Imperialism of Human Rights?" *Past and Present* 199, no. 1 (May 2008): 175–205.

———. *Moses Montefiore: Jewish Liberator, Imperial Hero.* Cambridge, MA: Belknap Press of Harvard University Press, 2010.

———. "Rethinking Sir Moses Montefiore: Religion, Nationhood, and International Philanthropy in the Nineteenth Century." *American Historical Review* 110 (June 2005): 631–58.

Gyani, Gabor. "Uses and Misuses of Public Space in Budapest: 1873–1914." In *Budapest and New York: Studies in Metropolitan Transformation, 1870–1930*. Edited by Thomas Bender and Carl E. Schorske. New York: Russell Sage Foundation, 1994.

Habermas, Jürgen. *The Structural Transformation of the Public Sphere: An Inquiry into a Category of Bourgeois Society*. Translated by Thomas Burger. Cambridge, MA: MIT Press, 1989.

Haidt, Jonathan. *The Righteous Mind: Why Good People Are Divided by Politics and Religion*. New York: Pantheon, 2012.

Halfmann, Drew, and Michael P. Young. "War Pictures: The Grotesque as a Mobilizing Tactic." *Mobilization: An International Quarterly* 15, no. 1 (2010): 1–24.

Harris, Ruth. *Dreyfus: Politics, Emotion, and the Scandal of the Century*. New York: Henry Holt, 2010.

Hart, Mitchell B. "The Unbearable Lightness of Britain: Anglo-Jewish Historiography and the Anxiety of Success." *Journal of Modern Jewish Studies* 6, no. 2 (July 2007): 145–65.

Hazlitt, W. Carew. *The Livery Companies of the City of London: Their Origin, Character, Development, and Social and Political Importance*. London: Swan Sonnenschein, 1892.

Healy, Ann E. "Tsarist Anti-Semitism and Russian-American Relations." *Slavic Review* 42, no. 3 (Fall 1983): 408–25.

Henriques, Ursula. *Religious Toleration in England, 1787–1833*. Toronto: University of Toronto Press, 1961.

Hepworth, Mike. "Privacy, Security and Respectability: The Ideal Victorian Home." In *Ideal Homes? Social Change and Domestic Life*. Edited by Tony Chapman and Jenny Hockey. London: Routledge, 1999.

Hersh, Blanche Glassman. "'Am I Not a Woman and a Sister?' Abolitionist Beginnings of Nineteenth-Century Feminism." In *Antislavery Reconsidered: New Perspectives on the Abolitionists*. Edited by Lewis Perry and Michael Fellman. Baton Rouge: Louisiana State University Press, 1979.

Hibbert, Christopher. *Wellington: A Personal History*. New York: Da Capo Press, 1997.

Highet, Gilbert. *The Classical Tradition: Greek and Roman Influences on Western Literature*. New York: Oxford University Press, 1985.

Higman, B.W. "To Begin the World Again." In *Jamaica in Slavery and Freedom: History, Heritage and Culture*. Edited by Kathleen E.A. Monteith and Glenn Richards. Kingston, Jamaica: University of the West Indies Press, 2002.

Hill, George Birkbeck, ed. *Boswell's Life of Johnson Including Boswell's Journal of a Tour of Hibrides and Johnson's Diary of a Journey into North Wales*. Vol. 5. New York, 1891.

Hilton, Boyd. *Age of Atonement, The Influence of Evangelicalism on Social and Economic Thought, 1785–1865*. Oxford: Oxford University Press, 1986.

———. *A Mad, Bad, and Dangerous People? England, 1783–1846*. Oxford: Oxford University Press, 2006.

Himmelfarb, Gertrude. "The Idea of Compassion: The British versus the French Enlightenment." *Public Interest* 145 (Fall 2001): 3–24.

Hochschild, Adam. *Bury the Chains: Prophets and Rebels in the Fight to Free an Empire's Slaves*. New York: Houghton Mifflin, 2005.

Hofmeester, Karin. *Jewish Workers and the Labour Movement: A Comparative Study of Amsterdam, London, and Paris, 1870–1914*. Hants, UK: Ashgate, 2004.

Hosking, Geoffrey. *Russia and the Russians: A History*. Cambridge, MA: Harvard University Press, 2001.

Ioanid, Radu. "The Holocaust in Romania: The Iasi Pogrom of June 1941." In *Holocaust: Critical Concepts in Historical Studies*. Edited by David Cesarani. Vol. 3. London: Routledge, 2004.
Isser, Natalie. *Antisemitism during the French Second Empire*. New York: Peter Lang, 1991.
Jacobs, Joseph. "The Damascus Affair of 1840 and the Jews of America." *Publications of the American Jewish Historical Society* 10 (1902): 119–28.
Janowitz, Anne F. "'Wild Outcasts of Society': The Transit of the Gypsies in Romantic Period Poetry." In *The Country and the City Revisited: England and the Politics of Culture, 1550–1850*. Edited by Gerald Maclean, Donna Landry, and Joseph P. Ward. Cambridge: Cambridge University Press, 1999.
Jensen, Ronald J. "The Politics of Discrimination: America, Russia, and the Jewish Question." *American Jewish History* 75 (March 1986): 280–95.
Jick, Leon A. *The Americanization of the Synagogue, 1820–1870*. Hanover, NH: University Press of New England, 1976.
Johnson, Nan. "The Popularization of Nineteenth-Century Rhetoric: Elocution and the Private Learner." In *Oratorical Culture in Nineteenth Century America: Transformations in the Theory and Practice of Rhetoric*. Carbondale: Southern Illinois University Press, 1993.
Johnson, Victoria. "The Strategic Determinants of a Countermovement: The Emergence and Impact of Operation Rescue Blockades." In *Waves of Protest: Social Movements Since the Sixties*. Edited by Jo Freeman and Victoria Johnson. Lanham, MD: Rowman & Littlefield, 1999.
Johnston, Hank. "Verification and Proof in Frame and Discourse Analysis." In *Methods of Social Movement Research*. Edited by Bert Klandermans and Suzanne Staggenborg. Minneapolis: University of Minnesota Press, 2002.
Judge, Edward H. *Easter in Kishinev: Anatomy of a Pogrom*. New York: New York University Press, 1992.
Juergensmeyer, Mark. *Terror in the Mind of God: The Global Rise of Religious Violence*. 3rd ed. Berkeley: University of California Press, 2001.
Katz, David. "The Marginalization of Early Modern Anglo-Jewish History." In *The Jewish Heritage in British History: Englishness and Jewishness*. Edited by Tony Kushner. London: Frank Cass, 1992.
Katz, Jacob. "The Concept of Social History and Its Possible Use in Jewish Historical Research." *Scripta Hierosolymitana* 3 (1955): 292–312.
———. *Jewish Emancipation and Self-Emancipation*. Philadelphia: Jewish Publication Society, 1986.
———. *Tradition and Crisis: Jewish Society at the End of the Middle Ages*. New York: Free Press of Glencoe, 1961.
Kelly, Charles Stuart. *The American Consul: A History of the American Consular Service, 1776–1914*. Contributions in American History. New York: Greenwood Press, 1990.
Kelner, Shaul. "Ritualized Protest and Redemptive Politics: Cultural Consequences of the American Mobilization to Free Soviet Jews." *Jewish Social Studies* 14 (Spring–Summer 2008): 1–37.
Kemper, Theodore D. "A Structural Approach to Social Movement Emotions." In *Passionate Politics: Emotions and Social Movements*. Edited by Jeff Goodwin, James M. Jasper, and Francesca Polletta, 58–73. Chicago: University of Chicago Press, 2001.
Kendall, Diana Elizabeth. *Members Only: Elite Clubs and the Process of Exclusion*. Lanham, MD: Rowman & Littlefield, 2008.
Kenez, Peter. "Pogroms and White Ideology in the Russian Civil War." In *Pogroms: Anti-Jewish Violence in Modern Jewish History*. Edited by John D. Klier and Shlomo Lambroza, 293–313. Cambridge: Cambridge University Press, 1992.

Keogh, Dermot. *Jews in Twentieth-Century Ireland: Refugees, Anti-Semitism and the Holocaust.* Cork, Ireland: Cork University Press, 1998.

Kertzer, David I. *The Kidnapping of Edgardo Mortara.* New York: Vintage Books, 1998.

Klandermans, Bert. "The Demand and Supply of Participation: Social-Psychological Correlates of Participation in Social Movements." In *Blackwell Companion to Social Movements.* Edited by David A. Snow, Sarah A. Soule, and Hanspeter Kriesi. Malden, MA: Blackwell, 2004.

Klier, John D. "Russian Jewry of the Eve of the Pogroms." In *Pogroms: Anti-Jewish Violence in Modern Jewish History.* Edited by John D. Klier and Shlomo Lambroza, 3–12. Cambridge: Cambridge University Press, 1992.

———. *Russians, Jews, and the Pogroms of 1881–1882.* Cambridge: Cambridge University Press, 2011.

Kolb, Felix. *Protest and Opportunities: The Political Outcomes of Social Movements.* Frankfurt: Campus Verlag, 2007.

Koltun-Fromm, Kenneth. "A Narrative Reading of Moses Hess's Return to Judaism." *Modern Judaism* 19 (February 1999): 41–65.

Koopmans, Ruud. "Protest in Time and Space: The Evolution of Waves of Contention." In *The Blackwell Companion to Social Movements.* Edited by David A. Snow, Sarah A. Soule, and Hanspeter Kriesi. Malden, MA: Blackwell, 2004.

Korn, Bertram Wallace. *American Jewry and the Civil War.* Marietta, GA: R. Bemis, 1995.

———. *The American Reaction to the Mortara Case: 1858–1859.* Cincinnati: American Jewish Archives, 1957.

Kornberg, Jacques. *Theodor Herzl: From Assimilation to Zionism.* Bloomington: University of Indiana Press, 1993.

Korolenko, Vladimir. "Kishinev: The Medieval Outbreak Against the Jews." In *Great Events by Famous Historians.* Edited by C.F. Horne and J. Rossiter, 35–49. Vol. 20. N.p.: National Alumni, 1909.

Krinsky, Carol Herselle. *Synagogues of Europe: Architecture, History, Meaning.* Mineola, NY: Dover, 1996.

Kurzman, Charles, et al. "Celebrity Status." *Sociological Theory* 25, no. 4 (December 2007): 347–67.

LaKelly, Helen. *Abolitionist Feminists of the Anti-Slavery Convention of American Women of 1837: The Role of Theological Vision and the Ethic of Sympathy.* PhD diss., Union Theological Seminary, 2003.

Lambroza, Shlomo. "Jewish Responses to Pogroms in Late Imperial Russia." In *Living with Antisemitism: Modern Jewish Responses.* Edited by Jehuda Reinharz. Hanover, NH: University of New England Press, 1987.

Lang, Ariella. *Converting a Nation: A Modern Inquisition and the Unification of Italy.* New York: Palgrave Macmillan, 2008.

Lederhendler, Eli. *Jewish Responses to Modernity: New Voices in America and Eastern Europe.* New York: New York University Press, 1994.

———. *The Road to Modern Jewish Politics: Political Tradition and Political Reconstruction in the Jewish Community of Tsarist Russia.* New York: Oxford University Press, 1989.

Lee, Alan J. *The Origins of the Popular Press in England, 1855–1914.* London: Croom Helm, 1976.

Lee, Alfred McClung. *The Daily Newspaper in America: The Evolution of a Social Instrument.* London: Routledge/Thoemmes Press, 2000.

Leff, Lisa Moses. "Jewish Solidarity in Nineteenth-Century France: The Evolution of a Concept." *Journal of Modern History* 74 (March 2002): 33–61.

———. *Sacred Bonds of Solidarity: The Rise of Jewish Internationalism in Nineteenth-Century France.* Stanford, CA: Stanford University Press, 2006.

Lewis, Clyde J. "The Disintegration of the Tory-Anglican Alliance in the Struggle for Catholic Emancipation." *Church History* 29, no. 1 (March 1960): 25–43.

Lewis, Donald M. *The Origins of Christian Zionism: Lord Shaftesbury and Evangelical Support for a Jewish Homeland*. Cambridge: Cambridge University Press, 2010.

Liddle, Dallas. "Anatomy of a 'Nine Days Wonder': Sensational Journalism in the Decade of the Sensational Novel." In *Victorian Crime, Madness, and Sensation*. Edited by Andrew Maunder and Grace Moore. Hampshire, UK: Ashgate, 2004.

Lindemann, Albert S. *Esau's Tears: Modern Anti-Semitism and the Rise of the Jews*. Cambridge: Cambridge University Press, 1997.

———. *The Jew Accused: Three Anti-Semitic Affairs (Dreyfus, Beilis, Frank), 1894–1915*. Cambridge: Cambridge University Press, 1991.

Loeb, Lori Anne. *Consuming Angels: Advertising and Victorian Women*. New York: Oxford University Press, 1994.

Lofland, John. *Social Movement Organizations: Guide to Research on Insurgent Realities*. New York: Aldine de Gruyter, 1996.

Löwe, Heinz-Dietrich. "Pogroms in Russia: Explanations, Comparisons, Suggestions." *Jewish Social Studies* 11 (Fall 2004): 16–24.

Lukacs, John. "The Evolving Relationship of History and Sociology." *International Journal of Politics, Culture and Society* 1 (1987): 79–88.

Marcus, Jacob Rader. *United States Jewry, 1776–1985*. Vol. 1. Detroit: Wayne State University Press, 1989.

Marty, Martin E. *When Faiths Collide*. Malden, MA: Blackwell, 2005.

McAdam, Doug. "Initiator and Spin-Off Movements: Diffusion Processes in Protest Cycles." In *Repertoires and Cycles of Collective Action*. Edited by Mark Traugott. Durham, NC: Duke University Press, 1995.

McCalman, Iain. *Radical Underworld: Prophets, Revolutionaries, and Pornographers in London, 1795–1840*. Cambridge: Cambridge University Press, 1988.

McLintock, John, and James Strong, eds. *Cyclopaedia of Biblical, Theological, and Ecclesiastical Literature*. Vol. 7. New York: Harper and Brothers, 1894.

Medoff, Rafael. *Jewish Americans and Political Participation*. Santa Barbara, CA: ABC-CLIO, 2002.

Mishkova, Diana. "The Interesting Anomaly of Balkan Liberalism." In *Liberty and the Search for Identity: Liberal Nationalism and the Legacy of Empires*. Edited by Iván Zoltan Dénes, 399–453. Budapest: Central European University Press, 2006.

Monaco, C. S. "The Extraordinary Movement of the Jews of Great Britain, 1827–1831." *Journal of Modern Jewish Studies* 8, no. 3 (November 2009): 337–59.

———. *Moses Levy of Florida: Jewish Utopian and Antebellum Reformer*. Baton Rouge: Louisiana State University Press, 2005.

Morais, Henry Samuel. *Eminent Israelites of the Nineteenth Century*. Philadelphia: Edward Stern, 1880.

Morris, Edmund. *Colonel Roosevelt*. New York: Random House, 2010.

Moss, Walter G. *A History of Russia, Since 1855*. 2nd ed. London: Anthem Press, 2005.

Murphy, Sean D. *Humanitarian Intervention: The United Nations in an Evolving World Order*. Philadelphia: University of Pennsylvania Press, 1996.

Nathans, Benjamin. *Beyond the Pale: The Jewish Encounter with Late Imperial Russia*. Berkeley: University of California Press, 2002.

Oisteanu, Andrei. *Inventing the Jew: Antisemitic Stereotypes in Romanian and Other Central-East European Cultures*. Translated by Mirela Adascalitei. Lincoln: University of Nebraska Press, 2009.

Oldson, William O. "Rationalizing Anti-Semitism: The Romanian Gambit." *Proceedings of the American Philosophical Society* 138 (March 1994): 25–30.

Opp, Karl-Dieter. *Theories of Political Protest and Social Movements: A Multidisciplinary Introduction, Critique, and Synthesis.* New York: Routledge, 2009.
Osofsky, George. "The Hebrew Emigrant Aid Society of the United States (1881–1883)." In *Politics and the Immigrant.* Edited by George E. Pozzetta. New York: Garland, 1991.
Page, Judith W. *Imperfect Sympathies: Jews and Judaism in British Romantic Literature and Culture.* New York: Palgrave Macmillan, 2004.
Panitz, Esther L. *Simon Wolf: Private Conscience and Public Image.* Cranbury, NJ: Associated University Presses, 1987.
Passy, Florence. "Political Altruism and the Solidarity Movement." Introduction to *Political Altruism? Solidarity Movements in International Perspective.* Edited by Marco Giugni and Florence Passy, 3–25. Lanham, MD: Rowman & Littlefield, 2001.
Patterson, Mark, and Andrew Walker. "'Our Unspeakable Comfort,' Irving, Albury, and the Origins of the Pre-Tribulation Rapture." In *Christian Millenarianism: From the Early Church to Waco.* Bloomington: Indiana University Press, 2001.
Penkower, Monty Noam. "The Kishinev Pogrom of 1903: A Turning Point in Jewish History." *Modern Judaism* 24, no. 3 (2004): 187–225.
Penn, Virginia. "Philhellenism in England (1821–1827)." *Slavonic and East European Review* 14 (January 1936): 363–71.
Penslar, Derek J. *Shylock's Children: Economics and Jewish Identity in Modern Europe.* Berkeley: University of California Press, 2001.
Perlmann, Moshe. "The British Embassy in St. Petersburg on Russian Jewry, 1890–92." *Proceedings of the American Academy for Jewish Research* 48 (1981): 297–323.
Peters, Edward. *Torture.* Philadelphia: University of Pennsylvania Press, 1985.
Philipp, Thomas. "The Farhi Family and the Changing Position of the Jews of Syria, 1750–1860." *Middle Eastern Studies* 20 (October 1984): 37–52.
Pierrard, Pierre. *Louis Veuillot.* Paris: Beauchesne Editeur, 1998.
Pinney, Thomas, ed. *Letters of Thomas Babington Macaulay.* Vol. 2. Cambridge: Cambridge University Press, 2008.
Po-Chia Hsia, R. *The Myth of Ritual Murder: Jews and Magic in Reformation Germany.* New Haven, CT: Yale University Press, 1988.
Polletta, Francesca. "Contending Stories: Narrative in Social Movements." *Qualitative Sociology* 21 (1998): 419–46.
Polletta, Francesca, and James M. Jasper. "Collective Identity and Social Movements." *Annual Review of Sociology* 27 (2001): 283–305.
Polunov, Alexander. *Russia in the Nineteenth-Century: Autocracy, Reform, and Social Change, 1814–1914.* Edited by Thomas C. Owen and Larissa G. Zakharova. Translated by Marshall Schatz. Armonk, NY: M. E. Sharpe, 2005.
Posener, S. *Adolphe Crémieux: A Biography.* Translated by Eugene Golob. Philadelphia: Jewish Publication Society of America, 1940.
Repousis, Angelo. "'The Cause of the Greeks': Philadelphia and the Greek War for Independence, 1821–1828." *Pennsylvania Magazine of History and Biography* 123, no. 4 (October 1999): 333–63.
Roberts, F. David. *The Social Conscience of the Early Victorians.* Stanford, CA: Stanford University Press, 2002.
Rockaway, Robert, and Arnon Gutfeld. "Demonic Images of the Jew in the Nineteenth Century United States." *American Jewish History* 89 (December 2001): 355–81.
Rodrigue, Aron. "Abraham de Camondo of Istanbul; The Transformation of Jewish Philanthropy." In *Profiles in Diversity: Jews in a Changing Europe, 1750–1870.* Edited by Frances Malino and David Sorkin. Detroit: Wayne State University Press, 1998.

Rogger, Hans. "Conclusion and Overview." In *Pogroms: Anti-Jewish Violence in Modern Russian History*. Edited by John D. Klier and Shlomo Lambroza, 314–72. Cambridge: Cambridge University Press, 1992.

———. "Government, Jews, Peasants, and Land in Post-Emancipation Russia: Two Specters: Peasant Violence and Jewish Exploitation." *Cahiers du Monde russe et soviétique* 17 (April–September 1976): 171–211.

———. *Jewish Policies and Right-Wing Politics in Imperial Russia*. Berkeley: University of California Press, 1986.

Rosenthall, William A. *The Damascus Affair: Its Impact on the United States of America*. MA thesis, Hebrew Union College—Jewish Institute of Religion, 1956.

Rosenwein, Barbara H. "Worrying About Emotions in History." *American Historical Review* 107, no. 3 (June 2002), 821–45.

Rozin, Mordechai. *The Rich and the Poor: Jewish Philanthropy and Social Control in Nineteenth-Century London*. Brighton, UK: Sussex Academic Press, 1999.

Rubery, Matthew. *The Novelty of Newspapers: Victorian Fiction After the Invention of the News*. New York: Oxford University Press, 2009.

Rubinstein, William D., and Hilary L. Rubinstein. *Philosemitism: Admiration and Support in the English-Speaking World for Jews, 1840–1939*. New York: St. Martin's Press, 1999.

Ruderman, David B. *Jewish Enlightenment in an English Key: Anglo-Jewry's Construction of Modern Jewish Thought*. Princeton, NJ: Princeton University Press, 2002.

Sacks, Jonathan. *To Heal a Fractured World: The Ethics of Responsibility*. New York: Schocken Books, 2007.

Salbstein, M.C.N. *The Emancipation of the Jews in Britain: The Question of the Admission of the Jews to Parliament, 1828–1860*. Rutherford, NJ: Fairleigh Dickinson University Press, 1982.

Sarna, Jonathan D., ed. *The American Jewish Experience*. 2nd ed. New York: Holmes & Meier, 1997.

———. "The American Jewish Response to Nineteenth-Century Jewish Missions." *Journal of American History* 68, no. 1 (June 1981): 35–51.

———. *American Judaism*. New Haven, CT: Yale University Press, 2004.

———. *Jacksonian Jew: The Two Worlds of Mordecai Noah*. New York: Holmes and Meier, 1981.

Sawyers, Traci M., and David S. Meyer. "Missed Opportunities: Social Movement Abeyance and Public Policy." *Social Problems* 46, no. 2 (1999): 187–206.

Schoenberg, Philip Ernest. "The American Reaction to the Kishinev Pogrom of 1903." *American Jewish Historical Quarterly* 63 (March 1974): 262–83.

Schreiber, Elliot. "Tainted Sources: The Subversion of the Grimms' Ideology of the Folktale in Heinrich Heine's 'Der Rabbi von Bacherach.'" *German Quarterly* 78 (Winter 2005): 23–44.

Scult, Mel. *Millennial Expectations and Jewish Liberties: A Study of the Efforts to Convert the Jews in Britain, up to the Mid-Nineteenth Century*. Leiden: Brill, 1978.

Seigel, Jerrold. *Bohemian Paris: Culture, Politics, and the Boundaries of Bourgeois Life, 1830–1930*. Baltimore: Johns Hopkins University Press, 1986.

Semenoff, E. *The Russian Government and the Massacres: A Page of the Russian-Counter Revolution*. London: John Murray, 1907.

Serry, Herve. "Littérature et religion catholique (1880–1914). Contribution à une socio-histoire de la croyance." *Cahiers d'histoire. Revue d'histoire critique* 87 (2002): 37–59.

Silberstein, Laurence J. "Historical Sociology and Jewish Historiography: A Review Essay." *Journal of the American Academy of Religion* 42, no. 4 (1974): 692–98.

246 Selected Bibliography

Skocpol, Theda. "Sociology's Historical Imagination." In *Vision and Method in Historical Sociology*. Edited by T. Skocpol. New York: Cambridge University Press, 1985.

Smith, Timothy B. "In Defense of Privilege: The City of London and the Challenge of Municipal Reform, 1875–1890." *Journal of Social History* 27, no. 1 (Fall 1993): 59–83.

Smithy, Lee A., and Michael P. Young. "Parading Protest: Orange Parades in Northern Ireland and Temperance Parades in Antebellum America." *Social Movement Studies* 9 (November 2010): 393–410.

Sombart, Werner. *Jews and Modern Capitalism*. Translated by M. Epstein. New York: E.P. Dutton, 1913.

Sorin, Gerald. *A Time for Building: The Third Migration, 1880–1920*. The Jewish People in America Series. Baltimore: Johns Hopkins University Press, 1992.

Stanislawski, Michael. *For Whom Do I Toil? Judah Leib Gordon and the Crisis of Russian Jewry*. New York: Oxford University Press, 1988.

———. Review of *The Road to Modern Jewish Politics: Political Tradition and Political Reconstruction in the Jewish Community of Tsarist Russia*, by Eli Lederhendler. *Slavic Review* 51 (Spring 1992): 173–74.

Stern, Fritz. *Gold and Iron: Bismarck, Bleichroder, and the Building of the German Empire*. New York: Knopf, 1977.

Stock, Eugene. *The History of the Church Missionary Society*. Vol. 1. London: Church Missionary Society, 1899.

Stone, Harry. "Dickens and the Jews." *Victorian Studies* 2 (March 1959): 223–53.

Strack, Hermann L. *The Jews and Human Sacrifice: Human Blood and Jewish Ritual, An Historical and Sociological Inquiry*. Translated by Henry Blamchamp. London: n.p., 1909.

Sussman, Lance. *Isaac Leeser and the Making of American Judaism*. Detroit: Wayne State University Press, 1995.

Szajkowski, Zosa. "The Jewish Saint-Simonians and Socialist Antisemites in France." *Jewish Social Studies* 9, no. 1 (January 1947): 33–60.

———. "Paul Nathan, Lucien Wolf, Jacob H. Schiff and the Jewish Revolutionary Movements in Eastern Europe 1903–1917." *Jewish Social Studies* 29 (January 1967): 3–26.

Szajkowski, Zoza. "How the Mass Migration to America Began." *Jewish Social Studies* 4, no. 4 (October 1942): 291–310.

Tarrow, Sidney. *The New Transnational Activism*. Cambridge: Cambridge University Press, 2008.

———. *Power in Movement: Social Movements and Contentious Politics*. 2nd ed. Cambridge: Cambridge University Press, 1998.

———. "States and Opportunities: The Political Structuring of Social Movements." In *Comparative Perspectives on Social Movements: Political Opportunities, Mobilizing Structures, and Cultural Framing*. Edited by Doug McAdams, John D. McCarthy, and Mayer Zald. Cambridge: Cambridge University Press, 1996.

Tarshish, Allan. "The Board of Delegates of American Israelites (1859–1878)." In *American Jewish History*. Edited by Jeffrey S. Gurock. Vol. 6. New York: Routledge, 1998.

Taylor, Verta. "Social Movement Continuity: The Women's Movement in Abeyance." *American Sociological Review* 54 (October 1989): 761–75.

Taylor, Verta, and Nella Van Dyke. "'Get Up, Stand Up,' Tactical Repertoires of Social Movements." In *Blackwell Companion to Social Movements*. Edited by David A. Snow, Sarah A. Soule, and Hanspeter Kriesi. Malden, MA: Blackwell, 2004.

Tilly, Charles. *The Politics of Collective Violence*. Cambridge: Cambridge University Press, 2003.

———. *Popular Contention in Great Britain, 1758–1834*. Boulder, CO: Paradigm, 2005.
Tilly, Charles, and Sidney Tarrow. *Contentious Politics*. Boulder, CO: Paradigm Press, 2007.
Tosh, John. "Gentlemanly Politeness and Manly Simplicity in Victorian England." *Transactions of the Royal Historical Society*, 6th ser., 12 (2002): 455–72.
Toury, Jacob. "M. E. Levy's Plan for a Jewish Colony in Florida—1825." In *Michael: On the History of the Jews in the Diaspora*. Edited by Lloyd P. Gartner. Tel Aviv: Diaspora Research Institute, 1975.
Turley, David. *The Culture of English Antislavery, 1780–1860*. London: Routledge, 1991.
VanBurkleo, Sandra F. *'Belonging to the World,' Women's Rights and American Constitutional Culture*. New York: Oxford University Press, 2001.
Vance, Norman. *The Sinews of the Spirit: The Ideal of Christian Manliness in Victorian Literature and Religious Thought*. Cambridge: Cambridge University Press, 1985.
Vital, David. *The Origins of Zionism*. Oxford: Oxford University Press, 1975.
———. *A People Apart: The Jews in Europe, 1789–1939*. Oxford History of Modern Europe. Oxford: Oxford University Press, 1999.
Weinberg, Robert. "The Russian Right Responds to 1905: Visual Depictions of Jews in Post Revolutionary Russia." In *The Revolution of 1905 and Russia's Jews*. Edited by Stefanie Hofman and Ezra Mendelsohn. Philadelphia: University of Pennsylvania Press, 2008.
Weissbrodt, David. "Human Rights: An Historical Perspective." In *Human Rights*. Edited by Peter Davies. London: Routledge, 1988.
Whittier, Nancy. "The Consequences of Social Movements for Each Other." In *Blackwell Companion to Social Movements*. Edited by David A. Snow, Sarah A. Soule, and Hanspeter Kriesi. Malden, MA: Blackwell, 2004.
Whooley, Owen. "Masterframes and Movement Trajectory: A Case Study of the American Abolitionist Movement." Paper presented at the annual meeting of the American Sociological Association, San Francisco, 2004.
Wilson, Mary C. "The Damascus Affair and the Beginnings of France's Empire in the Middle East." In *Histories of the Modern Middle East: New Directions*. Edited by Israel Gershoni, Hakan Erdem, and Ursula Wokock. Boulder, CO: Lynne Reinner, 2002.
Wistrich, Robert S. "The Old-New Anti-Semitism." In *Those Who Forget the Past: The Question of Anti-Semitism*. Edited by Ron Rosenbaum. New York: Random House, 2004.
Woocher, Jonathan. "'Sacred Survival' Revisited: American Jewish Civil Religion in the New Millennium." In *Cambridge Companion to American Judaism*. Edited by Dana Evan Kaplan. New York: Cambridge University Press, 2005.
Young, Michael P. *Bearing Witness Against Sin: The Evangelical Birth of the American Social Movement*. Chicago: University of Chicago Press, 2006.
Zald, Mayer, and Bert Useem. "Movement and Countermovement Interaction: Mobilization, Tactics, and State Involvement." In *Social Movements in an Organizational Society: Collected Essays*. Edited by Mayer N. Zald and John D. McCarthy. New Brunswick, NJ: Transaction, 2003.
Zenner, Walter P. "Middleman Minorities in the Syrian Mosaic: Trade, Conflict, and Image Management." *Sociological Perspectives* 30 (October 1987): 400–21.
Zipperstein, Steven J. *The Jews of Odessa: A Cultural History, 1794–1881*. Stanford, CA: Stanford University Press, 1986.

Index

A
abeyance, during social movements 2, 3, 6, 47, 52, 57, 83, 91, 101, 123, 185n5; *see also* Taylor, Verta
abolitionist movement, and emergence of Jewish rights movement 12–13, 28, 33–4, 79
Addams, Jane 165
"Address to the Captive Children of Israel, inhabiting the Dominions of his Britannic Majesty" (Levy) 42
Adler, Cyrus 164–5
Adler, Hermann 2, 148–9
agents provocateurs 143, 161
Ahad Ha'am 196n38
Albury conferences 27, 190n8, 192n46; *see also* London prophetic revival; Drummond, Henry; millennialism
Alexander, David L. 163–4
Alexander III, Tsar 142
Ali, Mehmed (viceroy of Egypt) 63, 65–7, 84–6
Allgemeine Zeitung des Judentums (Leipzig) 101, 205n4
Alliance Israelite Universelle: activities of 123–5, 127–8, 149, 153, 163, 173, 181; founding of 10, 114, 118, 158; vital role during abeyance phase 6
Anglo-Jewish Association 6, 123, 146, 148, 164, 173, 218n53
Anglo-Jews: admittance to Parliament 52, 98–9; ambiguous standing of Jewish magnates 22–3; and animosity toward evangelical proselytizers 24, 26–9; ascendance of working-class as Jewish rights activists 168–70; bias of communal historians 7; and Coleridge's ambiguity toward 22, 179; cooptation of movement by elites 7, 9; "cousinhood" 12, 22–3, 41, 48–9; early nineteenth-century disabilities 12, 23; freedom of the City 52, 74; and the importance of Jewish rights to self-esteem 3–4, 168, 180; inferior status vis-à-vis Continental Jews 21–2; the intellectual class 21; manliness 43–4; marginality of the poor 20–1; negative image of "stockjobbers" 22–3; provincial Jews versus London elite 102, 148; rise in social standing 53, 179–80 ; and "street Jews" 20–1
Anglo-Protestantism, crisis and fragmentation 19–20
Anti-Slavery Society 25, 30; in America 109
Antonelli, Cardinal 114
anti-Nazi boycott 173, 178
Ashley, Lord *see* Earl of Shaftesbury
Austria 63, 67, 85, 86, 93, 99, 100, 103, 116, 126, 134, 200n22, 208n61
Auto-Emancipation (Pinsker) 8, 146

B
"barefoot brigades" 143, 145; *see also* agents provocateurs
Barondess, Joseph 172
Battle of Navarino 19, 46
Benisch, Abraham, as newspaper editor and Jewish rights leader

250 *Index*

91, 104–5, 109, 113, 114–16, 125–6, 132, 146
Bentwich, Herbert 3–4, 164, 169, 172
"Berlinskys" 100
Bessarabia 131–3, 141, 160–61
Bexley, Lord 27, 47, 52, 192n44
Biale, David 8, 182–3
Bialik, Hayim Nahman 160
B'nai B'rith 130, 131, 137, 163; and adoption of "dignified silence" 174; petition to Tsar Nicholas II 167
B'nai Jeshurun (New York City congregation) 80, 109, 111
blood libel, as tactic of stigmatization 2, 60, 64–6, 83, 85, 86, 98, 161, 200n28
Board of Delegates of American Israelites 113, 130
Board of Deputies of British Jews 3, 23, 49, 52, 65–8, 76, 87, 92, 99, 102, 104, 112, 113, 118, 123, 132, 146, 163, 169, 172, 173, 181
Bologna 93–4, 102, 111, 116
Bourdieu, Pierre 23
Bourne, Stephen (editor of *World* newspaper) 34, 36, 45, 193n71
Bratianu, Ion 125, 131, 138
Brody (Galicia) 153
Brown, John Aquila 28, 36, 39, 51–2, 191n42, 198n84
Bucharest and the Jewish elite 133–6
Bund, as self-defense network 168, 171

C
Cahen, Isidore 116, 118
Carlyle, Thomas 21, 101
Carnegie Hall: as protest venue 165
Carol, Prince (Karl von Hohenzollern) 124, 126, 129, 131, 137, 138
Catholic emancipation 2, 9, 37, 48–9
Cavour, Count Camillo 102–3
Central Consistory of French Jews: and role during Damascus affair 60, 61, 66, 67; Mortara affair 84, 98, 102, 116, 117, 118, 158; limitations of 181
Charleston protest meetings 82–3, 108, 203n34; and "Israelites" 83
Chickering Hall (New York City) 149
Chinese immigrant support 163
City of London: actions on behalf of Jewish rights 71, 73–6, 132–3,

148–9, 153, 156; as self-serving oligarchy 73; unique powers of 72–3
"City of Slaughter" (Bialik) 160
Cleveland, Grover 164, 165
Collective violence as social control 144–5, 213n20
Cousinhood *see* Anglo-Jews
Crémieux, Adolphe: caution during Mortara affair 98; initial reaction to Damascus blood libel 61, 64–5; leadership of International Roumanian Conference 134; president of Alliance Israelite Universelle 123–5; status as transnational activist 9, 85; trip to Alexandria with Montefiore 66, 69, 77, 84–5; triumphant journey through Europe 86–7; visit to Bucharest 124–5
Crooll, Joseph 24, 26, 73
Crosby, Howard 149–50
"Cultural capital" 23, 74

D
Damascus: disappearance of Père Thomas 61–4; economic rivalries 63, 200n32; *see also* blood libel; Crémieux, Adolphe; Pasha, Sherif; Pieritz, George; Ratti-Menton, Comte de; torture
Darrow, Clarence 165
debating societies (England) 38–9
De Hirsch, Baron Maurice 156; *see also* emigration movement
Delacouture, Abbé Vincent 97
Derby, Lord 99
De Rothschild, Baron Lionel 52, 65, 98
Dickens, Charles 58, 93; *see also* humanitarianism
"diplomacy of humanity" 167
Dreyfus affair 158–9
Drummond, Henry 20, 27, 28, 52, 191n42
Drumont, Edouard 98, 158
Druze 59, 83

E
Eardley, Cullen 103–4, 116
East End (London) 20–1, 24, 26, 168
Easter, prominence during pogrom violence 142, 161

Egyptian Hall *see* Mansion House
Einhorn, David 113
Elisavetgrad (Ukraine), as scene of pogrom violence 142–4
Emigration movement: initial antagonism toward 133–7; proliferation during Russian pogroms 149, 152–3, 156; *see also* de Hirsch, Baron Maurice; Peixotto, Benjamin
Endelman, Todd M. 11, 27
Englishmen and Jews: Social Relations and Political Culture, 1840–1914 (Feldman) 11
English Zionist Federation *see* Gollancz, Herman
"European Uncle Tom" (Edgardo Mortara) 93
Evangelical Alliance 103–4, 116–17
Evangelical schism *see* millennialism

F

Faneuil Hall (Boston) 165
Feldman, David 11
Firman: edict of Sultan Abdul-Mejid 86
Frankel, Jonathan 8, 67, 85, 144, 146, 154, 185n9
Franco-Prussian War 123, 136
freedom of the City 12; admittance of Jews, 52, 74
Freemasons' Hall, as movement venue 30–4

G

Gamson, William M. 178
Gaster, Moses 164, 169, 172
George IV 19
Gintsburg, Goratsii 152, 163
Gladstone, William 135–6, 146
Goderich, Lord 19, 46
Goldsmid, Francis H. 3, 49, 52, 129, 132, 138, 146–7
Goldsmid, Isaac L. 9, 22, 25, 48–9, 52–3, 65
Goldsmid, Louisa 148
Gollancz, Herman 169
Gordon, J. E. 37
Gottheil, Richard 166
Grant, Ulysses S. 130
Great Assembly Hall (London): as protest venue 168–9
Great Synagogue (London): as protest venue 67–71, 76
Green, Abigail 5

Guildhall (London), as protest venue 156–7, 168
gypsies and Anglo-Jewry, social equivalence during early nineteenth-century 12, 29, 52

H

Habermas, Jurgen 7
Ha-Maggid (Lyck) 130, 155
Haskalah 38, 154, 156
Hay, John (U.S. secretary of state) 163, 167
hazzans, and their function in the United States 78
hearth and home: in Victorian sentiment 95, 180
Hebrew Congregation of Birmingham 109, 148
Hebrew Emigrant Aid Society 153
Henry, Michael 136, 212n41
Henriques, Joseph G. 65
Herzl, Theodor 158–9, 216 n90, n92
Hess, Moses 60
Hilton, Boyd 20, 34
Hirschell, Solomon 23, 47
honor: and its relation to Jewish rights 29, 64–5, 74–5, 99, 118, 158, 179
Hotel Otettaliano (Bucharest) 127–8
"Howlers" 169, 177
House of Catechumens (Rome) 94
Hugo, Victor 35, 151
humanitarianism 57–9, 74, 88
Hurwitz, Hyman 21, 22
Hyde Park (London): as protest venue 159, 169, 173, 176

I

Ignatiev, Nikolai 145, 149, 150, 152
Initiator movement 10, 59, 164, 186n12
"Insurgent reality," during social movements 7, 42, 78, 152
International Roumanian Conference 134–6; list of delegates, 212n52
Inquisition 93, 95, 96, 107, 110, 110, 114
Isaacs, Samuel M. 107, 110–11, 113; *see also Jewish Messenger*; United Congregations of Israelites of the City of New York
Israelite (Cincinnati) 107, 112–13; *see also* Wise, Isaac
"Israelites" of Virginia 78, 79

J

Jackson-Vanik Amendment 176
Jasper, James M. 178
Jewish-Christian debates (London) 37–40, 46, 47
Jewish Chronicle, as Jewish rights periodical 4, 91, 93, 104–5, 112–16, 125–6, 132, 135–6, 147–8, 151–2, 162, 164, 168–9, 179–80; *see also* Benisch, Abraham; Myers, Asher
Jewish Defense League (JDL) 175
Jewish Messenger (New York) 107, 133
"Jewish power" 181–2
Jewish press: emergence of 91, 116, 154, 156; *see also Allgemeine Zeitung des Judentums*; *Ha-Maggid*; *Israelite*; *Jewish Chronicle*; *Jewish Messenger*; *Razsvet*; *Voice of Jacob*
Jewish rights movement: and the antipathy of Catholic press 85, 96–7, 107, 158; backing of Van Buren's administration 80–1; boycotts as a tactic 173–4, 176, 178; and the British Foreign Office 65, 67, 99, 103, 105, 116, 123, 146, 167, 180; coalitions with Christians 9, 11, 15, 28, 30–4, 38–9, 45, 47–9, 51–2, 66–7, 73–6, 82–3, 109–10, 132–3, 148–51, 156–7, 164–5, 167–8, 173; co-optation by Anglo-Jewish elite 7, 9; definition of social movement 14–15; disengagement by the Anglo-Jewish magnates 4, 146–8, 163–4, 168, 170, 182; and the emergence of the formal protest meeting 1–2, 5, 30–2, 39–46, 67–71, 73–6; face-to-face arbitration 85–6, 114, 123–4, 126, 131; formal organizations 118, 123; and humor 111; impact in America 77–84, 104–5, 106–14, 129–30, 133, 149–51, 157–8, 162–8, 172–6; influence in Britain 3–4, 52–3, 179–80; influence in Pale of Settlement 154–6; and "modular forms" of collective action 77; movement continuity in England 3–4, 147–8, 164, 168; parliamentary petitions 14, 36, 47, 49, 52; refutation of quietism 1, 7–8, 10; rise of Jewish newspapers 6, 91, 151, 155; role of emotions, 5, 8, 32, 69, 75, 81, 95, 161–3, 165–6, 186n20; and Russian Ukase (1827) 39–41, 46; shift of contentious center to United States 167–8; street marches 169–70, 172, 173, 177, 179, 219n7; and support of Theodore Roosevelt, 166–7; tactic of civil disobedience, 175; and theme of unity, 10, 15, 16, 33, 58, 60, 70–1, 79, 83, 84, 95, 99, 101, 107, 109, 111–12, 115–18, 131, 148, 180; transition to more egalitarian strategies, 163, 165–6, 168–70, 172–6, 181; use of melodrama, 94–5, 111; use of grotesque imagery, 160–3; Zionist participation, 11, 164–6, 169–70, 172–4
Jewish Territorial Organization *see* Israel Zangwill
Jews' Free School 24
Jick, Leon 78
Journal des Débats (Paris) 64, 76, 81, 95, 97
Judenhetze 150
"Jurisconsultus," pseudonymous author during Russian Crisis 147–8

K

Kahal 154, 156, 182
Kahane, Meir *see* Jewish Defense League
Katz, Jacob 14, 189n76
Kelal Yisrael 15, 83, 135
"King of the City" (London) 72
King's Head tavern, as movement venue 45, 47
Kertzer, David I. 206n14
Kishinev, details of massacre 161–2; *see also* Bessarabia
Klier, John xiii, 145, 151, 213n3
Know-Nothing Party (United States) 107, 110
Korn, Bertram W. 94, 108
Korolenko, Vladimir 161

L

lachrymose history 5
LaGuardia, Fiorello 174

Lederhendler, Eli 154
Leeser, Isaac 15, 81, 83, 91, 95, 107–8, 112–13, 129, 192n59
Leo XII, Pope 36, 40
Levi, David 26
Levi, Leo N. 167
Levy, Jacob C. (Charleston) 83
Levy, Moses (of Great Alie Street, London) 49
Levy, Moses E.: as abolitionist 8–9, 13, 33, 34, 79, 188n69; biographical details 24–5; celebrity standing 33; Florida colonist 25, 50–1, 79; Freemasons' Hall speech 30–4, 221–9; social movement leader 1, 6, 7, 8–9, 12–14, 30–4, 36–48, 50–1, 53, 69, 182, 185n2, 193n65, 194n3, 196n38
Lilienblum, Moshe 144–5
Lilienthal, Max 107
liquor laws (Romania) 137–8
Loewe, Louis: with Montefiore on European tour 100; in Bucharest 127–9
London Magazine 29, 45
London prophetic revival 20; *see also* Millennialism
London protest meetings *see* Freemasons' Hall; Great Assembly Hall; Great Synagogue; Guildhall; Hyde Park; London Tavern; Mansion House; Salvador House; and Queen's Hall
London Society for the Promotion of Christianity among the Jews (London Society) 28, 47, 60, 66–7, 73, 199n13; *see also* Philo-Judacan Society
London Tavern, as protest venue 41–4
Lower East Side (New York), as center of American Jewry 162–3, 172

M
Macaulay, Thomas Babington 22, 30, 179
McNeile, Hugh 27, 33, 191n42
Madison Square Garden, as movement venue 173–4
Malmesbury, Lord 99, 103, 105, 208n61
Mandeville, Viscount 27, 30, 221
Manning, Cardinal 148–50

Mansion House, as protest venue 71, 75–6, 132–3, 148–9; Committee, 153
Marcus, Jacob R. 83–4
Maronites 59, 61, 63
"mask of quietism" 1, 44, 155, 177, 185n4
maskilim 21, 42, 144, 154–6
Masliansky, Zvi Hirsch 165, 166
master frame, as constructed during the Jewish rights campaign 15, 33, 49, 59
Mikveh Israel *see* Leeser, Isaac; Philadelphia protests
millenarianism *see* millennialism
millennialism: importance during "extraordinary movement" 13, 27–8; post-millennialism 20; pre-millennialism 20, 25, 27–8, 33, 60; *see also* Philo-Judaean Society
Moldavia 124, 125, 161
"moral capital" 13
"moral shocks," within Jewish rights movement 75, 163, 182, 220n10
Mortara affair: agitation of Louis Veuillot and *L'Univers* 97–8; American protests 106–14; and anti-Catholic sentiment 104, 106–7, 110; and the growth of sensational journalism 94–5; the issue of Italian unification 93, 116; Montefiore's mission to the Vatican 114–16; Mortara family 93–5, 116; and the move toward formal organizations 113–14, 117–19; muted response in England 99, 103–5; petition of the Jews of Piedmont-Sardinia 102; and the reaction of Louis Napoleon 103–4, 116, 208n61; and the role of Abraham Benisch and the *Jewish Chronicle* 91, 93, 104–5, 109, 113–16; "theater of tears," 93–5
Montagu, Samuel 163–4
Montefiore, Moses: during Damascus affair 65, 66, 67–71, 74–7, 85–8, 118; as idealized hero 101, 125; and Lady Judith 88, 100, 114, 128; mission to Romania 125–9; Morocco, 123–4; Mortara affair 91, 99, 103–5, 107, 108, 114, 116;

as outmoded Jewish champion 126; and positive attributes of social movement leadership 3, 9, 61, 69–70; trip to Russia and Eastern Europe 100–01; uneasy relations with Adolphe Crémieux 86
Morisi, Anna 93, 97, 207n34
Mortara, Edgardo 93–4, 96, 97, 110, 112, 114, 116, 178, 180
movement for Soviet Jews 174–6
Mozart Hall (New York City), as protest venue 109–12
Myers, Asher 147–8, 151

N
Napoleon III 93, 99, 102–4, 116, 208n61
"natural rights" (natural law) 43, 93, 95, 97, 149, 182
Newman, Selig 25–7, 29, 31, 36–8, 47, 191n34
New York City protests: during Damascus affair 79–81; Kishinev massacre 162–3, 165; Mortara affair 34–5, 98, 109–12; Russian pogroms (1881–1882) 149–50
Nicholas I, Tsar 1, 39, 41, 100; see also Russophobia
Nicholas II, Tsar 161, 167
nihilism 142, 150, 169
Noah, Mordecai M.: as activist 79, 80; orator 38, 78; failed Jewish colonizer 25, 32

O
O'Connell, Daniel 9, 13, 49, 75, 95
Oratory, importance of 13, 34, 38, 69, 181
Ottoman Empire 58, 63, 65, 67, 76, 86, 125, 138, 180

P
Pale of Settlement 2, 39, 100, 141–3, 145–6, 152, 154–5, 156, 171
Palmerston, Lord 65, 67, 76
Papal States 93–4, 99, 102–3, 116; map of; 92; see also Bologna
Paris Commune (1871) 136
Paris Convention (1858) 126
Pasha, Sherif 61–2, 66
Peel, Robert 53, 74, 101

Peixotto, Benjamin: consular appointment by Grant 130; specific achievements in Romania 136–7; promotion of Jewish immigration 133–4, 137; role as transnational activist 129–38; and testy relations with Bucharest elite 134–6; negative reaction from International Roumanian Conference 135–6
Pellatt, Apsley 51–2
Pereira Mendes, Rev. Henry 157–8
"persecution of contempt" 9, 12, 32
Philadelphia protests: during Damascus affair 79, 81–2; Kishinev massacre 166; and Mortara affair 108, 110, 112; see also Leeser, Isaac
Philhellenic movement 76–7
Philo-Judaean Society: and actions on behalf of Jews 27, 30–3, 36, 37, 45, 47, 51–2; anti-liberalism of leadership 28; dissolution 52; founding 25, 27; and Ladies Association 28, 47; merger with Abrahamic Association 192n51; and pre-millennial orientation 27–8
Philo-Semitism 5; and conceptual shift within 28, 192n50; see also millennialism
Pieritz, George W.: journey to Middle East 66; influential report of, 74–5, 78, 203n20
pilgrimage plantation 25, 51
Pinckney, Henry L. (mayor of Charleston) 82
Pinsker, Leo 8, 9, 146, 158
Pius IX, Pope: actions throughout Mortara affair 95–7, 99, 102–3, 105, 114, 115, 117; "adoption" of Edgardo Mortara 96; caricature in *Punch* 117; intransigence of 96, 103; and opposition to modernity 93; see also Papal States
Plombières-les-Baine 103
Poland, Kingdom of 82, 100, 141, 154
postmodernism and Jewish history 4
Prag, Joseph 164, 172
print culture (Britain) 13

Q

Queen's Hall (London), as movement venue 17
quietism *see* "mask of quietism"

R

Ramsgate (England) 3, 151, 168
Raphall, Morris 26, 98, 109, 110, 111
Ratti-Menton, Comte de: actions in Damascus 62–3; and Thiers' defense in Chamber of Deputies 64–65
Razsvet (St. Petersburg) 151–2, 215n60
Reformed Society of Israelites (Charleston) 83
Rhodes 65–7
The Road to Modern Jewish Politics (Lederhendler) 154–6
Rodrigue, Aron 118
Roosevelt, Theodore 163, 166–7
Romania (United Principalities) 124; and endemic antisemitism 124–5, 127, 130–1, 134, 138; laws against "vagabondage" 138; *see also* Bratianu, Ion; "liquor laws"; Carol, Prince
Roumanian Committees, proliferation of 132, 134, 138, 212n62
Romanticism, and evangelicalism 13, 20
rough music (shaming ritual) 26, 28, 29
Russell, Lord John 116
Russian pogroms (1881–1882) 142–8
Russian Revolution 171
Russophobia (in Britain) 41, 195n28
Russo-Turkish War 138, 143

S

Salomons, David 3, 68, 74, 132, 168
Salvador, Joseph 64, 201n38
Salvador House, as movement venue 36–9, 194n3
San Francisco 112, 165
Schiff, Jacob H. 163, 165
"seatholders," in London synagogues 23
Seligman, Joseph 110, 130, 211n31
Shaftesbury, Earl of 27, 36, 58, 94, 133, 148–9
Shandel, Herman 3, 168
shtadlan 51, 154–5
Silbermann, Eliezer 155
"signs of the times" *see* millennialism
slave mentality, and the Jews, 9, 33–4, 44, 95, 182
social movement: definition 14–15; "success" or "failure" 178
solidarity movements 15
spin-off movement 10, 48, 152, 159, 186n12
Straus, Oscar 163, 167, 218n43

T

Taylor, Verta, and concept of abeyance 3, 185n5; 185n10
taverns: Jewish management as source of conflict 137, 141, 142, 144; and alcoholism 144, 214n21
Test and Corporation Acts 9, 47, 48, 57
Thiers, Adolphe 60, 64–5
Tilly, Charles 9, 15, 49
Times (London): as advocate during the "extraordinary movement" 37, 45; adversarial role throughout Damascus affair 65–6; position during Mortara affair 103, 114; active support during Russian pogroms (1881–1882) 143, 146, 148
torture 2, 12, 59, 62, 200n25; psychosocial ramifications 63–4; *see also* Pasha, Sherif; Ratti-Menton, Comte de

U

Ukase (1827), and reaction in London 39–41
Ultramontane Catholics, 97 180
Union of American Hebrew Congregations 163
United Congregations of Israelites of the City of New York 113

V

Vallentine, Isaac 38, 91
Van Buren, Martin 80–1, 106
Van Oven, Barnard 68, 70, 95, 99, 202n15
Veuillot, Louis 97–8, 207n31
Vilna 100, 142, 153
Voice of Jacob (London) 4, 101, 180

W

Wellington, Duke of: appointment as prime minister 19; opposition

to Jewish rights 46, 48, 197n51
Wilberforce, William 13, 20, 30
Wise, Isaac M. 107, 112, 113, 137, 150; *see also Israelite*
Wise, Stephen 173–4
Wolf, Lucien 164, 217n28
Wolff, Joseph 26–30, 33, 37, 191n38; "debate" with Selig Newman 26–7; as Jewish "turncoat" 29; and reaction of Isaac Leeser 81, 192n59
women's rights movement 2, 6, 14, 167, 179, 193n74

World (London), and influence during the "extraordinary movement" 33–4, 36, 37, 39, 46, 193n65; *see also* Bourne, Stephen

Y
Yulee, David 25, 112, 209n26

Z
Zangwill, Israel 169, 172
Zionists 8, 11, 31, 43, 164, 165–6, 169, 172–3, 174, 181, 217n26
Zion Society (Romania) 131, 137

For Product Safety Concerns and Information please contact our EU
representative GPSR@taylorandfrancis.com
Taylor & Francis Verlag GmbH, Kaufingerstraße 24, 80331 München, Germany

www.ingramcontent.com/pod-product-compliance
Lightning Source LLC
Chambersburg PA
CBHW060558230426
43670CB00011B/1870